# FROG™

KERORO GUNSOU

## Volume # 4 by Mine Yoshizaki

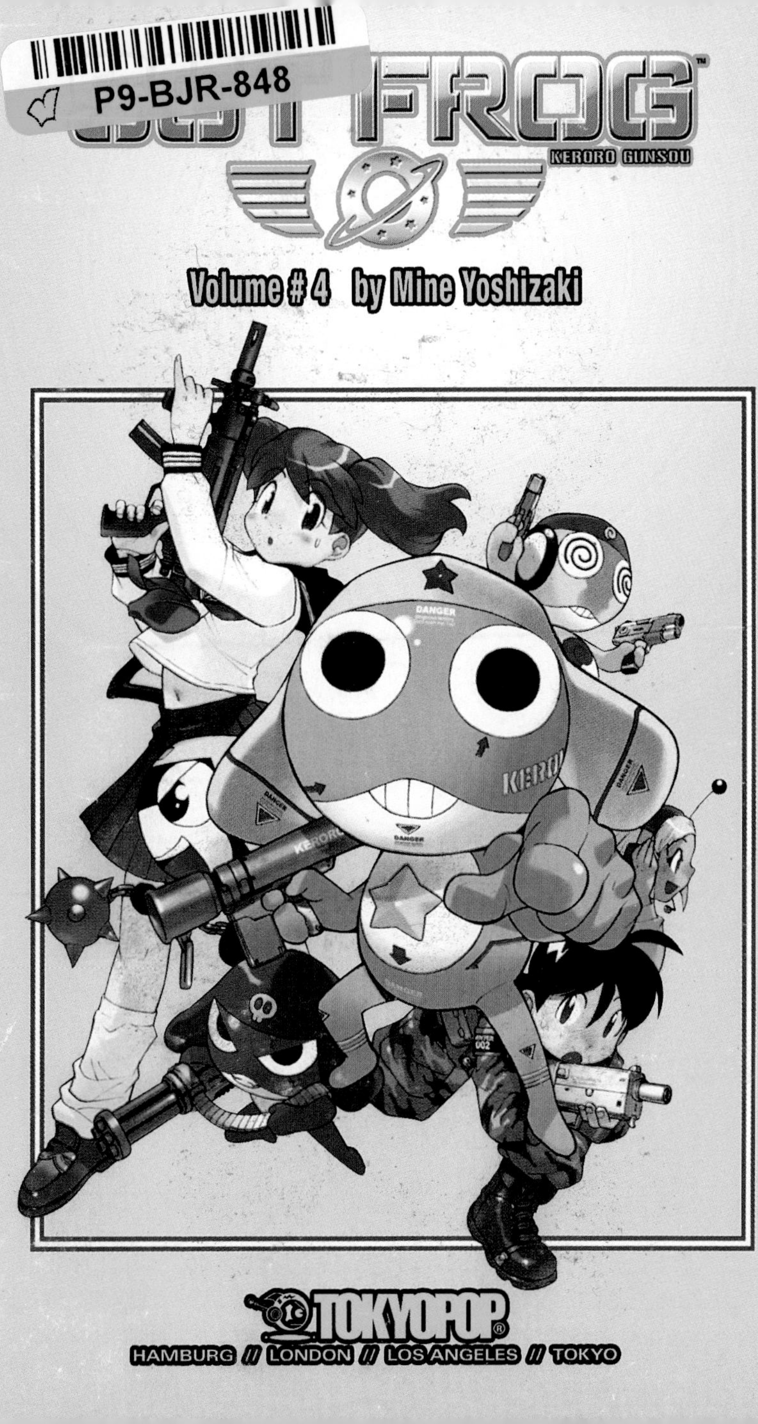

TOKYOPOP®
HAMBURG // LONDON // LOS ANGELES // TOKYO

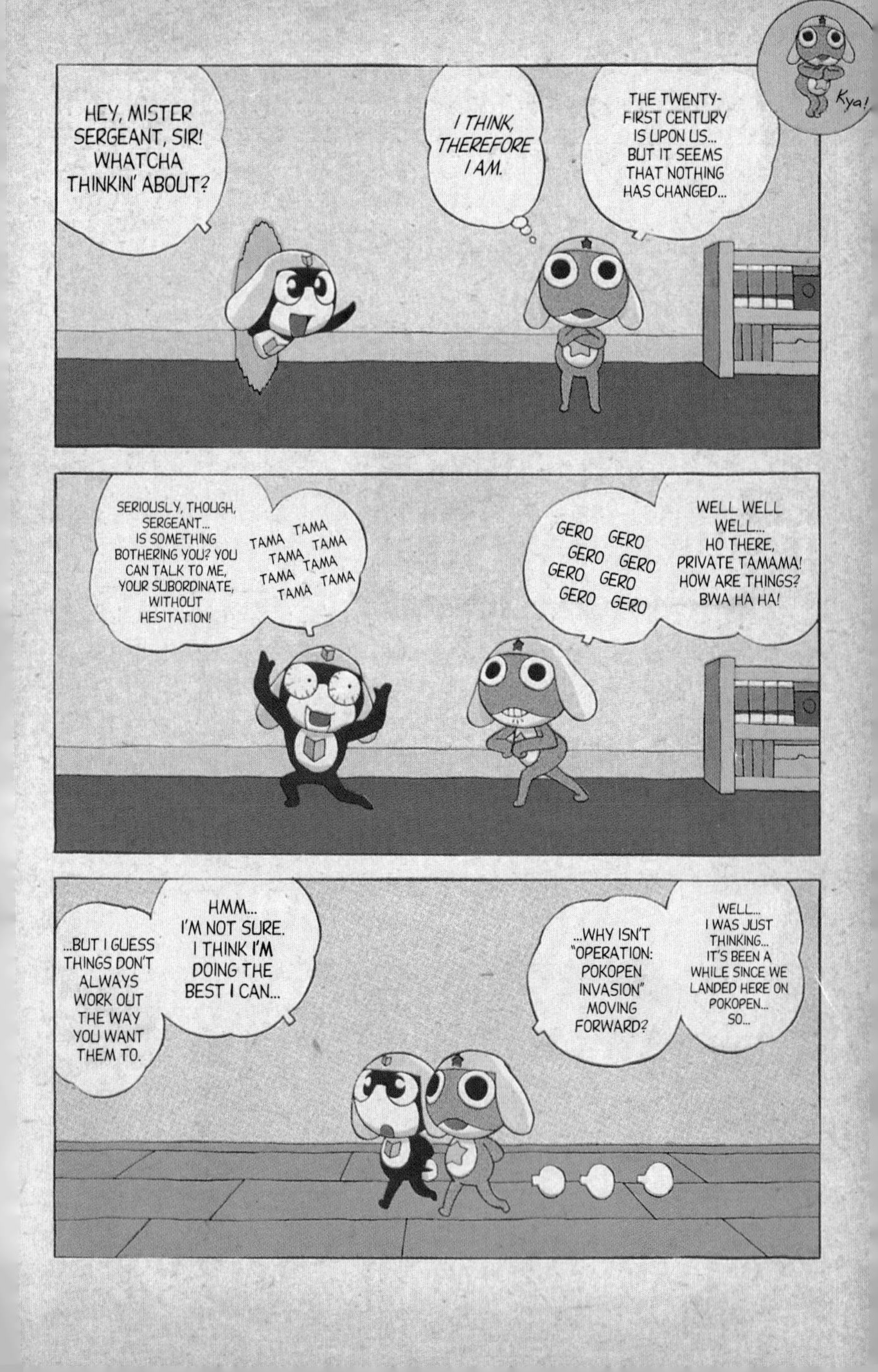
Kya!
THE TWENTY-FIRST CENTURY IS UPON US... BUT IT SEEMS THAT NOTHING HAS CHANGED...
I THINK, THEREFORE I AM.
HEY, MISTER SERGEANT, SIR! WHATCHA THINKIN' ABOUT?
WELL WELL WELL... HO THERE, PRIVATE TAMAMA! HOW ARE THINGS? BWA HA HA!
GERO GERO GERO GERO GERO GERO GERO GERO
TAMA TAMA TAMA TAMA TAMA TAMA TAMA TAMA
SERIOUSLY, THOUGH, SERGEANT... IS SOMETHING BOTHERING YOU? YOU CAN TALK TO ME, YOUR SUBORDINATE, WITHOUT HESITATION!
WELL... I WAS JUST THINKING... IT'S BEEN A WHILE SINCE WE LANDED HERE ON POKOPEN... SO...
...WHY ISN'T "OPERATION: POKOPEN INVASION" MOVING FORWARD?
HMM... I'M NOT SURE. I THINK I'M DOING THE BEST I CAN...
...BUT I GUESS THINGS DON'T ALWAYS WORK OUT THE WAY YOU WANT THEM TO.

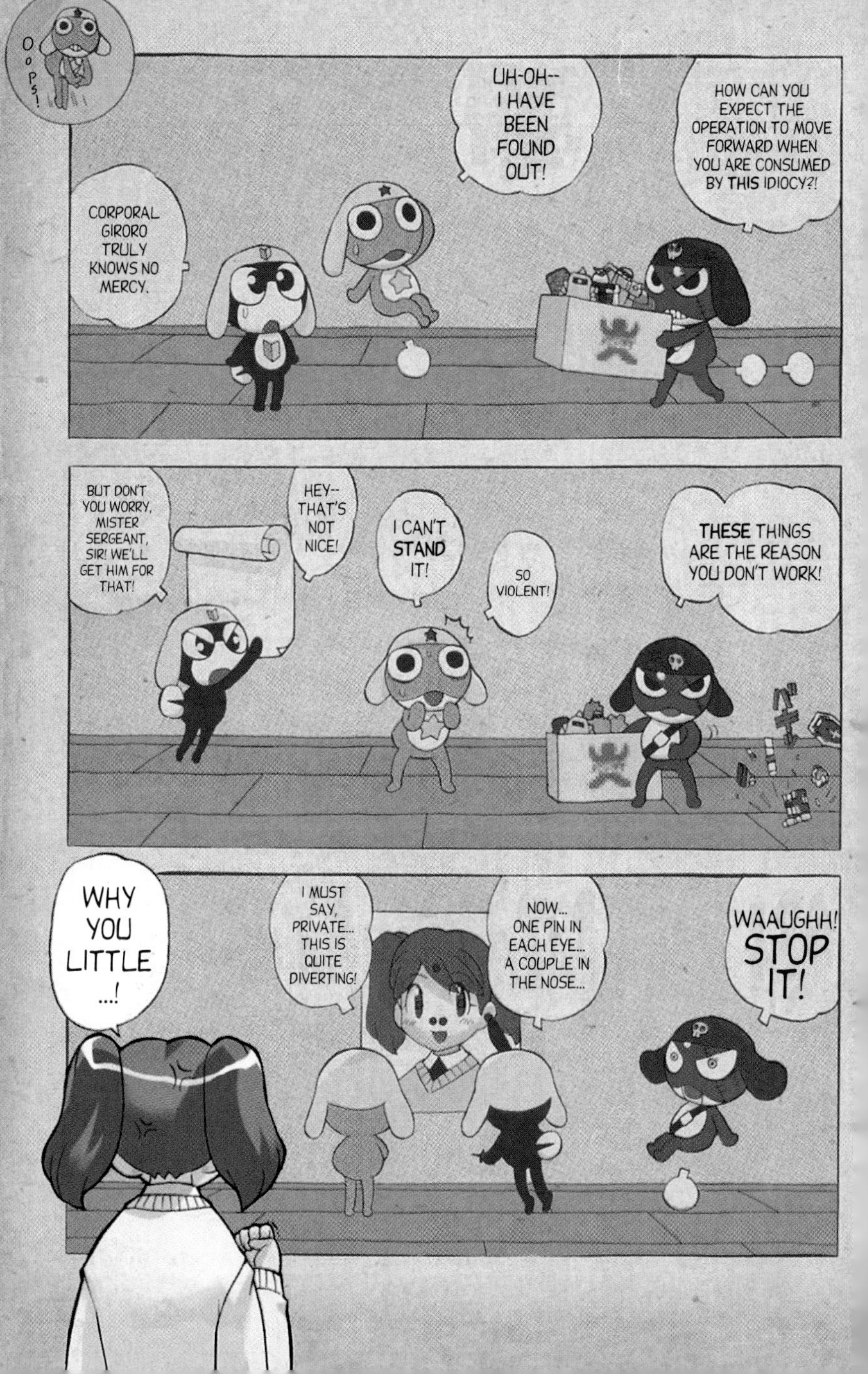
HOW CAN YOU EXPECT THE OPERATION TO MOVE FORWARD WHEN YOU ARE CONSUMED BY THIS IDIOCY?!
UH-OH-- I HAVE BEEN FOUND OUT!
CORPORAL GIRORO TRULY KNOWS NO MERCY.
OOPS!
THESE THINGS ARE THE REASON YOU DON'T WORK!
SO VIOLENT!
I CAN'T STAND IT!
HEY-- THAT'S NOT NICE!
BUT DON'T YOU WORRY, MISTER SERGEANT, SIR! WE'LL GET HIM FOR THAT!
WAAUGHH! STOP IT!
NOW... ONE PIN IN EACH EYE... A COUPLE IN THE NOSE...
I MUST SAY, PRIVATE... THIS IS QUITE DIVERTING!
WHY YOU LITTLE ...!

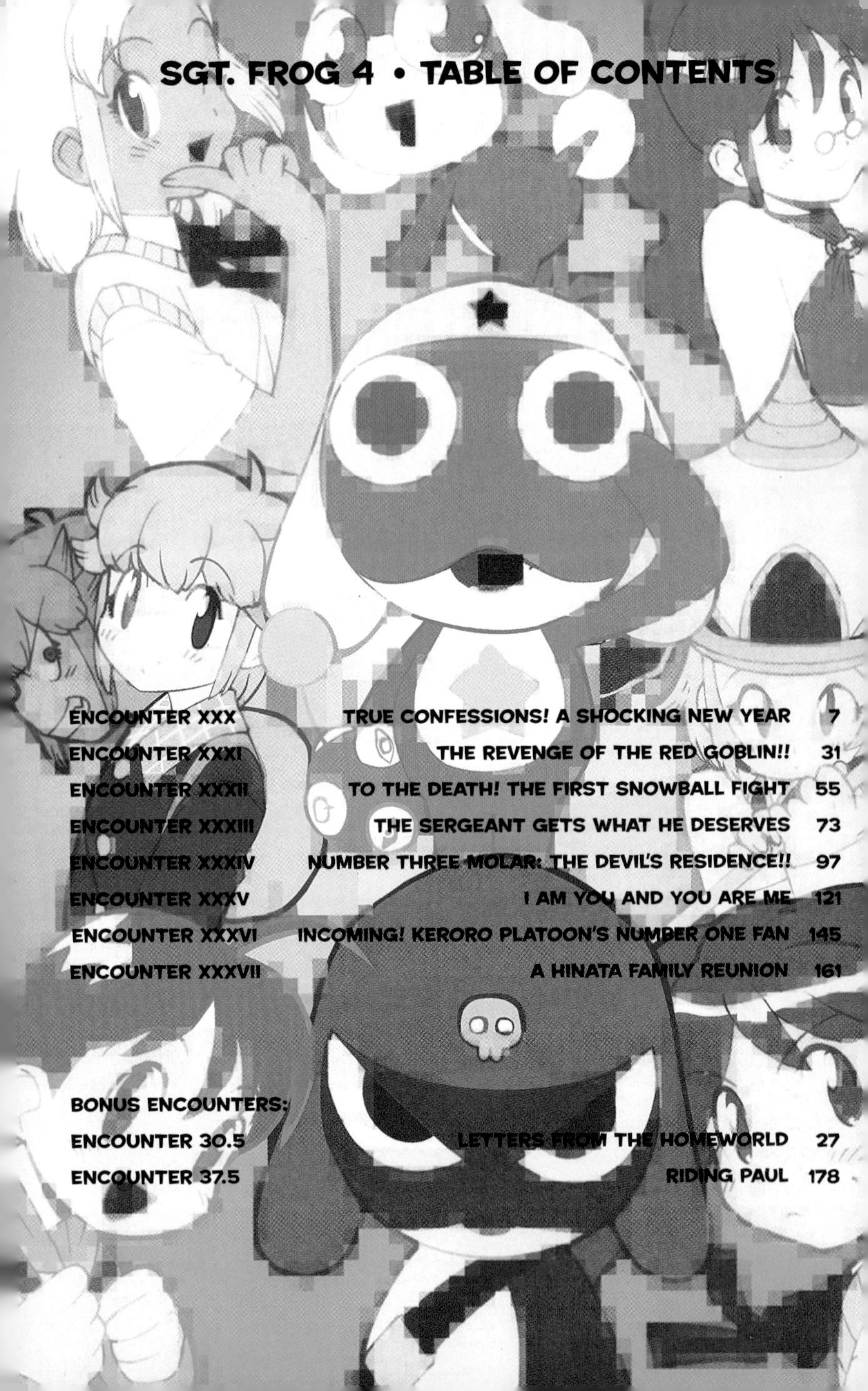

# SGT. FROG 4 • TABLE OF CONTENTS

# SGT FROG

KERORO GUNSOU

## CHARACTER RELATIONSHIPS AND THE STORY SO FAR

(FACT-CHECKING PERFORMED BY SHONEN ACE MAGAZINE)

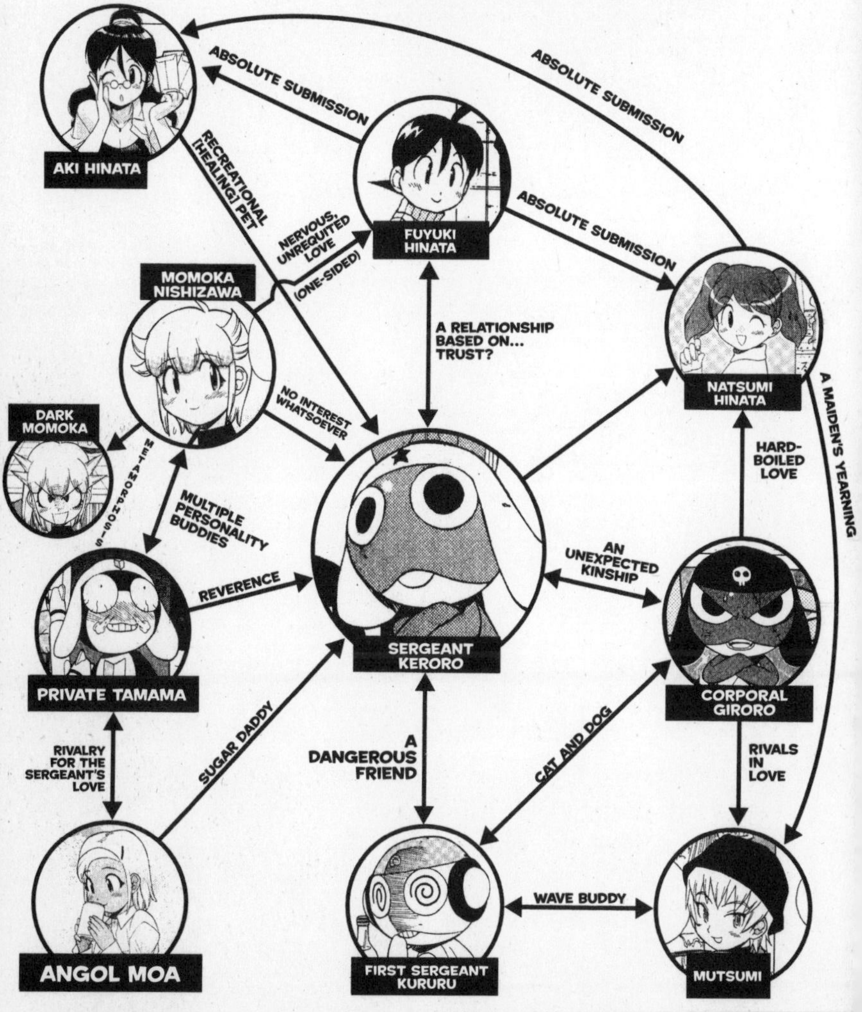

AKI HINATA
ABSOLUTE SUBMISSION
ABSOLUTE SUBMISSION
RECREATIONAL [HEALING] PET
FUYUKI HINATA
ABSOLUTE SUBMISSION
NERVOUS, UNREQUITED LOVE
(ONE-SIDED)
MOMOKA NISHIZAWA
A RELATIONSHIP BASED ON... TRUST?
NATSUMI HINATA
A MAIDEN'S YEARNING
NO INTEREST WHATSOEVER
DARK MOMOKA
METAMORPHOSIS
MULTIPLE PERSONALITY BUDDIES
HARD-BOILED LOVE
AN UNEXPECTED KINSHIP
REVERENCE
PRIVATE TAMAMA
SERGEANT KERORO
CORPORAL GIRORO
RIVALRY FOR THE SERGEANT'S LOVE
SUGAR DADDY
A DANGEROUS FRIEND
CAT AND DOG
RIVALS IN LOVE
ANGOL MOA
WAVE BUDDY
FIRST SERGEANT KURURU
MUTSUMI


SERGEANT KERORO, CAPTAIN OF THE SPACE INVASION FORCE'S SPECIAL ADVANCE TEAM OF THE 58TH PLANET OF THE GAMMA STORM CLOUD SYSTEM, CAME TO THE HINATA HOUSEHOLD AS A PRE-ATTACK PREPARATION FOR THE INVASION OF EARTH... UNFORTUNATELY, HE WAS EASILY CAPTURED BY THE HINATA CHILDREN, FUYUKI AND NATSUMI. HOWEVER, THANKS TO FUYUKI'S GENEROSITY--OR, RATHER, HIS FASCINATION WITH ALIENS--SGT. KERORO BECAME A FREELOADER IN THE HINATA HOUSE. OF COURSE, THE SERGEANT'S SUBORDINATES--PRIVATE "SPLIT PERSONALITY" TAMAMA, BLAZING MILITARY MAN CORPORAL GIRORO, MAD INVENTOR/D.J. FIRST SERGEANT KURURU, AND ANGOL MOA, THE MUCH-HERALDED "LORD OF TERROR"--HAD TO JOIN HIM... AND TO TOP IT ALL OFF, THEY EVEN BUILT THEIR OWN SECRET BASE.

AND SO WE CONTINUE OUR CHRONICLE OF THE HINATAS AND THE SERGEANT'S PLATOON... WHO ARE, OF COURSE, DEAD-SET ON INVADING THE EARTH...

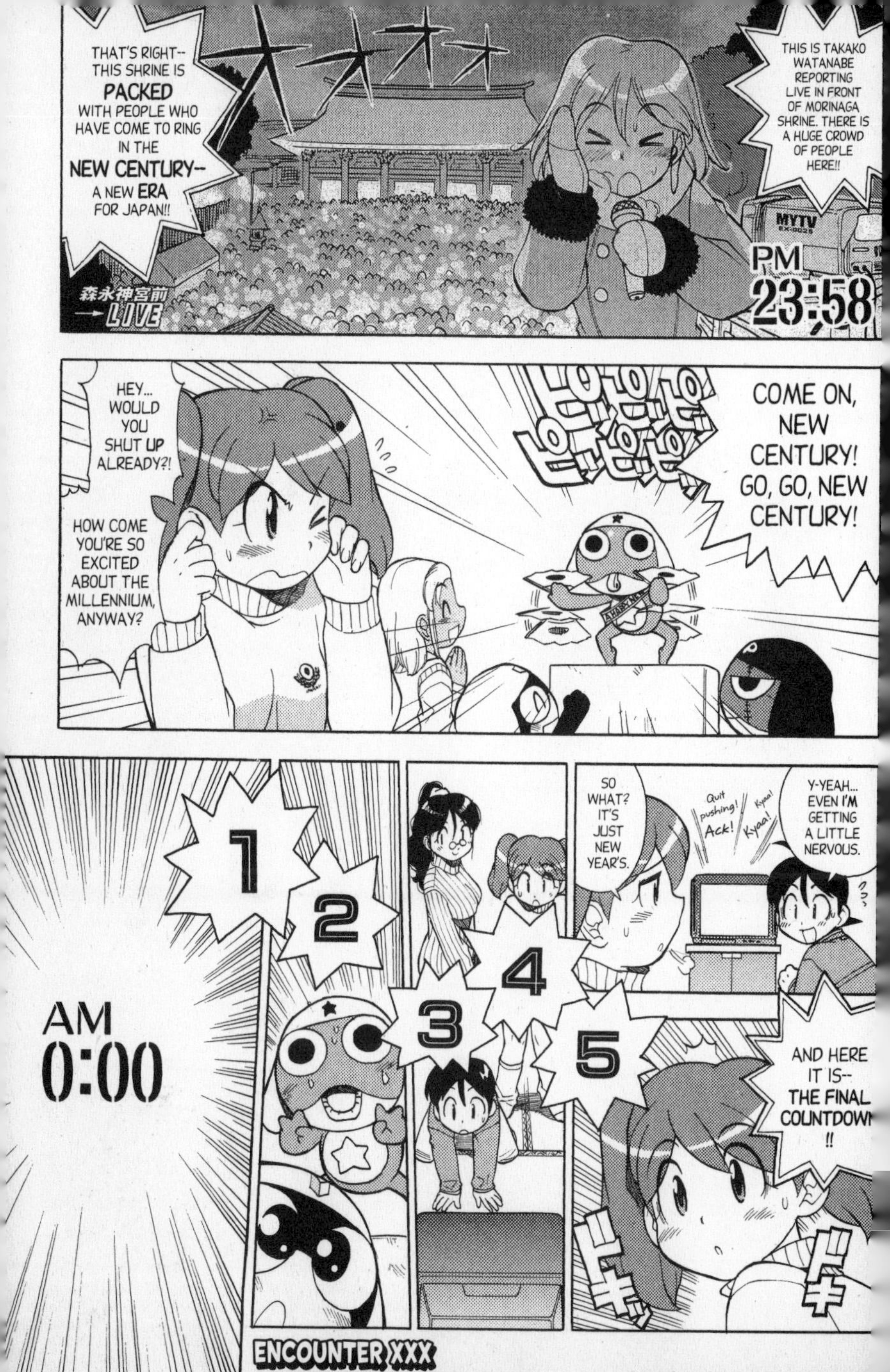
THIS IS TAKAKO WATANABE REPORTING LIVE IN FRONT OF MORINAGA SHRINE. THERE IS A HUGE CROWD OF PEOPLE HERE!!
オオオオ
THAT'S RIGHT-- THIS SHRINE IS PACKED WITH PEOPLE WHO HAVE COME TO RING IN THE NEW CENTURY-- A NEW ERA FOR JAPAN!!
MYTV
森永神宮前 LIVE
PM 23:58
COME ON, NEW CENTURY! GO, GO, NEW CENTURY!
HEY... WOULD YOU SHUT UP ALREADY?!
HOW COME YOU'RE SO EXCITED ABOUT THE MILLENNIUM, ANYWAY?
Y-YEAH... EVEN I'M GETTING A LITTLE NERVOUS.
Kyaa!
Kyaa!
Quit pushing!
Ack!
SO WHAT? IT'S JUST NEW YEAR'S.
5
4
3
2
1
AND HERE IT IS-- THE FINAL COUNTDOWN!!
ドキ
ドキッ
AM 0:00

## ENCOUNTER XXX
## TRUE CONFESSIONS! A SHOCKING NEW YEAR

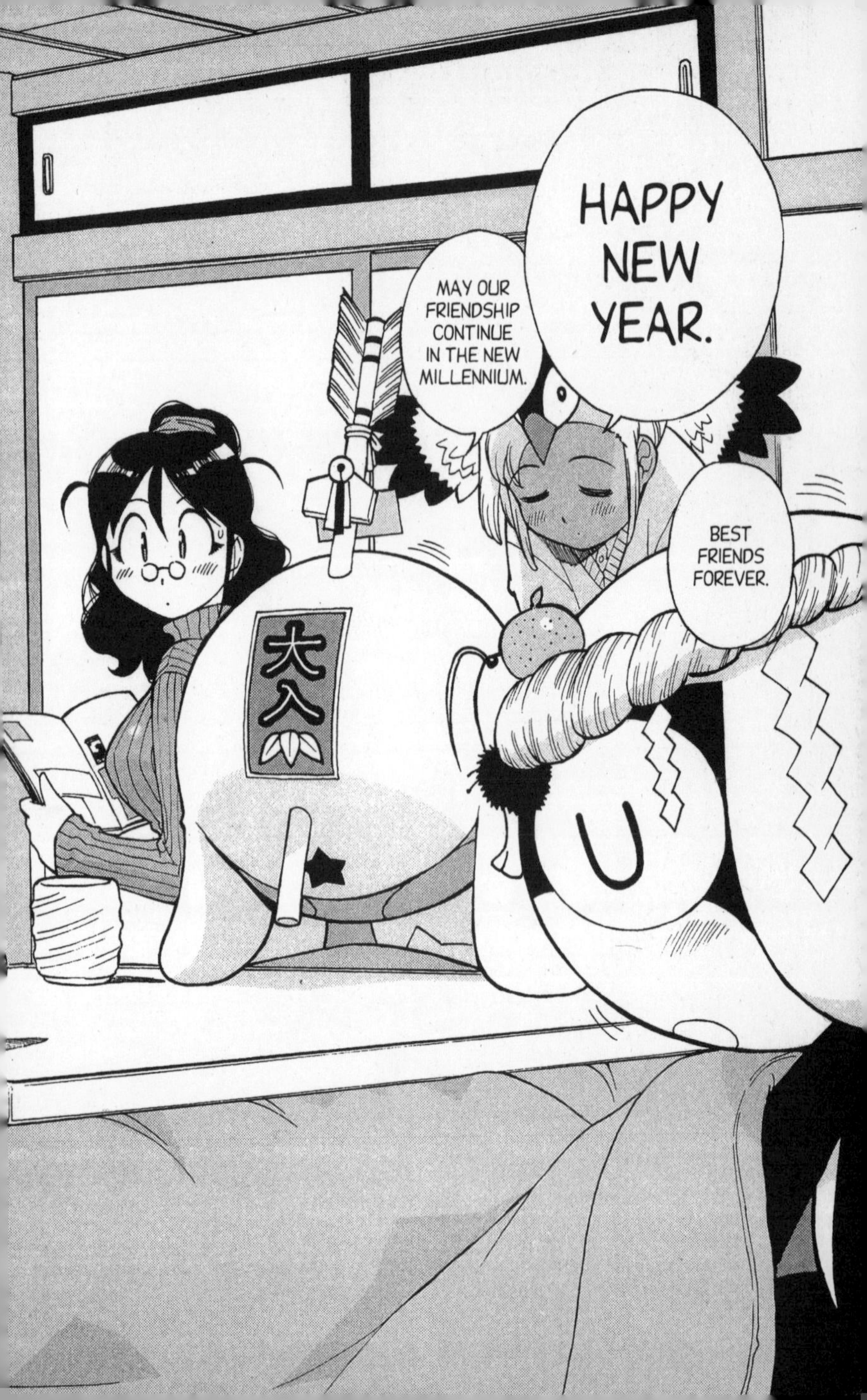
HAPPY NEW YEAR.
MAY OUR FRIENDSHIP CONTINUE IN THE NEW MILLENNIUM.
BEST FRIENDS FOREVER.
大入

## ENCOUNTER XXX
## TRUE CONFESSIONS! A SHOCKING NEW YEAR

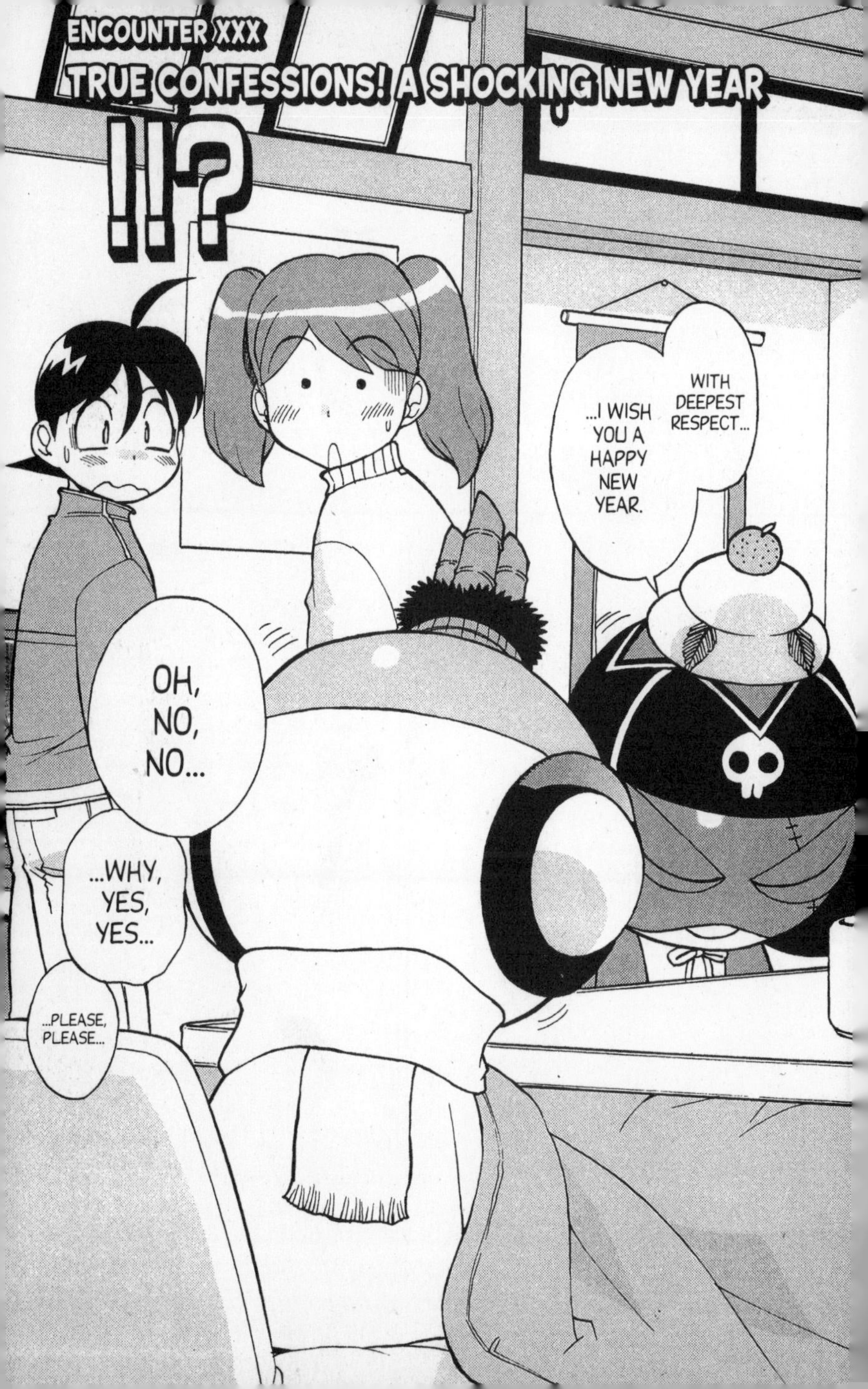
WITH DEEPEST RESPECT...
...I WISH YOU A HAPPY NEW YEAR.
!!?
OH, NO, NO...
...WHY, YES, YES...
...PLEASE, PLEASE...

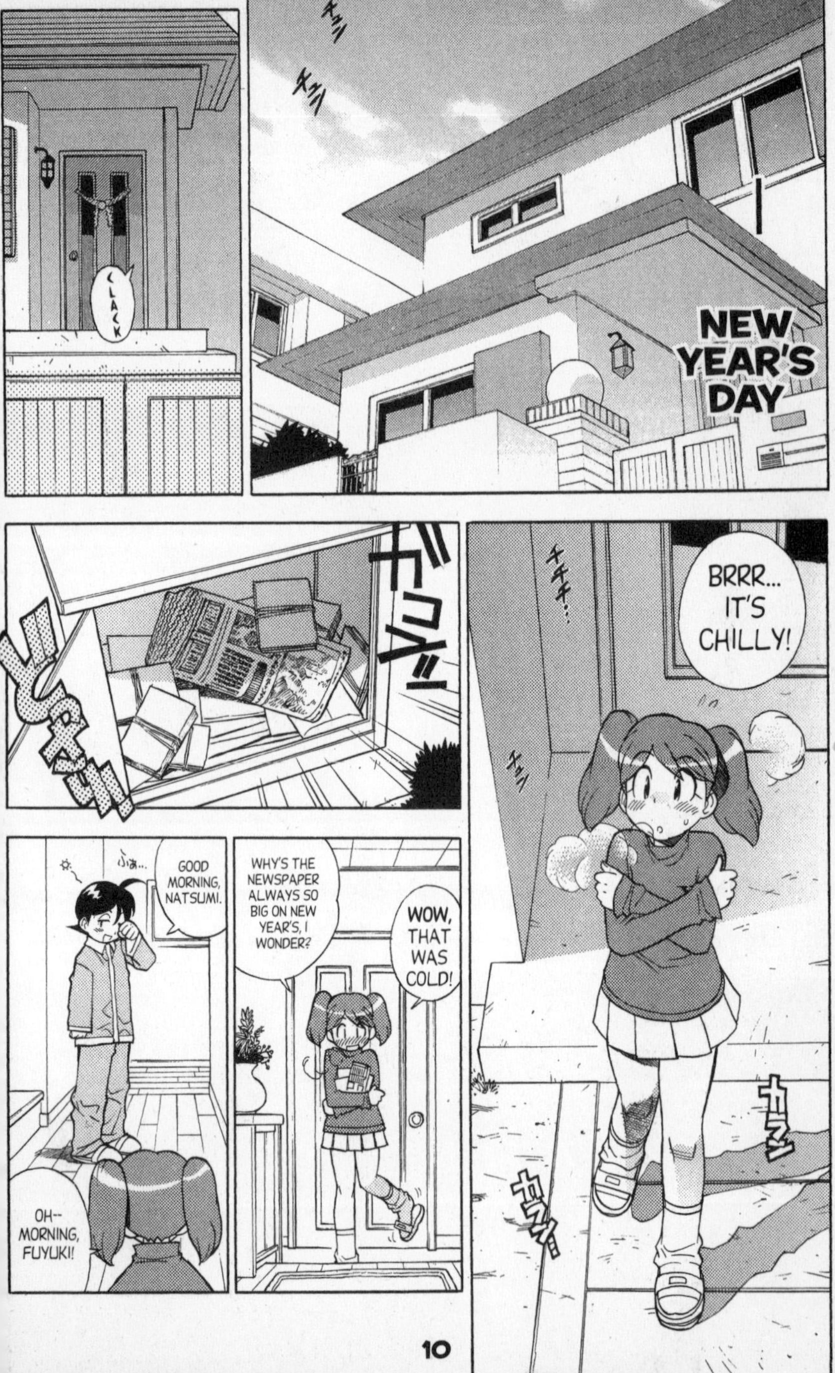
チュン
チュン
NEW YEAR'S DAY
CLACK
チチチ...
BRRR... IT'S CHILLY!
チュン
WHY'S THE NEWSPAPER ALWAYS SO BIG ON NEW YEAR'S, I WONDER?
WOW, THAT WAS COLD!
ふぁ...
GOOD MORNING, NATSUMI.
OH-- MORNING, FUYUKI!

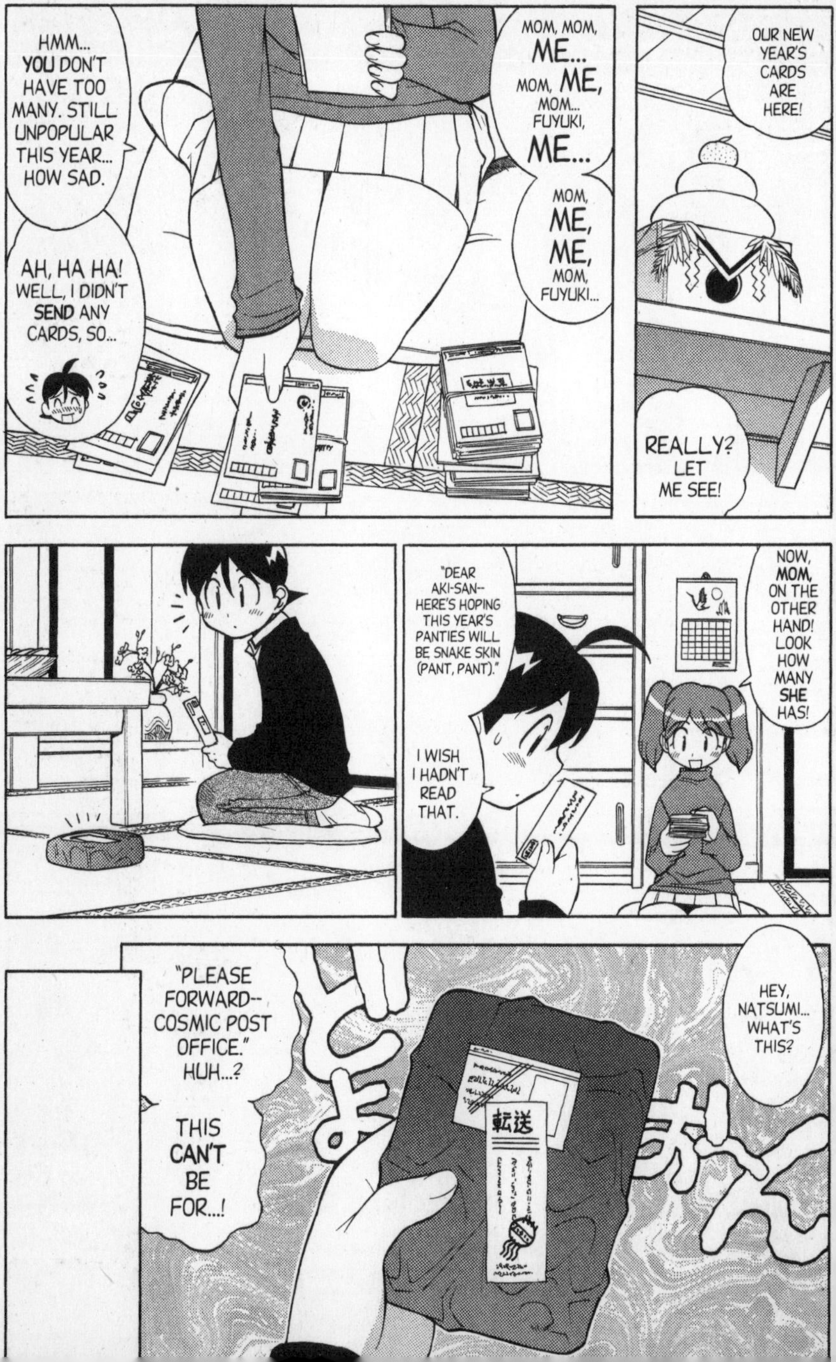
OUR NEW YEAR'S CARDS ARE HERE!
REALLY? LET ME SEE!
MOM, MOM, ME... MOM, ME, MOM... FUYUKI, ME...
MOM, ME, ME, MOM, FUYUKI...
HMM... YOU DON'T HAVE TOO MANY. STILL UNPOPULAR THIS YEAR... HOW SAD.
AH, HA HA! WELL, I DIDN'T SEND ANY CARDS, SO...
NOW, MOM, ON THE OTHER HAND! LOOK HOW MANY SHE HAS!
"DEAR AKI-SAN-- HERE'S HOPING THIS YEAR'S PANTIES WILL BE SNAKE SKIN (PANT, PANT)."
I WISH I HADN'T READ THAT.
HEY, NATSUMI... WHAT'S THIS?
"PLEASE FORWARD-- COSMIC POST OFFICE." HUH...?
THIS CAN'T BE FOR...!
転送

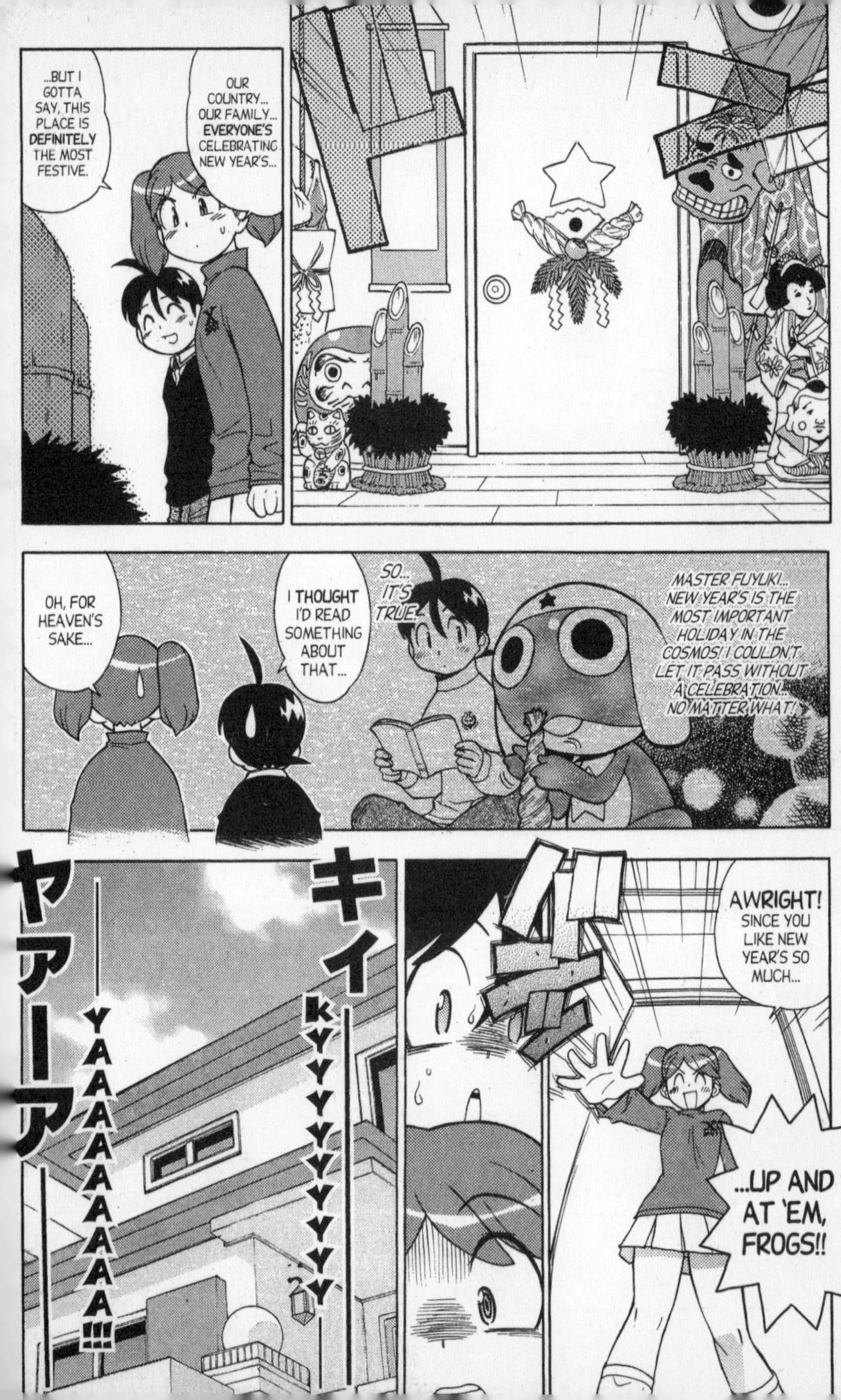
OUR COUNTRY... OUR FAMILY... EVERYONE'S CELEBRATING NEW YEAR'S...
...BUT I GOTTA SAY, THIS PLACE IS DEFINITELY THE MOST FESTIVE.
MASTER FUYUKI... NEW YEAR'S IS THE MOST IMPORTANT HOLIDAY IN THE COSMOS! I COULDN'T LET IT PASS WITHOUT A CELEBRATION... NO MATTER WHAT!
SO... IT'S TRUE.
I THOUGHT I'D READ SOMETHING ABOUT THAT...
OH, FOR HEAVEN'S SAKE...
AWRIGHT! SINCE YOU LIKE NEW YEAR'S SO MUCH...
...UP AND AT 'EM, FROGS!!
キィ
KYYYYYYYYYY
ヤァーア
YAAAAAAAAAA!!!

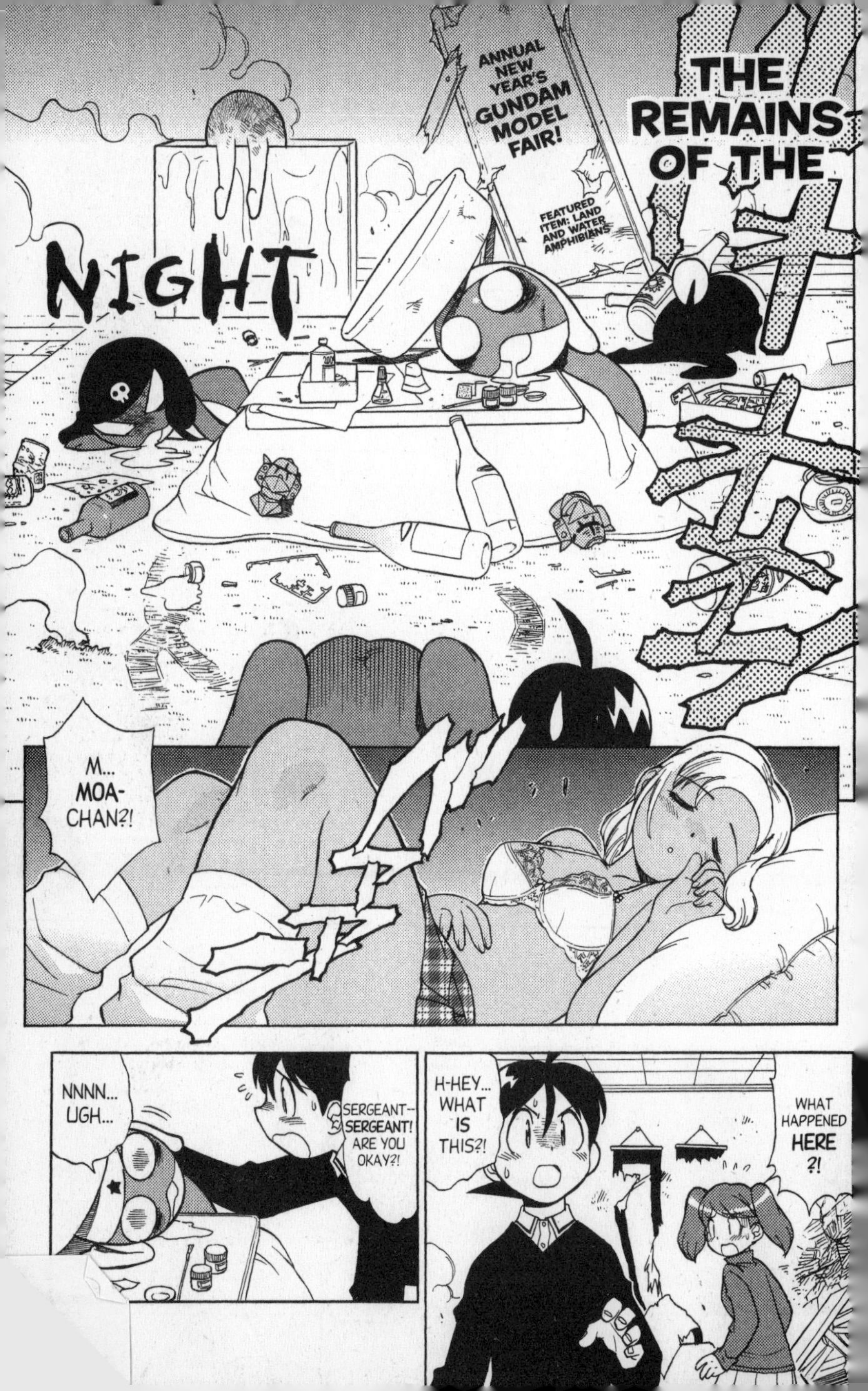
THE REMAINS OF THE
NIGHT
ANNUAL NEW YEAR'S GUNDAM MODEL FAIR!
FEATURED ITEM: LAND AND WATER AMPHIBIANS
M... MOA-CHAN?!
WHAT HAPPENED HERE?!
H-HEY... WHAT IS THIS?!
SERGEANT--SERGEANT! ARE YOU OKAY?!
NNNN... UGH...

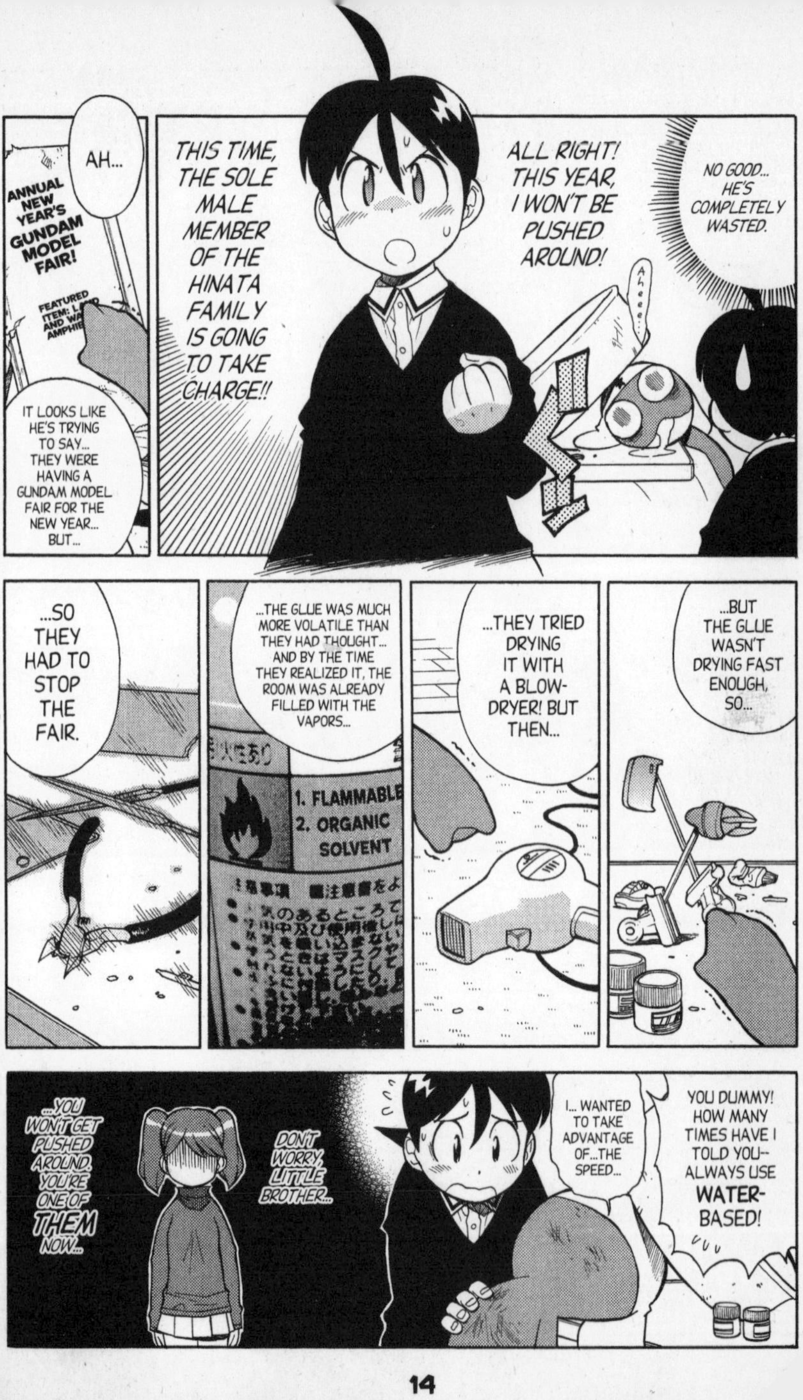
NO GOOD... HE'S COMPLETELY WASTED.
ALL RIGHT! THIS YEAR, I WON'T BE PUSHED AROUND!
THIS TIME, THE SOLE MALE MEMBER OF THE HINATA FAMILY IS GOING TO TAKE CHARGE!!
Aheee...
AH...
ANNUAL NEW YEAR'S GUNDAM MODEL FAIR!
FEATURED ITEM:
IT LOOKS LIKE HE'S TRYING TO SAY... THEY WERE HAVING A GUNDAM MODEL FAIR FOR THE NEW YEAR... BUT...
...BUT THE GLUE WASN'T DRYING FAST ENOUGH, SO...
...THEY TRIED DRYING IT WITH A BLOW-DRYER! BUT THEN...
...THE GLUE WAS MUCH MORE VOLATILE THAN THEY HAD THOUGHT... AND BY THE TIME THEY REALIZED IT, THE ROOM WAS ALREADY FILLED WITH THE VAPORS...
1. FLAMMABLE
2. ORGANIC SOLVENT
...SO THEY HAD TO STOP THE FAIR.
YOU DUMMY! HOW MANY TIMES HAVE I TOLD YOU-- ALWAYS USE WATER-BASED!
I... WANTED TO TAKE ADVANTAGE OF...THE SPEED...
DON'T WORRY, LITTLE BROTHER...
...YOU WON'T GET PUSHED AROUND. YOU'RE ONE OF THEM NOW...

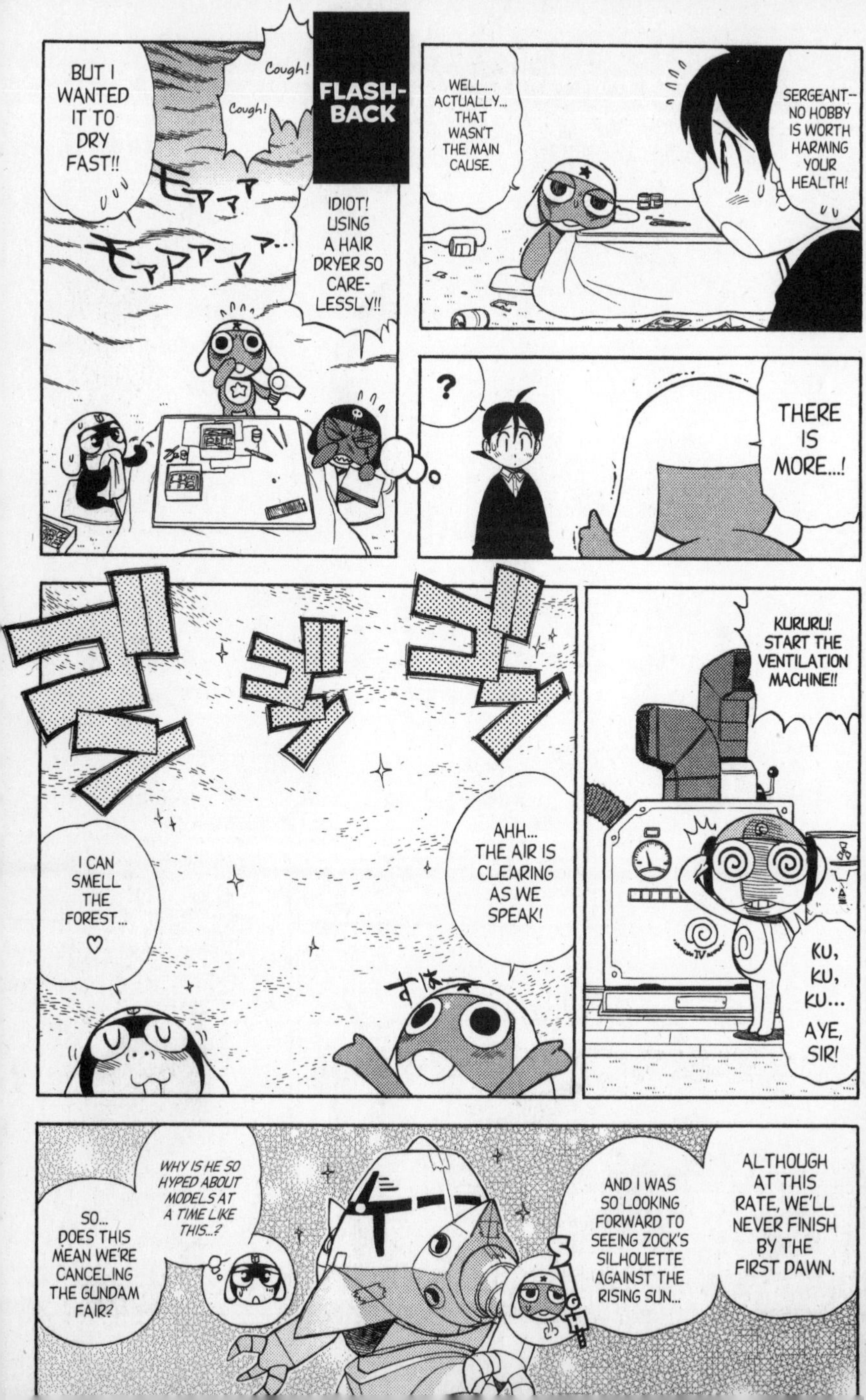
SERGEANT—NO HOBBY IS WORTH HARMING YOUR HEALTH!
WELL... ACTUALLY... THAT WASN'T THE MAIN CAUSE.
THERE IS MORE...!
?
FLASHBACK
Cough!
Cough!
IDIOT! USING A HAIR DRYER SO CARE-LESSLY!!
BUT I WANTED IT TO DRY FAST!!
モヤァァァ
モヤァァァァ…
KURURU! START THE VENTILATION MACHINE!!
KU, KU, KU... AYE, SIR!
AHH... THE AIR IS CLEARING AS WE SPEAK!
すはー
I CAN SMELL THE FOREST... ♡
ALTHOUGH AT THIS RATE, WE'LL NEVER FINISH BY THE FIRST DAWN.
AND I WAS SO LOOKING FORWARD TO SEEING ZOCK'S SILHOUETTE AGAINST THE RISING SUN...
SIGH
WHY IS HE SO HYPED ABOUT MODELS AT A TIME LIKE THIS...?
SO... DOES THIS MEAN WE'RE CANCELING THE GUNDAM FAIR?

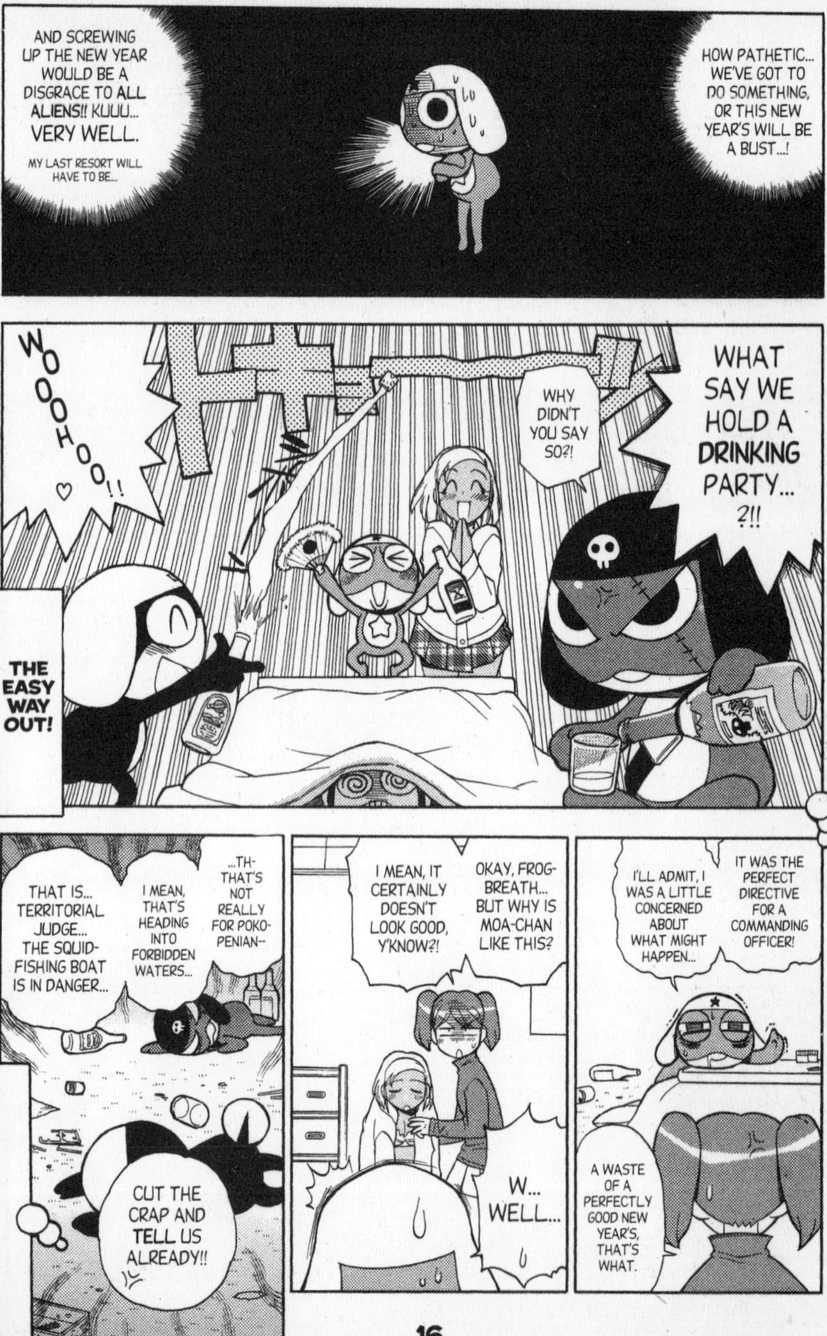
HOW PATHETIC... WE'VE GOT TO DO SOMETHING, OR THIS NEW YEAR'S WILL BE A BUST...!
AND SCREWING UP THE NEW YEAR WOULD BE A DISGRACE TO ALL ALIENS!! KUUU... VERY WELL.
MY LAST RESORT WILL HAVE TO BE...
WHAT SAY WE HOLD A DRINKING PARTY... ?!!
WHY DIDN'T YOU SAY SO?!
WOOOHOOO!! ♡
THE EASY WAY OUT!
IT WAS THE PERFECT DIRECTIVE FOR A COMMANDING OFFICER!
I'LL ADMIT, I WAS A LITTLE CONCERNED ABOUT WHAT MIGHT HAPPEN...
A WASTE OF A PERFECTLY GOOD NEW YEAR'S, THAT'S WHAT.
OKAY, FROG-BREATH... BUT WHY IS MOA-CHAN LIKE THIS?
I MEAN, IT CERTAINLY DOESN'T LOOK GOOD, Y'KNOW?!
W... WELL...
...TH-THAT'S NOT REALLY FOR POKO-PENIAN--
I MEAN, THAT'S HEADING INTO FORBIDDEN WATERS...
THAT IS... TERRITORIAL JUDGE... THE SQUID-FISHING BOAT IS IN DANGER...
CUT THE CRAP AND TELL US ALREADY!!

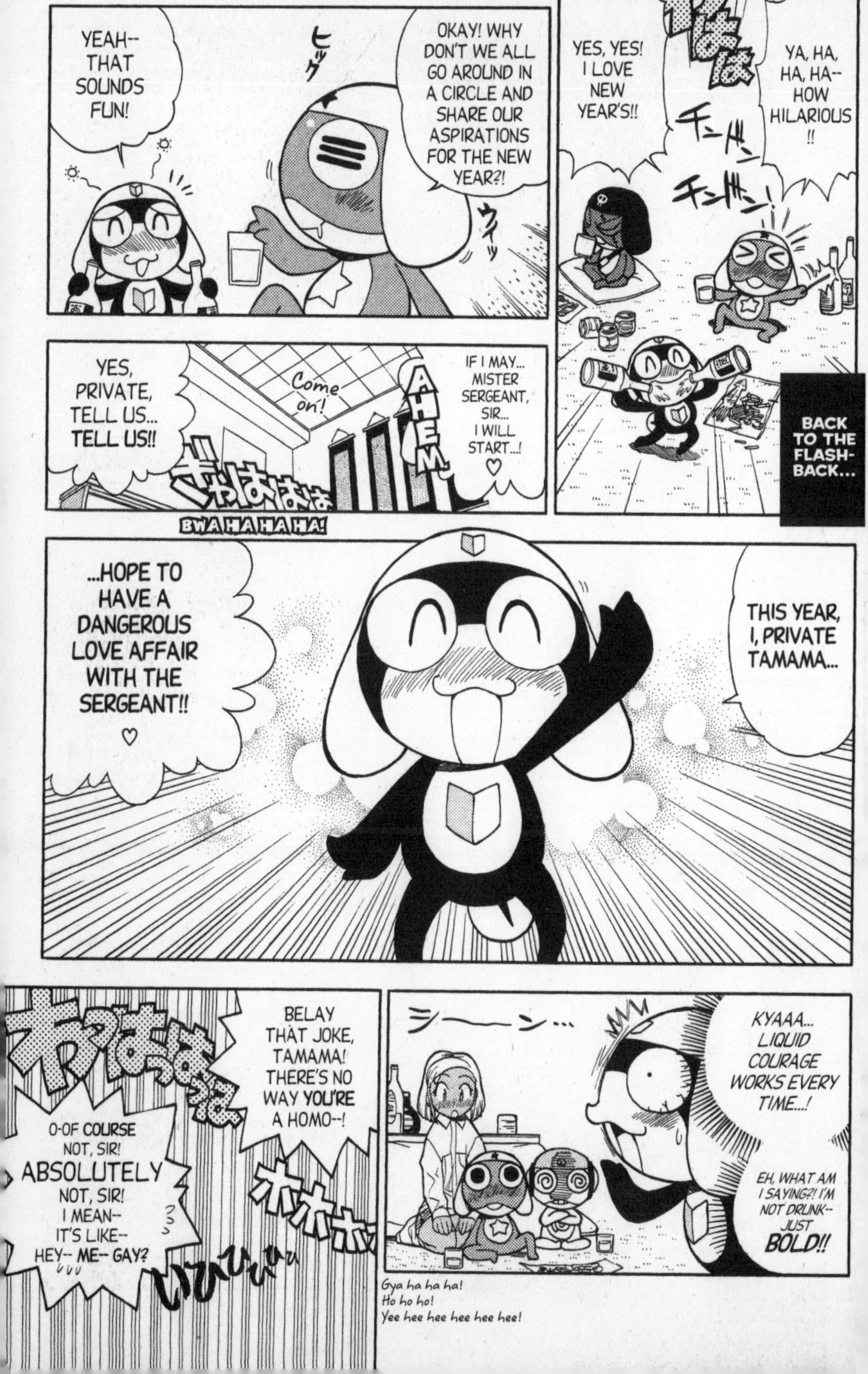
YA, HA, HA, HA-- HOW HILARIOUS !!
YES, YES! I LOVE NEW YEAR'S!!
BACK TO THE FLASH-BACK...
OKAY! WHY DON'T WE ALL GO AROUND IN A CIRCLE AND SHARE OUR ASPIRATIONS FOR THE NEW YEAR?!
YEAH-- THAT SOUNDS FUN!
IF I MAY... MISTER SERGEANT, SIR... I WILL START...! ♡
AHEM
Come on!
YES, PRIVATE, TELL US... TELL US!!
BWA HA HA HA!
THIS YEAR, I, PRIVATE TAMAMA...
...HOPE TO HAVE A DANGEROUS LOVE AFFAIR WITH THE SERGEANT!! ♡
KYAAA... LIQUID COURAGE WORKS EVERY TIME...!
EH, WHAT AM I SAYING?! I'M NOT DRUNK-- JUST BOLD!!
Gya ha ha ha!
Ho ho ho!
Yee hee hee hee hee hee!
BELAY THAT JOKE, TAMAMA! THERE'S NO WAY YOU'RE A HOMO--!
O-OF COURSE NOT, SIR! ABSOLUTELY NOT, SIR! I MEAN-- IT'S LIKE-- HEY-- ME-- GAY?

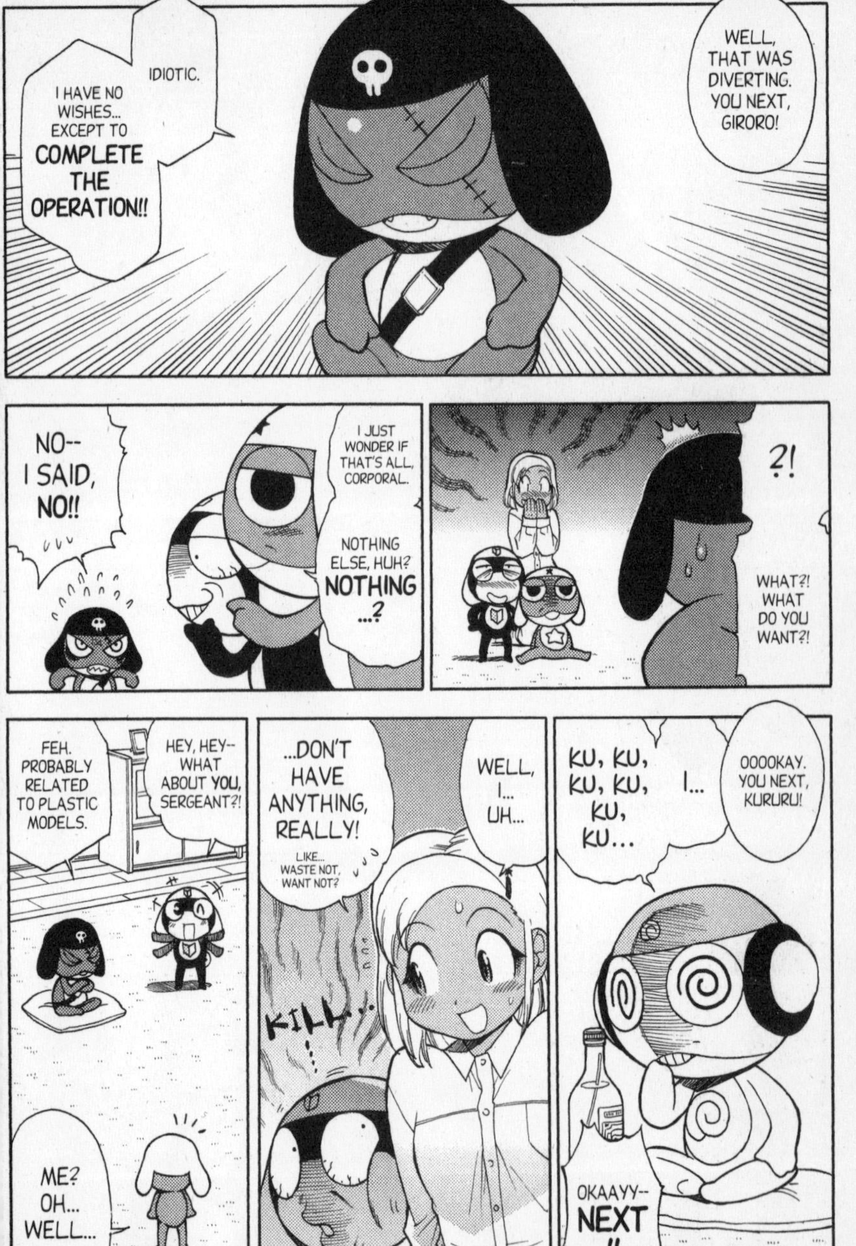
WELL, THAT WAS DIVERTING. YOU NEXT, GIRORO!
IDIOTIC.
I HAVE NO WISHES... EXCEPT TO COMPLETE THE OPERATION!!
?!
WHAT?! WHAT DO YOU WANT?!
I JUST WONDER IF THAT'S ALL, CORPORAL.
NOTHING ELSE, HUH? NOTHING ...?
NO-- I SAID, NO!!
OOOOKAY. YOU NEXT, KURURU!
I...
KU, KU, KU, KU, KU, KU...
OKAAYY-- NEXT !!
WELL, I... UH...
...DON'T HAVE ANYTHING, REALLY!
LIKE... WASTE NOT, WANT NOT?
KILL...
HEY, HEY-- WHAT ABOUT YOU, SERGEANT?!
FEH. PROBABLY RELATED TO PLASTIC MODELS.
ME? OH... WELL...

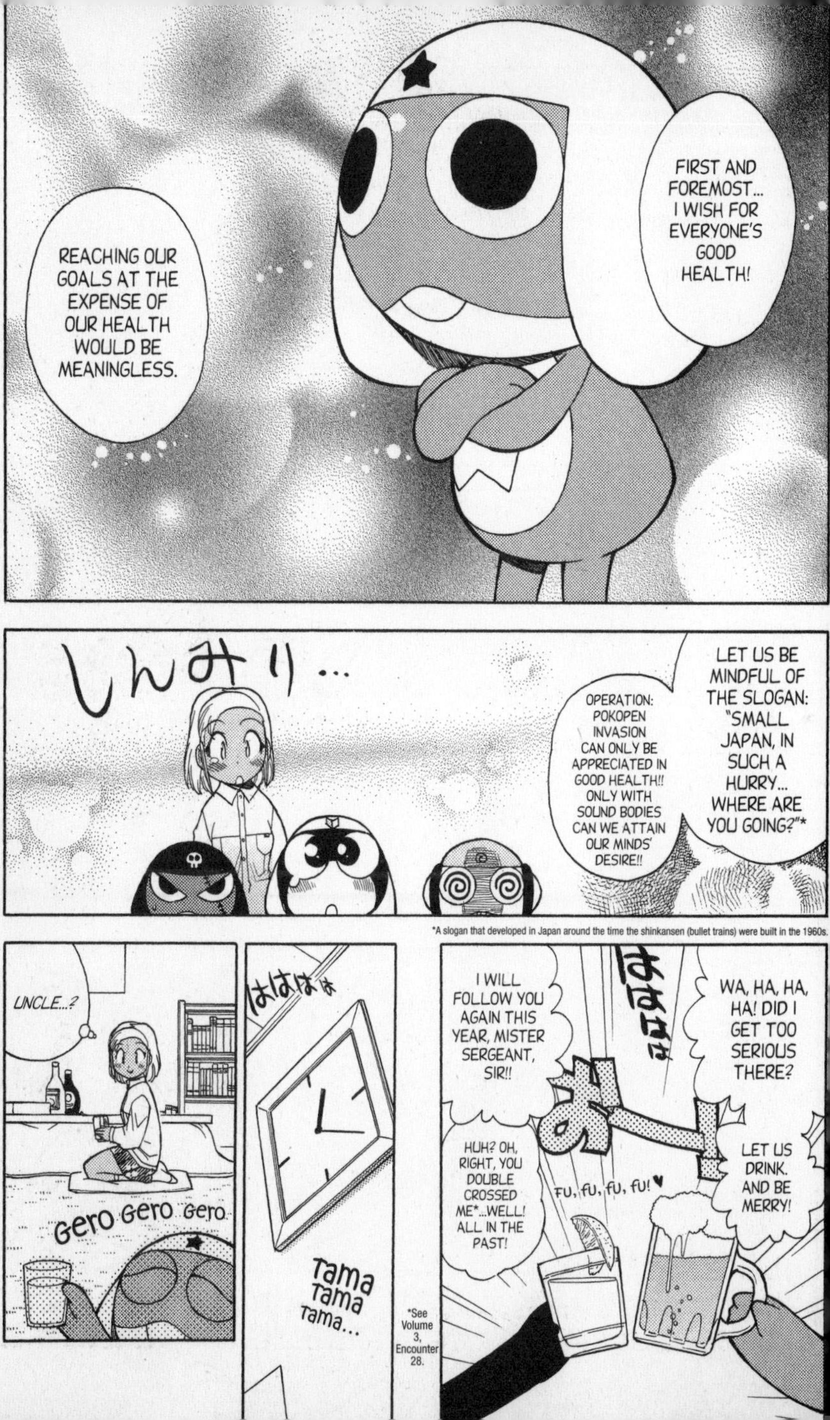
FIRST AND FOREMOST... I WISH FOR EVERYONE'S GOOD HEALTH!
REACHING OUR GOALS AT THE EXPENSE OF OUR HEALTH WOULD BE MEANINGLESS.
LET US BE MINDFUL OF THE SLOGAN: "SMALL JAPAN, IN SUCH A HURRY... WHERE ARE YOU GOING?"*
OPERATION: POKOPEN INVASION CAN ONLY BE APPRECIATED IN GOOD HEALTH!! ONLY WITH SOUND BODIES CAN WE ATTAIN OUR MINDS' DESIRE!!
しんみり...
WA, HA, HA, HA! DID I GET TOO SERIOUS THERE?
I WILL FOLLOW YOU AGAIN THIS YEAR, MISTER SERGEANT, SIR!!
ははは
LET US DRINK. AND BE MERRY!
HUH? OH, RIGHT, YOU DOUBLE CROSSED ME*...WELL! ALL IN THE PAST!
FU, fU, fU, fU!♥
ははは
Tama Tama Tama...
UNCLE...?
Gero Gero Gero

*A slogan that developed in Japan around the time the shinkansen (bullet trains) were built in the 1960s.

*See Volume 3, Encounter 28.

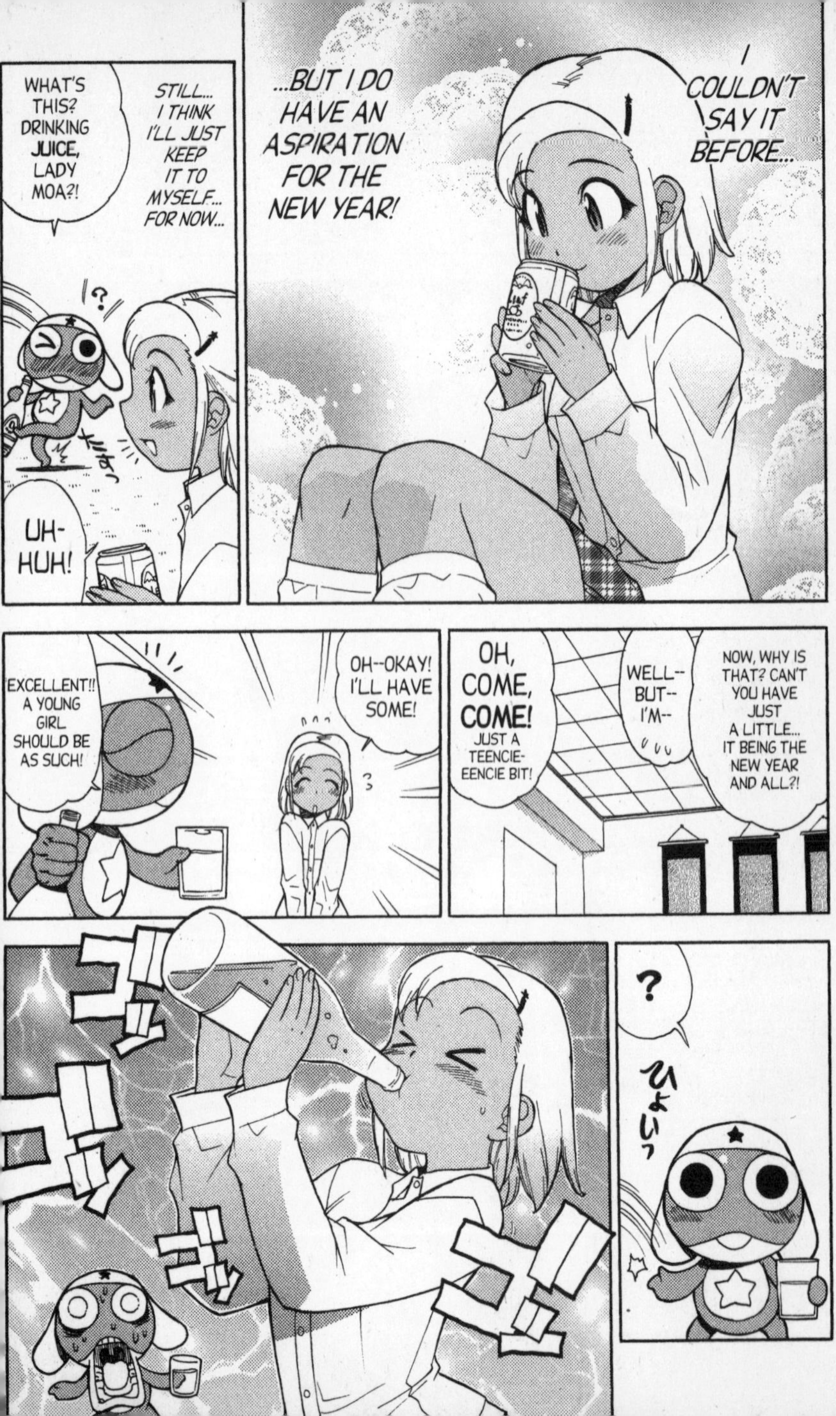

I COULDN'T SAY IT BEFORE...
...BUT I DO HAVE AN ASPIRATION FOR THE NEW YEAR!
STILL... I THINK I'LL JUST KEEP IT TO MYSELF... FOR NOW...
WHAT'S THIS? DRINKING JUICE, LADY MOA?!
UH-HUH!
NOW, WHY IS THAT? CAN'T YOU HAVE JUST A LITTLE... IT BEING THE NEW YEAR AND ALL?!
WELL-- BUT-- I'M--
OH, COME, COME! JUST A TEENCIE-EENCIE BIT!
OH--OKAY! I'LL HAVE SOME!
EXCELLENT!! A YOUNG GIRL SHOULD BE AS SUCH!
?
ひょいっ

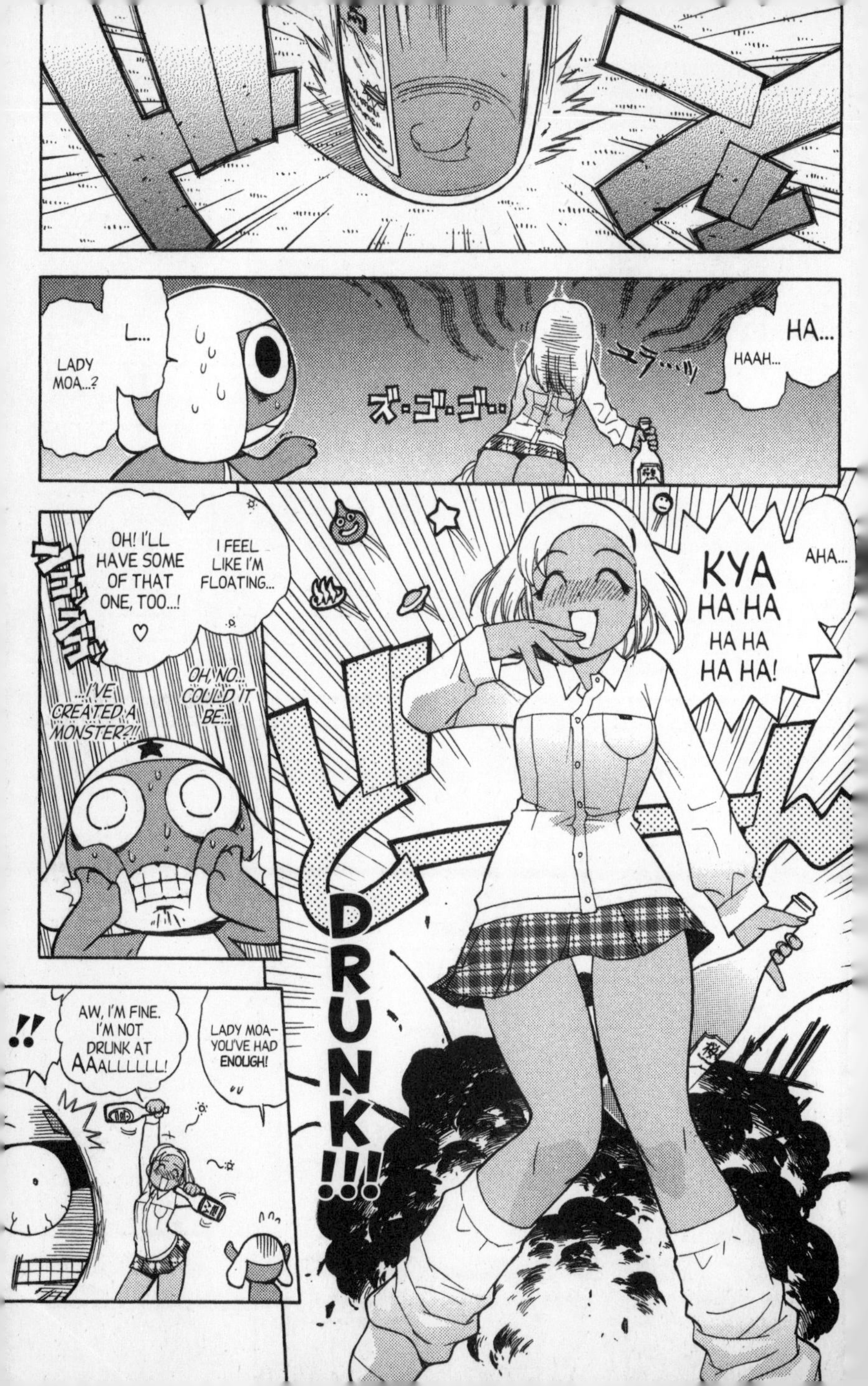
HA...
HAAH...
ユラ…ッ
ズ・ゴ・ゴ・・
L...
LADY MOA...?
AHA...
KYA HA HA HA HA HA HA!
DRUNK!!!
I FEEL LIKE I'M FLOATING...
OH! I'LL HAVE SOME OF THAT ONE, TOO...! ♡
OH, NO... COULD IT BE...
...I'VE CREATED A MONSTER?!!
LADY MOA- YOU'VE HAD ENOUGH!
AW, I'M FINE. I'M NOT DRUNK AT AAALLLLLL!
!!

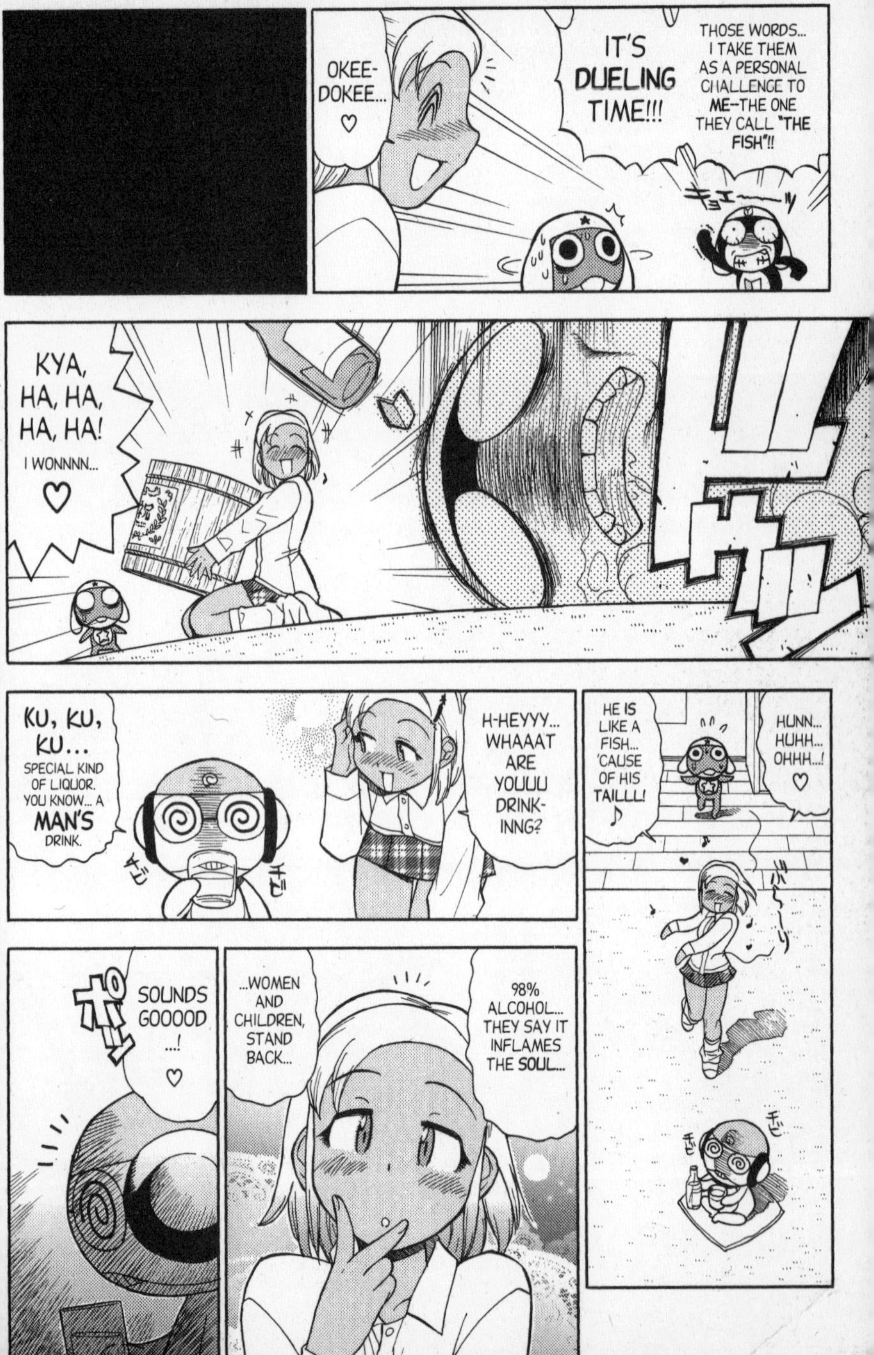
THOSE WORDS... I TAKE THEM AS A PERSONAL CHALLENGE TO ME--THE ONE THEY CALL "THE FISH"!!
IT'S DUELING TIME!!!
OKEE-DOKEE... ♡
KYA, HA, HA, HA, HA! I WONNNN... ♡
HUNN... HUHH... OHHH...! ♡
HE IS LIKE A FISH... 'CAUSE OF HIS TAILLL! ♪
H-HEYYY... WHAAAT ARE YOUUU DRINK-INNG?
KU, KU, KU... SPECIAL KIND OF LIQUOR. YOU KNOW... A MAN'S DRINK.
98% ALCOHOL... THEY SAY IT INFLAMES THE SOUL...
...WOMEN AND CHILDREN, STAND BACK...
SOUNDS GOOOOD ...! ♡

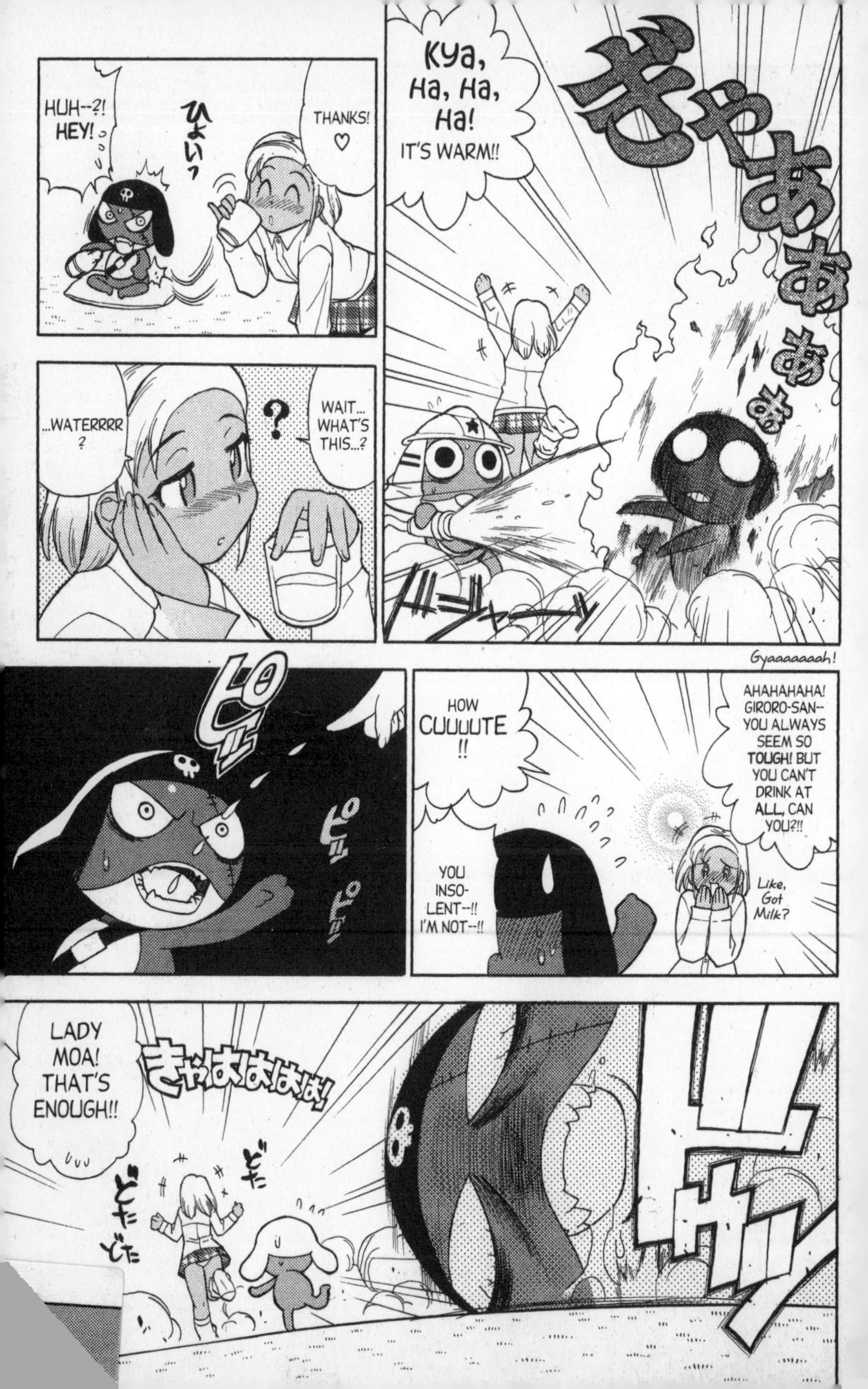

Kya, Ha, Ha, Ha!
IT'S WARM!!
ぎゃああああ
Gyaaaaaaah!
THANKS! ♡
ひょいっ
HUH--?! HEY!
WAIT... WHAT'S THIS...?
...WATERRRR?
AHAHAHAHA! GIROROSAN-- YOU ALWAYS SEEM SO TOUGH! BUT YOU CAN'T DRINK AT ALL, CAN YOU?!!
Like, Got Milk?
HOW CUUUUTE!!
YOU INSO-LENT--!! I'M NOT--!!
きゃはははは!
LADY MOA! THAT'S ENOUGH!!
どた どた どた

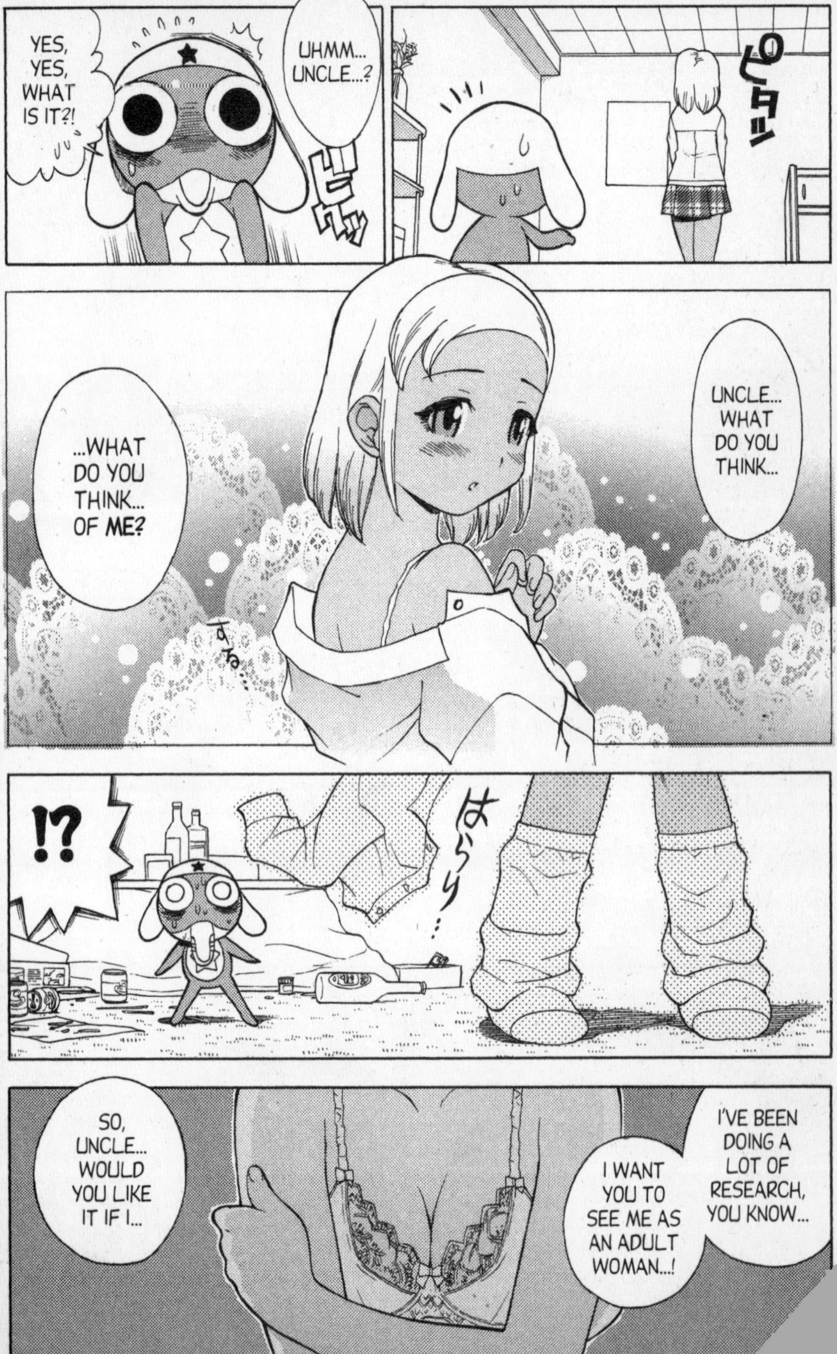
ピタッ
UHMM... UNCLE...?
YES, YES, WHAT IS IT?!
ビクッ
UNCLE... WHAT DO YOU THINK...
...WHAT DO YOU THINK... OF ME?
する...
はらり...
!?
I'VE BEEN DOING A LOT OF RESEARCH, YOU KNOW...
I WANT YOU TO SEE ME AS AN ADULT WOMAN...!
SO, UNCLE... WOULD YOU LIKE IT IF I...

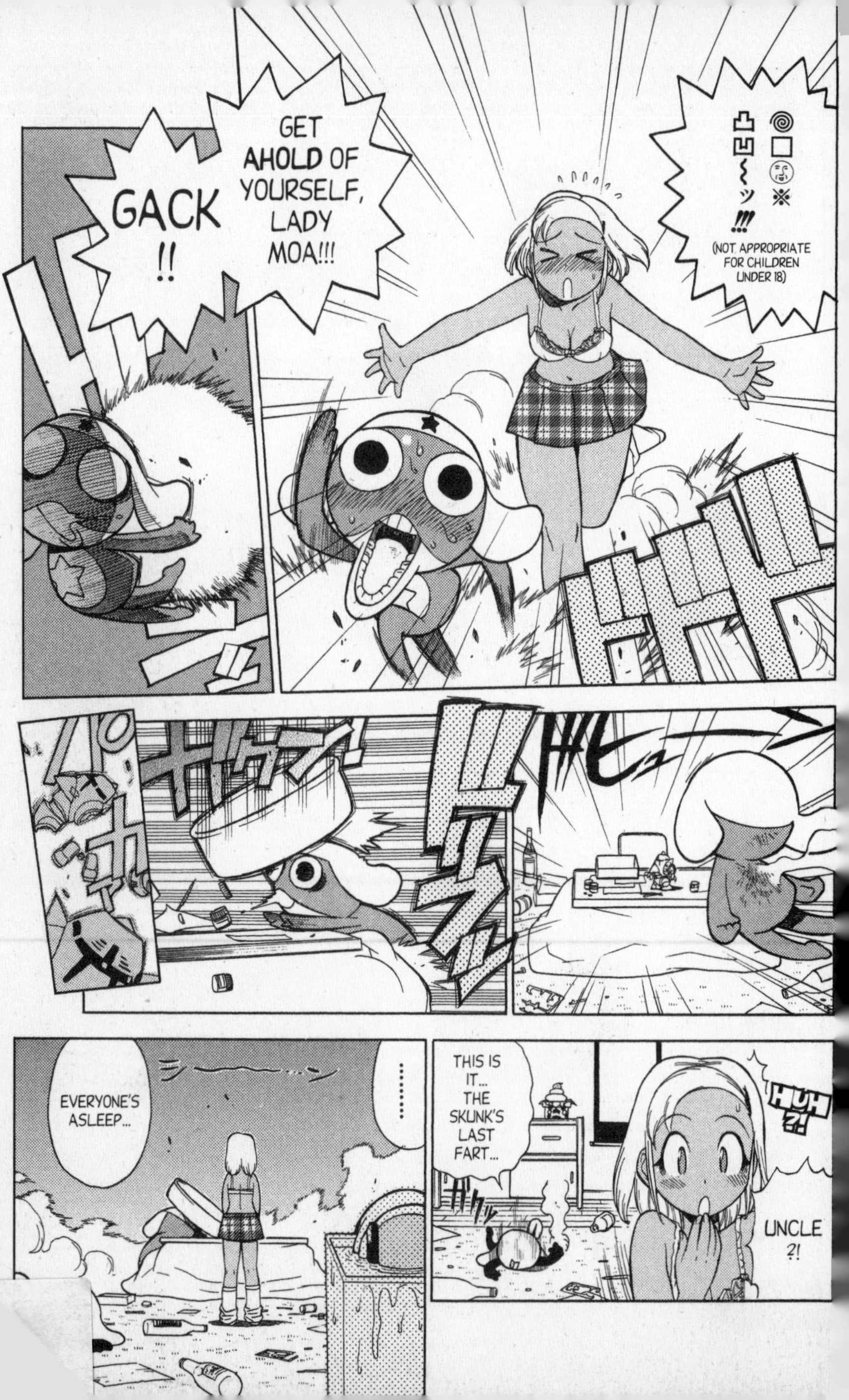

◎□※凸凹〜ッ!!!
(NOT APPROPRIATE FOR CHILDREN UNDER 18)
GET AHOLD OF YOURSELF, LADY MOA!!!
GACK !!
HUH ?!
THIS IS IT... THE SKUNK'S LAST FART...
UNCLE ?!
.......
EVERYONE'S ASLEEP...

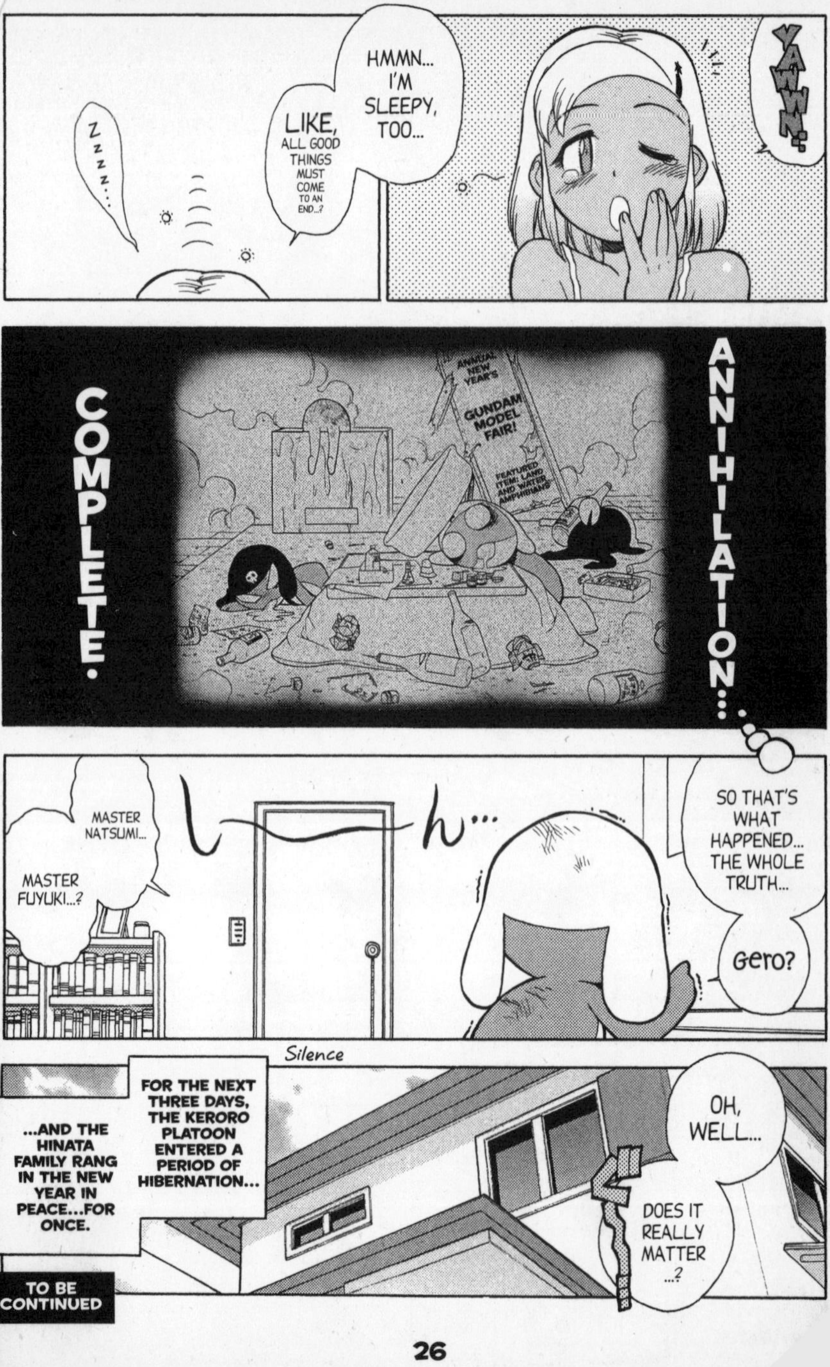
YAWWN...
HMMN... I'M SLEEPY, TOO...
LIKE, ALL GOOD THINGS MUST COME TO AN END...?
Z z z z...
ANNIHILATION...
ANNUAL NEW YEAR'S GUNDAM MODEL FAIR!
FEATURED ITEM: LAND AND WATER AMPHIBIANS
COMPLETE.
SO THAT'S WHAT HAPPENED... THE WHOLE TRUTH...
Gero?
MASTER NATSUMI...
MASTER FUYUKI...?
Silence
OH, WELL...
DOES IT REALLY MATTER...?
FOR THE NEXT THREE DAYS, THE KERORO PLATOON ENTERED A PERIOD OF HIBERNATION...
...AND THE HINATA FAMILY RANG IN THE NEW YEAR IN PEACE...FOR ONCE.
TO BE CONTINUED

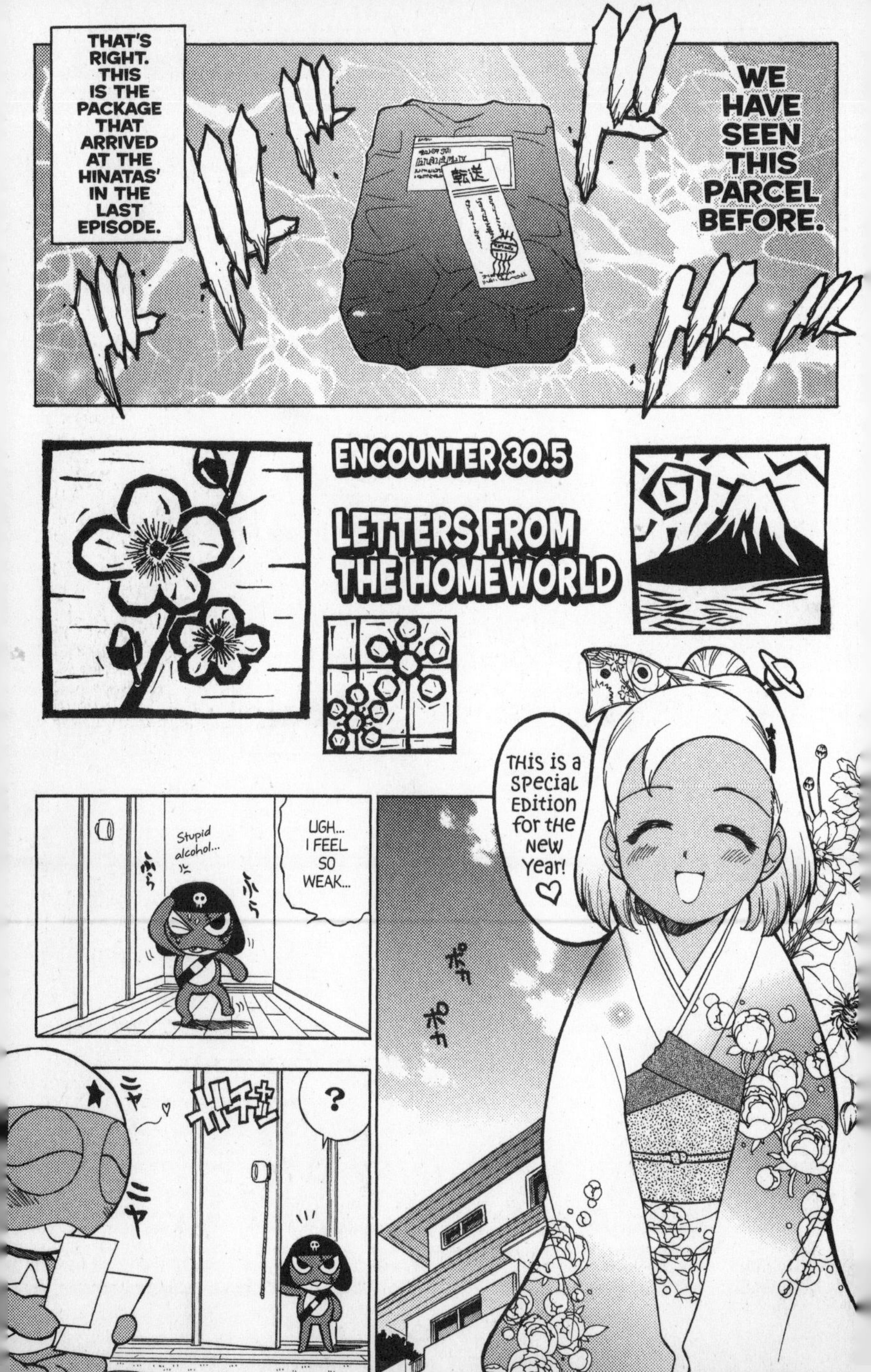

WE HAVE SEEN THIS PARCEL BEFORE.
THAT'S RIGHT. THIS IS THE PACKAGE THAT ARRIVED AT THE HINATAS' IN THE LAST EPISODE.
転送
ENCOUNTER 30.5
LETTERS FROM THE HOMEWORLD
THIS is a Special Edition for tHE NEW Year! ♡
UGH... I FEEL SO WEAK...
Stupid alcohol...
?

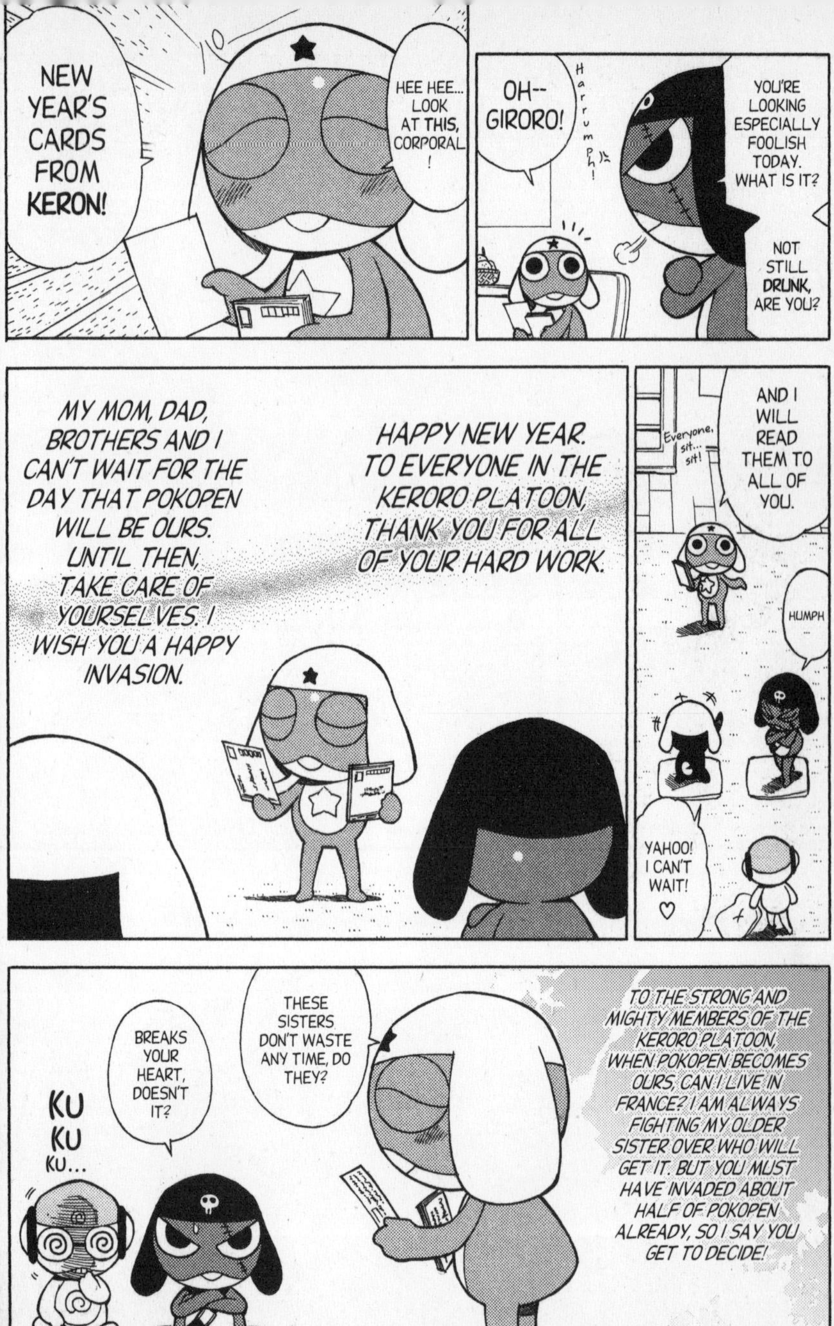
YOU'RE LOOKING ESPECIALLY FOOLISH TODAY. WHAT IS IT?
Harrumph!
OH-- GIRORO!
NOT STILL DRUNK, ARE YOU?
HEE HEE... LOOK AT THIS, CORPORAL!
NEW YEAR'S CARDS FROM KERON!
AND I WILL READ THEM TO ALL OF YOU.
Everyone, sit... sit!
HUMPH...
YAHOO! I CAN'T WAIT! ♡
HAPPY NEW YEAR. TO EVERYONE IN THE KERORO PLATOON, THANK YOU FOR ALL OF YOUR HARD WORK.
MY MOM, DAD, BROTHERS AND I CAN'T WAIT FOR THE DAY THAT POKOPEN WILL BE OURS. UNTIL THEN, TAKE CARE OF YOURSELVES. I WISH YOU A HAPPY INVASION.
TO THE STRONG AND MIGHTY MEMBERS OF THE KERORO PLATOON, WHEN POKOPEN BECOMES OURS, CAN I LIVE IN FRANCE? I AM ALWAYS FIGHTING MY OLDER SISTER OVER WHO WILL GET IT. BUT YOU MUST HAVE INVADED ABOUT HALF OF POKOPEN ALREADY, SO I SAY YOU GET TO DECIDE!
THESE SISTERS DON'T WASTE ANY TIME, DO THEY?
BREAKS YOUR HEART, DOESN'T IT?
KU KU KU...

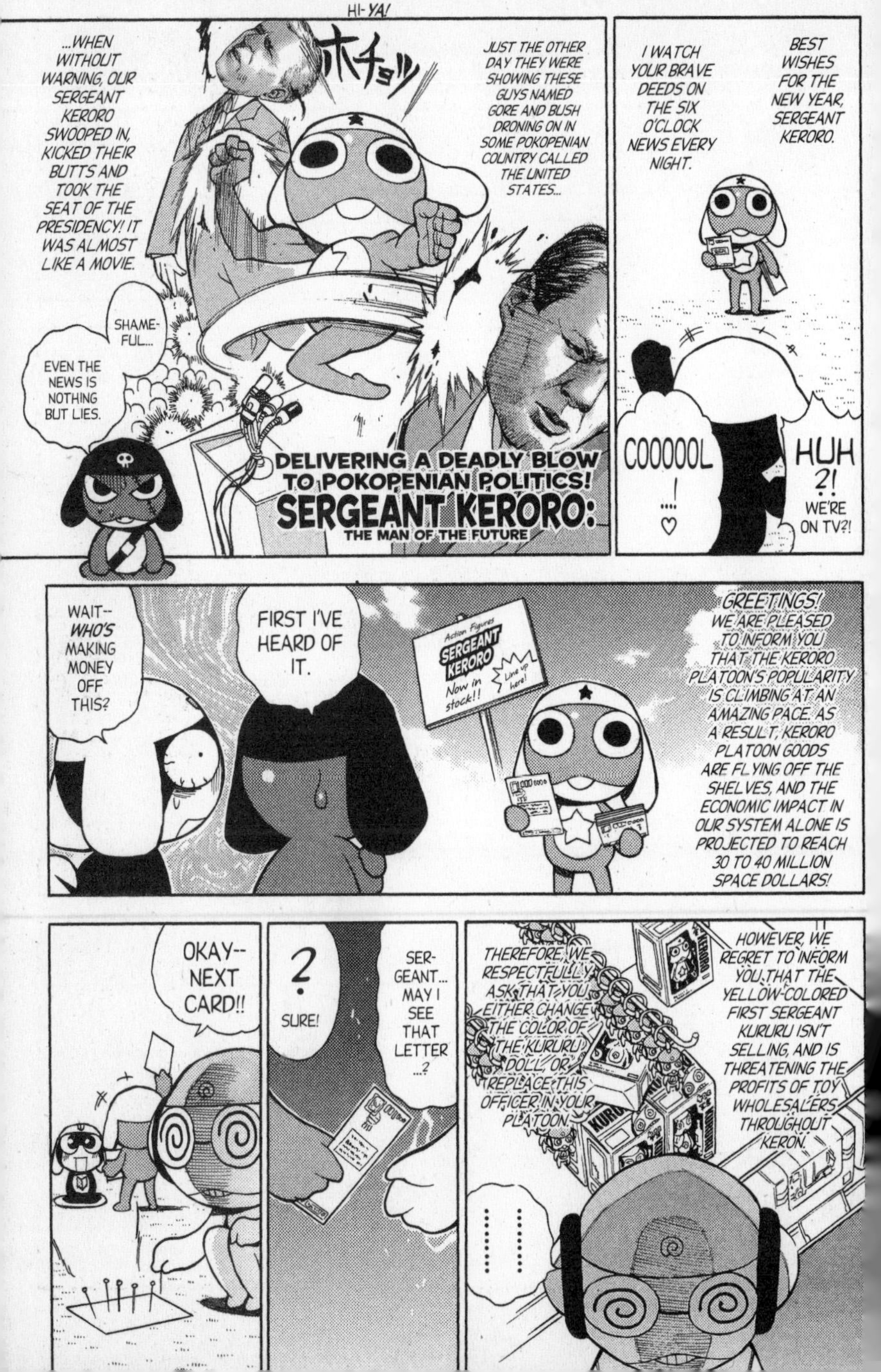
BEST WISHES FOR THE NEW YEAR, SERGEANT KERORO.
I WATCH YOUR BRAVE DEEDS ON THE SIX O'CLOCK NEWS EVERY NIGHT.
HUH?! WE'RE ON TV?!
COOOOOL...! ♡
HI-YA!
ホチョッ
JUST THE OTHER DAY THEY WERE SHOWING THESE GUYS NAMED GORE AND BUSH DRONING ON IN SOME POKOPENIAN COUNTRY CALLED THE UNITED STATES...
...WHEN WITHOUT WARNING, OUR SERGEANT KERORO SWOOPED IN, KICKED THEIR BUTTS AND TOOK THE SEAT OF THE PRESIDENCY! IT WAS ALMOST LIKE A MOVIE.
SHAME-FUL...
EVEN THE NEWS IS NOTHING BUT LIES.
DELIVERING A DEADLY BLOW TO POKOPENIAN POLITICS!
SERGEANT KERORO:
THE MAN OF THE FUTURE
GREETINGS! WE ARE PLEASED TO INFORM YOU THAT THE KERORO PLATOON'S POPULARITY IS CLIMBING AT AN AMAZING PACE. AS A RESULT, KERORO PLATOON GOODS ARE FLYING OFF THE SHELVES, AND THE ECONOMIC IMPACT IN OUR SYSTEM ALONE IS PROJECTED TO REACH 30 TO 40 MILLION SPACE DOLLARS!
Action Figures SERGEANT KERORO Now in stock!!
Line up here!
FIRST I'VE HEARD OF IT.
WAIT-- WHO'S MAKING MONEY OFF THIS?
HOWEVER, WE REGRET TO INFORM YOU THAT THE YELLOW-COLORED FIRST SERGEANT KURURU ISN'T SELLING, AND IS THREATENING THE PROFITS OF TOY WHOLESALERS THROUGHOUT KERON.
THEREFORE, WE RESPECTFULLY ASK THAT YOU EITHER CHANGE THE COLOR OF THE KURURU DOLL, OR REPLACE THIS OFFICER IN YOUR PLATOON.
......
SER-GEANT... MAY I SEE THAT LETTER...?
?
SURE!
OKAY-- NEXT CARD!!

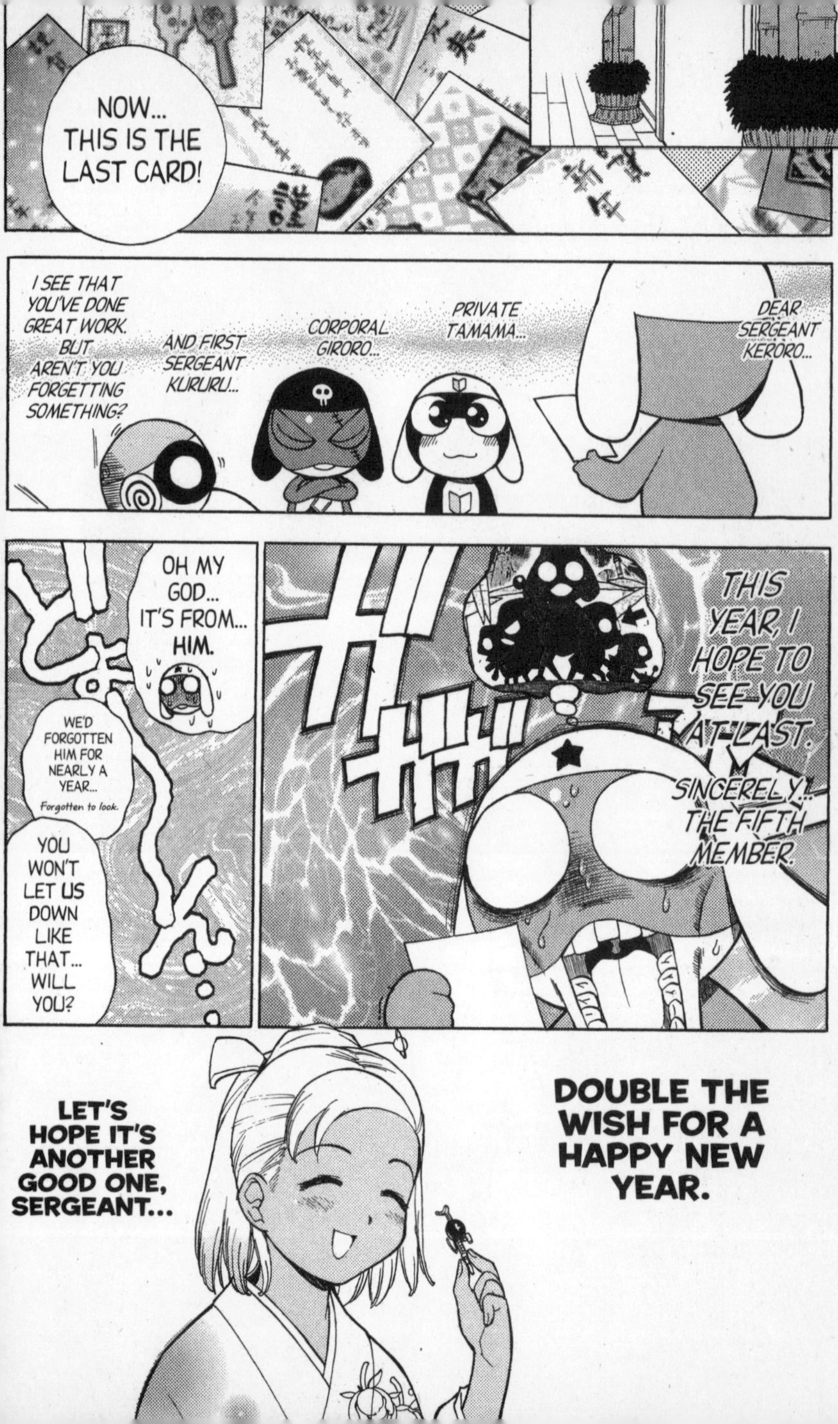
NOW... THIS IS THE LAST CARD!
DEAR SERGEANT KERORO...
PRIVATE TAMAMA...
CORPORAL GIRORO...
AND FIRST SERGEANT KURURU...
I SEE THAT YOU'VE DONE GREAT WORK. BUT AREN'T YOU FORGETTING SOMETHING?
THIS YEAR, I HOPE TO SEE YOU AT LAST.
SINCERELY... THE FIFTH MEMBER.
OH MY GOD... IT'S FROM... HIM.
WE'D FORGOTTEN HIM FOR NEARLY A YEAR...
Forgotten to look.
YOU WON'T LET US DOWN LIKE THAT... WILL YOU?
DOUBLE THE WISH FOR A HAPPY NEW YEAR.
LET'S HOPE IT'S ANOTHER GOOD ONE, SERGEANT...

## ENCOUNTER XXXI
# THE REVENGE OF THE RED GOBLIN!!

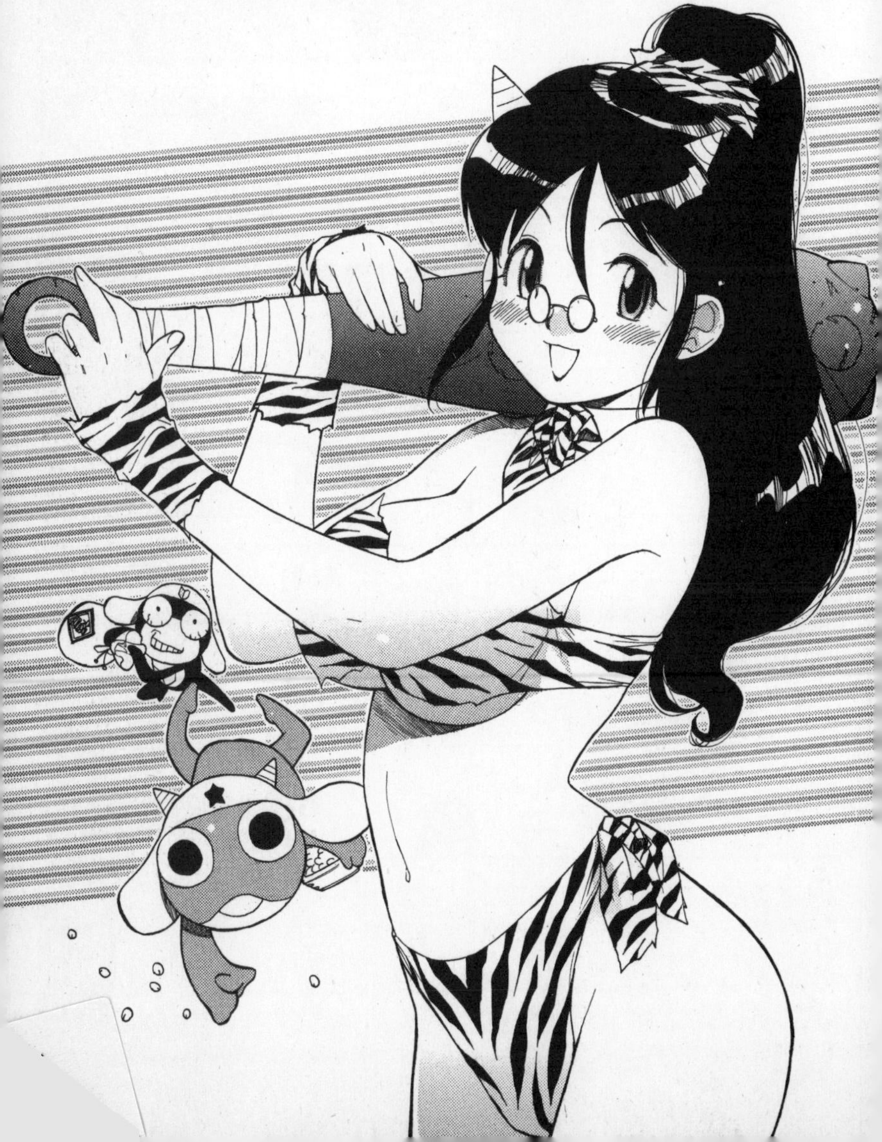

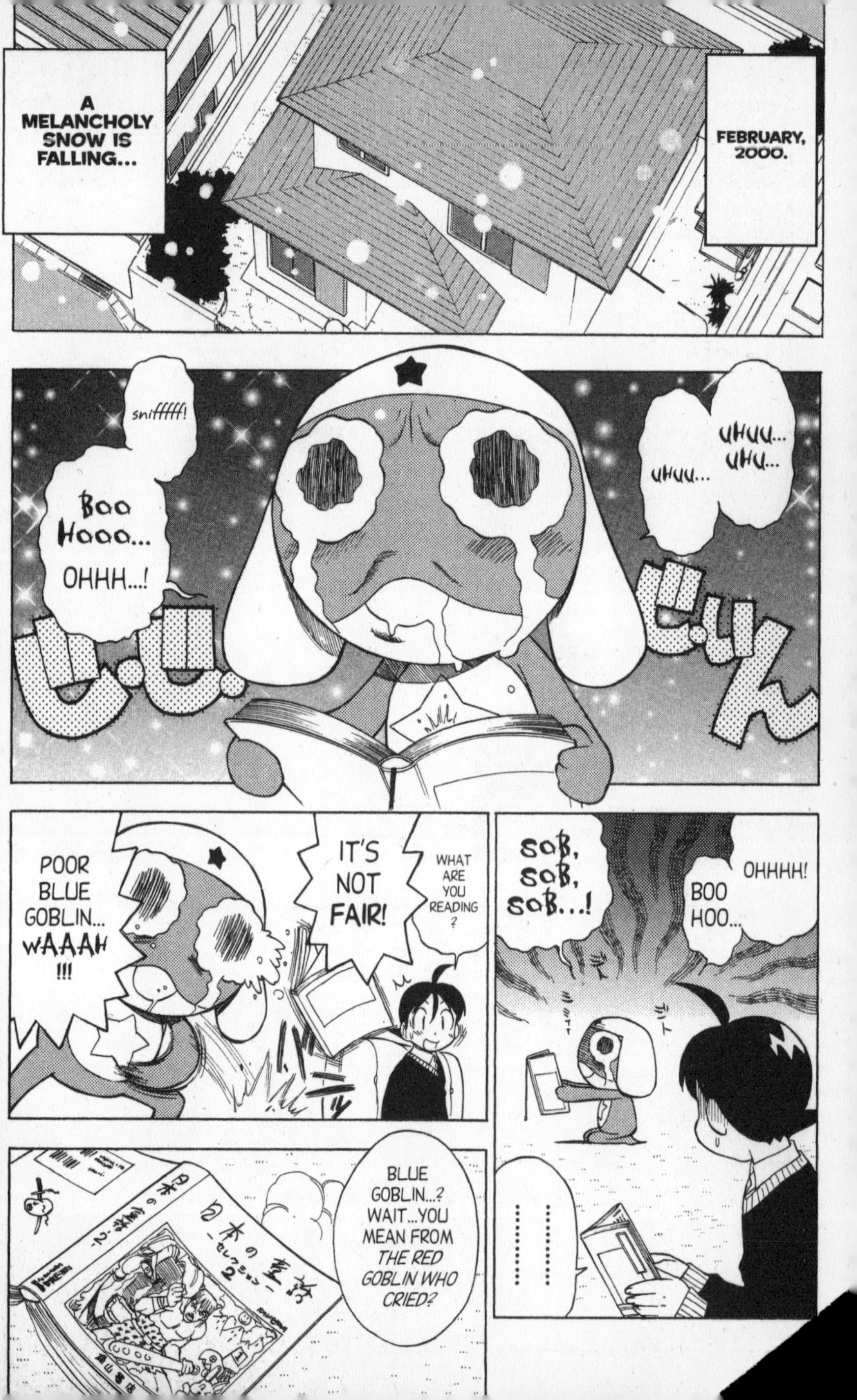
FEBRUARY, 2000.
A MELANCHOLY SNOW IS FALLING...
UHUU... UHU... UHUU...
sniffff!
Boo Haaa... OHHH...!
OHHHH! BOO HOO...
SoB, SoB, SoB...!
WHAT ARE YOU READING?
IT'S NOT FAIR!
POOR BLUE GOBLIN... WAAAH!!!
......
......
BLUE GOBLIN...? WAIT...YOU MEAN FROM *THE RED GOBLIN WHO CRIED?*

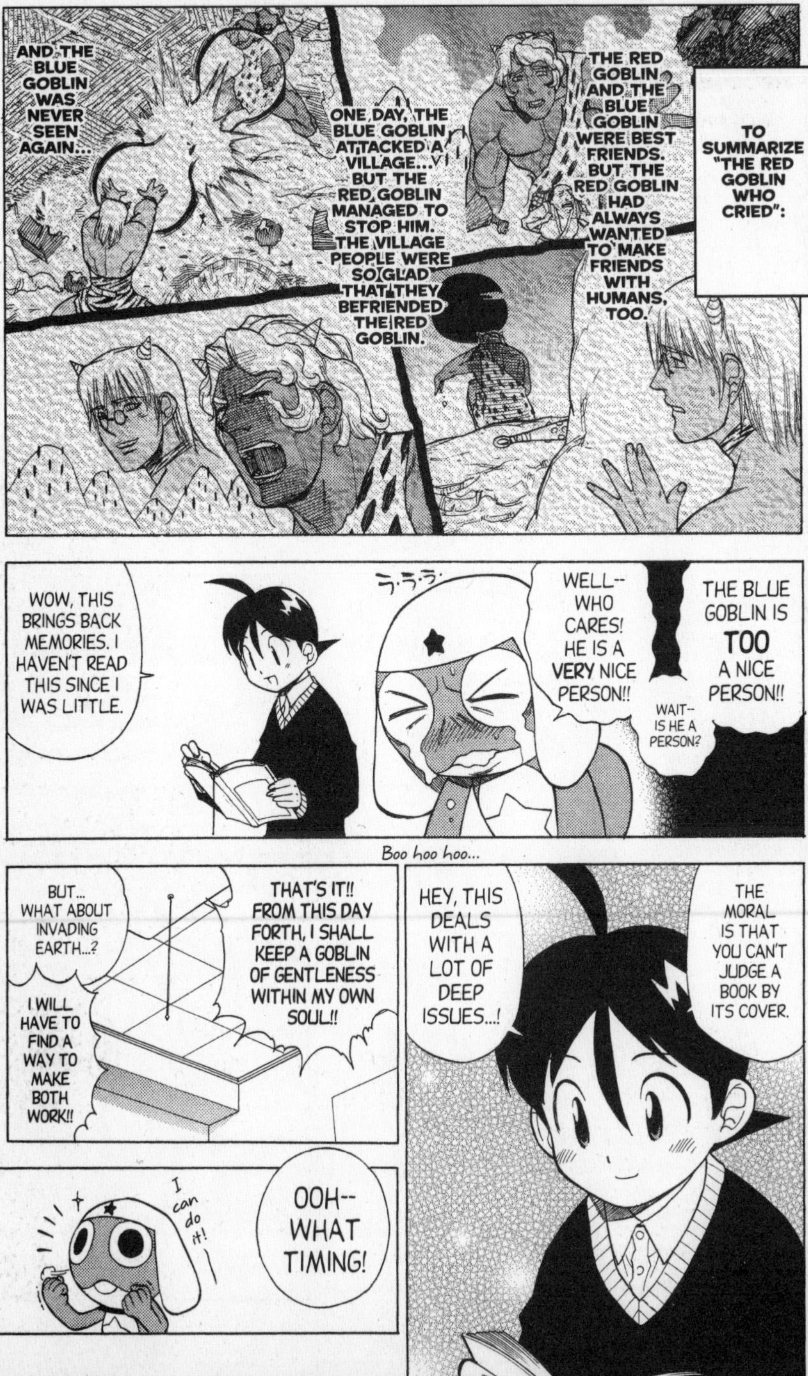
TO SUMMARIZE "THE RED GOBLIN WHO CRIED":
THE RED GOBLIN AND THE BLUE GOBLIN WERE BEST FRIENDS. BUT THE RED GOBLIN HAD ALWAYS WANTED TO MAKE FRIENDS WITH HUMANS, TOO.
ONE DAY, THE BLUE GOBLIN ATTACKED A VILLAGE... BUT THE RED GOBLIN MANAGED TO STOP HIM. THE VILLAGE PEOPLE WERE SO GLAD THAT THEY BEFRIENDED THE RED GOBLIN.
AND THE BLUE GOBLIN WAS NEVER SEEN AGAIN...
THE BLUE GOBLIN IS TOO A NICE PERSON!!
WAIT-- IS HE A PERSON?
WELL-- WHO CARES! HE IS A VERY NICE PERSON!!
ラ·ラ·ラ·
WOW, THIS BRINGS BACK MEMORIES. I HAVEN'T READ THIS SINCE I WAS LITTLE.
Boo hoo hoo...
THE MORAL IS THAT YOU CAN'T JUDGE A BOOK BY ITS COVER.
HEY, THIS DEALS WITH A LOT OF DEEP ISSUES...!
THAT'S IT!! FROM THIS DAY FORTH, I SHALL KEEP A GOBLIN OF GENTLENESS WITHIN MY OWN SOUL!!
BUT... WHAT ABOUT INVADING EARTH...?
I WILL HAVE TO FIND A WAY TO MAKE BOTH WORK!!
OOH-- WHAT TIMING!
I can do it!

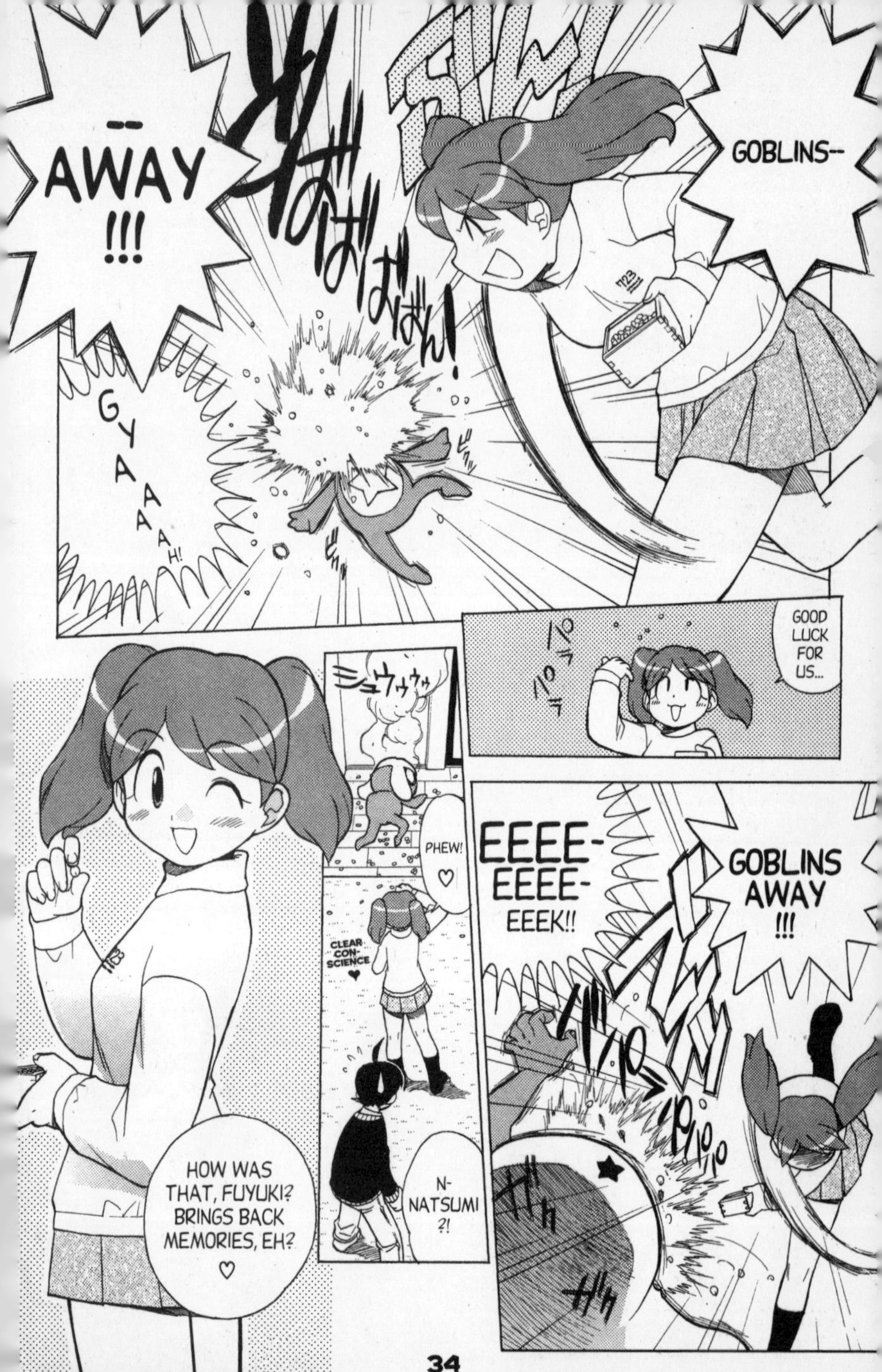
GOBLINS--
--AWAY!!!
GYAAAAAH!
GOOD LUCK FOR US...
GOBLINS AWAY!!!
EEEE-EEEE-EEEK!!
PHEW! ♡
CLEAR CON-SCIENCE ♥
N-NATSUMI?!
HOW WAS THAT, FUYUKI? BRINGS BACK MEMORIES, EH? ♡

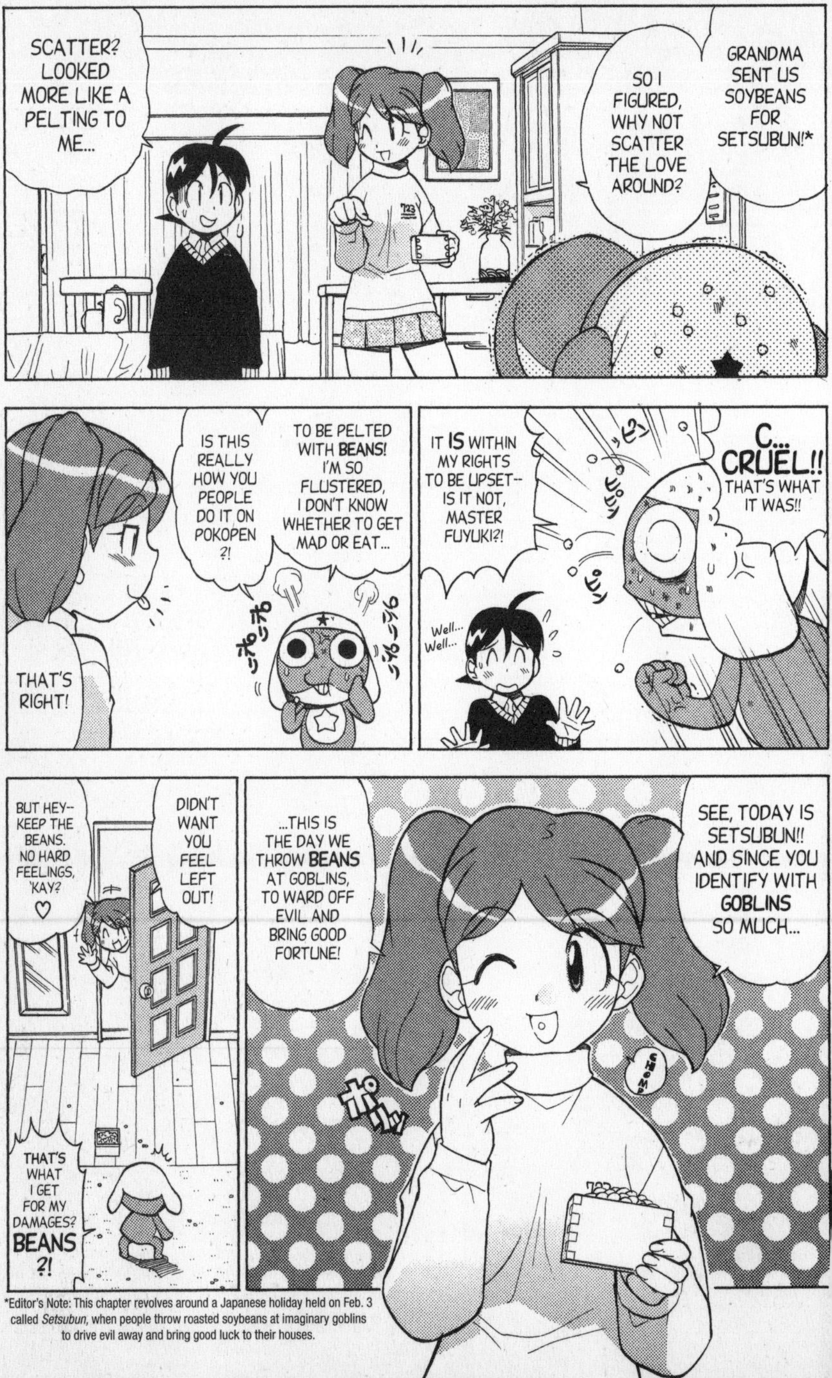
GRANDMA SENT US SOYBEANS FOR SETSUBUN!*
SO I FIGURED, WHY NOT SCATTER THE LOVE AROUND?
SCATTER? LOOKED MORE LIKE A PELTING TO ME...
C... CRUEL!! THAT'S WHAT IT WAS!!
IT IS WITHIN MY RIGHTS TO BE UPSET-- IS IT NOT, MASTER FUYUKI?!
Well... Well...
TO BE PELTED WITH BEANS! I'M SO FLUSTERED, I DON'T KNOW WHETHER TO GET MAD OR EAT...
IS THIS REALLY HOW YOU PEOPLE DO IT ON POKOPEN?!
THAT'S RIGHT!
SEE, TODAY IS SETSUBUN!! AND SINCE YOU IDENTIFY WITH GOBLINS SO MUCH...
...THIS IS THE DAY WE THROW BEANS AT GOBLINS, TO WARD OFF EVIL AND BRING GOOD FORTUNE!
CHOMP
DIDN'T WANT YOU FEEL LEFT OUT!
BUT HEY-- KEEP THE BEANS. NO HARD FEELINGS, 'KAY? ♡
THAT'S WHAT I GET FOR MY DAMAGES? BEANS?!

*Editor's Note: This chapter revolves around a Japanese holiday held on Feb. 3 called *Setsubun*, when people throw roasted soybeans at imaginary goblins to drive evil away and bring good luck to their houses.

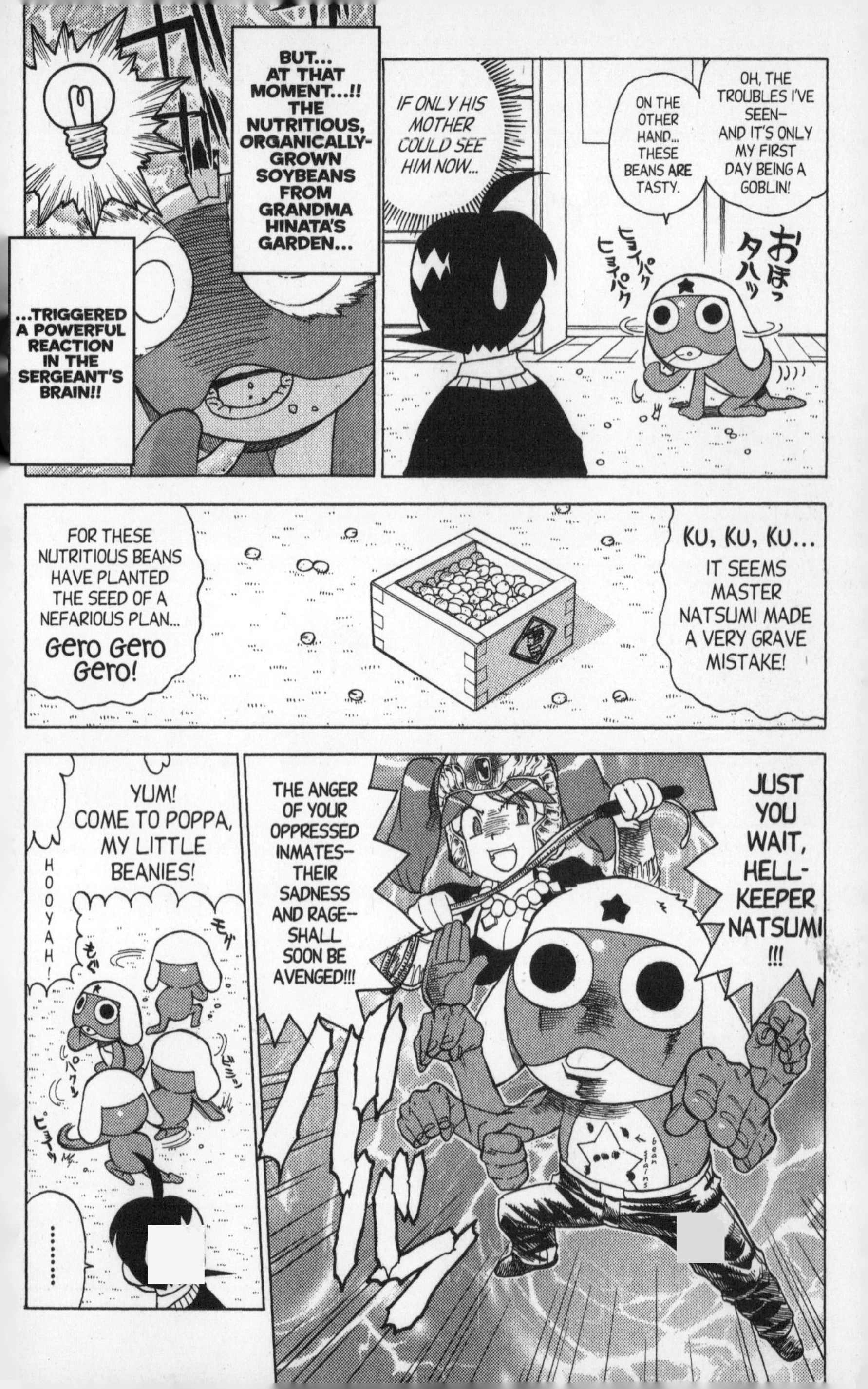
OH, THE TROUBLES I'VE SEEN— AND IT'S ONLY MY FIRST DAY BEING A GOBLIN!
ON THE OTHER HAND... THESE BEANS ARE TASTY.
おほっ タハッ
ヒョイパク ヒョイパク
IF ONLY HIS MOTHER COULD SEE HIM NOW...
BUT... AT THAT MOMENT...!! THE NUTRITIOUS, ORGANICALLY-GROWN SOYBEANS FROM GRANDMA HINATA'S GARDEN...
...TRIGGERED A POWERFUL REACTION IN THE SERGEANT'S BRAIN!!
KU, KU, KU... IT SEEMS MASTER NATSUMI MADE A VERY GRAVE MISTAKE!
FOR THESE NUTRITIOUS BEANS HAVE PLANTED THE SEED OF A NEFARIOUS PLAN... Gero Gero Gero!
JUST YOU WAIT, HELL-KEEPER NATSUMI!!!
THE ANGER OF YOUR OPPRESSED INMATES-- THEIR SADNESS AND RAGE-- SHALL SOON BE AVENGED!!!
bean stains
YUM! COME TO POPPA, MY LITTLE BEANIES!
HOOYAH!
.........

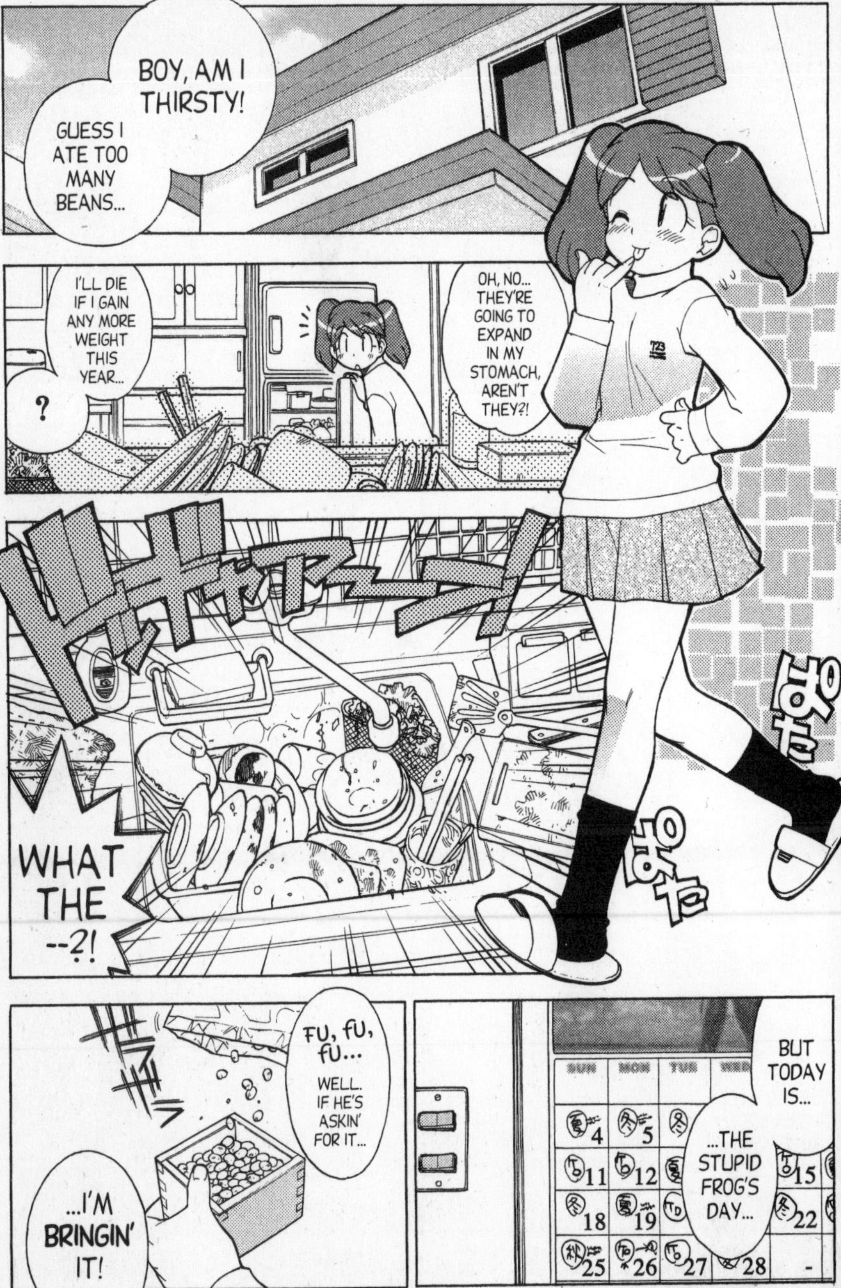
BOY, AM I THIRSTY!
GUESS I ATE TOO MANY BEANS...
OH, NO... THEY'RE GOING TO EXPAND IN MY STOMACH, AREN'T THEY?!
I'LL DIE IF I GAIN ANY MORE WEIGHT THIS YEAR...
?
ぽた
ぽた
WHAT THE --?!
BUT TODAY IS...
...THE STUPID FROG'S DAY...
FU, FU, FU...
WELL. IF HE'S ASKIN' FOR IT...
...I'M BRINGIN' IT!

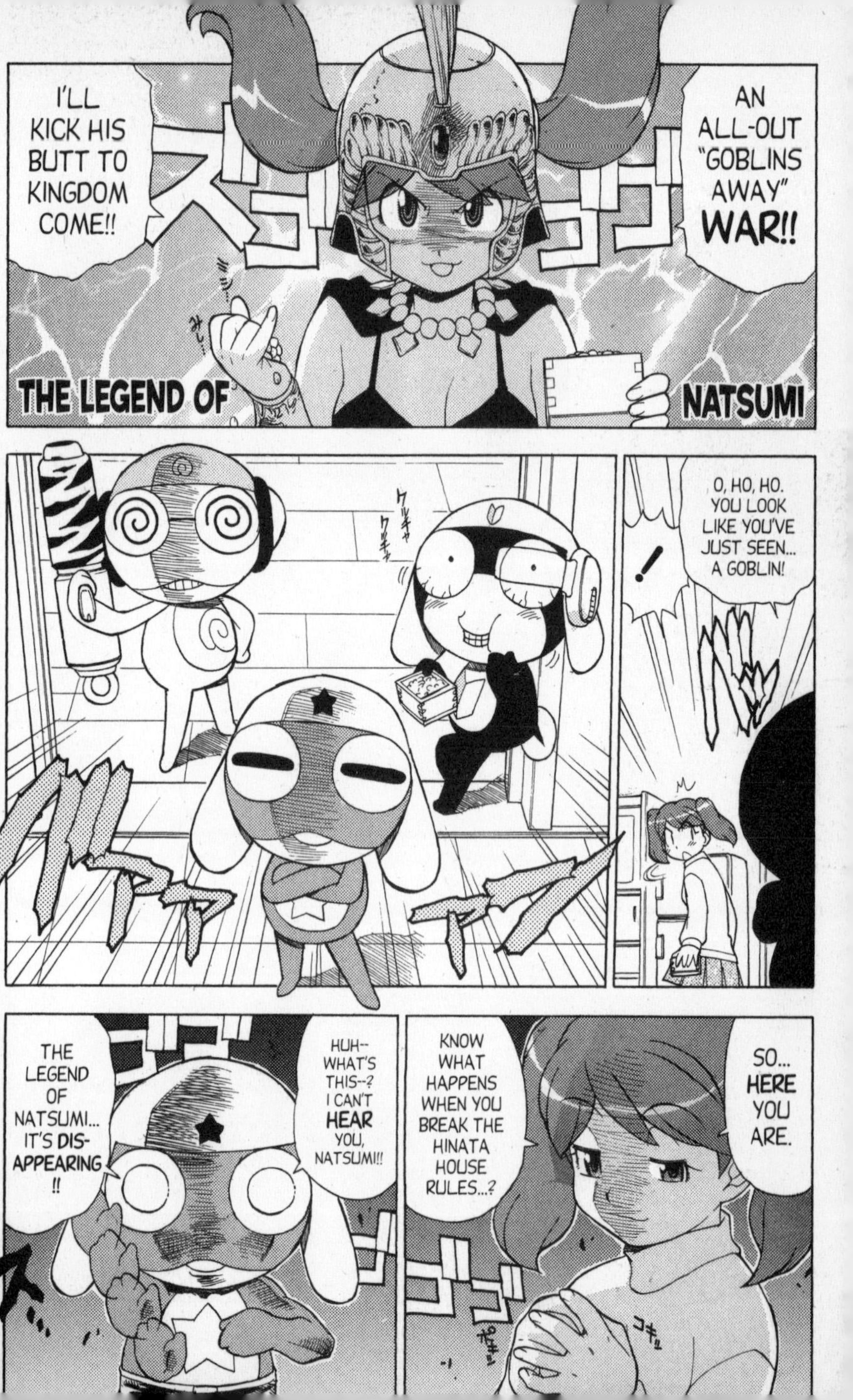
AN ALL-OUT "GOBLINS AWAY" WAR!!
I'LL KICK HIS BUTT TO KINGDOM COME!!
THE LEGEND OF NATSUMI
O, HO, HO. YOU LOOK LIKE YOU'VE JUST SEEN... A GOBLIN!
!
SO... HERE YOU ARE.
KNOW WHAT HAPPENS WHEN YOU BREAK THE HINATA HOUSE RULES...?
HUH-- WHAT'S THIS--? I CAN'T HEAR YOU, NATSUMI!!
THE LEGEND OF NATSUMI... IT'S DIS-APPEARING!!

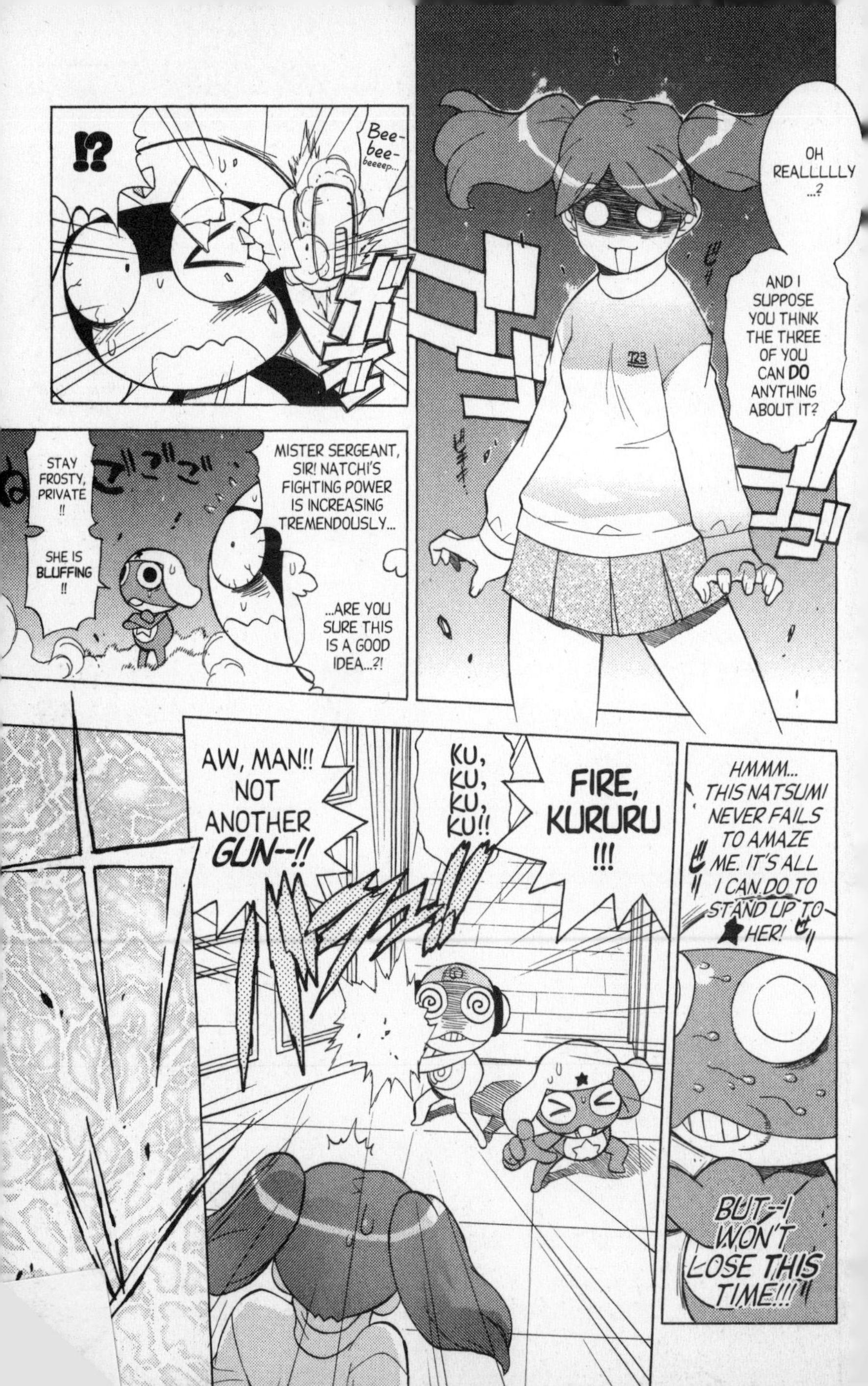
OH REALLLLLY ...?
AND I SUPPOSE YOU THINK THE THREE OF YOU CAN DO ANYTHING ABOUT IT?
Bee-bee-beeeep...
!?
MISTER SERGEANT, SIR! NATCHI'S FIGHTING POWER IS INCREASING TREMENDOUSLY...
...ARE YOU SURE THIS IS A GOOD IDEA...?!
STAY FROSTY, PRIVATE !!
SHE IS BLUFFING !!
HMMM... THIS NATSUMI NEVER FAILS TO AMAZE ME. IT'S ALL I CAN DO TO STAND UP TO HER!
BUT--I WON'T LOSE THIS TIME!!!
FIRE, KURURU !!!
KU, KU, KU, KU!!
AW, MAN!! NOT ANOTHER GUN--!!

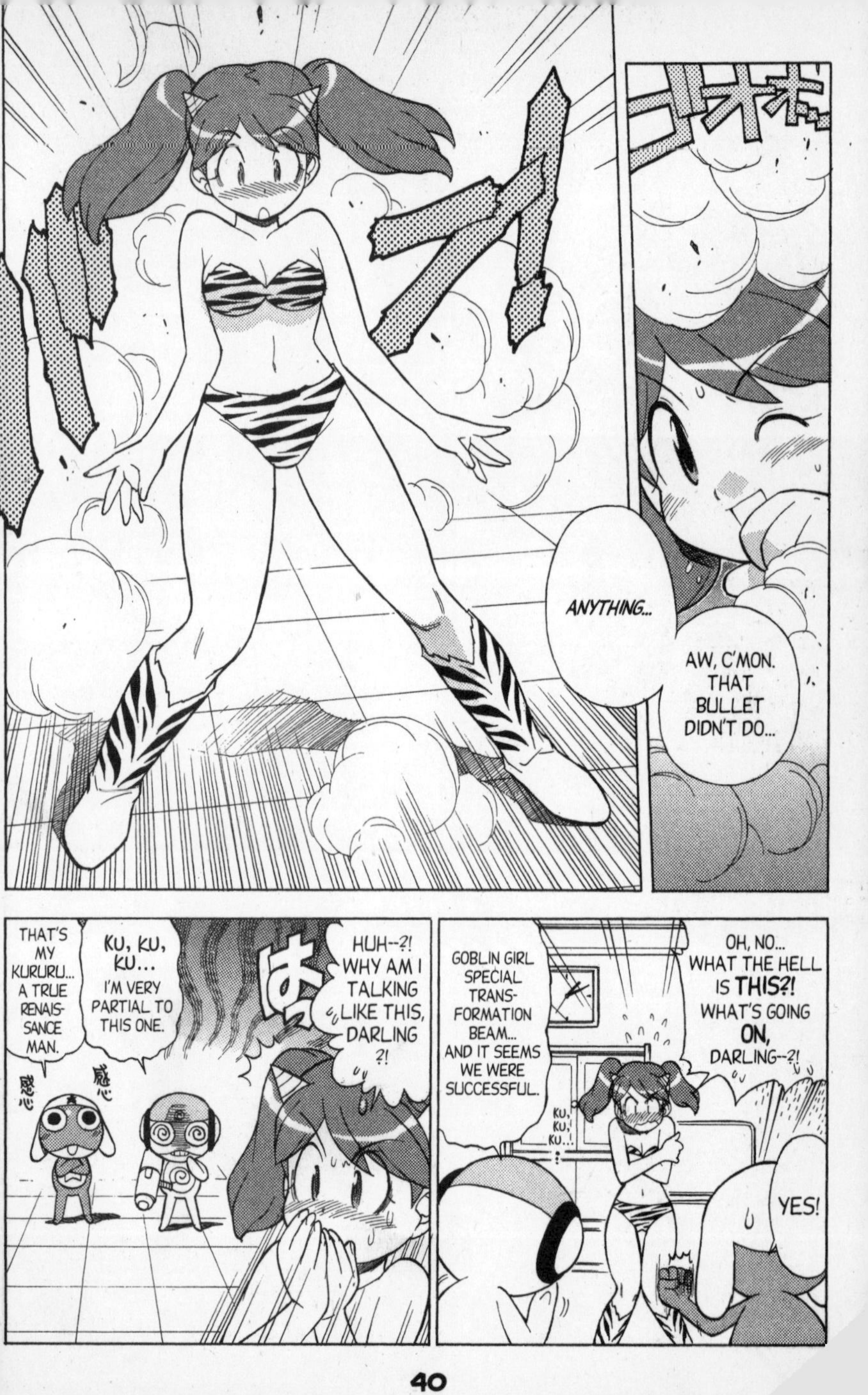
AW, C'MON. THAT BULLET DIDN'T DO...
ANYTHING...
OH, NO... WHAT THE HELL IS THIS?! WHAT'S GOING ON, Darling--?!
GOBLIN GIRL SPECIAL TRANS-FORMATION BEAM... AND IT SEEMS WE WERE SUCCESSFUL.
KU, KU, KU...!
YES!
HUH--?! WHY AM I TALKING LIKE THIS, DARLING?!
は
KU, KU, KU... I'M VERY PARTIAL TO THIS ONE.
THAT'S MY KURURU... A TRUE RENAIS-SANCE MAN.
感心
感心

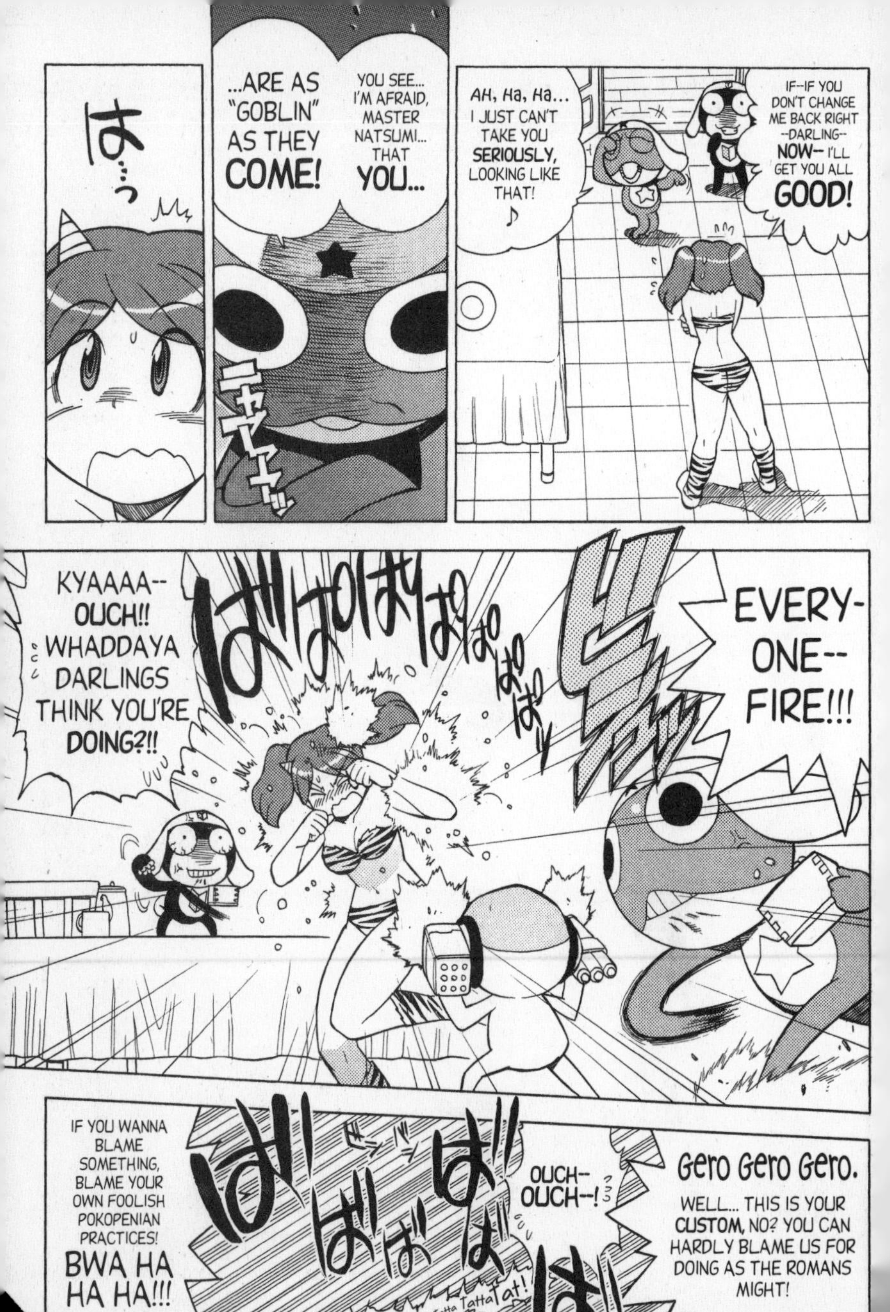

IF--IF YOU DON'T CHANGE ME BACK RIGHT --DARLING-- NOW-- I'LL GET YOU ALL GOOD!
AH, HA, HA... I JUST CAN'T TAKE YOU SERIOUSLY, LOOKING LIKE THAT! ♪
YOU SEE... I'M AFRAID, MASTER NATSUMI... THAT YOU...
...ARE AS "GOBLIN" AS THEY COME!
はっ
EVERY-ONE-- FIRE!!!
KYAAAA-- OUCH!! WHADDAYA DARLINGS THINK YOU'RE DOING?!!
Gero Gero Gero.
WELL... THIS IS YOUR CUSTOM, NO? YOU CAN HARDLY BLAME US FOR DOING AS THE ROMANS MIGHT!
OUCH-- OUCH--!
IF YOU WANNA BLAME SOMETHING, BLAME YOUR OWN FOOLISH POKOPENIAN PRACTICES!
BWA HA HA HA!!!
Ratta Tatta Tatta Tattatat!

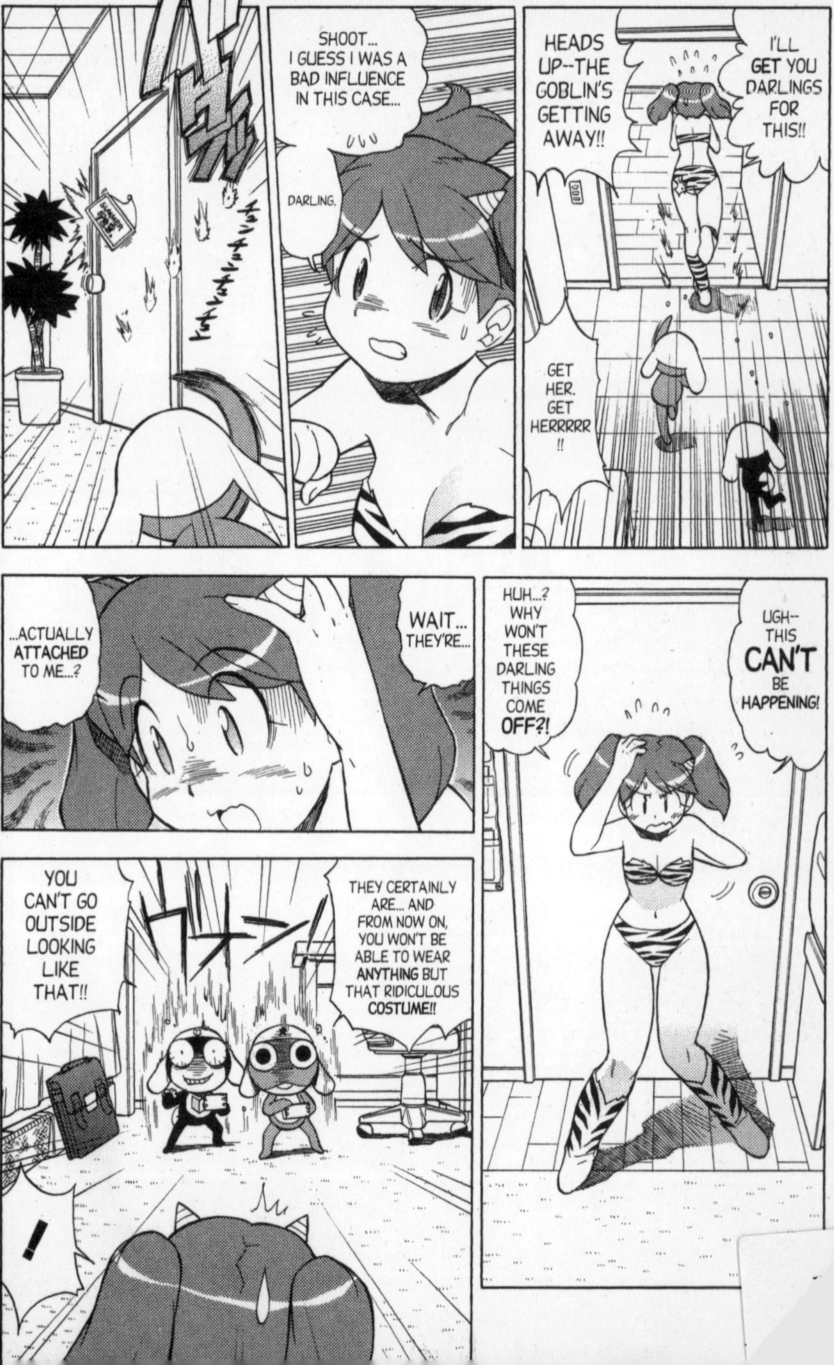
I'LL GET YOU DARLINGS FOR THIS!!
HEADS UP--THE GOBLIN'S GETTING AWAY!!
GET HER. GET HERRRRR!!
SHOOT... I GUESS I WAS A BAD INFLUENCE IN THIS CASE...
DARLING.
UGH-- THIS CAN'T BE HAPPENING!
HUH...? WHY WON'T THESE DARLING THINGS COME OFF?!
WAIT... THEY'RE...
...ACTUALLY ATTACHED TO ME...?
THEY CERTAINLY ARE... AND FROM NOW ON, YOU WON'T BE ABLE TO WEAR ANYTHING BUT THAT RIDICULOUS COSTUME!!
YOU CAN'T GO OUTSIDE LOOKING LIKE THAT!!
!

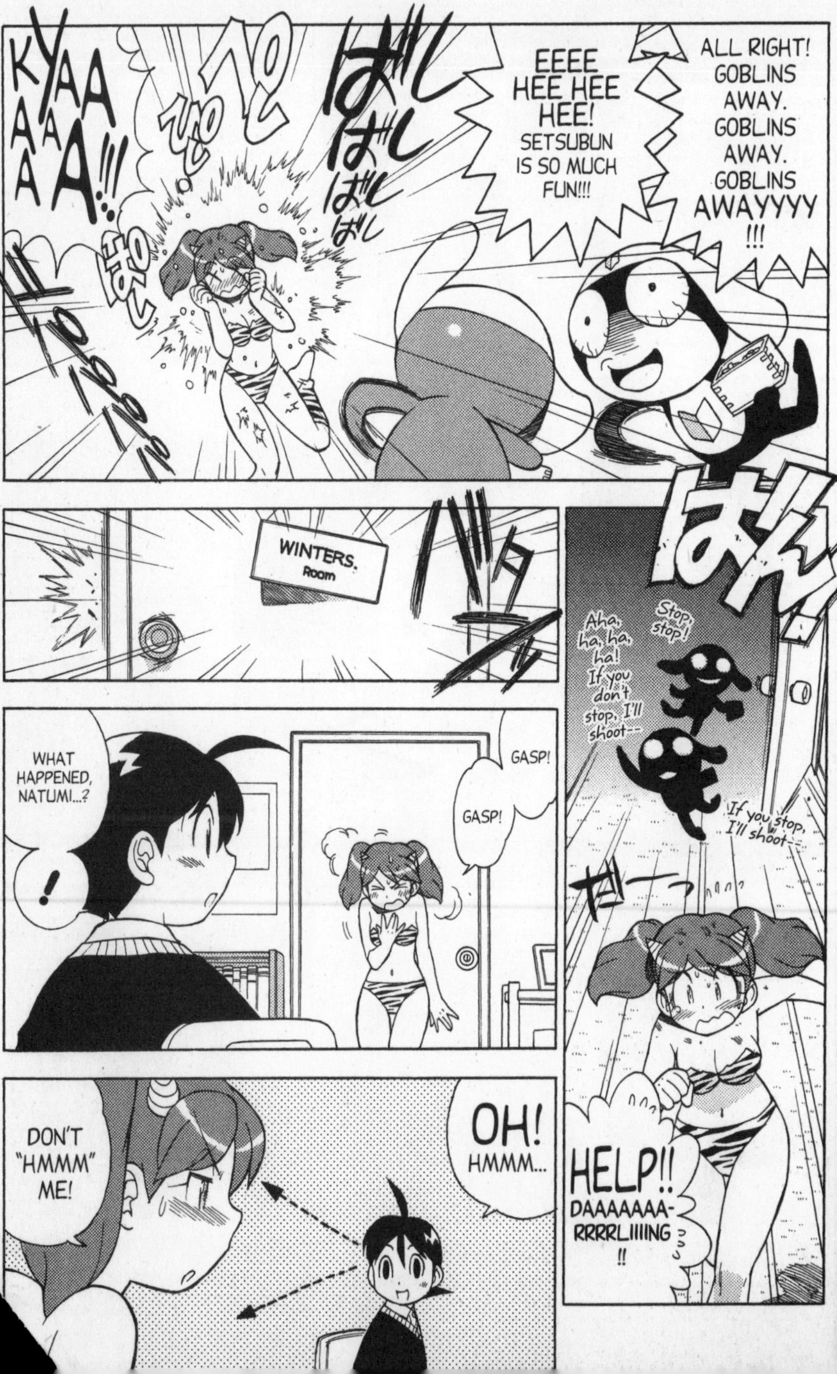

ALL RIGHT! GOBLINS AWAY. GOBLINS AWAY. GOBLINS AWAYYYY!!!
EEEE HEE HEE HEE! SETSUBUN IS SO MUCH FUN!!!
KYAAAAAAAA!!!
Stop, stop!
Aha, ha, ha, ha! If you don't stop, I'll shoot--
If you stop, I'll shoot--
HELP!! DAAAAAAA-RRRRLIIIING!!
WINTERS. Room
GASP!
GASP!
WHAT HAPPENED, NATUMI...?
!
OH! HMMM...
DON'T "HMMM" ME!

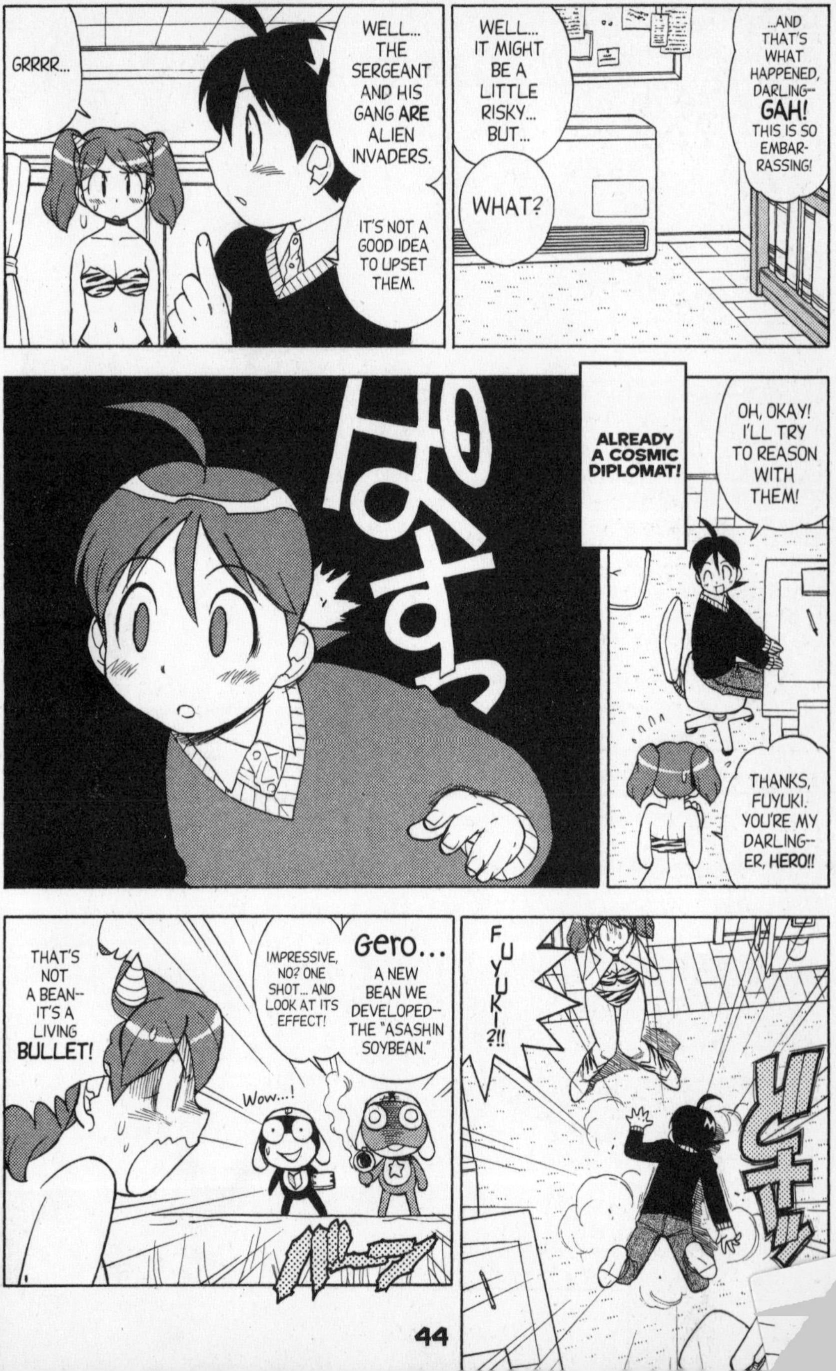
...AND THAT'S WHAT HAPPENED, DARLING-- GAH! THIS IS SO EMBARRASSING!
WELL... IT MIGHT BE A LITTLE RISKY... BUT...
WHAT?
WELL... THE SERGEANT AND HIS GANG ARE ALIEN INVADERS.
IT'S NOT A GOOD IDEA TO UPSET THEM.
GRRRR...
ALREADY A COSMIC DIPLOMAT!
OH, OKAY! I'LL TRY TO REASON WITH THEM!
THANKS, FUYUKI. YOU'RE MY DARLING-- ER, HERO!!
ぱすっ
FUYUKI?!!
Gero... A NEW BEAN WE DEVELOPED-- THE "ASASHIN SOYBEAN."
IMPRESSIVE, NO? ONE SHOT... AND LOOK AT ITS EFFECT!
THAT'S NOT A BEAN-- IT'S A LIVING BULLET!
Wow...!

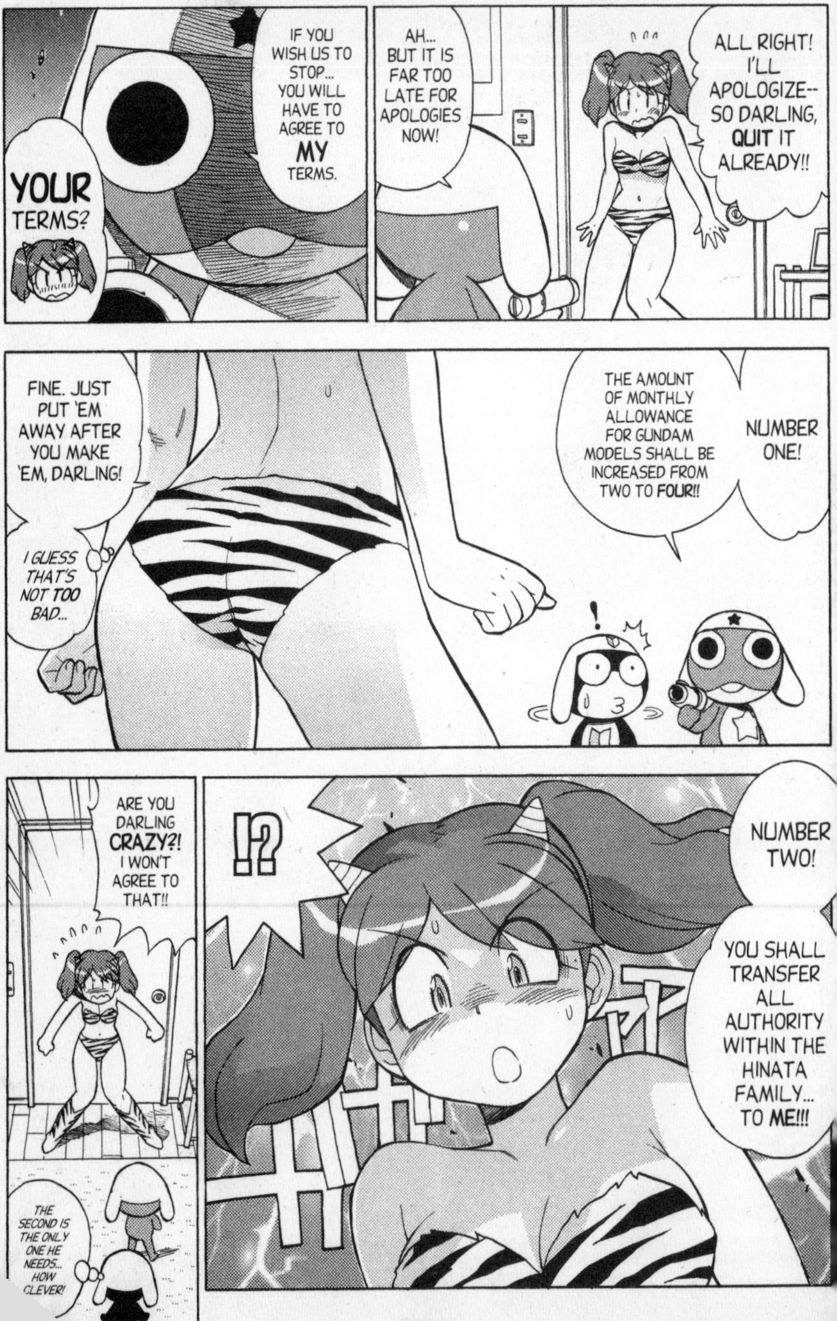
ALL RIGHT! I'LL APOLOGIZE-- SO DARLING, QUIT IT ALREADY!!
AH... BUT IT IS FAR TOO LATE FOR APOLOGIES NOW!
IF YOU WISH US TO STOP... YOU WILL HAVE TO AGREE TO MY TERMS.
YOUR TERMS?
NUMBER ONE!
THE AMOUNT OF MONTHLY ALLOWANCE FOR GUNDAM MODELS SHALL BE INCREASED FROM TWO TO FOUR!!
FINE. JUST PUT 'EM AWAY AFTER YOU MAKE 'EM, DARLING!
I GUESS THAT'S NOT TOO BAD...
NUMBER TWO!
YOU SHALL TRANSFER ALL AUTHORITY WITHIN THE HINATA FAMILY... TO ME!!!
!?
ARE YOU DARLING CRAZY?! I WON'T AGREE TO THAT!!
THE SECOND IS THE ONLY ONE HE NEEDS... HOW CLEVER!

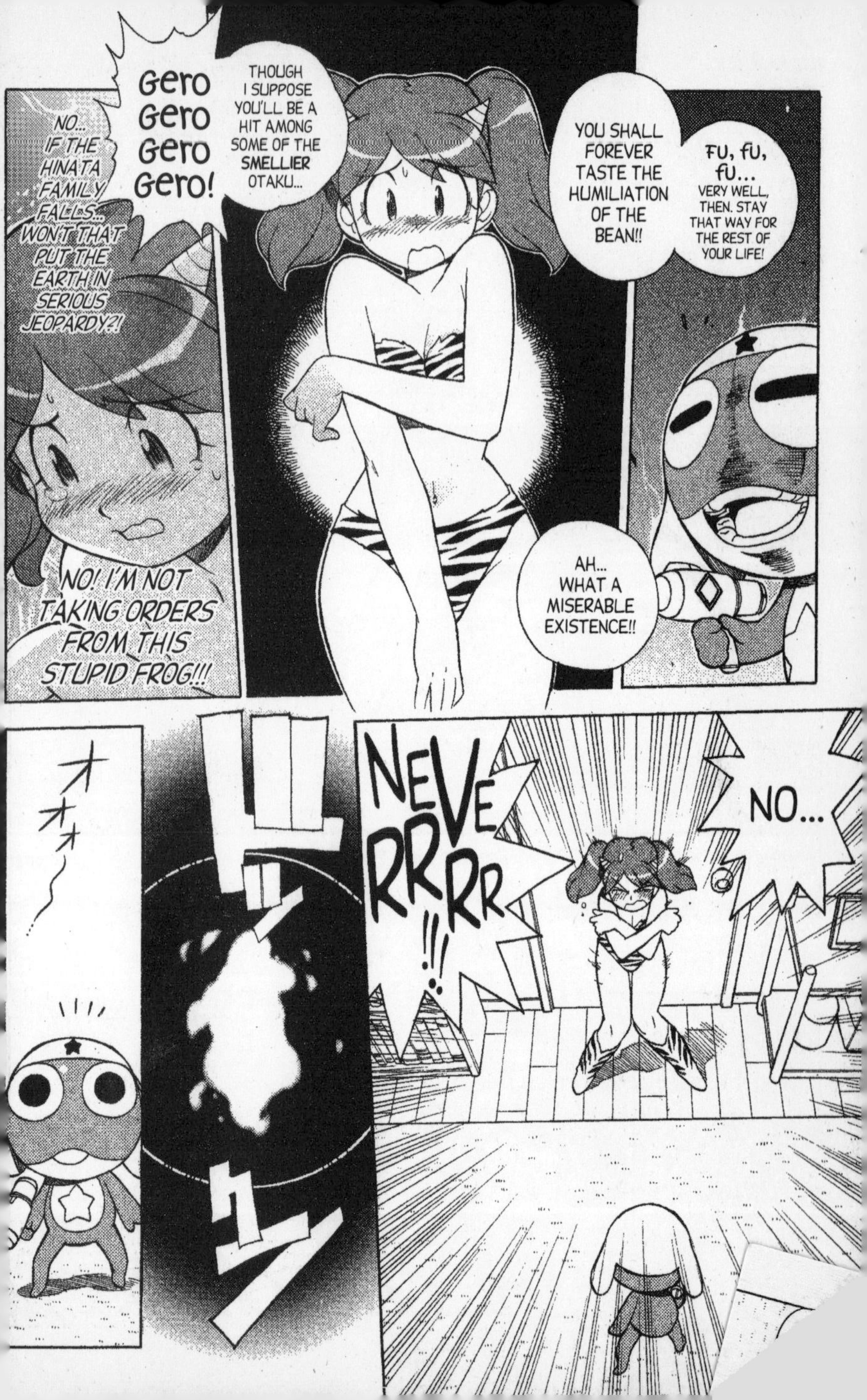
FU, FU, FU... VERY WELL, THEN. STAY THAT WAY FOR THE REST OF YOUR LIFE!
YOU SHALL FOREVER TASTE THE HUMILIATION OF THE BEAN!!
AH... WHAT A MISERABLE EXISTENCE!!
THOUGH I SUPPOSE YOU'LL BE A HIT AMONG SOME OF THE SMELLIER OTAKU...
Gero Gero Gero Gero!
NO... IF THE HINATA FAMILY FALLS... WON'T THAT PUT THE EARTH IN SERIOUS JEOPARDY?!
NO! I'M NOT TAKING ORDERS FROM THIS STUPID FROG!!!
NO...
NEVERRRRR!!!

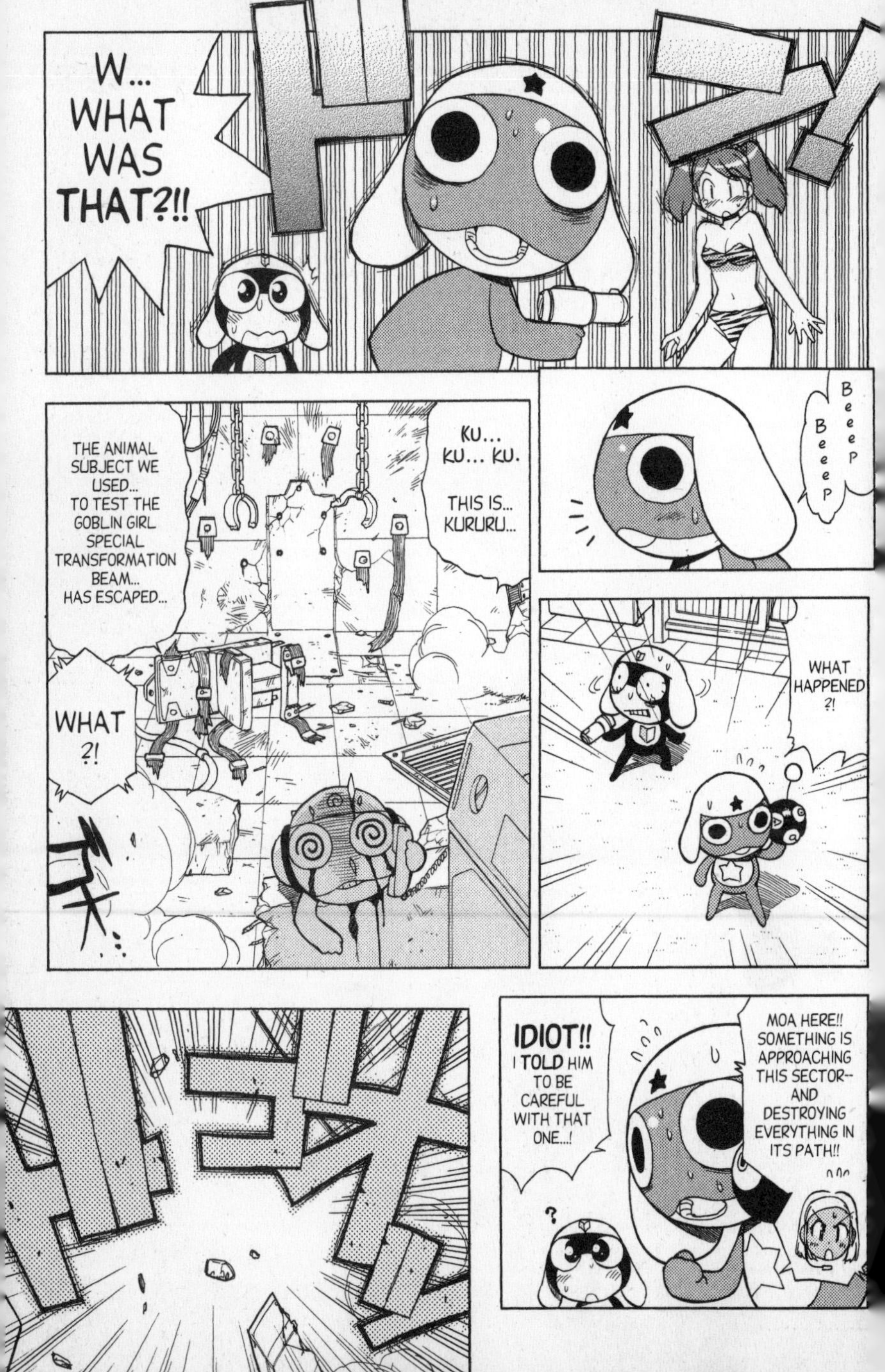
W... WHAT WAS THAT?!!
Beeep
Beeep
WHAT HAPPENED?!
KU... KU... KU.
THIS IS... KURURU...
THE ANIMAL SUBJECT WE USED... TO TEST THE GOBLIN GIRL SPECIAL TRANSFORMATION BEAM... HAS ESCAPED...
WHAT?!
MOA HERE!! SOMETHING IS APPROACHING THIS SECTOR-- AND DESTROYING EVERYTHING IN ITS PATH!!
IDIOT!! I TOLD HIM TO BE CAREFUL WITH THAT ONE...!

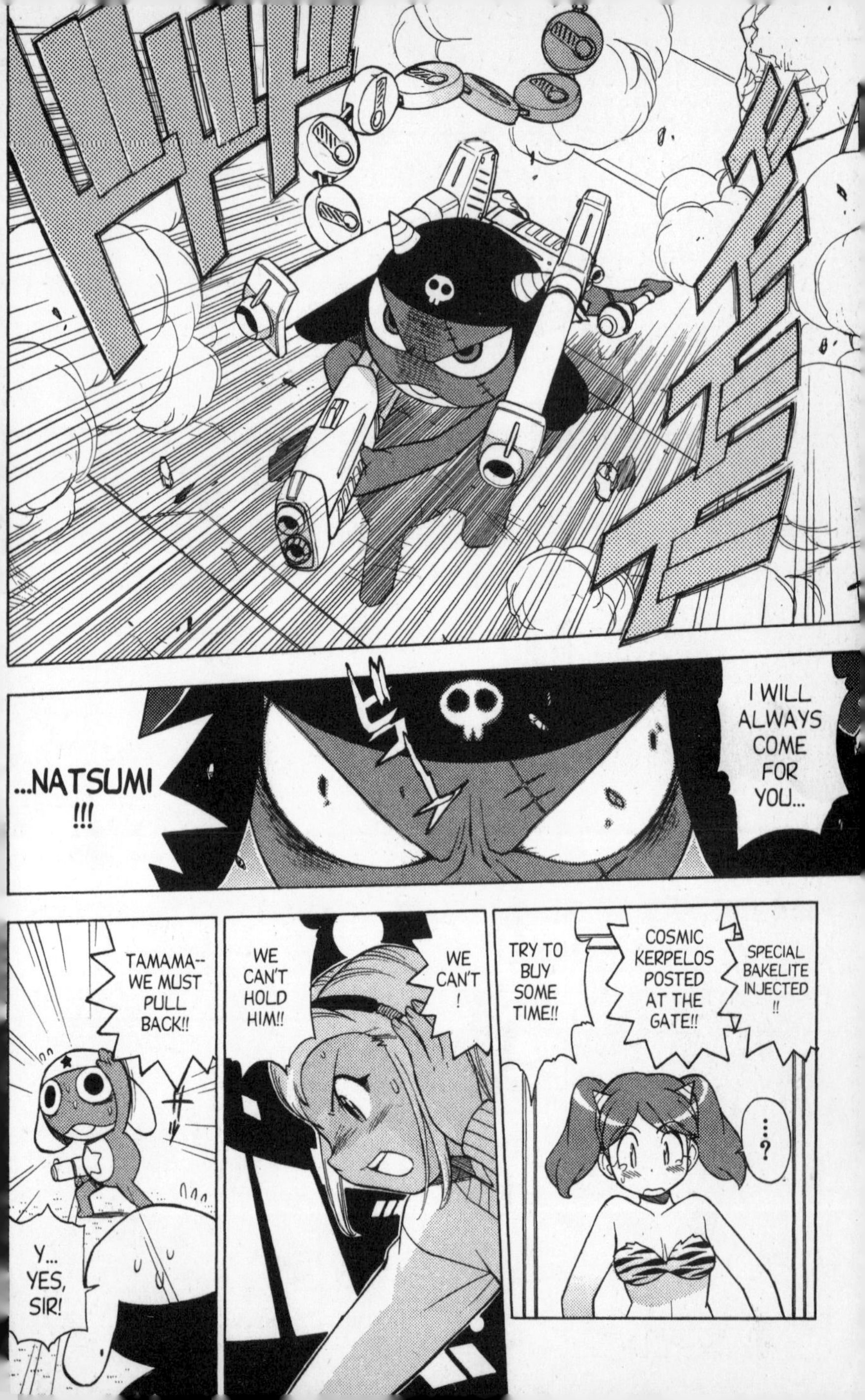
I WILL ALWAYS COME FOR YOU...
...NATSUMI !!!
SPECIAL BAKELITE INJECTED !!
COSMIC KERPELOS POSTED AT THE GATE!!
TRY TO BUY SOME TIME!!
...?
WE CAN'T !
WE CAN'T HOLD HIM!!
TAMAMA-- WE MUST PULL BACK!!
Y... YES, SIR!

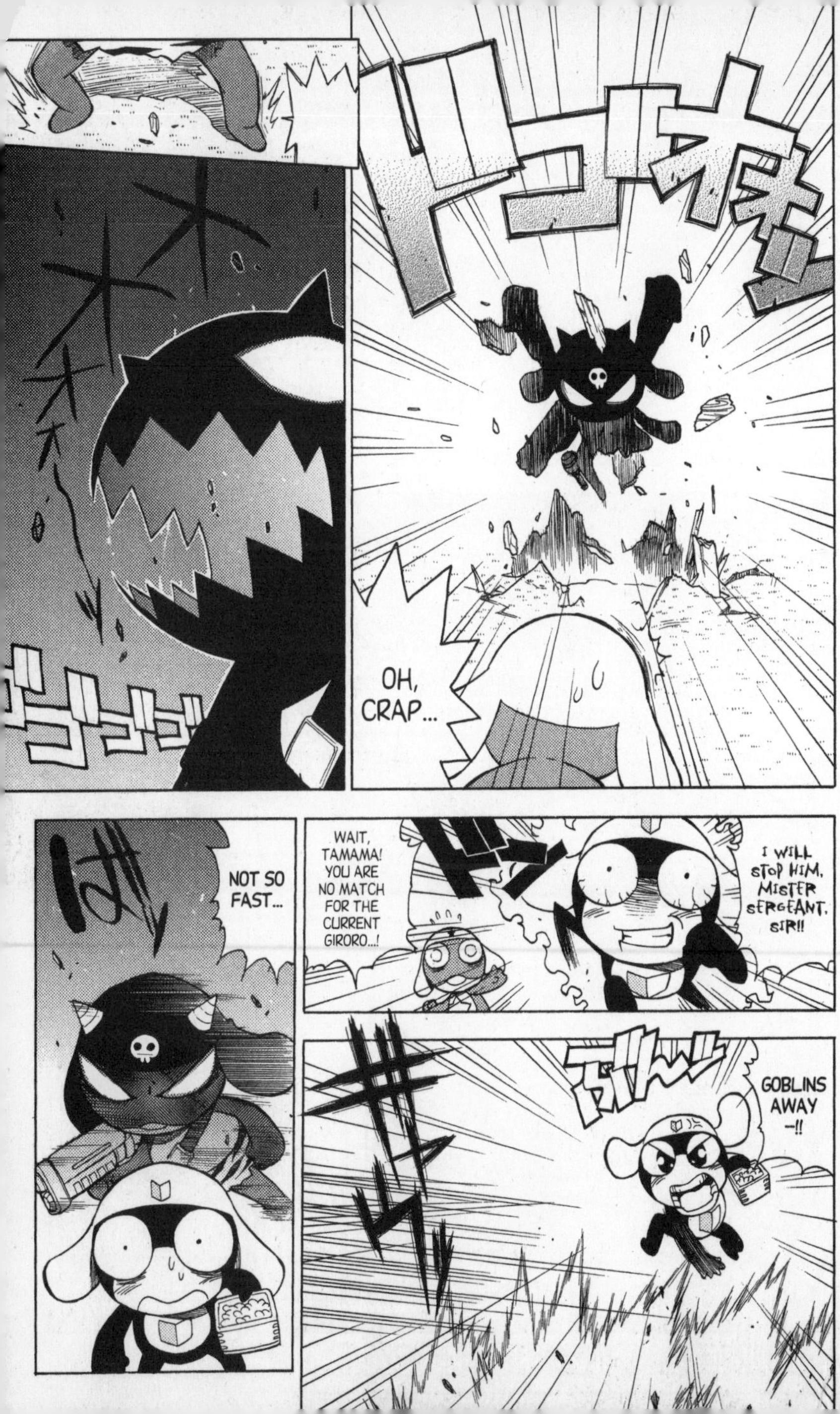
OH, CRAP...
I WILL STOP HIM, MISTER SERGEANT, SIR!!
WAIT, TAMAMA! YOU ARE NO MATCH FOR THE CURRENT GIRORO...!
GOBLINS AWAY—!!
NOT SO FAST...

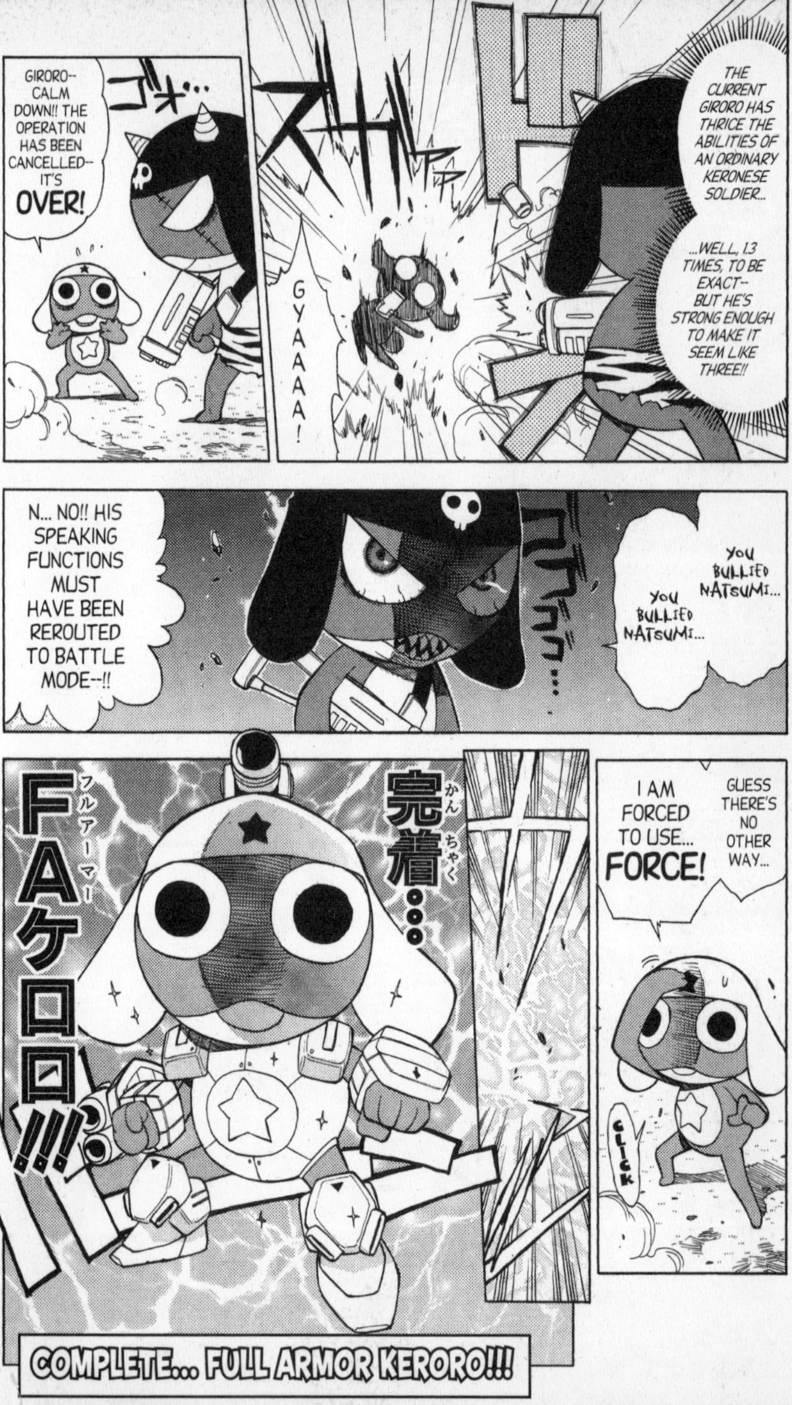
ド
THE CURRENT GIRORO HAS THRICE THE ABILITIES OF AN ORDINARY KERONESE SOLDIER...
...WELL, 1.3 TIMES, TO BE EXACT-- BUT HE'S STRONG ENOUGH TO MAKE IT SEEM LIKE THREE!!
GYAAAAA!
ゴォ…
GIRORO-- CALM DOWN!! THE OPERATION HAS BEEN CANCELLED-- IT'S **OVER!**
YOU BULLIED NATSUMI...
YOU BULLIED NATSUMI...
N... NO!! HIS SPEAKING FUNCTIONS MUST HAVE BEEN REROUTED TO BATTLE MODE--!!
GUESS THERE'S NO OTHER WAY...
I AM FORCED TO USE... **FORCE!**
CLICK
完着(かんちゃく)…
FA(フルアーマー)ケロロ!!!
COMPLETE... FULL ARMOR KERORO!!!

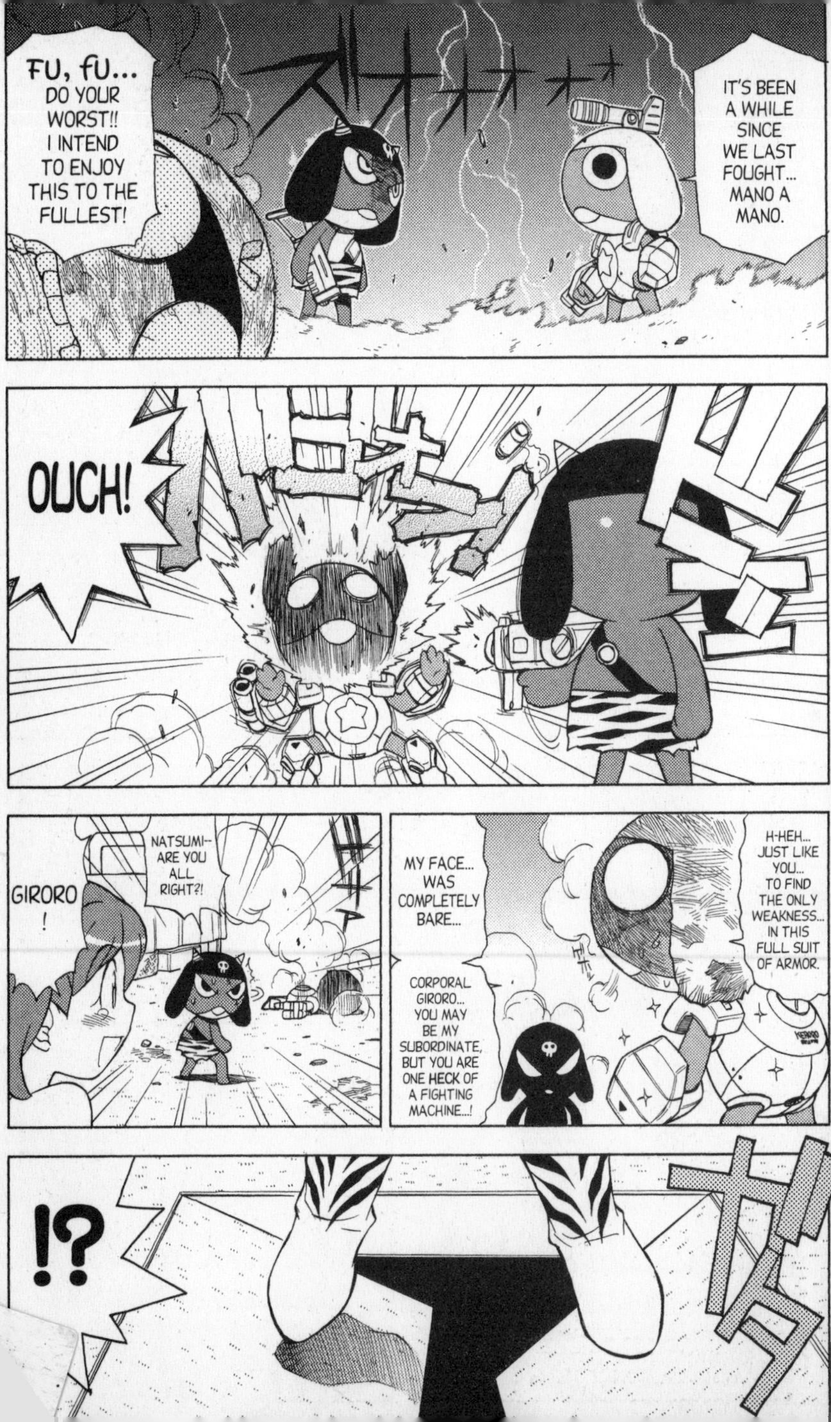
IT'S BEEN A WHILE SINCE WE LAST FOUGHT... MANO A MANO.
FU, FU... DO YOUR WORST!! I INTEND TO ENJOY THIS TO THE FULLEST!
OUCH!
H-HEH... JUST LIKE YOU... TO FIND THE ONLY WEAKNESS... IN THIS FULL SUIT OF ARMOR.
MY FACE... WAS COMPLETELY BARE...
CORPORAL GIRORO... YOU MAY BE MY SUBORDINATE, BUT YOU ARE ONE HECK OF A FIGHTING MACHINE...!
NATSUMI-- ARE YOU ALL RIGHT?!
GIRORO!
!?

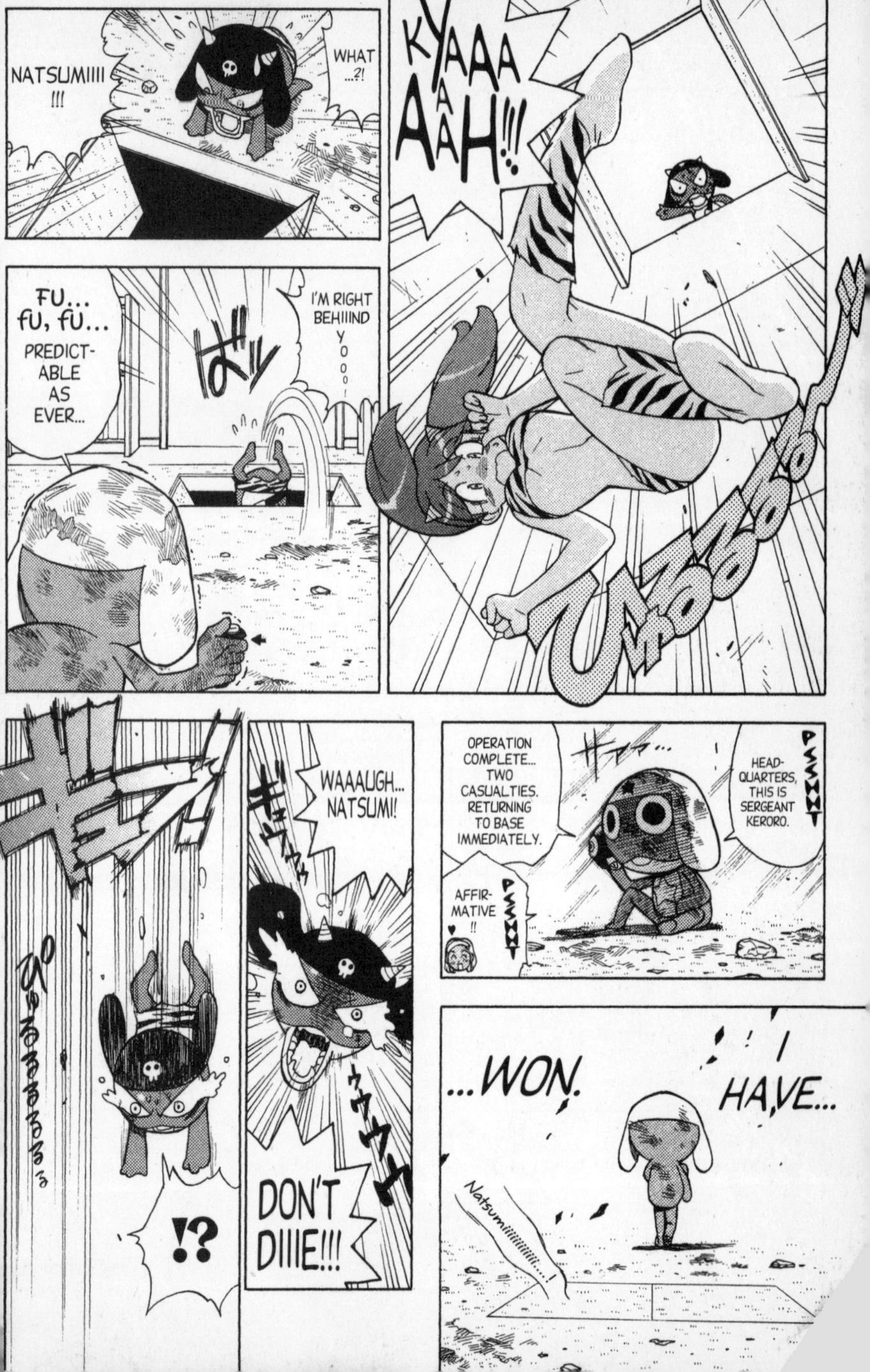
KYAAAAAH!!!
WHAT...?!
NATSUMIIII!!!
I'M RIGHT BEHIIIND YOOOO!
FU... fu, fu... PREDICTABLE AS EVER...
HEADQUARTERS, THIS IS SERGEANT KERORO.
OPERATION COMPLETE... TWO CASUALTIES. RETURNING TO BASE IMMEDIATELY.
AFFIRMATIVE!!
I HAVE...
...WON.
Natsumiiiiiiiiiiii...!
WAAAUGH... NATSUMI!
DON'T DIIIE!!!
!?

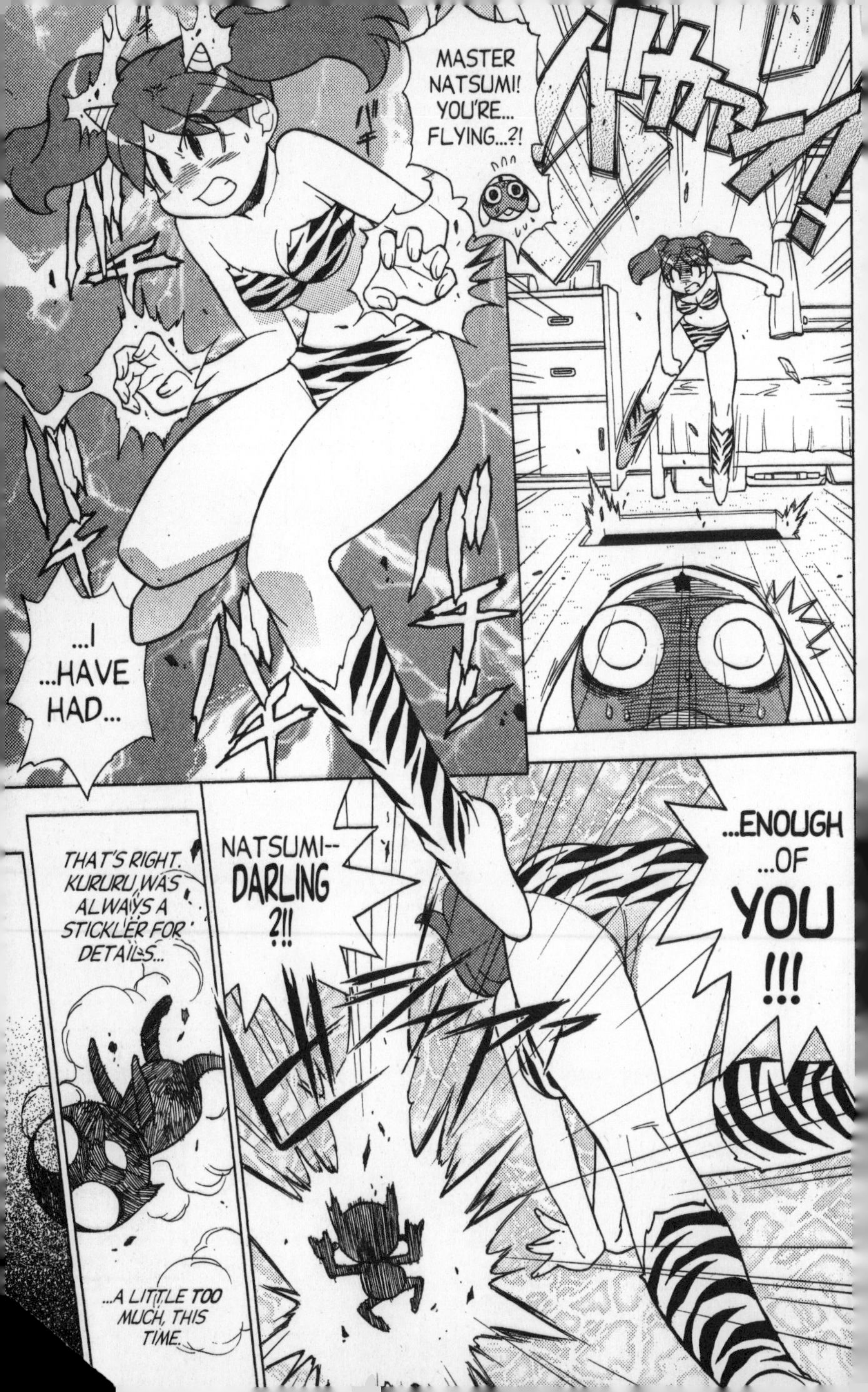
MASTER NATSUMI! YOU'RE... FLYING...?!
...I ...HAVE HAD...
...ENOUGH ...OF YOU !!!
NATSUMI-- DARLING ?!!
THAT'S RIGHT. KURURU WAS ALWAYS A STICKLER FOR DETAILS...
...A LITTLE TOO MUCH, THIS TIME.

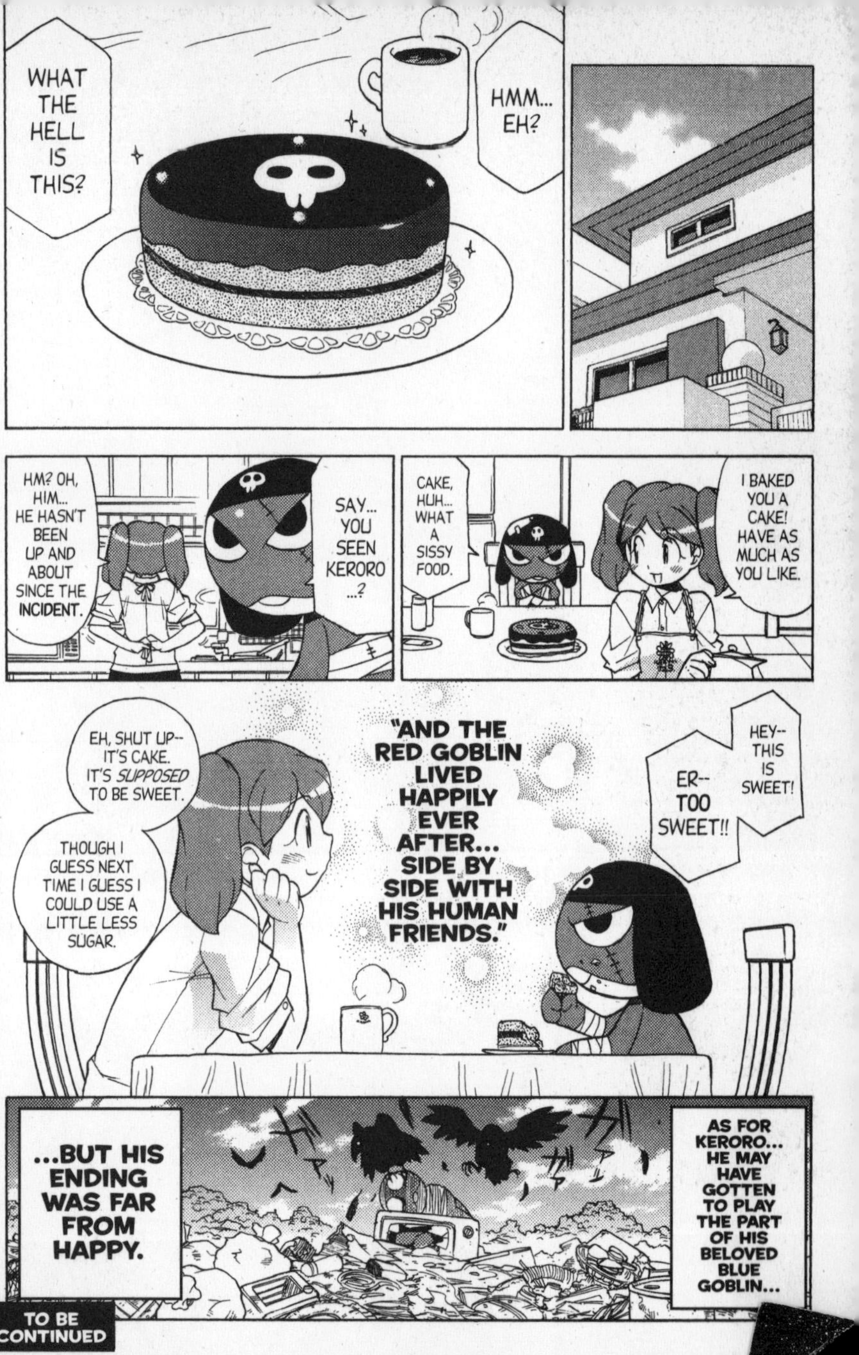
HMM... EH?
WHAT THE HELL IS THIS?
I BAKED YOU A CAKE! HAVE AS MUCH AS YOU LIKE.
CAKE, HUH... WHAT A SISSY FOOD.
SAY... YOU SEEN KERORO...?
HM? OH, HIM... HE HASN'T BEEN UP AND ABOUT SINCE THE INCIDENT.
HEY-- THIS IS SWEET!
ER-- TOO SWEET!!
"AND THE RED GOBLIN LIVED HAPPILY EVER AFTER... SIDE BY SIDE WITH HIS HUMAN FRIENDS."
EH, SHUT UP-- IT'S CAKE. IT'S SUPPOSED TO BE SWEET.
THOUGH I GUESS NEXT TIME I GUESS I COULD USE A LITTLE LESS SUGAR.
AS FOR KERORO... HE MAY HAVE GOTTEN TO PLAY THE PART OF HIS BELOVED BLUE GOBLIN...
...BUT HIS ENDING WAS FAR FROM HAPPY.
TO BE CONTINUED

## ENCOUNTER XXXII

# TO THE DEATH! THE FIRST SNOWBALL FIGHT

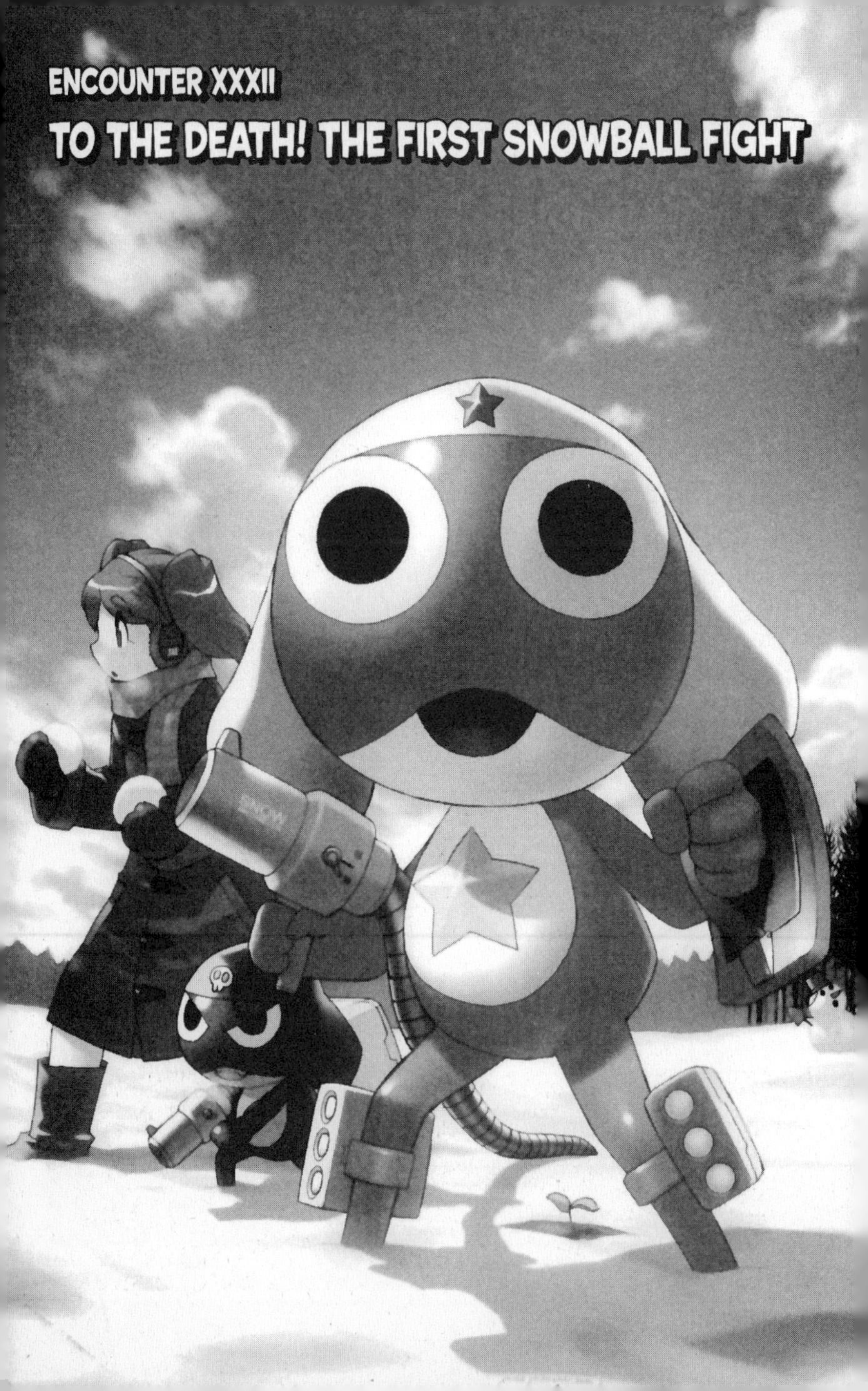
SNOW

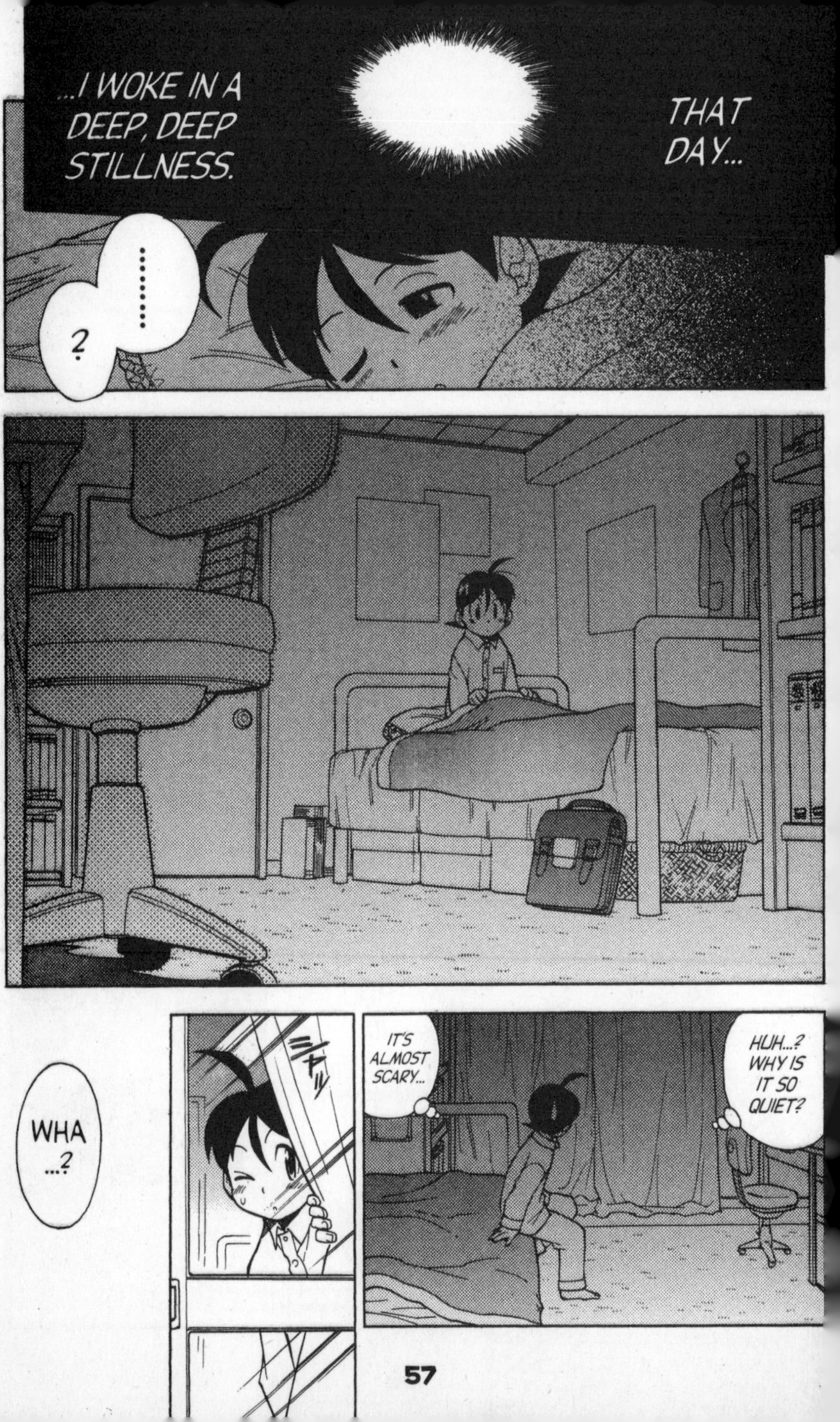
THAT DAY...
...I WOKE IN A DEEP, DEEP STILLNESS.
......?
HUH...? WHY IS IT SO QUIET?
IT'S ALMOST SCARY...
WHA...?

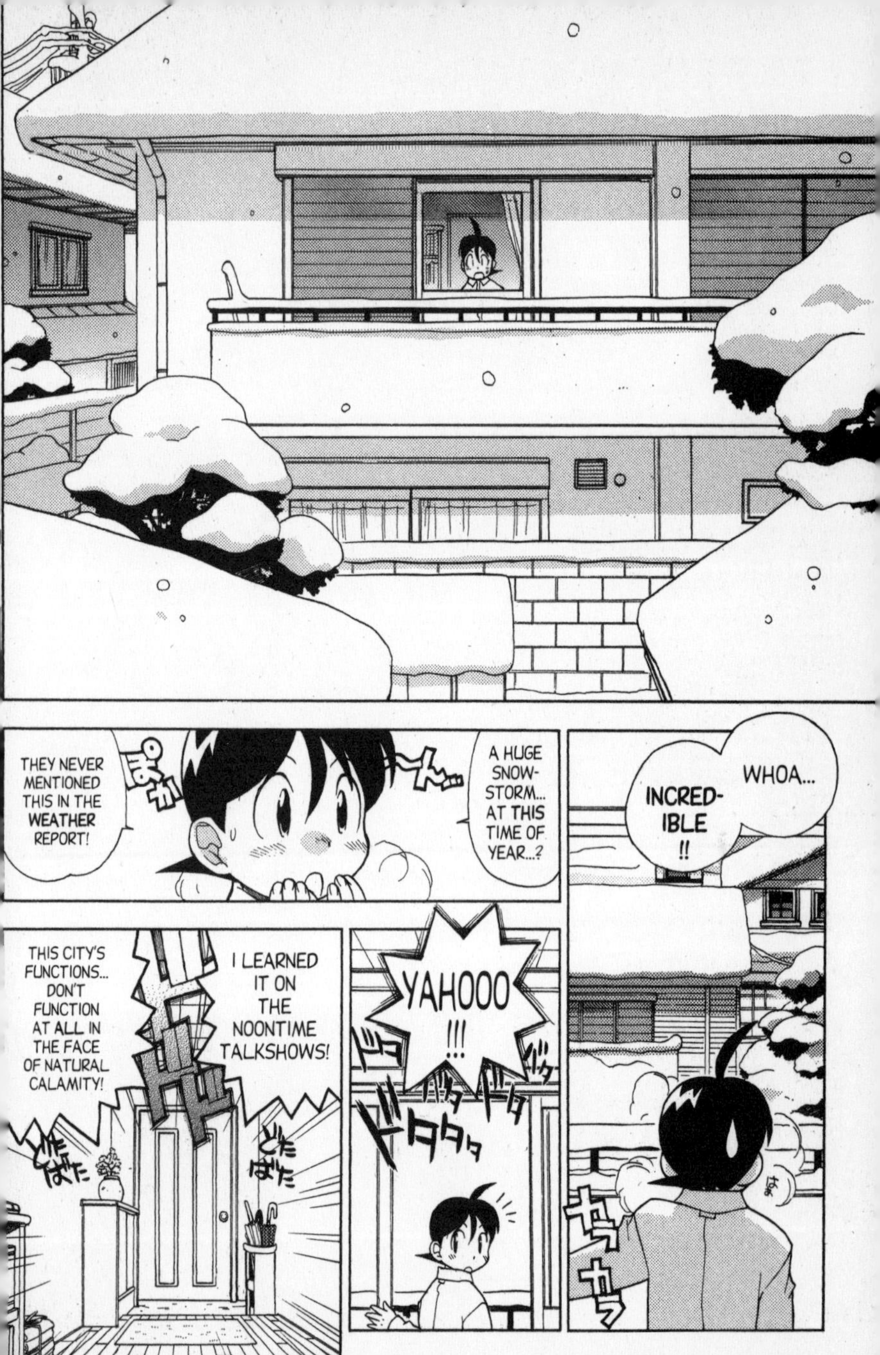
WHOA...
INCRED-IBLE !!
A HUGE SNOW-STORM... AT THIS TIME OF YEAR...?
THEY NEVER MENTIONED THIS IN THE WEATHER REPORT!
YAHOOO !!!
I LEARNED IT ON THE NOONTIME TALKSHOWS!
THIS CITY'S FUNCTIONS... DON'T FUNCTION AT ALL IN THE FACE OF NATURAL CALAMITY!

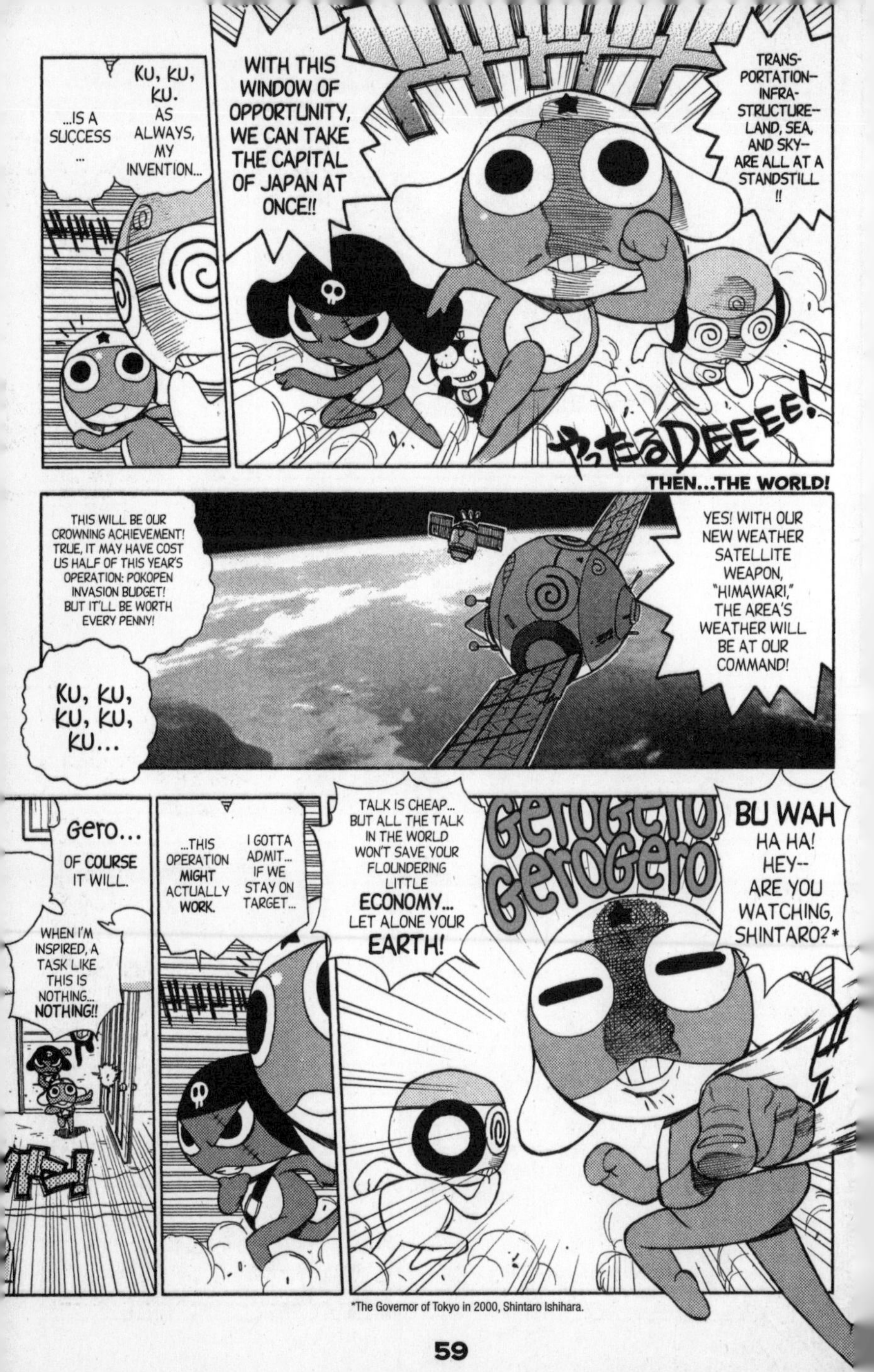
TRANSPORTATION—INFRASTRUCTURE—LAND, SEA, AND SKY—ARE ALL AT A STANDSTILL!!
WITH THIS WINDOW OF OPPORTUNITY, WE CAN TAKE THE CAPITAL OF JAPAN AT ONCE!!
やったるDEEEEE!
THEN...THE WORLD!
KU, KU, KU. AS ALWAYS, MY INVENTION...
...IS A SUCCESS...
YES! WITH OUR NEW WEATHER SATELLITE WEAPON, "HIMAWARI," THE AREA'S WEATHER WILL BE AT OUR COMMAND!
THIS WILL BE OUR CROWNING ACHIEVEMENT! TRUE, IT MAY HAVE COST US HALF OF THIS YEAR'S OPERATION: POKOPEN INVASION BUDGET! BUT IT'LL BE WORTH EVERY PENNY!
KU, KU, KU, KU, KU...
BU WAH HA HA! HEY-- ARE YOU WATCHING, SHINTARO?*
Gerogero Gerogero
TALK IS CHEAP... BUT ALL THE TALK IN THE WORLD WON'T SAVE YOUR FLOUNDERING LITTLE ECONOMY... LET ALONE YOUR EARTH!
I GOTTA ADMIT... IF WE STAY ON TARGET...
...THIS OPERATION MIGHT ACTUALLY WORK.
Gero... OF COURSE IT WILL.
WHEN I'M INSPIRED, A TASK LIKE THIS IS NOTHING... NOTHING!!

*The Governor of Tokyo in 2000, Shintaro Ishihara.

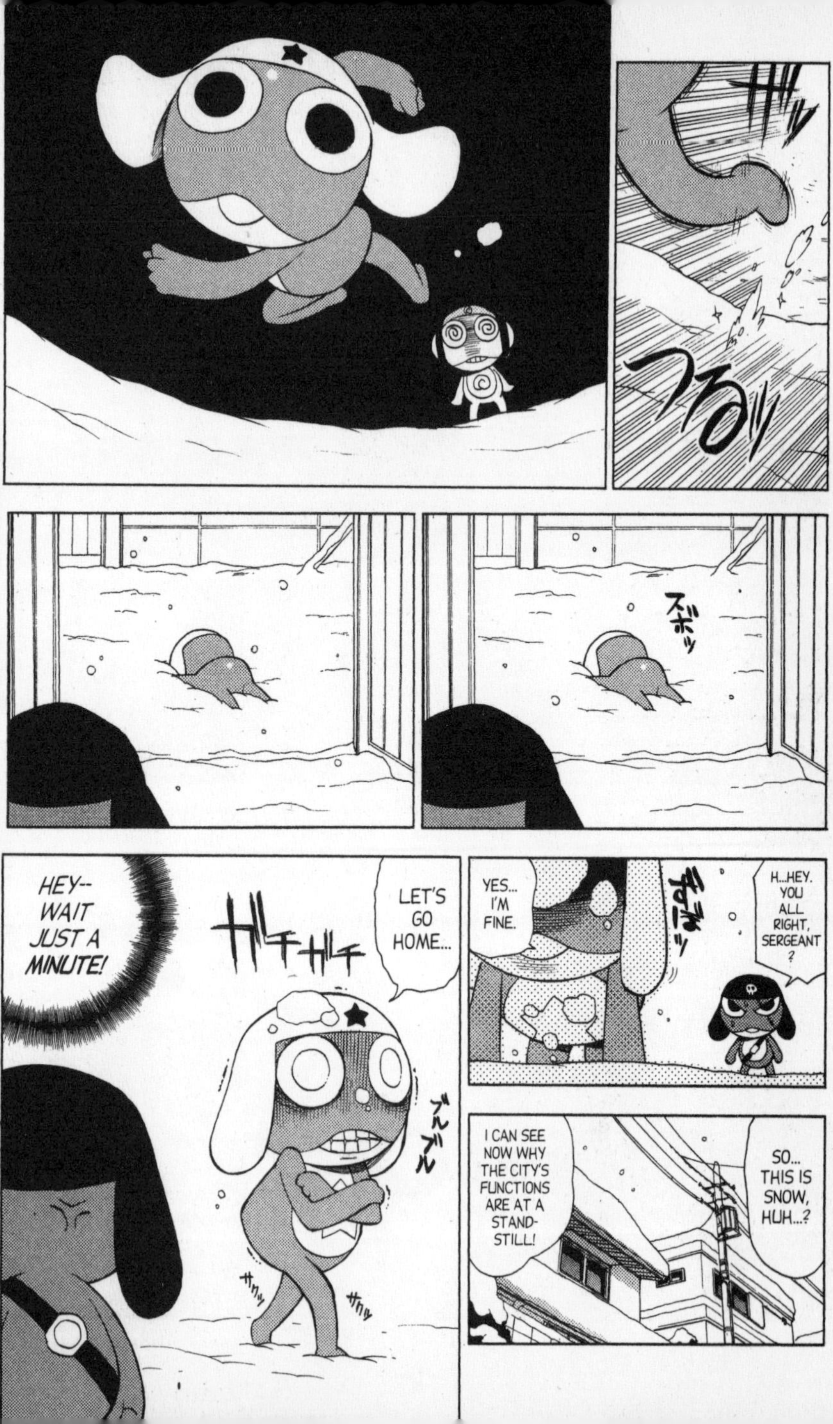
ガッ
つるッ
スポッ
H...HEY. YOU ALL RIGHT, SERGEANT?
ずぼッ
YES... I'M FINE.
SO... THIS IS SNOW, HUH...?
I CAN SEE NOW WHY THE CITY'S FUNCTIONS ARE AT A STANDSTILL!
LET'S GO HOME...
ガチガチ
ブルブル
サクッ
サクッ
HEY-- WAIT JUST A MINUTE!

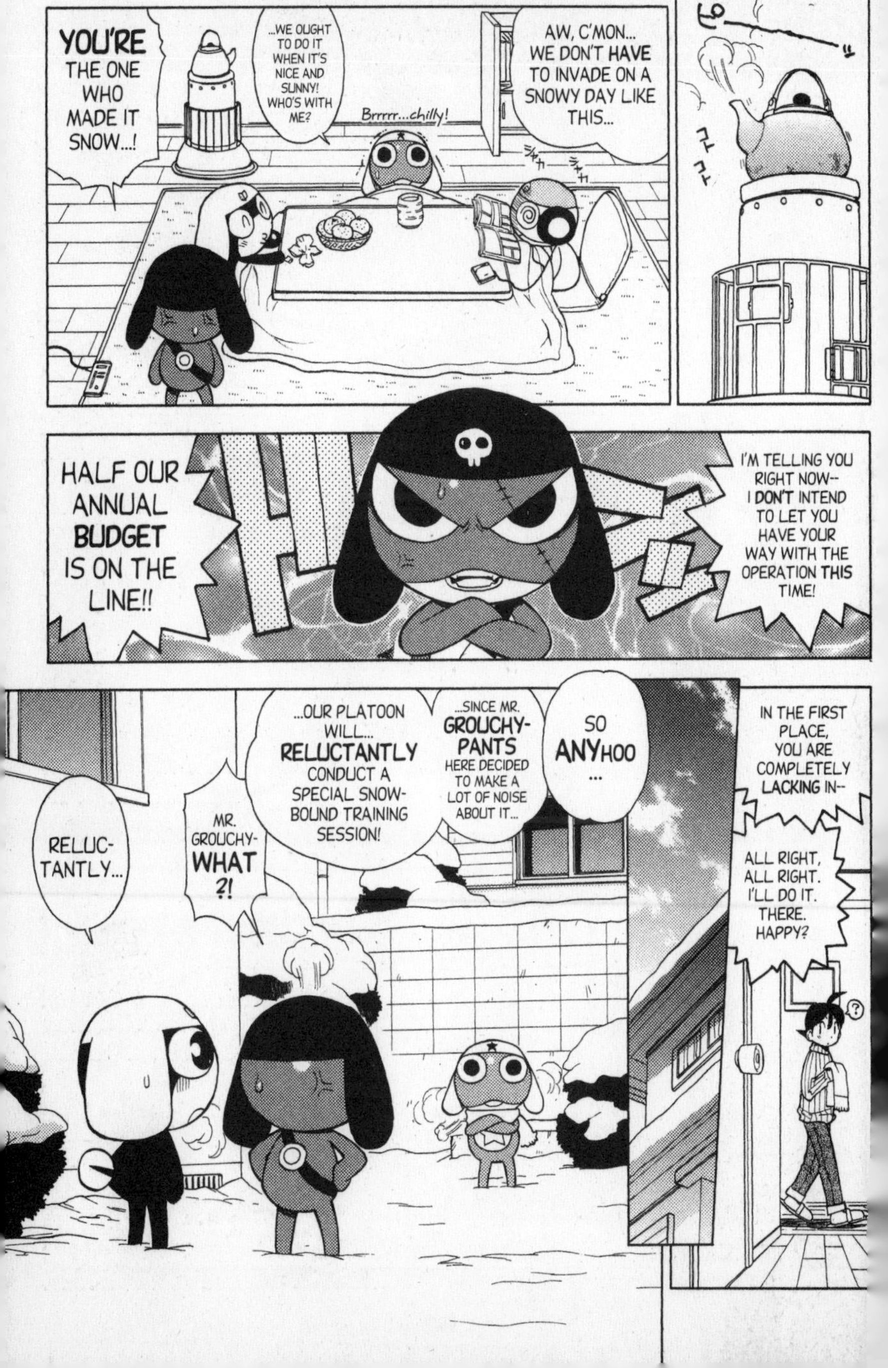
AW, C'MON... WE DON'T HAVE TO INVADE ON A SNOWY DAY LIKE THIS...
Brrrrr...chilly!
...WE OUGHT TO DO IT WHEN IT'S NICE AND SUNNY! WHO'S WITH ME?
YOU'RE THE ONE WHO MADE IT SNOW...!
I'M TELLING YOU RIGHT NOW-- I DON'T INTEND TO LET YOU HAVE YOUR WAY WITH THE OPERATION THIS TIME!
HALF OUR ANNUAL BUDGET IS ON THE LINE!!
IN THE FIRST PLACE, YOU ARE COMPLETELY LACKING IN--
ALL RIGHT, ALL RIGHT. I'LL DO IT. THERE. HAPPY?
SO ANYHOO ...
...SINCE MR. GROUCHY-PANTS HERE DECIDED TO MAKE A LOT OF NOISE ABOUT IT...
...OUR PLATOON WILL... RELUCTANTLY CONDUCT A SPECIAL SNOW-BOUND TRAINING SESSION!
MR. GROUCHY-WHAT?!
RELUC-TANTLY...

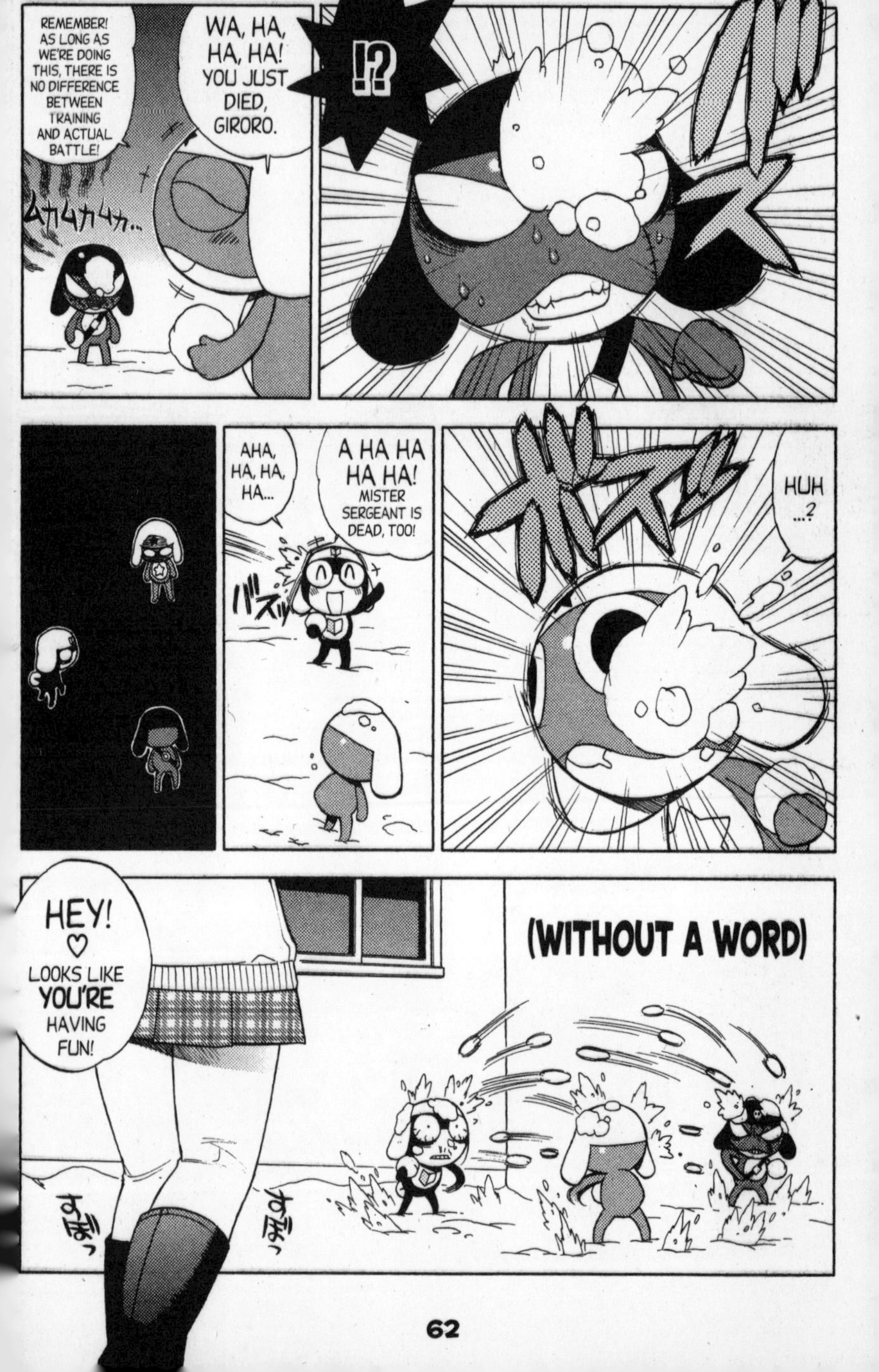
!?
WA, HA, HA, HA! YOU JUST DIED, GIRORO.
REMEMBER! AS LONG AS WE'RE DOING THIS, THERE IS NO DIFFERENCE BETWEEN TRAINING AND ACTUAL BATTLE!
ムカムカムカ...
HUH ...?
A HA HA HA HA! MISTER SERGEANT IS DEAD, TOO!
AHA, HA, HA, HA...
バズッ
(WITHOUT A WORD)
HEY! ♡ LOOKS LIKE YOU'RE HAVING FUN!
すぽっ
すぽっ

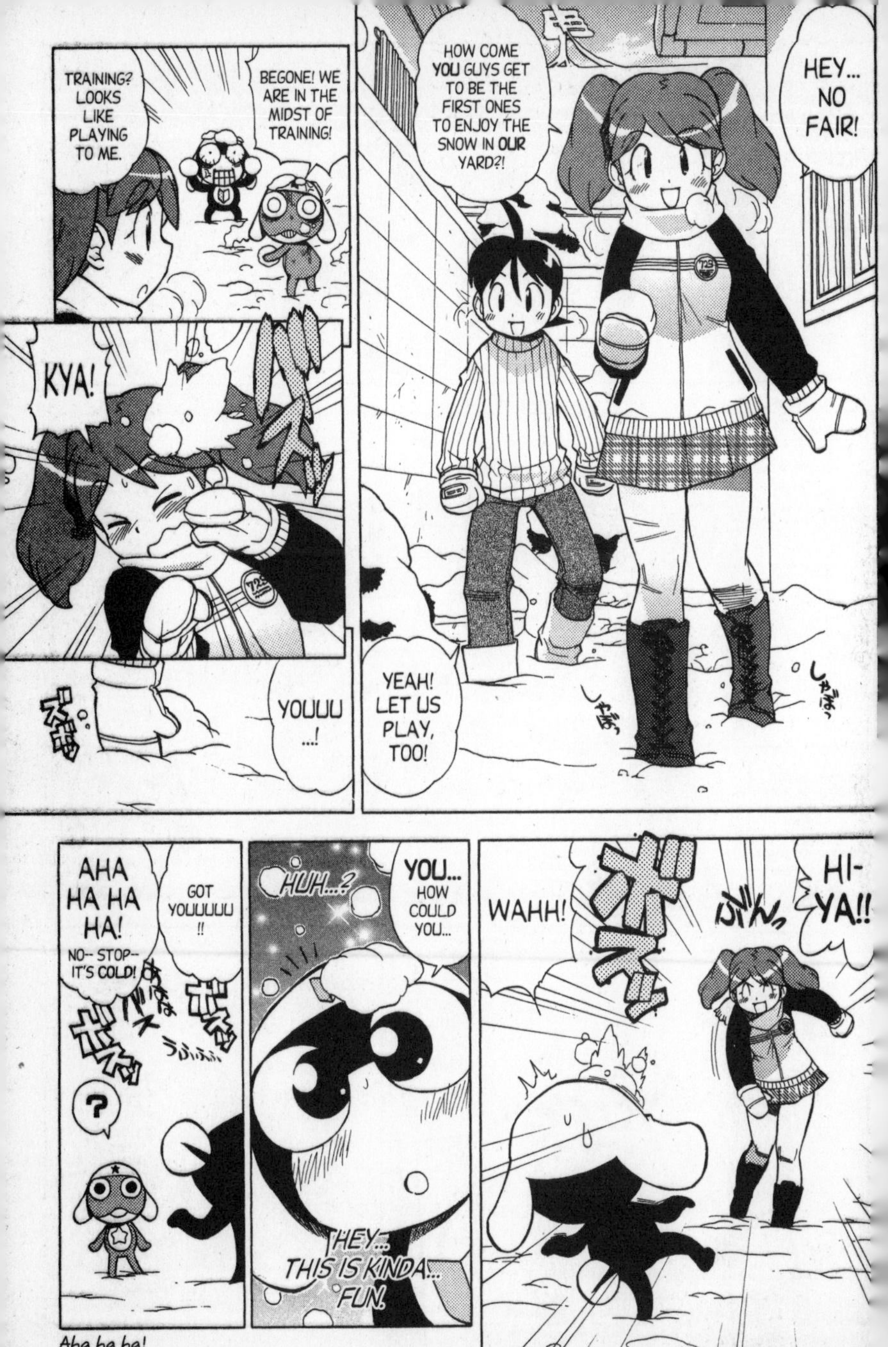
HEY... NO FAIR!
HOW COME YOU GUYS GET TO BE THE FIRST ONES TO ENJOY THE SNOW IN OUR YARD?!
YEAH! LET US PLAY, TOO!
BEGONE! WE ARE IN THE MIDST OF TRAINING!
TRAINING? LOOKS LIKE PLAYING TO ME.
KYA!
YOUUU ...!
HI-YA!!
WAHH!
YOU... HOW COULD YOU...
HUH...?
HEY... THIS IS KINDA... FUN.
AHA HA HA HA!
GOT YOUUUUU !!
NO-- STOP-- IT'S COLD!
?

Aha ha ha!
U fu fu fu fu!

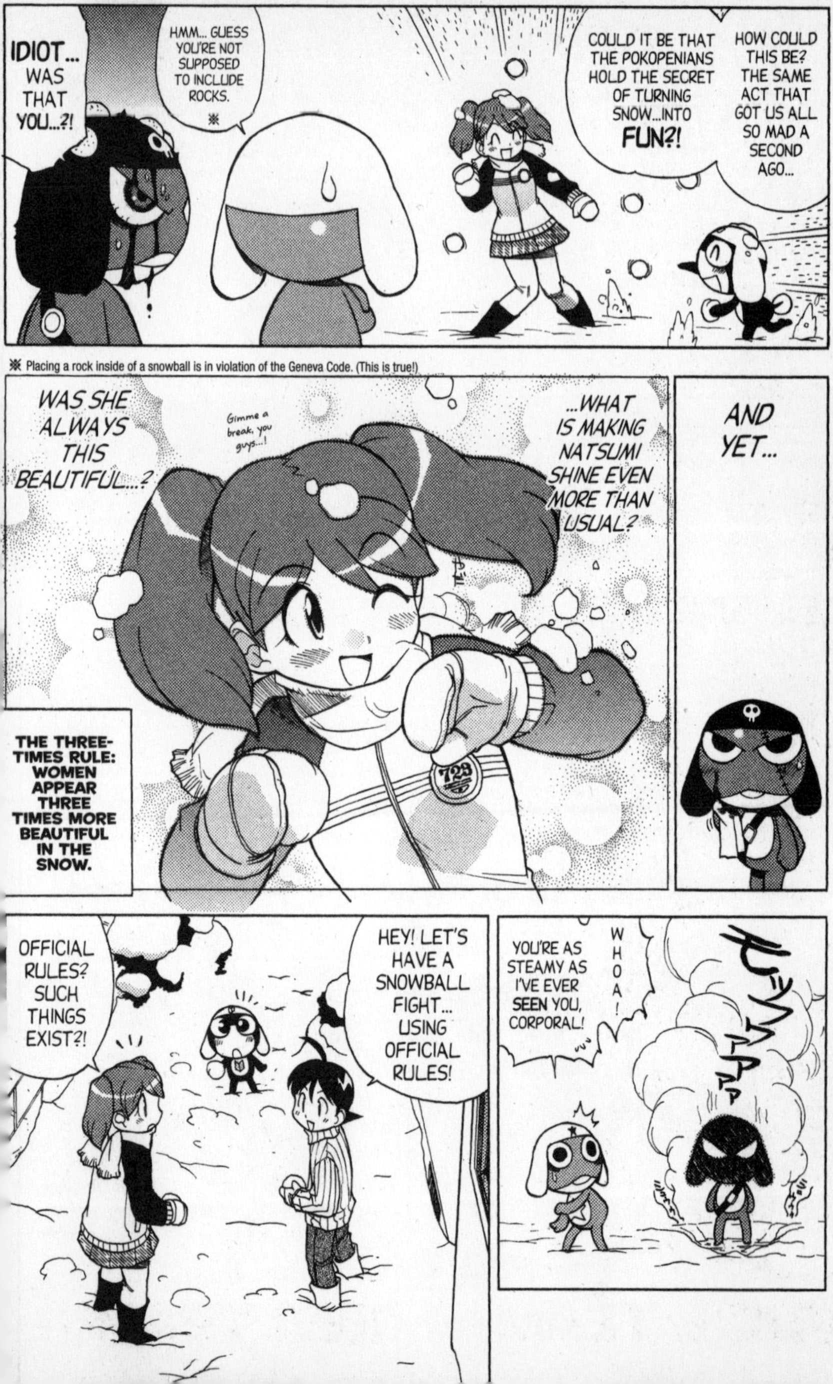
HOW COULD THIS BE? THE SAME ACT THAT GOT US ALL SO MAD A SECOND AGO...
COULD IT BE THAT THE POKOPENIANS HOLD THE SECRET OF TURNING SNOW...INTO FUN?!
HMM... GUESS YOU'RE NOT SUPPOSED TO INCLUDE ROCKS. ※
IDIOT... WAS THAT YOU...?!
※ Placing a rock inside of a snowball is in violation of the Geneva Code. (This is true!)
AND YET...
...WHAT IS MAKING NATSUMI SHINE EVEN MORE THAN USUAL?
Gimme a break, you guys...!
WAS SHE ALWAYS THIS BEAUTIFUL...?
THE THREE-TIMES RULE: WOMEN APPEAR THREE TIMES MORE BEAUTIFUL IN THE SNOW.
WHOA!
YOU'RE AS STEAMY AS I'VE EVER SEEN YOU, CORPORAL!
HEY! LET'S HAVE A SNOWBALL FIGHT... USING OFFICIAL RULES!
OFFICIAL RULES? SUCH THINGS EXIST?!

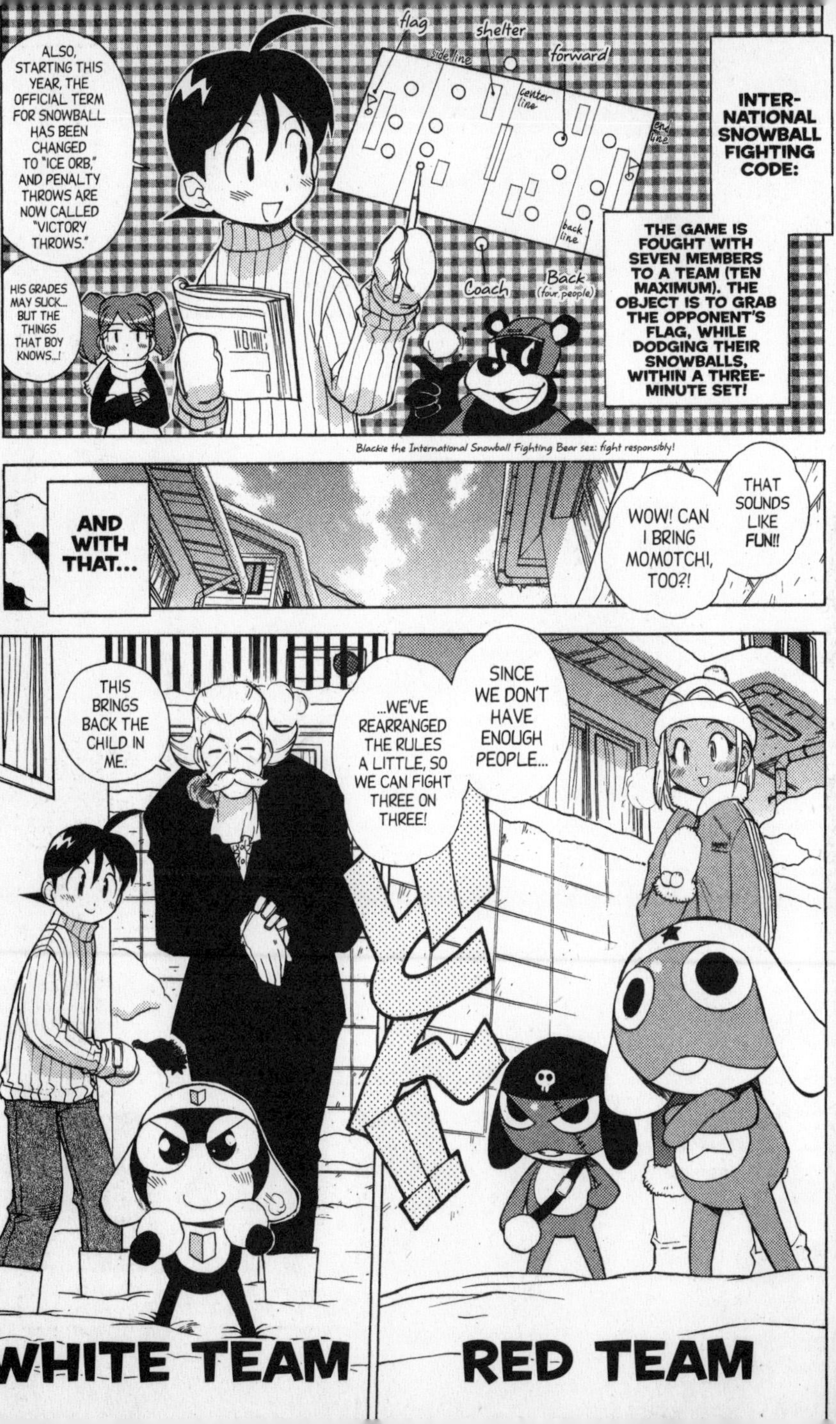
INTERNATIONAL SNOWBALL FIGHTING CODE:
THE GAME IS FOUGHT WITH SEVEN MEMBERS TO A TEAM (TEN MAXIMUM). THE OBJECT IS TO GRAB THE OPPONENT'S FLAG, WHILE DODGING THEIR SNOWBALLS, WITHIN A THREE-MINUTE SET!
flag
shelter
forward
side line
center line
end line
back line
Coach
Back (four people)
ALSO, STARTING THIS YEAR, THE OFFICIAL TERM FOR SNOWBALL HAS BEEN CHANGED TO "ICE ORB," AND PENALTY THROWS ARE NOW CALLED "VICTORY THROWS."
HIS GRADES MAY SUCK... BUT THE THINGS THAT BOY KNOWS...!
Blackie the International Snowball Fighting Bear sez: fight responsibly!
THAT SOUNDS LIKE FUN!!
WOW! CAN I BRING MOMOTCHI, TOO?!
AND WITH THAT...
SINCE WE DON'T HAVE ENOUGH PEOPLE...
...WE'VE REARRANGED THE RULES A LITTLE, SO WE CAN FIGHT THREE ON THREE!
RED TEAM
THIS BRINGS BACK THE CHILD IN ME.
WHITE TEAM

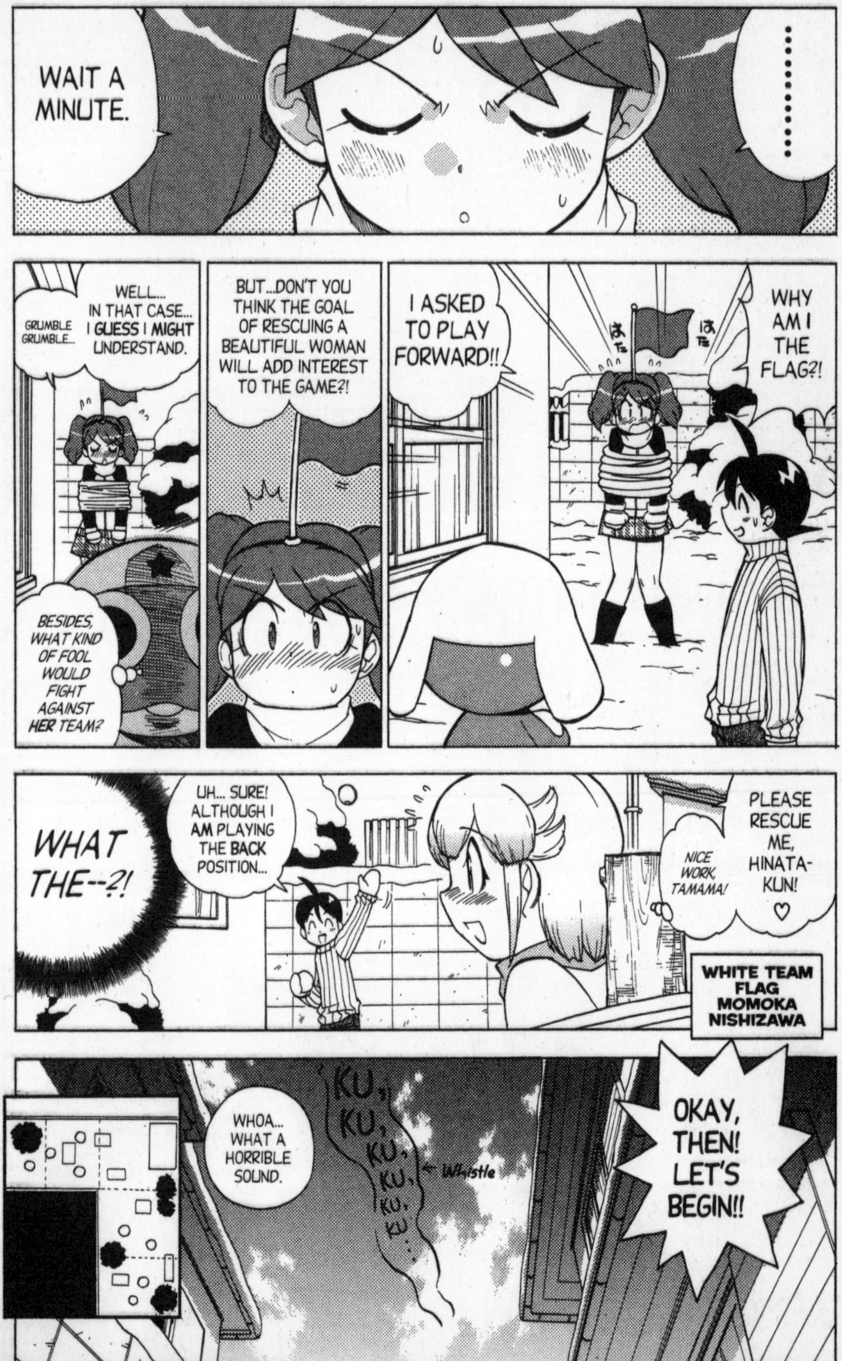
......
WAIT A MINUTE.
WHY AM I THE FLAG?!
はた
はた
I ASKED TO PLAY FORWARD!!
BUT...DON'T YOU THINK THE GOAL OF RESCUING A BEAUTIFUL WOMAN WILL ADD INTEREST TO THE GAME?!
WELL... IN THAT CASE... I GUESS I MIGHT UNDERSTAND.
GRUMBLE GRUMBLE...
BESIDES, WHAT KIND OF FOOL WOULD FIGHT AGAINST HER TEAM?
PLEASE RESCUE ME, HINATA-KUN! ♡
NICE WORK, TAMAMA!
WHITE TEAM FLAG MOMOKA NISHIZAWA
UH... SURE! ALTHOUGH I AM PLAYING THE BACK POSITION...
WHAT THE--?!
OKAY, THEN! LET'S BEGIN!!
KU, KU, KU, KU, KU, KU...
Whistle
WHOA... WHAT A HORRIBLE SOUND.

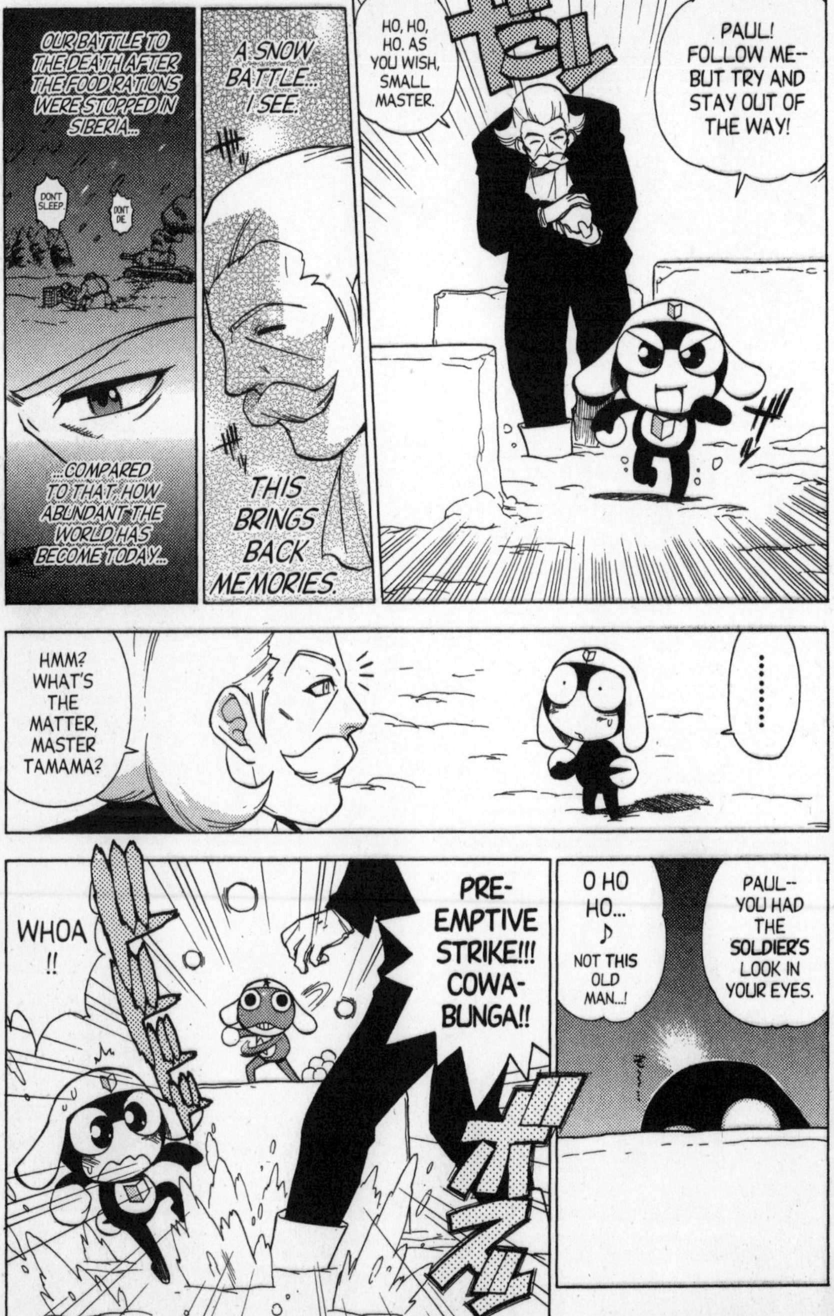
PAUL! FOLLOW ME-- BUT TRY AND STAY OUT OF THE WAY!
HO, HO, HO. AS YOU WISH, SMALL MASTER.
A SNOW BATTLE... I SEE.
THIS BRINGS BACK MEMORIES.
OUR BATTLE TO THE DEATH AFTER THE FOOD RATIONS WERE STOPPED IN SIBERIA...
DON'T SLEEP.
DON'T DIE.
...COMPARED TO THAT, HOW ABUNDANT THE WORLD HAS BECOME TODAY...
........
HMM? WHAT'S THE MATTER, MASTER TAMAMA?
PAUL-- YOU HAD THE SOLDIER'S LOOK IN YOUR EYES.
O HO HO... ♪ NOT THIS OLD MAN...!
PRE-EMPTIVE STRIKE!!! COWA-BUNGA!!
WHOA !!

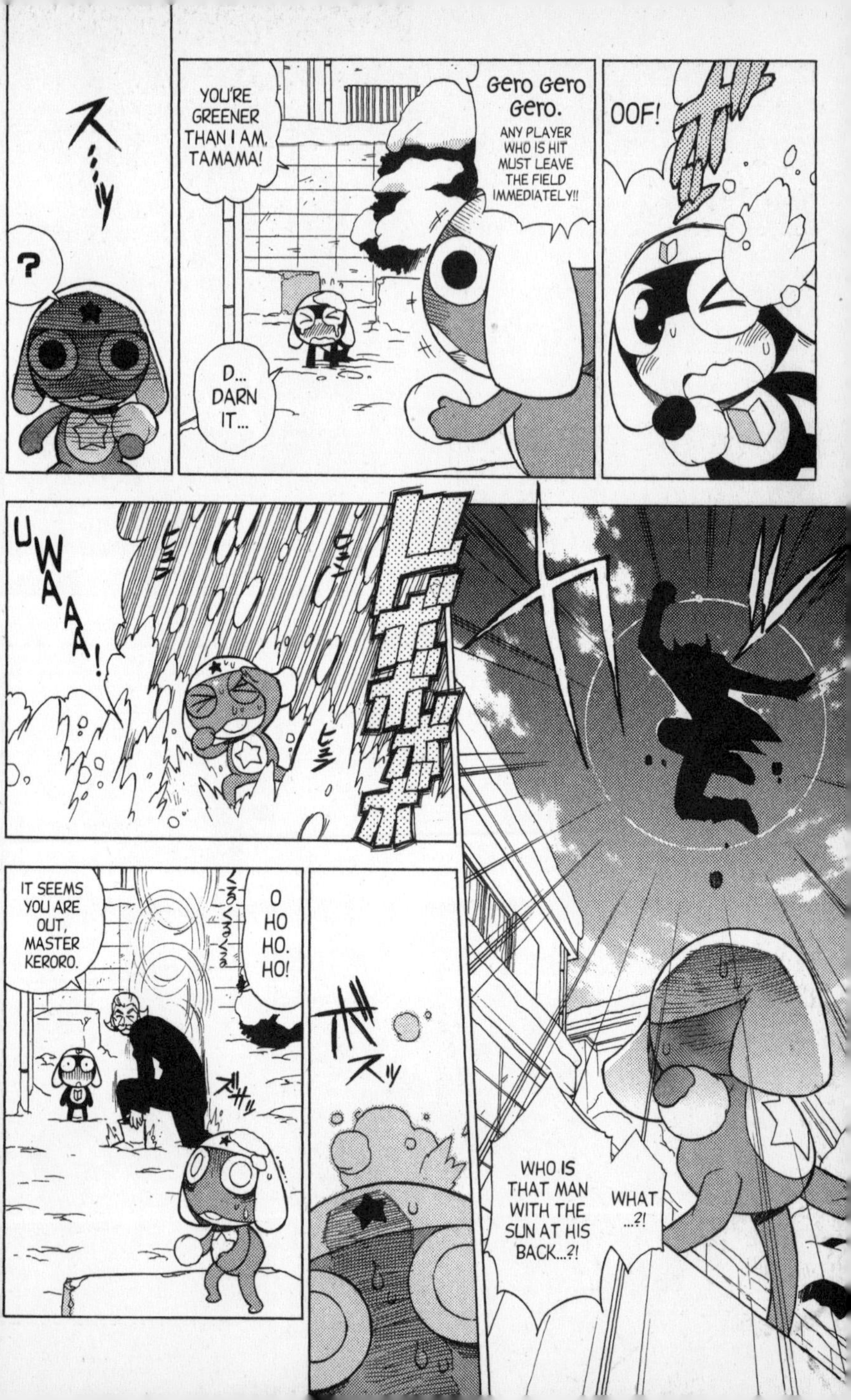
OOF!
Gero Gero Gero.
ANY PLAYER WHO IS HIT MUST LEAVE THE FIELD IMMEDIATELY!!
YOU'RE GREENER THAN I AM, TAMAMA!
D... DARN IT...
?
WHAT ...?!
WHO IS THAT MAN WITH THE SUN AT HIS BACK...?!
UWAAAA!
O HO HO. HO!
IT SEEMS YOU ARE OUT, MASTER KERORO.

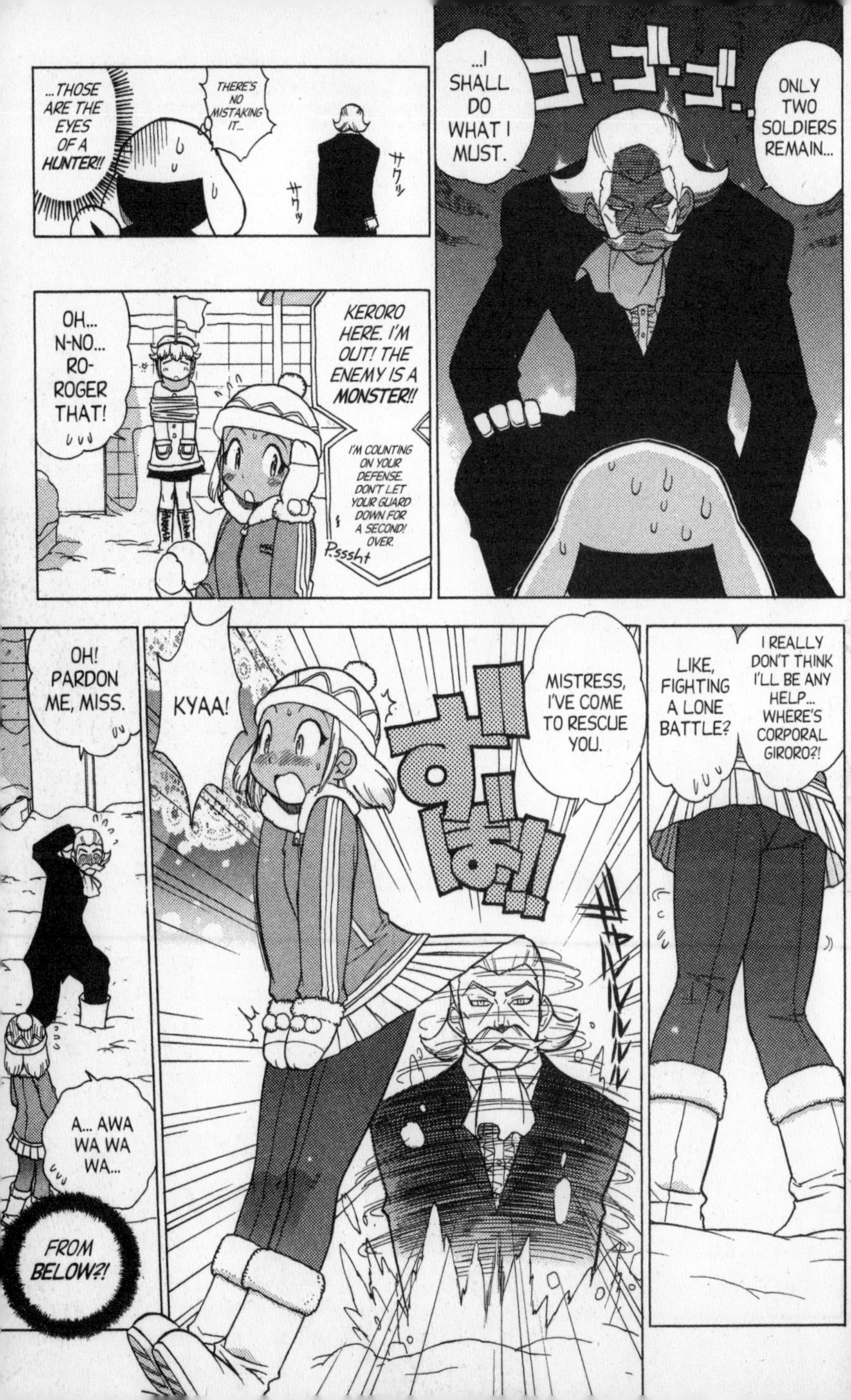
ONLY TWO SOLDIERS REMAIN...
...I SHALL DO WHAT I MUST.
...THOSE ARE THE EYES OF A HUNTER!!
THERE'S NO MISTAKING IT...
KERORO HERE. I'M OUT! THE ENEMY IS A MONSTER!!
I'M COUNTING ON YOUR DEFENSE. DON'T LET YOUR GUARD DOWN FOR A SECOND! OVER.
Pssssht
OH... N-NO... RO-ROGER THAT!
I REALLY DON'T THINK I'LL BE ANY HELP... WHERE'S CORPORAL GIRORO?!
LIKE, FIGHTING A LONE BATTLE?
MISTRESS, I'VE COME TO RESCUE YOU.
KYAA!
OH! PARDON ME, MISS.
A... AWA WA WA WA...
FROM BELOW?!

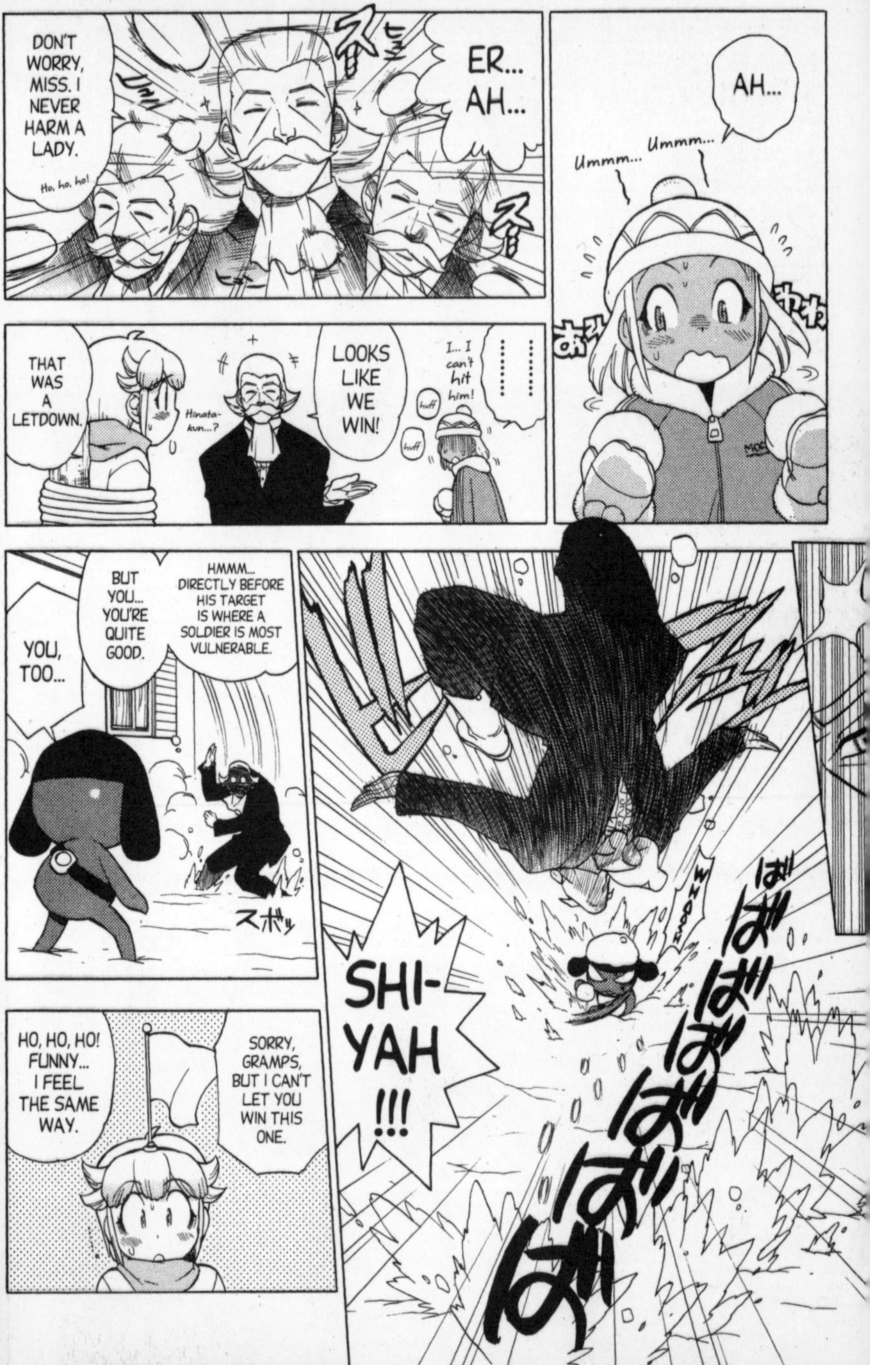
AH...
Ummm...
Ummm...
ER... AH...
DON'T WORRY, MISS. I NEVER HARM A LADY.
Ho, ho, ho!
......
I... I can't hit him!
huff
huff
LOOKS LIKE WE WIN!
Hinata-kun...?
THAT WAS A LETDOWN.
SHI-YAH!!!
HMMM... DIRECTLY BEFORE HIS TARGET IS WHERE A SOLDIER IS MOST VULNERABLE.
BUT YOU... YOU'RE QUITE GOOD.
YOU, TOO...
スボッ
SORRY, GRAMPS, BUT I CAN'T LET YOU WIN THIS ONE.
HO, HO, HO! FUNNY... I FEEL THE SAME WAY.

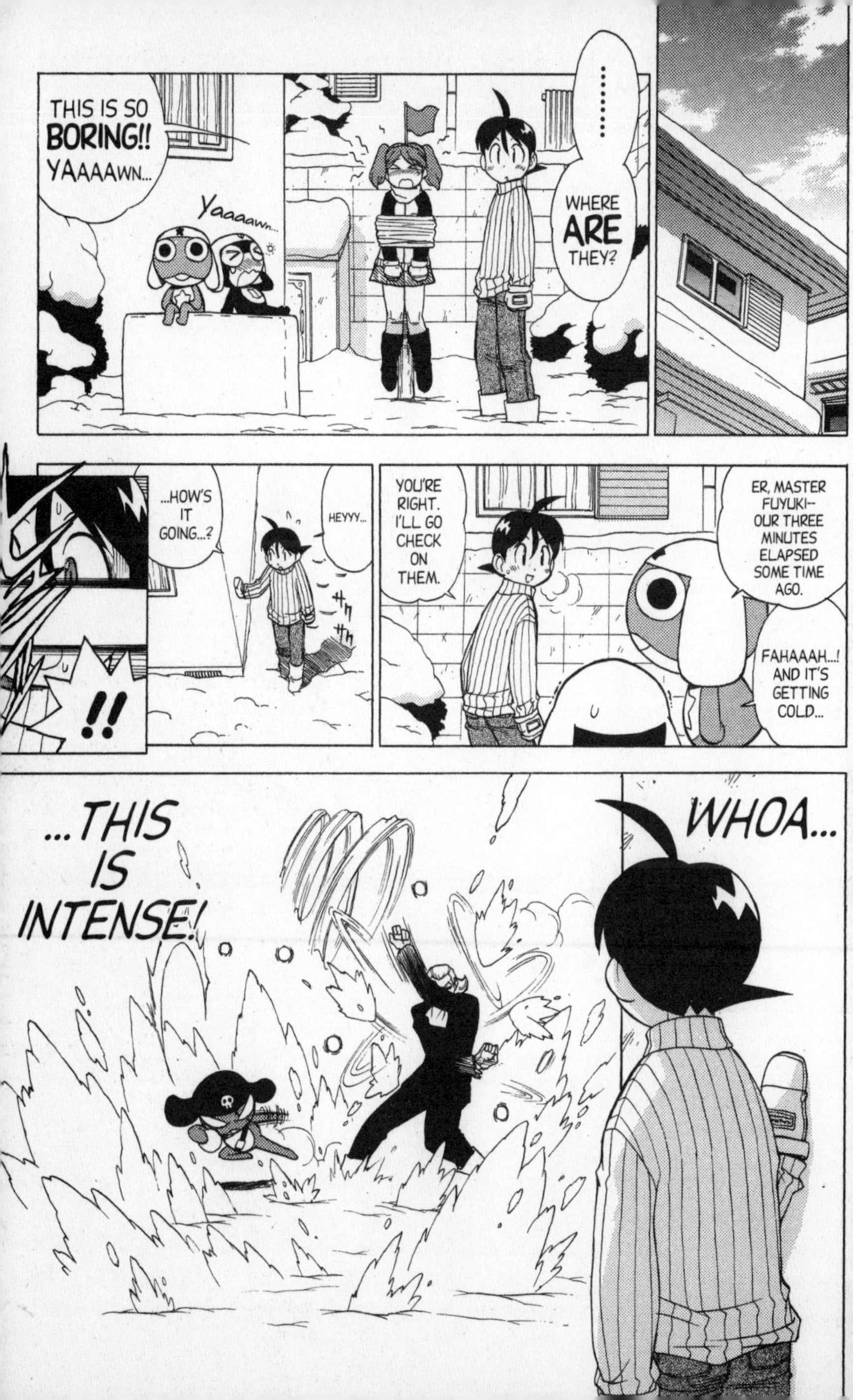
......
WHERE ARE THEY?
THIS IS SO BORING!! YAAAAWN...
Yaaaawn...
ER, MASTER FUYUKI-- OUR THREE MINUTES ELAPSED SOME TIME AGO.
FAHAAAH...! AND IT'S GETTING COLD...
YOU'RE RIGHT. I'LL GO CHECK ON THEM.
HEYYY...
...HOW'S IT GOING...?
!!
WHOA...
...THIS IS INTENSE!

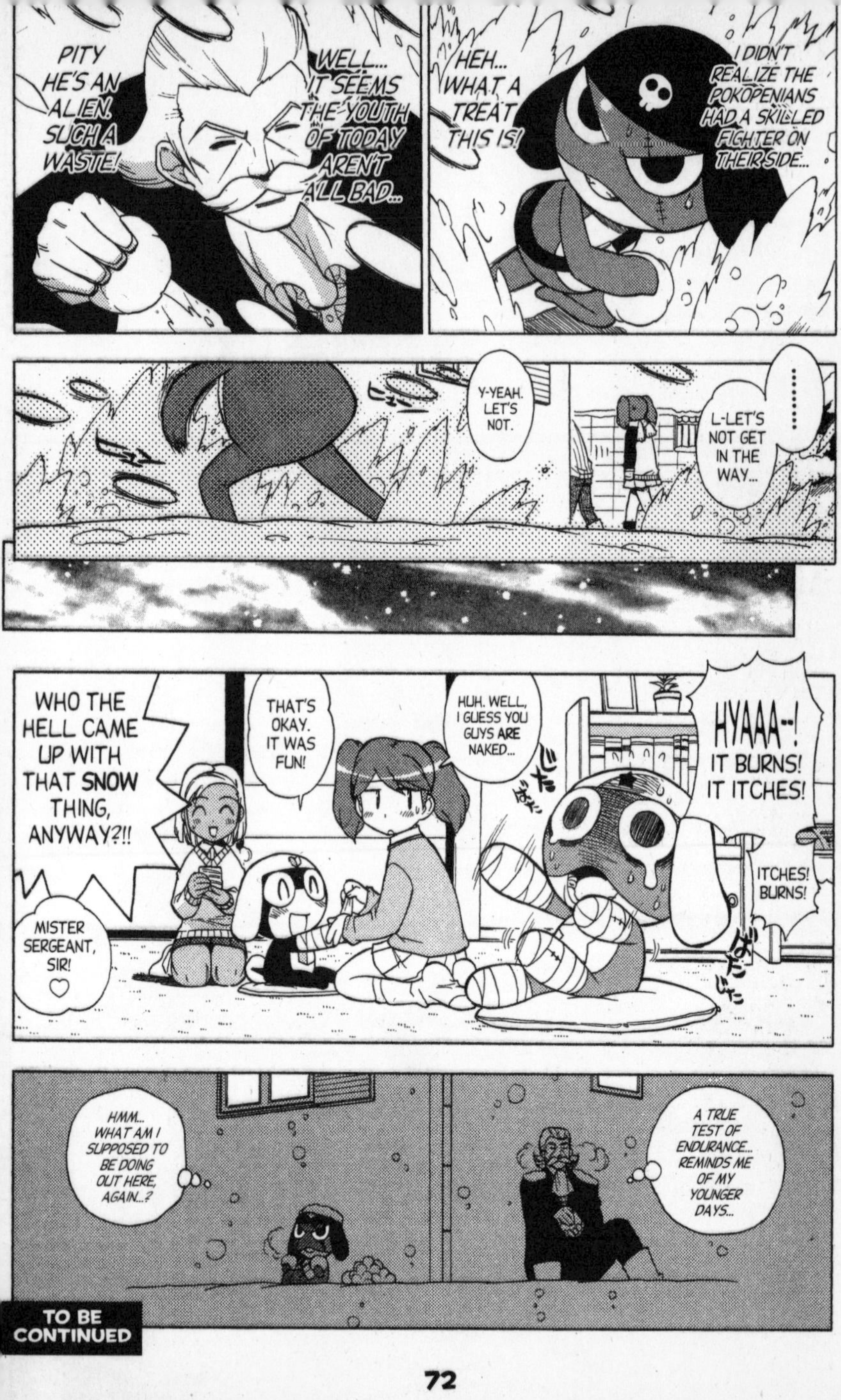
I DIDN'T REALIZE THE POKOPENIANS HAD A SKILLED FIGHTER ON THEIR SIDE...
HEH... WHAT A TREAT THIS IS!
WELL... IT SEEMS THE YOUTH OF TODAY AREN'T ALL BAD...
PITY HE'S AN ALIEN. SUCH A WASTE!
......
L-LET'S NOT GET IN THE WAY...
Y-YEAH. LET'S NOT.
HYAAA--! IT BURNS! IT ITCHES!
ITCHES! BURNS!
HUH. WELL, I GUESS YOU GUYS ARE NAKED...
THAT'S OKAY. IT WAS FUN!
WHO THE HELL CAME UP WITH THAT SNOW THING, ANYWAY?!!
MISTER SERGEANT, SIR! ♡
A TRUE TEST OF ENDURANCE... REMINDS ME OF MY YOUNGER DAYS...
HMM... WHAT AM I SUPPOSED TO BE DOING OUT HERE, AGAIN...?
TO BE CONTINUED

## ENCOUNTER XXXIII

# THE SERGEANT GETS WHAT HE DESERVES

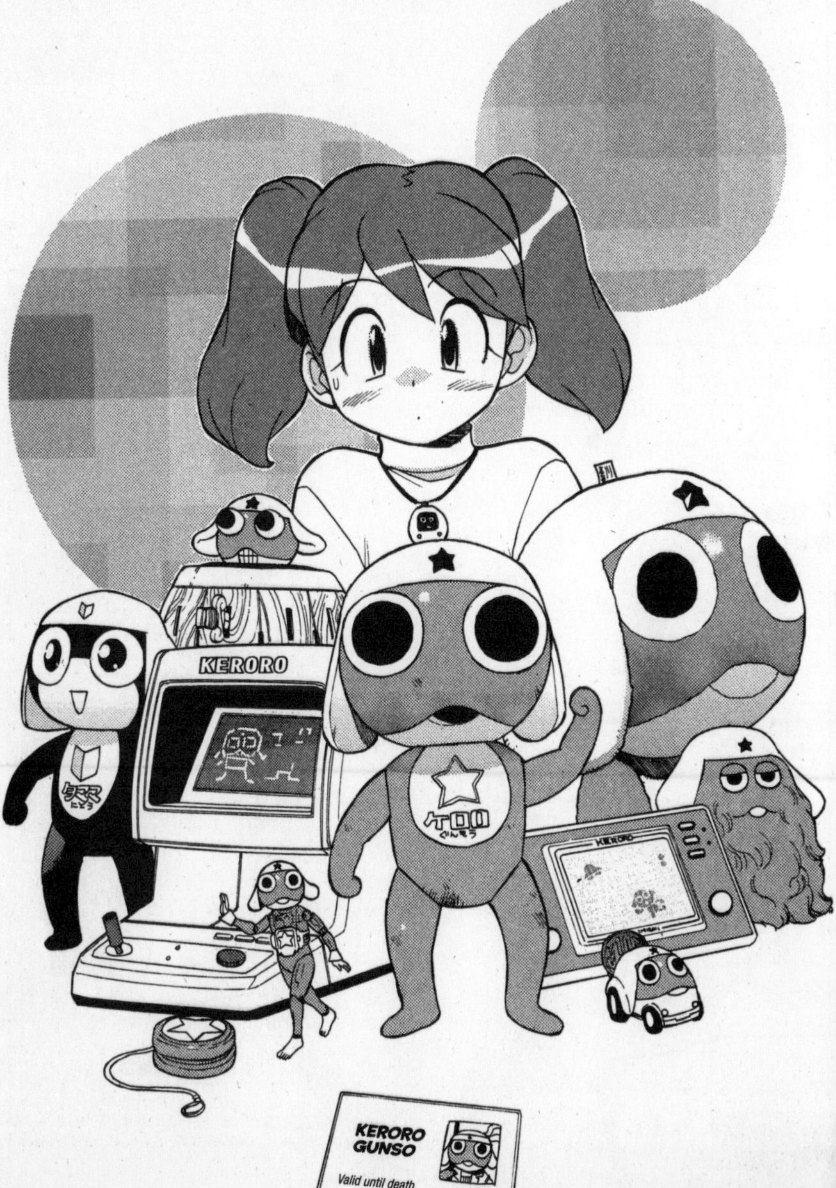
KERORO
ケロロ
KERORO
GUNSO
Valid until death

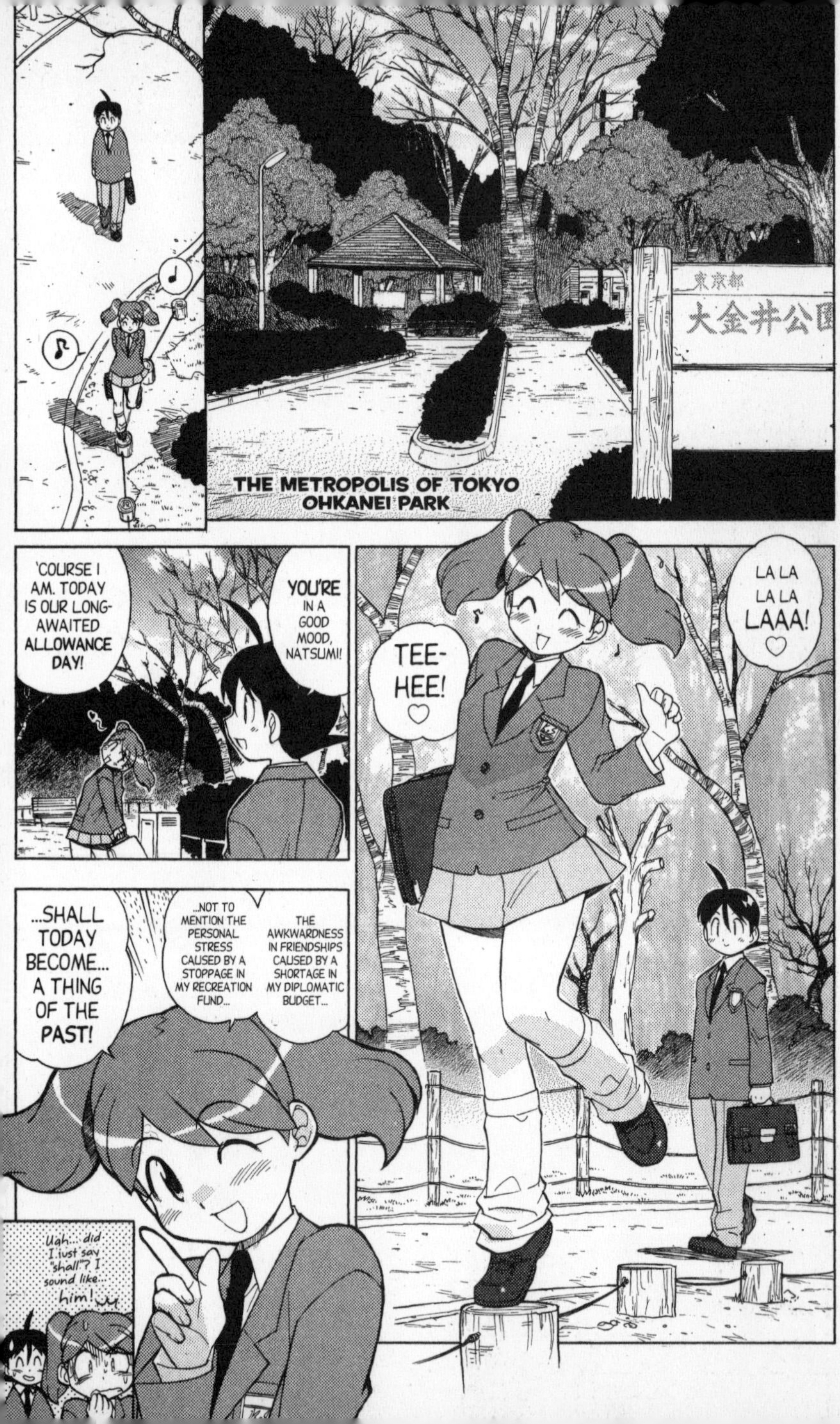
東京都
大金井公園
THE METROPOLIS OF TOKYO
OHKANEI PARK
LA LA LA LA LAAA!
TEE-HEE!
YOU'RE IN A GOOD MOOD, NATSUMI!
'COURSE I AM. TODAY IS OUR LONG-AWAITED ALLOWANCE DAY!
THE AWKWARDNESS IN FRIENDSHIPS CAUSED BY A SHORTAGE IN MY DIPLOMATIC BUDGET...
...NOT TO MENTION THE PERSONAL STRESS CAUSED BY A STOPPAGE IN MY RECREATION FUND...
...SHALL TODAY BECOME... A THING OF THE PAST!
Ugh... did I just say "shall"? I sound like... him!

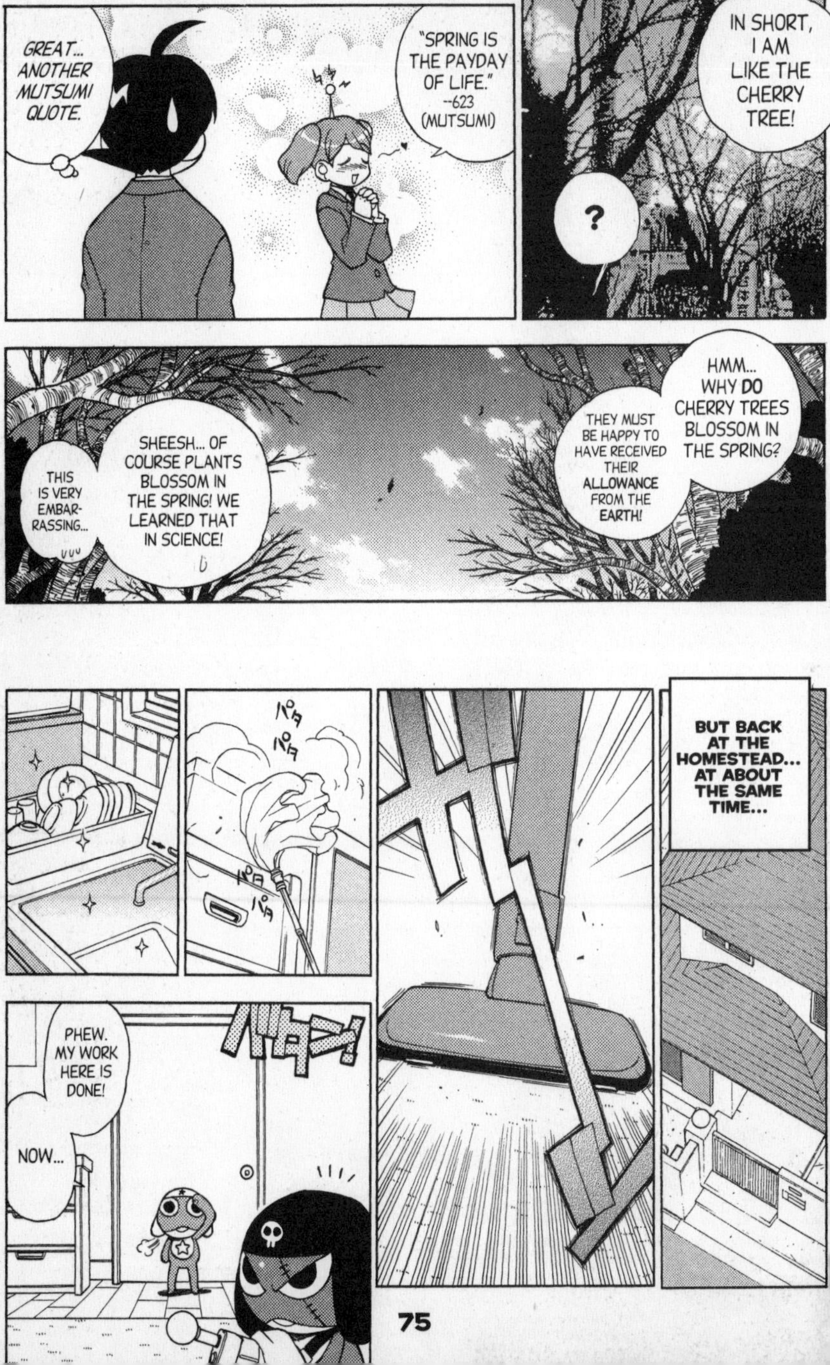
IN SHORT, I AM LIKE THE CHERRY TREE!
?
"SPRING IS THE PAYDAY OF LIFE." --623 (MUTSUMI)
GREAT... ANOTHER MUTSUMI QUOTE.
HMM... WHY DO CHERRY TREES BLOSSOM IN THE SPRING?
THEY MUST BE HAPPY TO HAVE RECEIVED THEIR ALLOWANCE FROM THE EARTH!
SHEESH... OF COURSE PLANTS BLOSSOM IN THE SPRING! WE LEARNED THAT IN SCIENCE!
THIS IS VERY EMBARRASSING...
BUT BACK AT THE HOMESTEAD... AT ABOUT THE SAME TIME...
PHEW. MY WORK HERE IS DONE!
NOW...

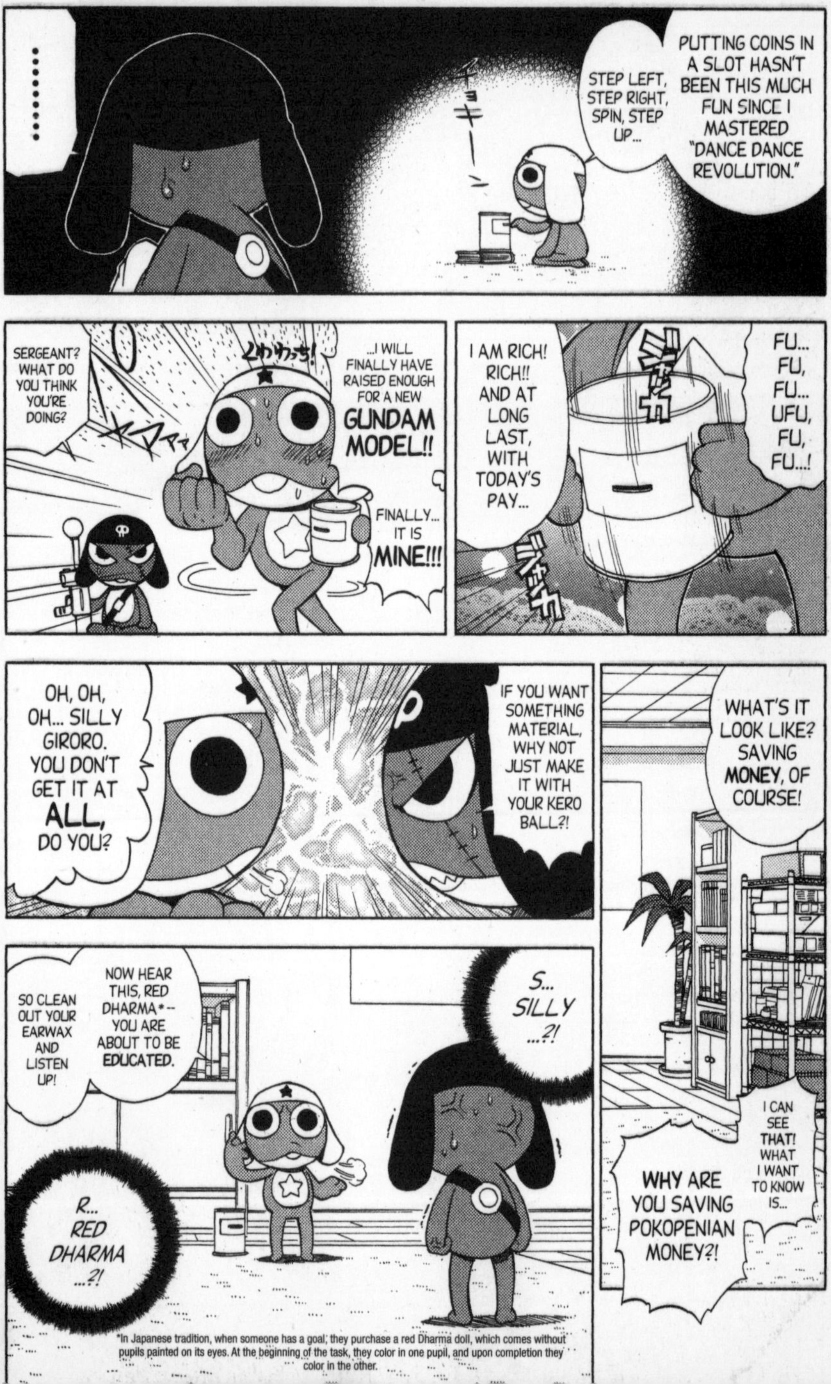
PUTTING COINS IN A SLOT HASN'T BEEN THIS MUCH FUN SINCE I MASTERED "DANCE DANCE REVOLUTION."
STEP LEFT, STEP RIGHT, SPIN, STEP UP...
........
FU... FU, FU... UFU, FU, FU...!
I AM RICH! RICH!! AND AT LONG LAST, WITH TODAY'S PAY...
...I WILL FINALLY HAVE RAISED ENOUGH FOR A NEW GUNDAM MODEL!!
FINALLY... IT IS MINE!!!
SERGEANT? WHAT DO YOU THINK YOU'RE DOING?
WHAT'S IT LOOK LIKE? SAVING MONEY, OF COURSE!
I CAN SEE THAT! WHAT I WANT TO KNOW IS...
WHY ARE YOU SAVING POKOPENIAN MONEY?!
IF YOU WANT SOMETHING MATERIAL, WHY NOT JUST MAKE IT WITH YOUR KERO BALL?!
OH, OH, OH... SILLY GIRORO. YOU DON'T GET IT AT ALL, DO YOU?
S... SILLY ...?!
NOW HEAR THIS, RED DHARMA*-- YOU ARE ABOUT TO BE EDUCATED.
SO CLEAN OUT YOUR EARWAX AND LISTEN UP!
R... RED DHARMA ...?!

*In Japanese tradition, when someone has a goal, they purchase a red Dharma doll, which comes without pupils painted on its eyes. At the beginning of the task, they color in one pupil, and upon completion they color in the other.

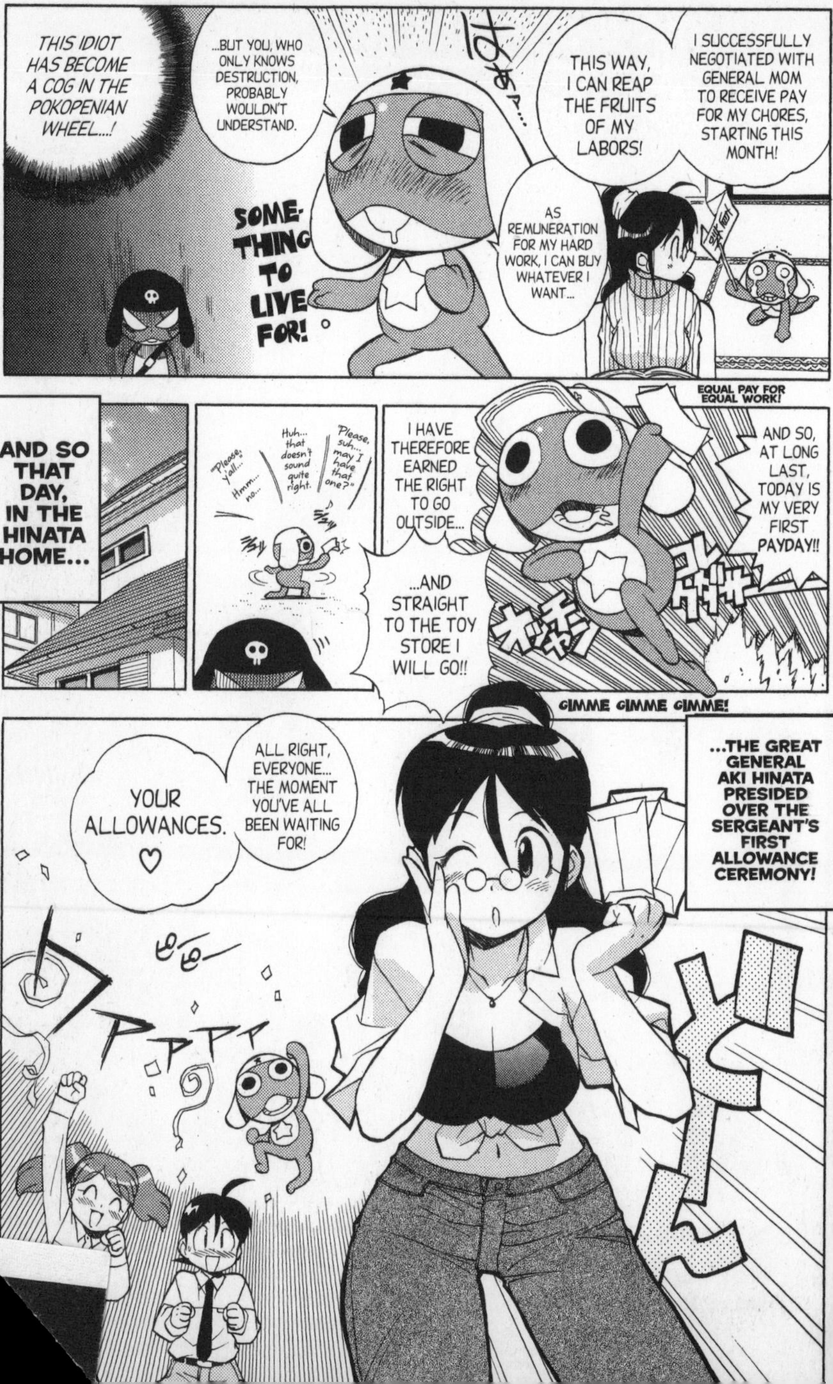
I SUCCESSFULLY NEGOTIATED WITH GENERAL MOM TO RECEIVE PAY FOR MY CHORES, STARTING THIS MONTH!
THIS WAY, I CAN REAP THE FRUITS OF MY LABORS!
AS REMUNERATION FOR MY HARD WORK, I CAN BUY WHATEVER I WANT...
...BUT YOU, WHO ONLY KNOWS DESTRUCTION, PROBABLY WOULDN'T UNDERSTAND.
SOME-THING TO LIVE FOR!
THIS IDIOT HAS BECOME A COG IN THE POKOPENIAN WHEEL...!
EQUAL PAY FOR EQUAL WORK!
AND SO, AT LONG LAST, TODAY IS MY VERY FIRST PAYDAY!!
I HAVE THEREFORE EARNED THE RIGHT TO GO OUTSIDE...
GIMME GIMME GIMME!
"Please, suh... may I have that one?"
Huh... that doesn't sound quite right.
"Please, y'all..."
Hmm... no...
...AND STRAIGHT TO THE TOY STORE I WILL GO!!
AND SO THAT DAY, IN THE HINATA HOME...
...THE GREAT GENERAL AKI HINATA PRESIDED OVER THE SERGEANT'S FIRST ALLOWANCE CEREMONY!
ALL RIGHT, EVERYONE... THE MOMENT YOU'VE ALL BEEN WAITING FOR!
YOUR ALLOWANCES. ♡

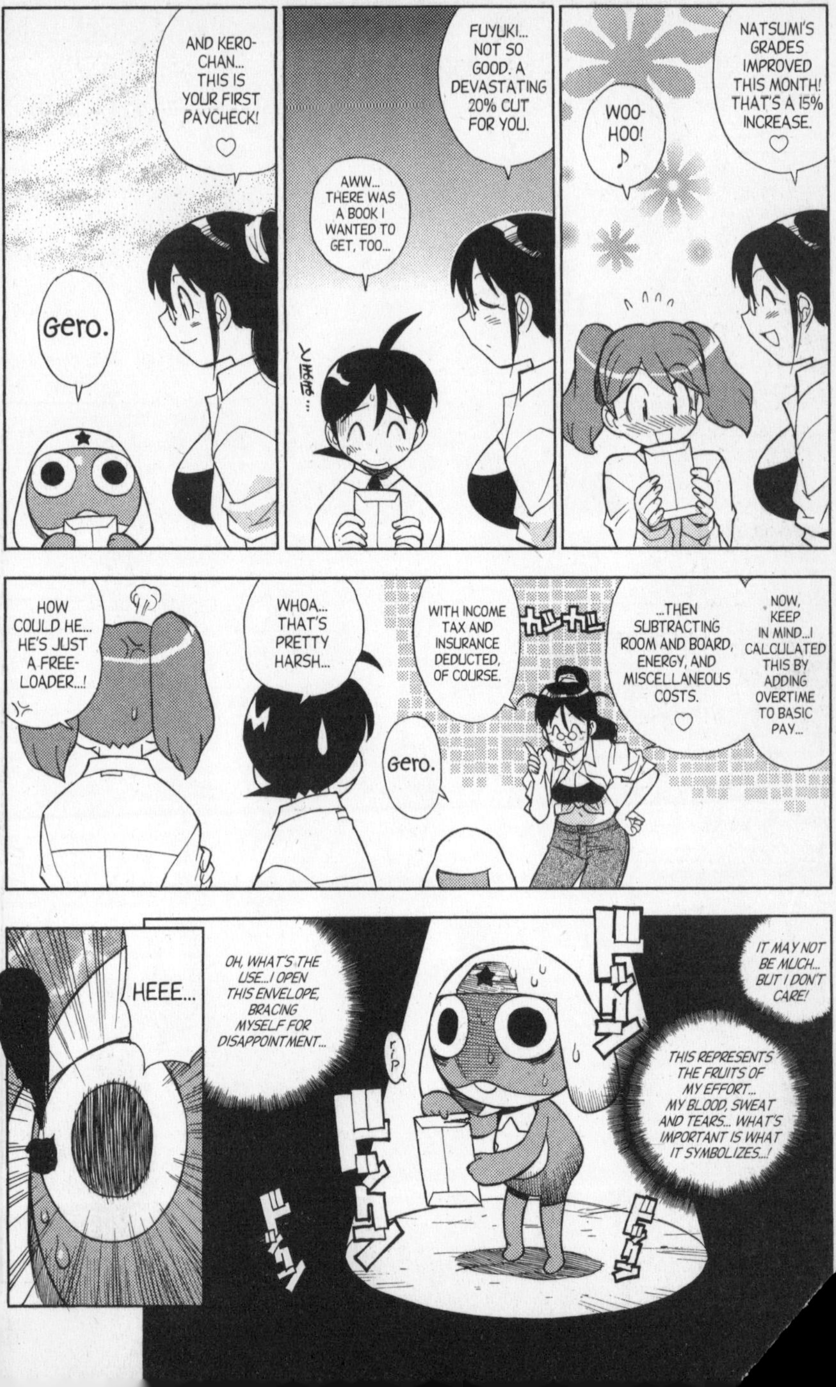
NATSUMI'S GRADES IMPROVED THIS MONTH! THAT'S A 15% INCREASE. ♡
WOO-HOO! ♪
FUYUKI... NOT SO GOOD. A DEVASTATING 20% CUT FOR YOU.
AWW... THERE WAS A BOOK I WANTED TO GET, TOO...
とほほ…
AND KERO-CHAN... THIS IS YOUR FIRST PAYCHECK! ♡
Gero.
NOW, KEEP IN MIND...I CALCULATED THIS BY ADDING OVERTIME TO BASIC PAY...
...THEN SUBTRACTING ROOM AND BOARD, ENERGY, AND MISCELLANEOUS COSTS. ♡
WITH INCOME TAX AND INSURANCE DEDUCTED, OF COURSE.
Gero.
WHOA... THAT'S PRETTY HARSH...
HOW COULD HE... HE'S JUST A FREE-LOADER...!
IT MAY NOT BE MUCH... BUT I DON'T CARE!
THIS REPRESENTS THE FRUITS OF MY EFFORT... MY BLOOD, SWEAT AND TEARS... WHAT'S IMPORTANT IS WHAT IT SYMBOLIZES...!
OH, WHAT'S THE USE...I OPEN THIS ENVELOPE, BRACING MYSELF FOR DISAPPOINTMENT...
RIP
HEEE...

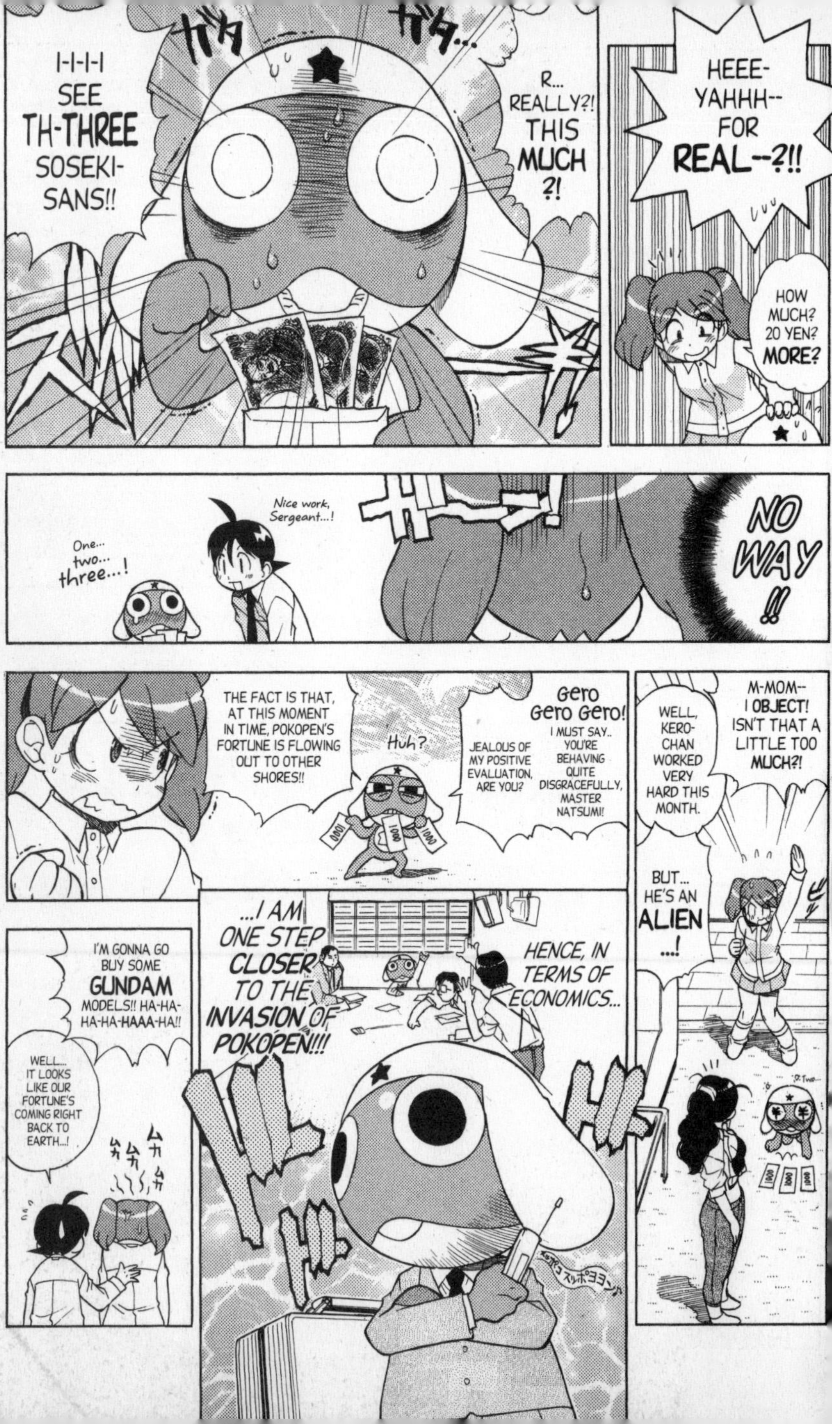
HEEE-YAHHH-- FOR REAL--?!!
HOW MUCH? 20 YEN? MORE?
ガタ
ガタ...
R... REALLY?! THIS MUCH ?!
I-I-I-I SEE TH-THREE SOSEKI-SANS!!
NO WAY !!
Nice work, Sergeant...!
One... two... three...!
M-MOM-- I OBJECT! ISN'T THAT A LITTLE TOO MUCH?!
WELL, KERO-CHAN WORKED VERY HARD THIS MONTH.
BUT... HE'S AN ALIEN ...!
Gero Gero Gero! I MUST SAY.. YOU'RE BEHAVING QUITE DISGRACEFULLY, MASTER NATSUMI!
JEALOUS OF MY POSITIVE EVALUATION, ARE YOU?
Huh?
THE FACT IS THAT, AT THIS MOMENT IN TIME, POKOPEN'S FORTUNE IS FLOWING OUT TO OTHER SHORES!!
HENCE, IN TERMS OF ECONOMICS...
...I AM ONE STEP CLOSER TO THE INVASION OF POKOPEN!!!
I'M GONNA GO BUY SOME GUNDAM MODELS!! HA-HA-HA-HA-HAAA-HA!!
WELL... IT LOOKS LIKE OUR FORTUNE'S COMING RIGHT BACK TO EARTH...!

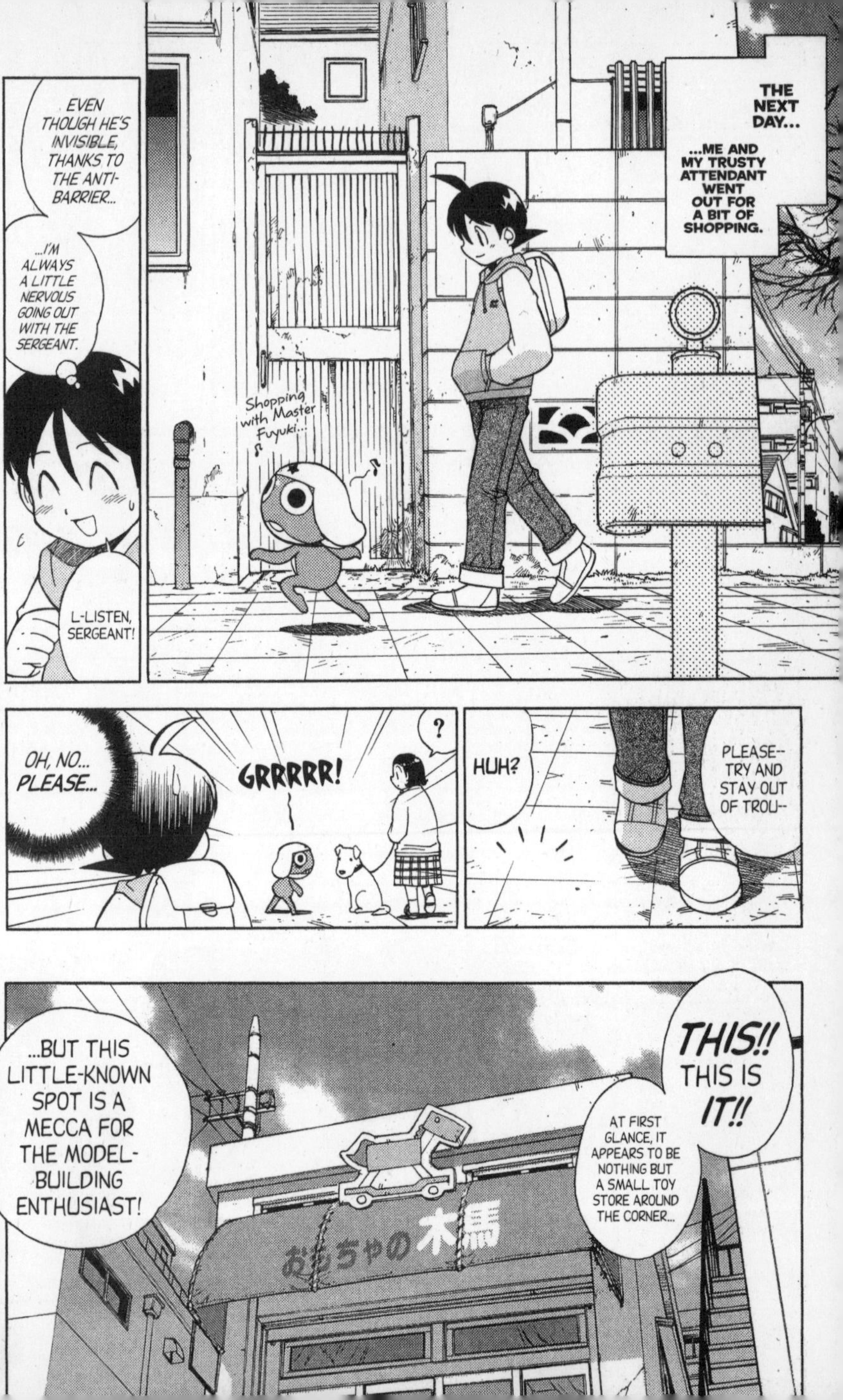
THE NEXT DAY...
...ME AND MY TRUSTY ATTENDANT WENT OUT FOR A BIT OF SHOPPING.
Shopping with Master Fuyuki...
EVEN THOUGH HE'S INVISIBLE, THANKS TO THE ANTI-BARRIER...
...I'M ALWAYS A LITTLE NERVOUS GOING OUT WITH THE SERGEANT.
L-LISTEN, SERGEANT!
PLEASE-- TRY AND STAY OUT OF TROU--
HUH?
?
GRRRRR!
OH, NO... PLEASE...
THIS!! THIS IS IT!!
AT FIRST GLANCE, IT APPEARS TO BE NOTHING BUT A SMALL TOY STORE AROUND THE CORNER...
...BUT THIS LITTLE-KNOWN SPOT IS A MECCA FOR THE MODEL-BUILDING ENTHUSIAST!
おもちゃの木馬

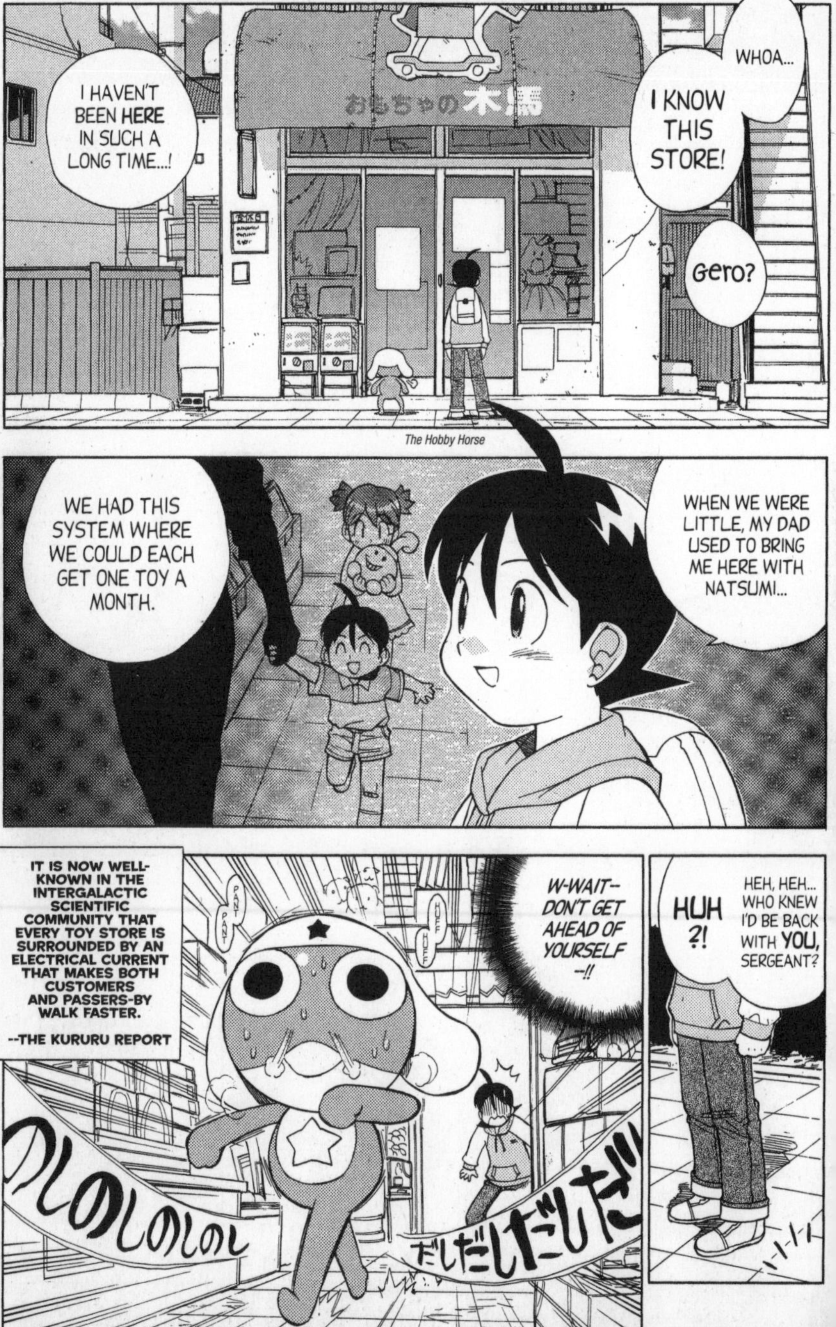
WHOA...
I KNOW THIS STORE!
Gero?
I HAVEN'T BEEN HERE IN SUCH A LONG TIME...!
おもちゃの木馬
The Hobby Horse
WHEN WE WERE LITTLE, MY DAD USED TO BRING ME HERE WITH NATSUMI...
WE HAD THIS SYSTEM WHERE WE COULD EACH GET ONE TOY A MONTH.
HEH, HEH... WHO KNEW I'D BE BACK WITH YOU, SERGEANT?
HUH ?!
W-WAIT-- DON'T GET AHEAD OF YOURSELF --!!
IT IS NOW WELL-KNOWN IN THE INTERGALACTIC SCIENTIFIC COMMUNITY THAT EVERY TOY STORE IS SURROUNDED BY AN ELECTRICAL CURRENT THAT MAKES BOTH CUSTOMERS AND PASSERS-BY WALK FASTER.
--THE KURURU REPORT
PANT PANT
HUFF HUFF
のしのしのしのしのし
だしだしだしだ

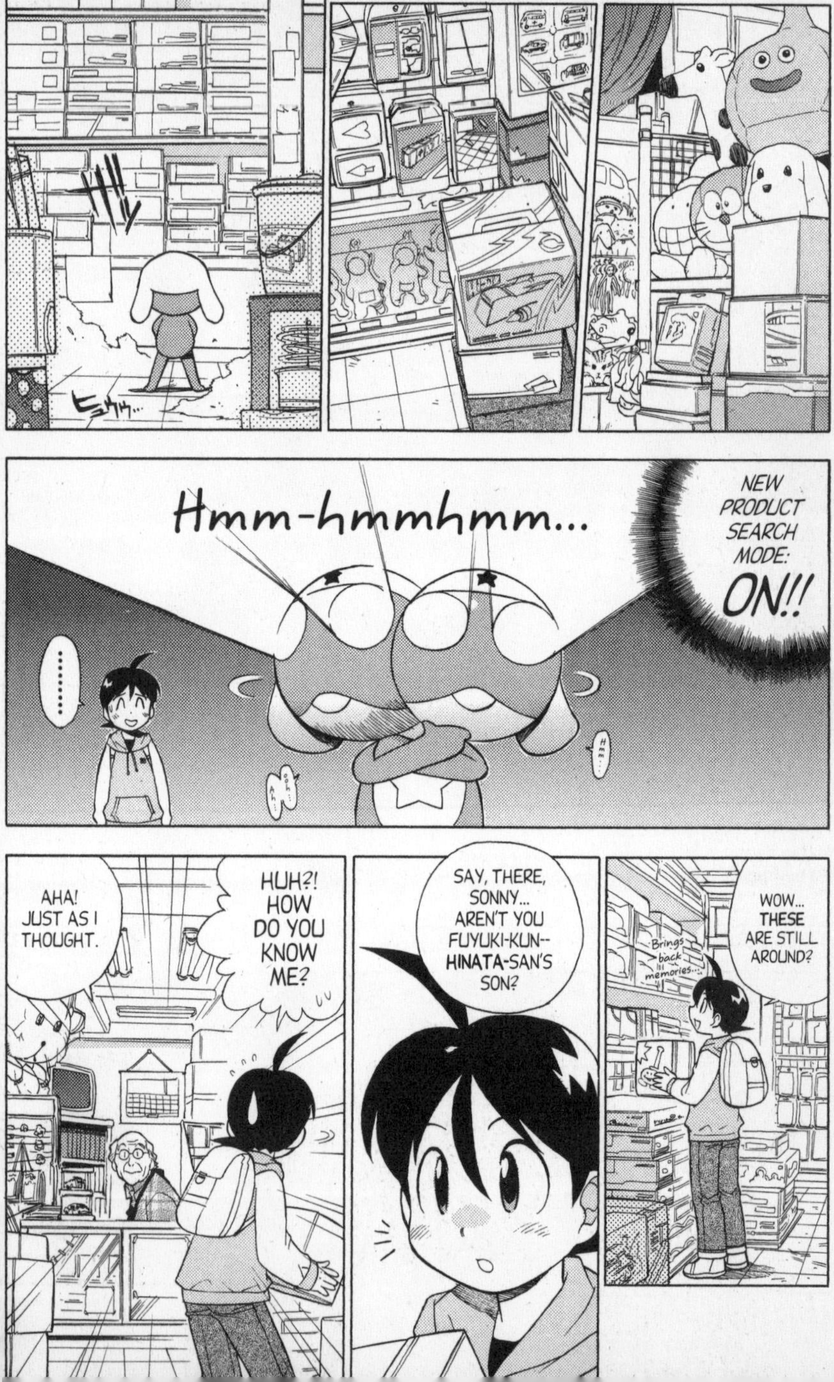
NEW PRODUCT SEARCH MODE: ON!!
Hmm-hmmhmm...
......
WOW... THESE ARE STILL AROUND?
Brings back memories...
SAY, THERE, SONNY... AREN'T YOU FUYUKI-KUN-- HINATA-SAN'S SON?
HUH?! HOW DO YOU KNOW ME?
AHA! JUST AS I THOUGHT.

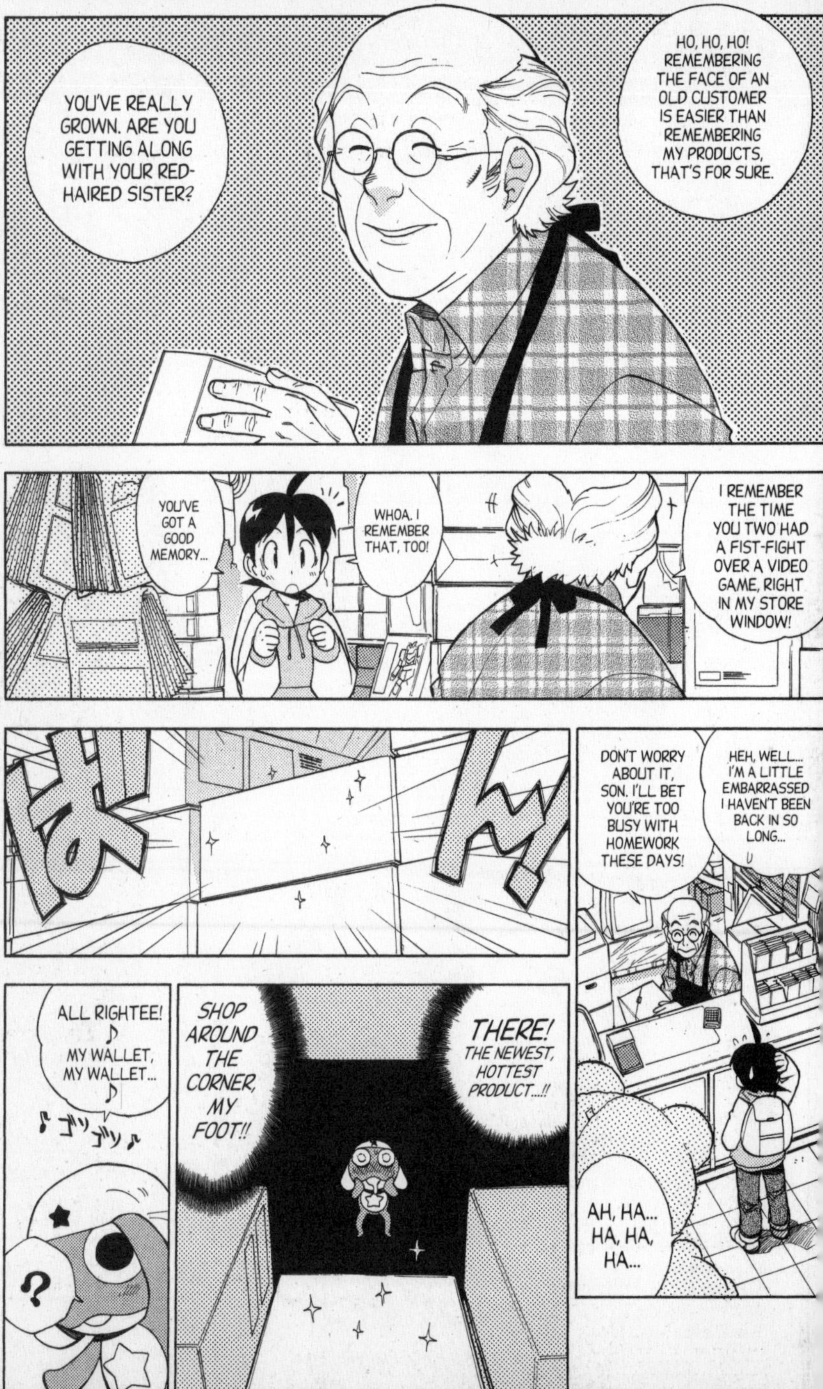
HO, HO, HO! REMEMBERING THE FACE OF AN OLD CUSTOMER IS EASIER THAN REMEMBERING MY PRODUCTS, THAT'S FOR SURE.
YOU'VE REALLY GROWN. ARE YOU GETTING ALONG WITH YOUR RED-HAIRED SISTER?
I REMEMBER THE TIME YOU TWO HAD A FIST-FIGHT OVER A VIDEO GAME, RIGHT IN MY STORE WINDOW!
WHOA. I REMEMBER THAT, TOO!
YOU'VE GOT A GOOD MEMORY...
HEH, WELL... I'M A LITTLE EMBARRASSED I HAVEN'T BEEN BACK IN SO LONG...
DON'T WORRY ABOUT IT, SON. I'LL BET YOU'RE TOO BUSY WITH HOMEWORK THESE DAYS!
AH, HA... HA, HA, HA...
THERE! THE NEWEST, HOTTEST PRODUCT...!!
SHOP AROUND THE CORNER, MY FOOT!!
ALL RIGHTEE! ♪ MY WALLET, MY WALLET... ♪
♪ゴソゴソ♪

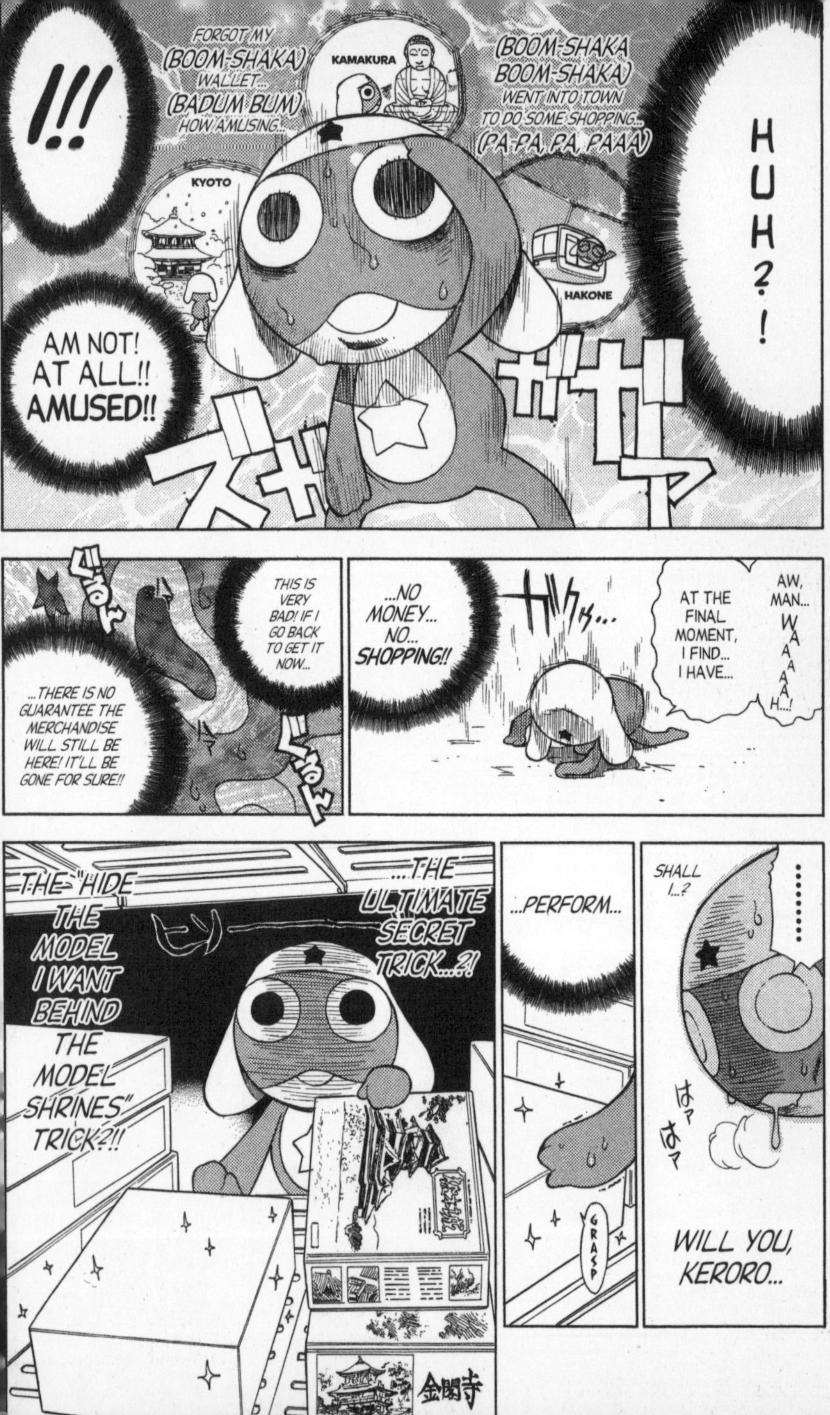
HUH?!
(BOOM-SHAKA BOOM-SHAKA) WENT INTO TOWN TO DO SOME SHOPPING... (PA-PA, PA, PAAA)
HAKONE
KAMAKURA
FORGOT MY (BOOM-SHAKA) WALLET... (BADUM BUM) HOW AMUSING...
KYOTO
!!!
AM NOT! AT ALL!! AMUSED!!
AW, MAN... WAAAAAH...!
AT THE FINAL MOMENT, I FIND... I HAVE...
...NO MONEY... NO... SHOPPING!!
THIS IS VERY BAD! IF I GO BACK TO GET IT NOW...
...THERE IS NO GUARANTEE THE MERCHANDISE WILL STILL BE HERE! IT'LL BE GONE FOR SURE!!
........
SHALL I...?
はァ はァ
WILL YOU, KERORO...
...PERFORM...
GRASP
...THE ULTIMATE SECRET TRICK...?!
THE "HIDE THE MODEL I WANT BEHIND THE MODEL SHRINES" TRICK?!!
ヒソ
金閣寺

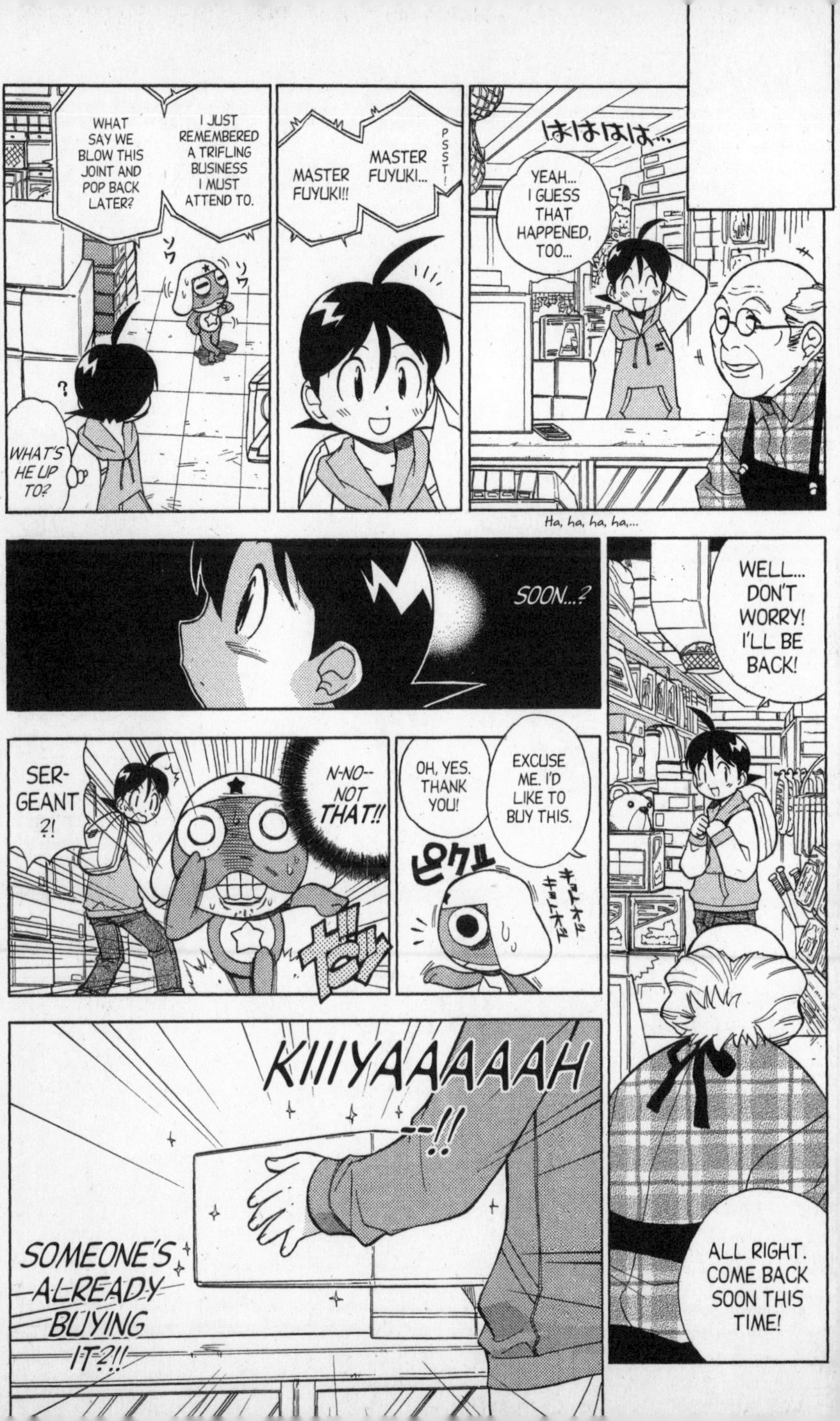
はははは...
YEAH... I GUESS THAT HAPPENED, TOO...
Ha, ha, ha, ha,...
PSST!
MASTER FUYUKI...
MASTER FUYUKI!!!
I JUST REMEMBERED A TRIFLING BUSINESS I MUST ATTEND TO.
WHAT SAY WE BLOW THIS JOINT AND POP BACK LATER?
ソワ
ソワ
?
WHAT'S HE UP TO?
WELL... DON'T WORRY! I'LL BE BACK!
ALL RIGHT. COME BACK SOON THIS TIME!
SOON...?
EXCUSE ME. I'D LIKE TO BUY THIS.
OH, YES. THANK YOU!
ピクッ
キョトオド キョトオド
N-NO-- NOT THAT!!
SER-GEANT?!
KIIIYAAAAAH --!!
SOMEONE'S ALREADY BUYING IT?!!

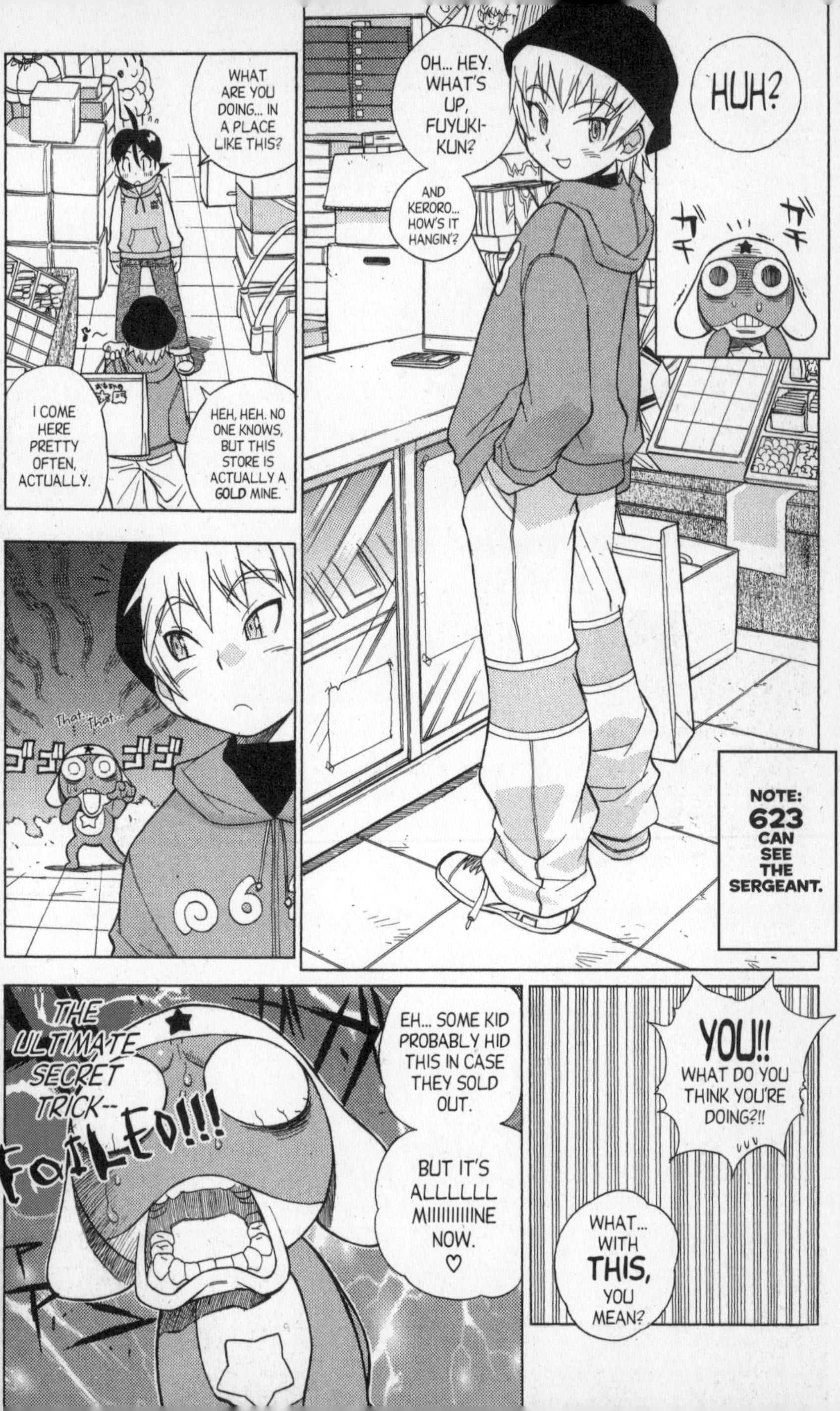
HUH?
OH... HEY. WHAT'S UP, FUYUKI-KUN?
AND KERORO... HOW'S IT HANGIN'?
NOTE: 623 CAN SEE THE SERGEANT.
WHAT ARE YOU DOING... IN A PLACE LIKE THIS?
HEH, HEH. NO ONE KNOWS, BUT THIS STORE IS ACTUALLY A GOLD MINE.
I COME HERE PRETTY OFTEN, ACTUALLY.
That... That...
YOU!! WHAT DO YOU THINK YOU'RE DOING?!!
WHAT... WITH THIS, YOU MEAN?
EH... SOME KID PROBABLY HID THIS IN CASE THEY SOLD OUT.
BUT IT'S ALLLLLL MIIIIIIIIINE NOW. ♡
THE ULTIMATE SECRET TRICK--
FAILED!!!

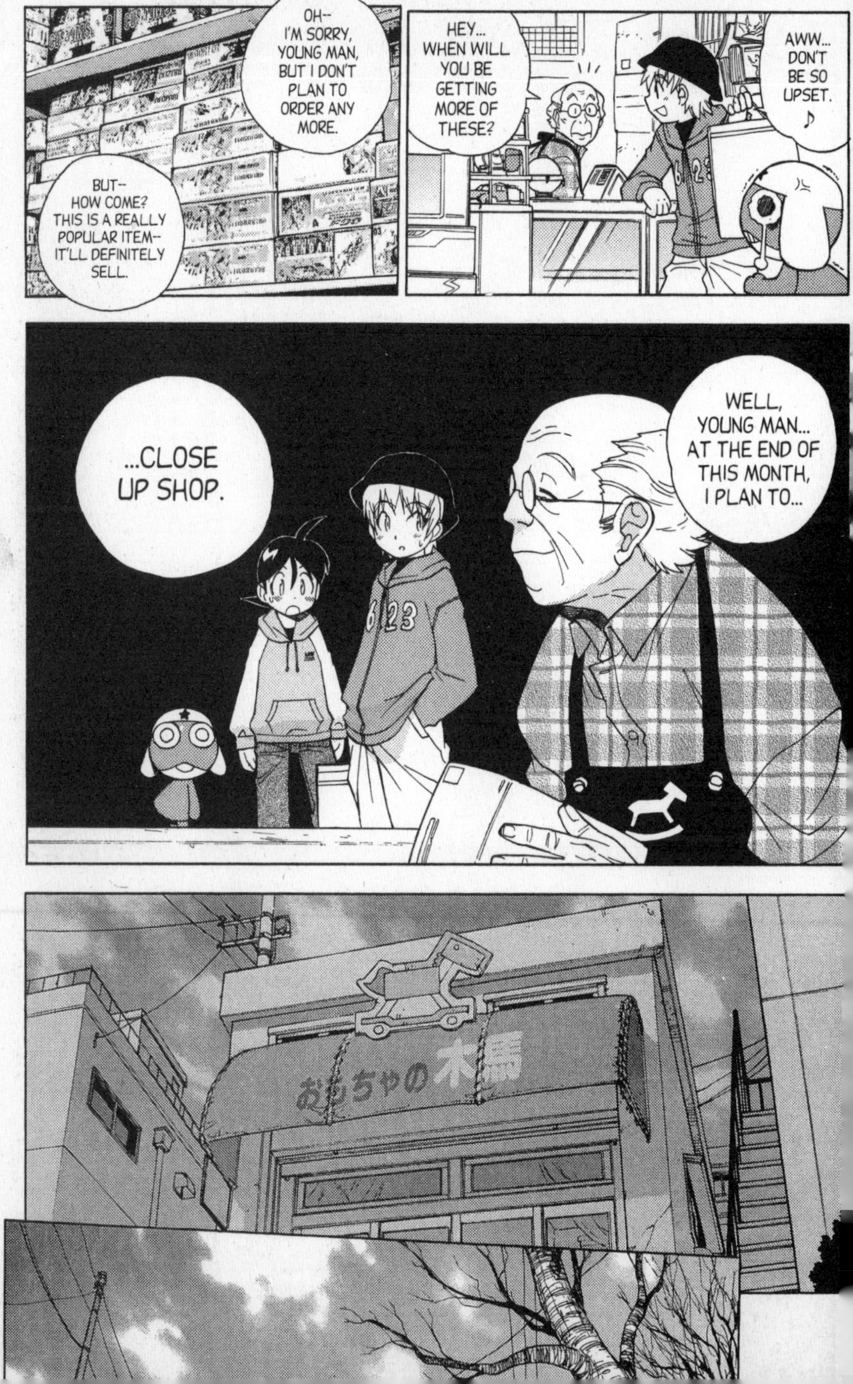
AWW... DON'T BE SO UPSET. ♪
HEY... WHEN WILL YOU BE GETTING MORE OF THESE?
OH-- I'M SORRY, YOUNG MAN, BUT I DON'T PLAN TO ORDER ANY MORE.
BUT-- HOW COME? THIS IS A REALLY POPULAR ITEM-- IT'LL DEFINITELY SELL.
WELL, YOUNG MAN... AT THE END OF THIS MONTH, I PLAN TO...
...CLOSE UP SHOP.
おもちゃの木馬

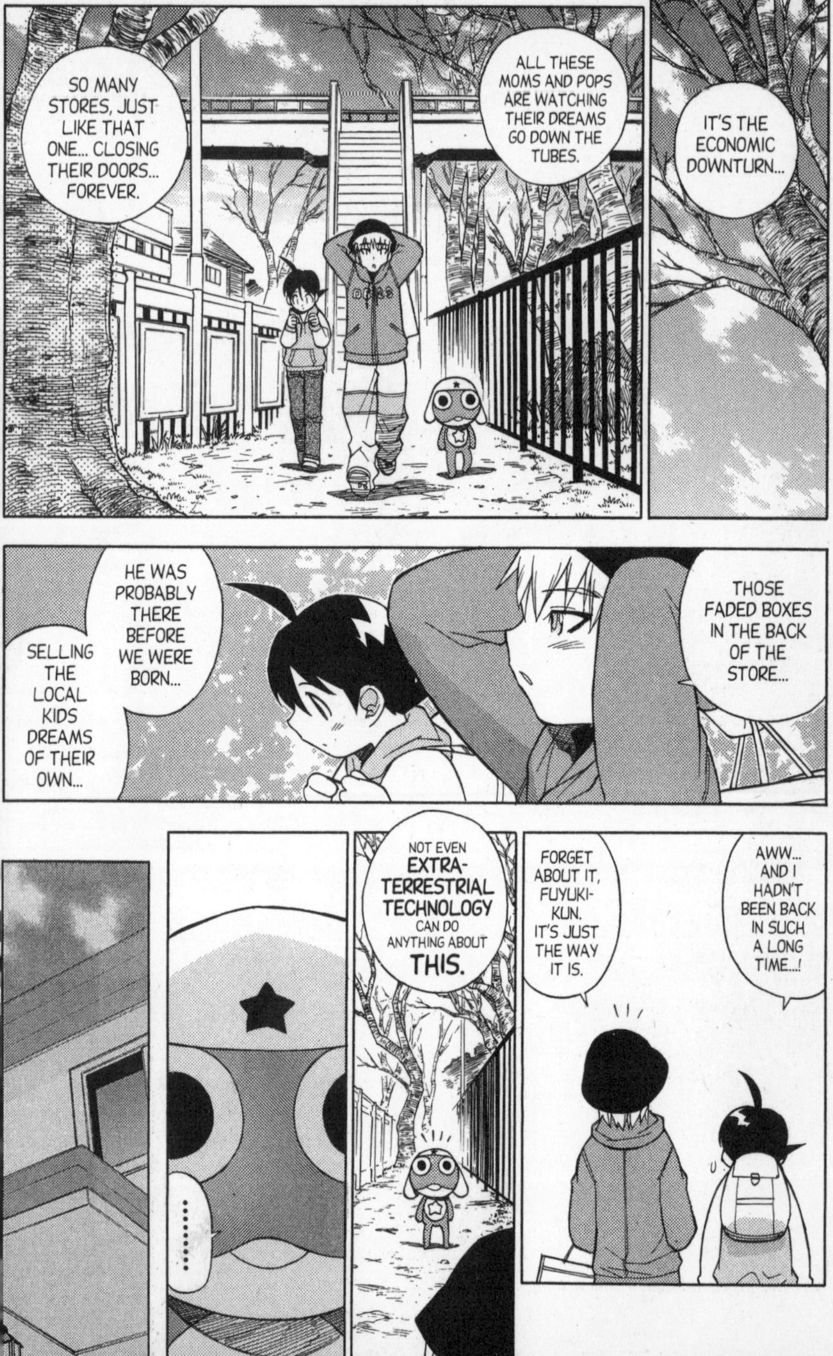
IT'S THE ECONOMIC DOWNTURN...
ALL THESE MOMS AND POPS ARE WATCHING THEIR DREAMS GO DOWN THE TUBES.
SO MANY STORES, JUST LIKE THAT ONE... CLOSING THEIR DOORS... FOREVER.
THOSE FADED BOXES IN THE BACK OF THE STORE...
HE WAS PROBABLY THERE BEFORE WE WERE BORN...
SELLING THE LOCAL KIDS DREAMS OF THEIR OWN...
AWW... AND I HADN'T BEEN BACK IN SUCH A LONG TIME...!
FORGET ABOUT IT, FUYUKI-KUN. IT'S JUST THE WAY IT IS.
NOT EVEN EXTRA-TERRESTRIAL TECHNOLOGY CAN DO ANYTHING ABOUT THIS.
.......

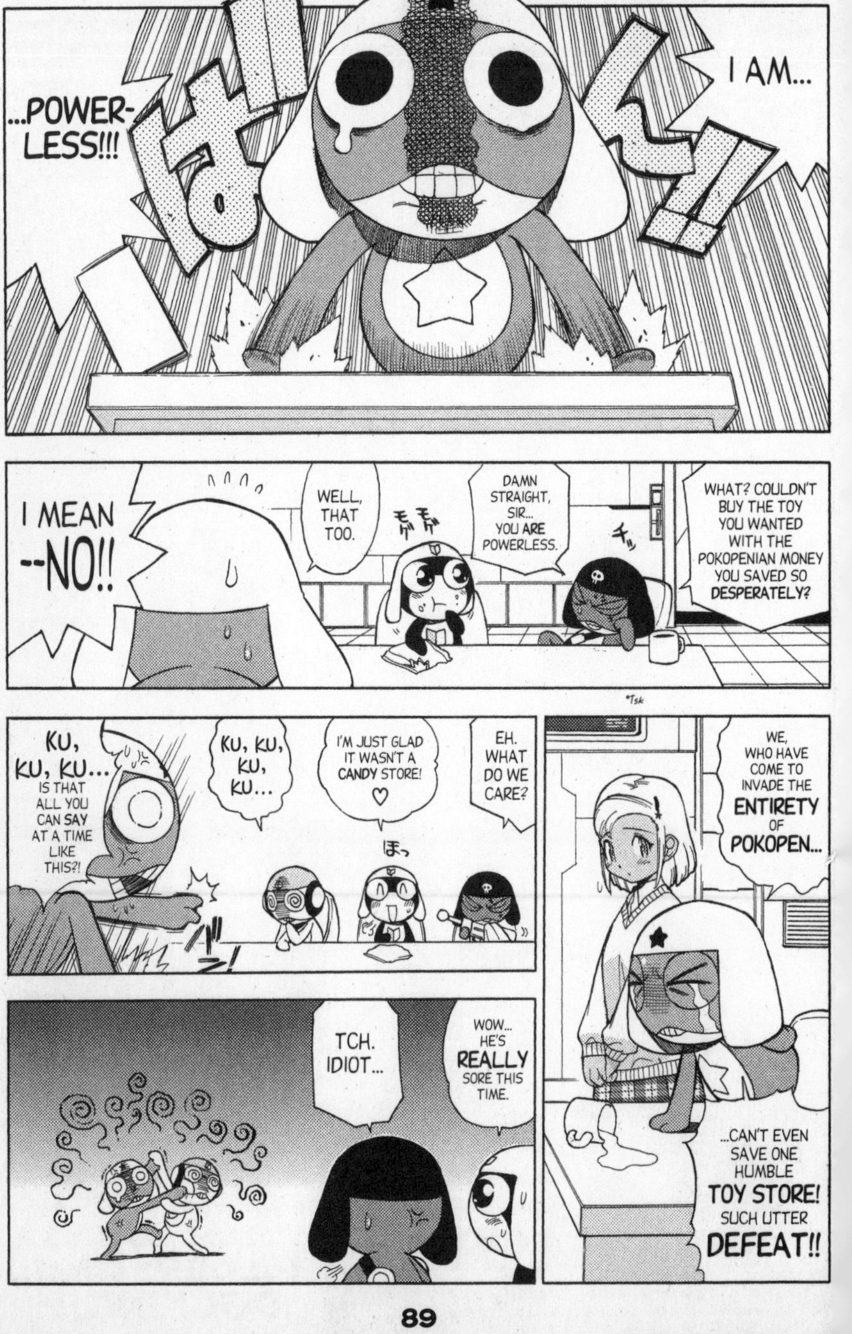
I AM...
...POWER-LESS!!!
WHAT? COULDN'T BUY THE TOY YOU WANTED WITH THE POKOPENIAN MONEY YOU SAVED SO DESPERATELY?
DAMN STRAIGHT, SIR... YOU ARE POWERLESS.
WELL, THAT TOO.
I MEAN --NO!!
*Tsk
WE, WHO HAVE COME TO INVADE THE ENTIRETY OF POKOPEN...
...CAN'T EVEN SAVE ONE HUMBLE TOY STORE! SUCH UTTER DEFEAT!!
EH. WHAT DO WE CARE?
I'M JUST GLAD IT WASN'T A CANDY STORE! ♡
KU, KU, KU, KU...
KU, KU, KU... IS THAT ALL YOU CAN SAY AT A TIME LIKE THIS?!
WOW... HE'S REALLY SORE THIS TIME.
TCH. IDIOT...

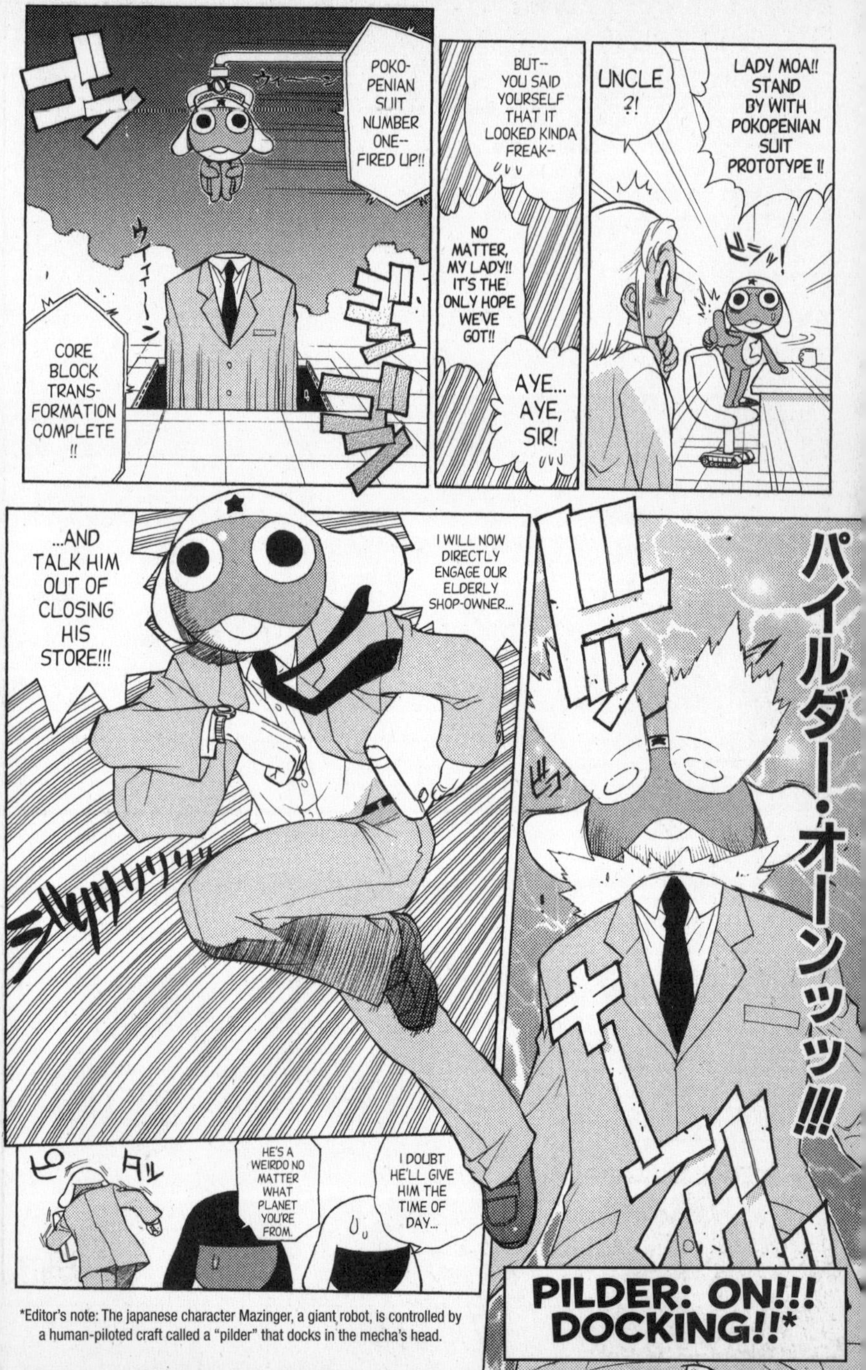
LADY MOA!! STAND BY WITH POKOPENIAN SUIT PROTOTYPE 1!
UNCLE ?!
BUT-- YOU SAID YOURSELF THAT IT LOOKED KINDA FREAK--
NO MATTER, MY LADY!! IT'S THE ONLY HOPE WE'VE GOT!!
AYE... AYE, SIR!
POKO-PENIAN SUIT NUMBER ONE-- FIRED UP!!
CORE BLOCK TRANS-FORMATION COMPLETE !!
パイルダー・オーンッッ!!!
PILDER: ON!!! DOCKING!!*
I WILL NOW DIRECTLY ENGAGE OUR ELDERLY SHOP-OWNER...
...AND TALK HIM OUT OF CLOSING HIS STORE!!!
I DOUBT HE'LL GIVE HIM THE TIME OF DAY...
HE'S A WEIRDO NO MATTER WHAT PLANET YOU'RE FROM.

*Editor's note: The japanese character Mazinger, a giant robot, is controlled by a human-piloted craft called a "pilder" that docks in the mecha's head.

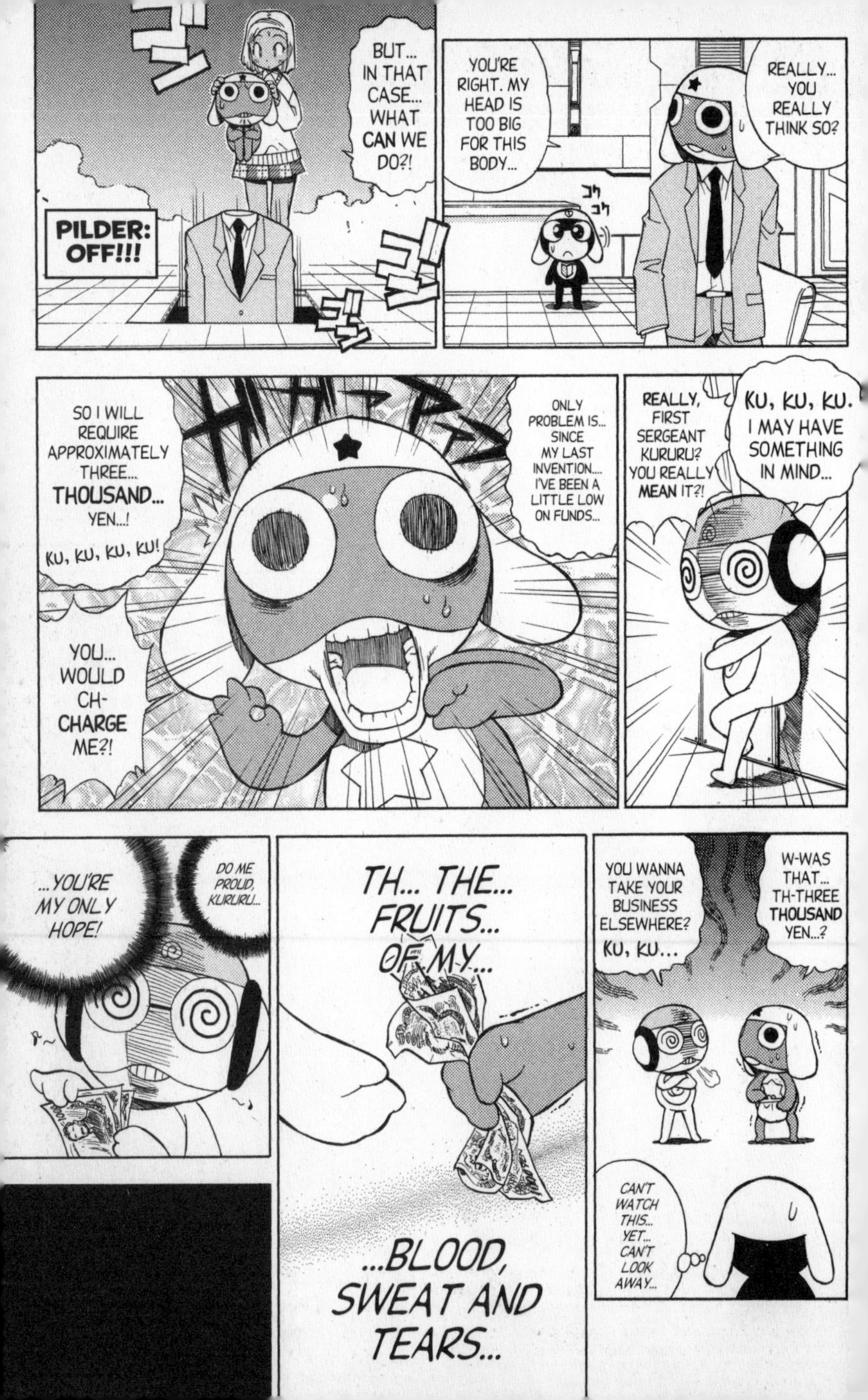
REALLY... YOU REALLY THINK SO?
YOU'RE RIGHT. MY HEAD IS TOO BIG FOR THIS BODY...
BUT... IN THAT CASE... WHAT CAN WE DO?!
PILDER: OFF!!!
KU, KU, KU. I MAY HAVE SOMETHING IN MIND...
REALLY, FIRST SERGEANT KURURU? YOU REALLY MEAN IT?!
ONLY PROBLEM IS... SINCE MY LAST INVENTION.... I'VE BEEN A LITTLE LOW ON FUNDS...
SO I WILL REQUIRE APPROXIMATELY THREE... THOUSAND... YEN...!
KU, KU, KU, KU!
YOU... WOULD CH-CHARGE ME?!
W-WAS THAT... TH-THREE THOUSAND YEN...?
YOU WANNA TAKE YOUR BUSINESS ELSEWHERE? KU, KU...
CAN'T WATCH THIS... YET... CAN'T LOOK AWAY...
TH... THE... FRUITS... OF MY...
...BLOOD, SWEAT AND TEARS...
DO ME PROUD, KURURU...
...YOU'RE MY ONLY HOPE!

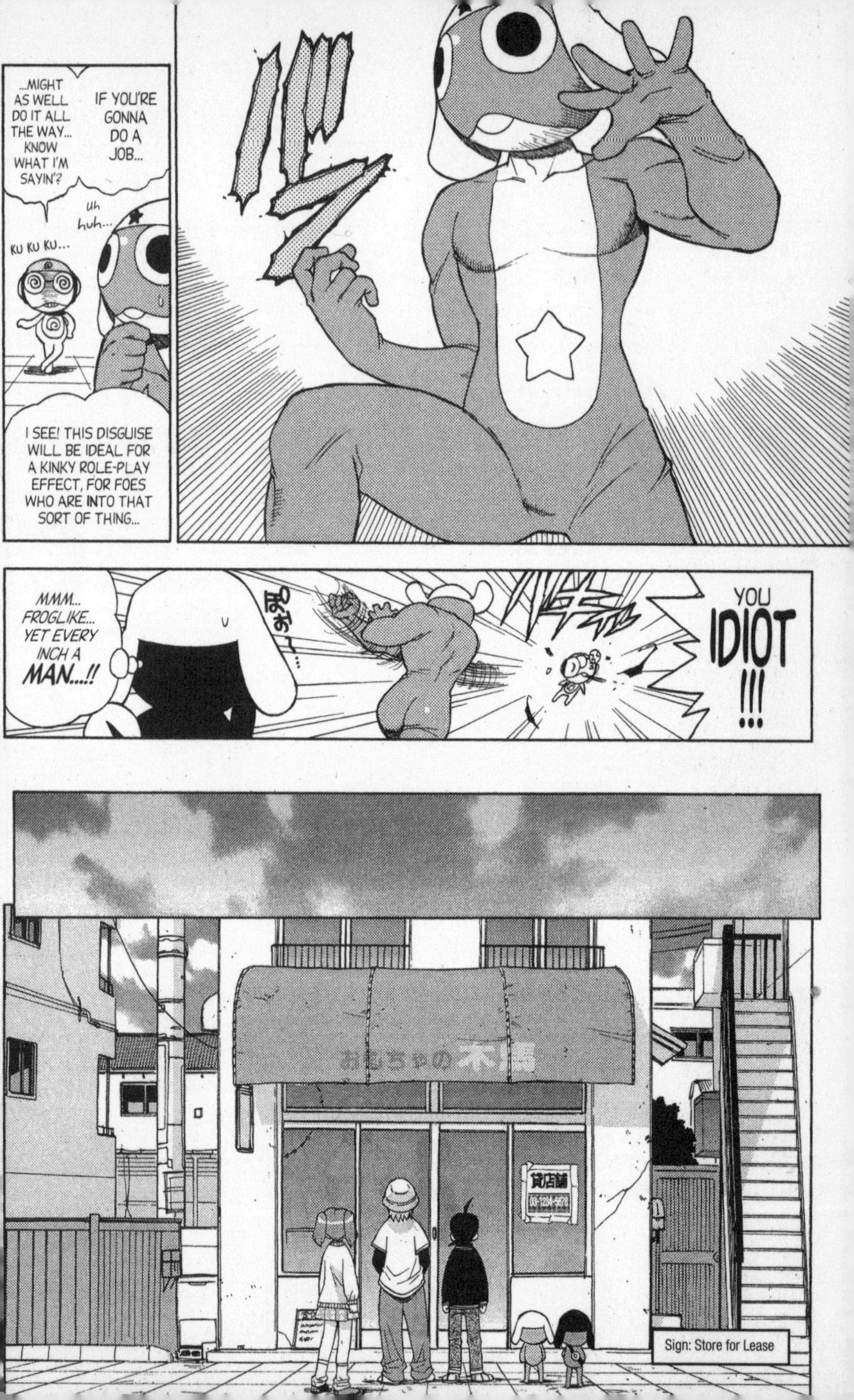
IF YOU'RE GONNA DO A JOB...
...MIGHT AS WELL DO IT ALL THE WAY... KNOW WHAT I'M SAYIN'?
uh huh...
KU KU KU...
I SEE! THIS DISGUISE WILL BE IDEAL FOR A KINKY ROLE-PLAY EFFECT, FOR FOES WHO ARE INTO THAT SORT OF THING...
YOU IDIOT!!!
MMM... FROGLIKE... YET EVERY INCH A MAN...!!
貸店舗
Sign: Store for Lease

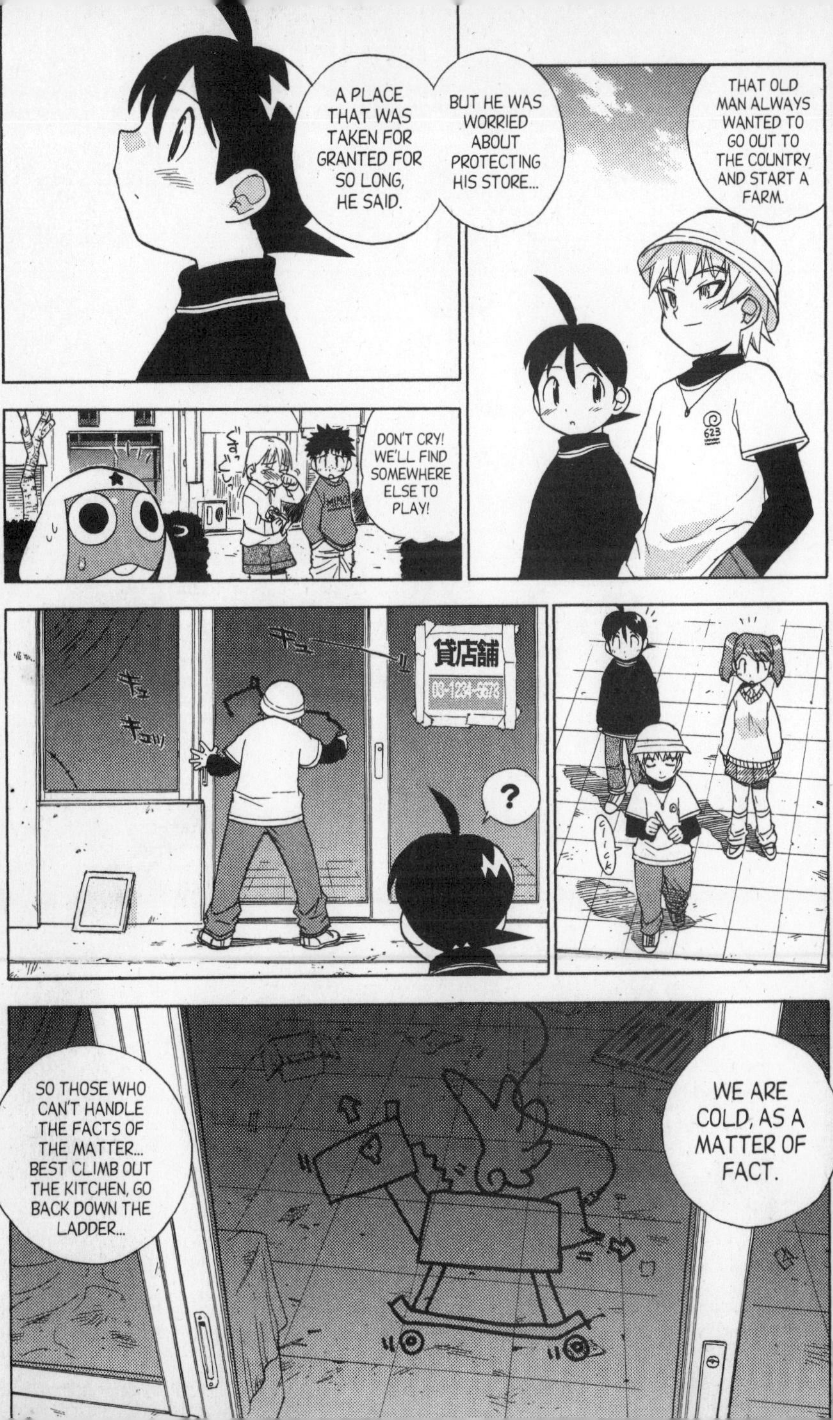
THAT OLD MAN ALWAYS WANTED TO GO OUT TO THE COUNTRY AND START A FARM.
BUT HE WAS WORRIED ABOUT PROTECTING HIS STORE...
A PLACE THAT WAS TAKEN FOR GRANTED FOR SO LONG, HE SAID.
DON'T CRY! WE'LL FIND SOMEWHERE ELSE TO PLAY!
click
?
貸店舗
03-1234-5678
WE ARE COLD, AS A MATTER OF FACT.
SO THOSE WHO CAN'T HANDLE THE FACTS OF THE MATTER... BEST CLIMB OUT THE KITCHEN, GO BACK DOWN THE LADDER...

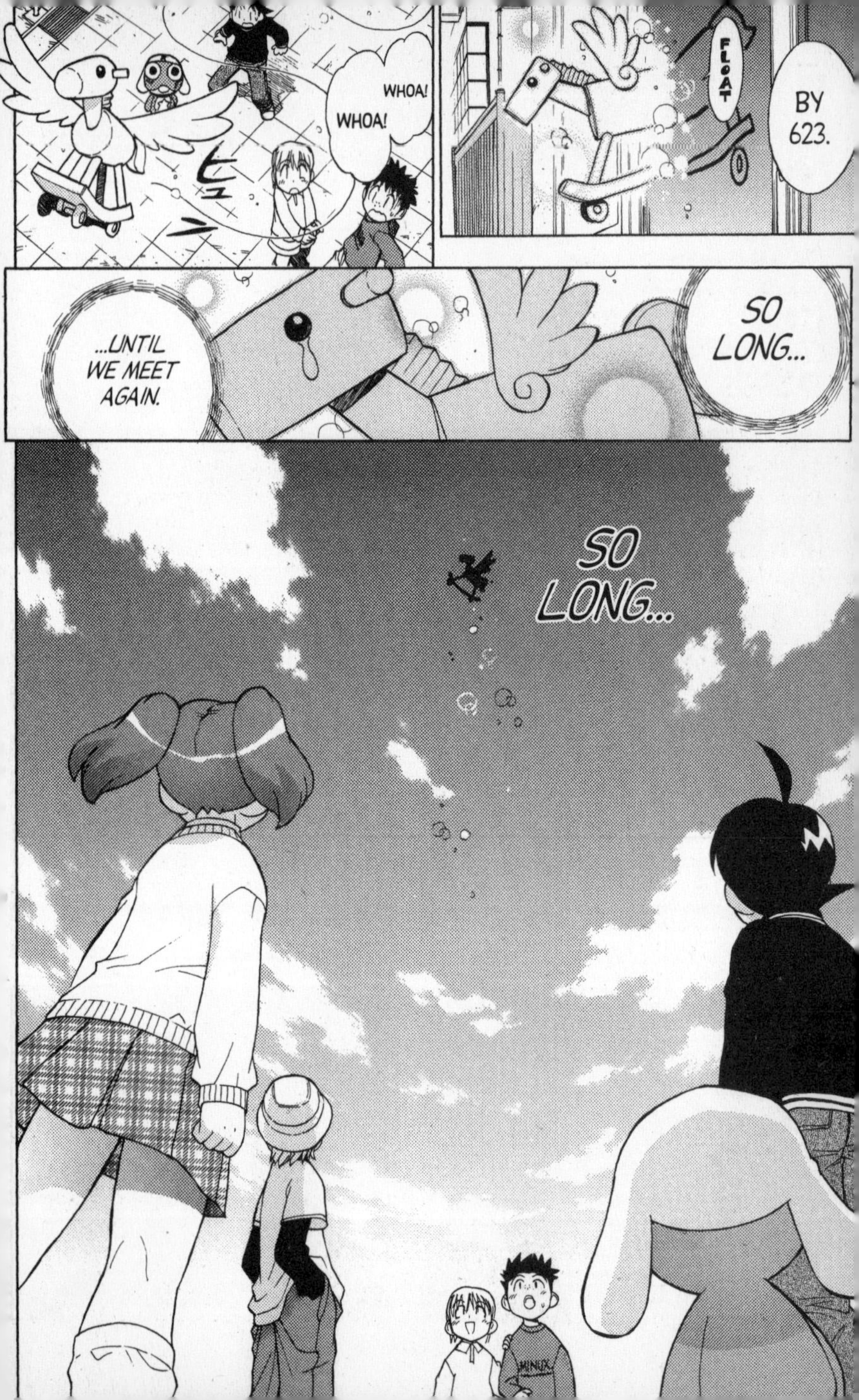
FLOAT
BY 623.
WHOA!
WHOA!
ヒュ
SO LONG...
...UNTIL WE MEET AGAIN.
SO LONG...

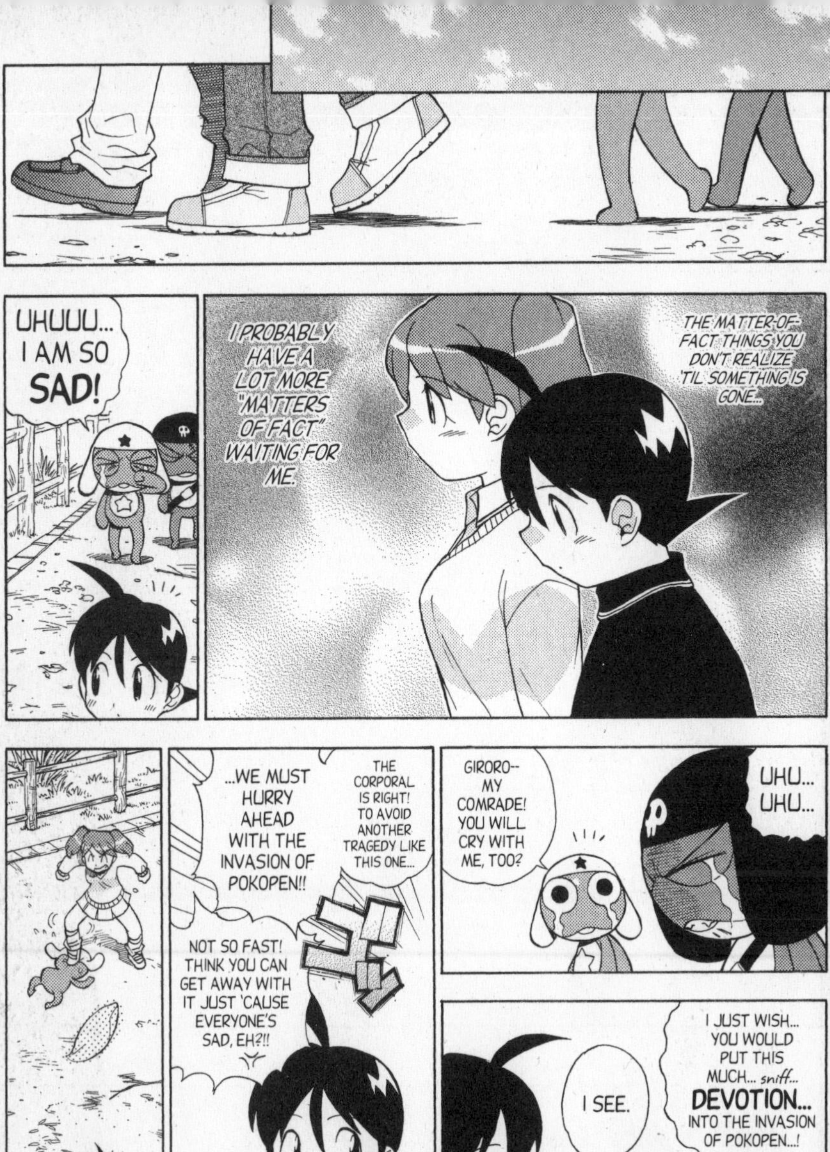
THE MATTER-OF-FACT THINGS YOU DON'T REALIZE 'TIL SOMETHING IS GONE...
I PROBABLY HAVE A LOT MORE "MATTERS OF FACT" WAITING FOR ME.
UHUUU... I AM SO SAD!
UHU... UHU...
GIRORO-- MY COMRADE! YOU WILL CRY WITH ME, TOO?
I JUST WISH... YOU WOULD PUT THIS MUCH... sniff... DEVOTION... INTO THE INVASION OF POKOPEN...!
Uhuu...
I SEE.
THE CORPORAL IS RIGHT! TO AVOID ANOTHER TRAGEDY LIKE THIS ONE...
...WE MUST HURRY AHEAD WITH THE INVASION OF POKOPEN!!
NOT SO FAST! THINK YOU CAN GET AWAY WITH IT JUST 'CAUSE EVERYONE'S SAD, EH?!!
OH, WELL...

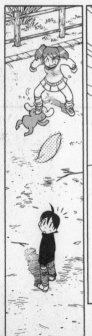

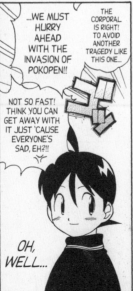

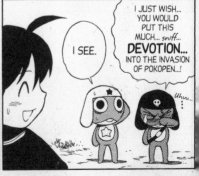

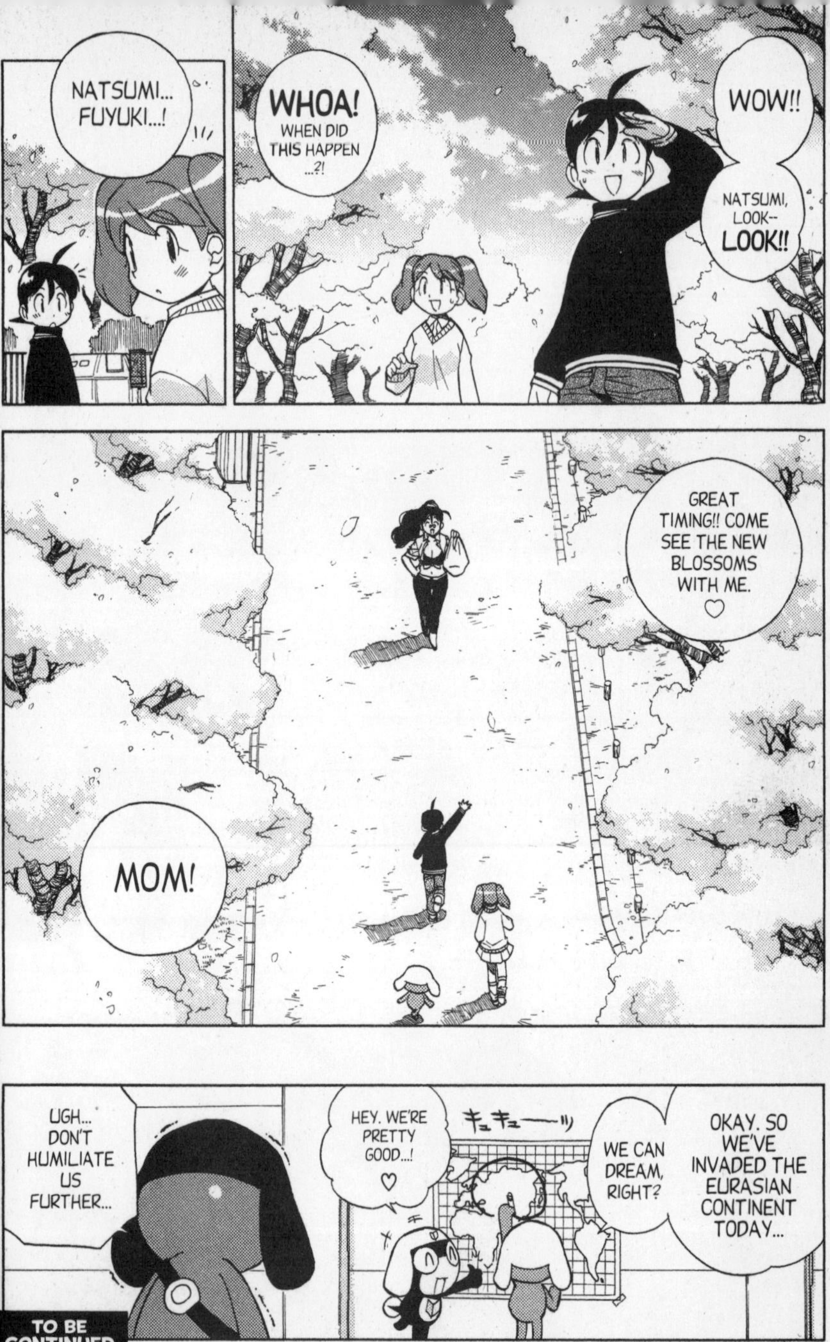
WOW!!
NATSUMI, LOOK-- LOOK!!
WHOA! WHEN DID THIS HAPPEN ...?!
NATSUMI... FUYUKI...!
GREAT TIMING!! COME SEE THE NEW BLOSSOMS WITH ME. ♡
MOM!
OKAY. SO WE'VE INVADED THE EURASIAN CONTINENT TODAY...
キュキューーッ
WE CAN DREAM, RIGHT?
HEY. WE'RE PRETTY GOOD...! ♡
UGH... DON'T HUMILIATE US FURTHER...
TO BE CONTINUED

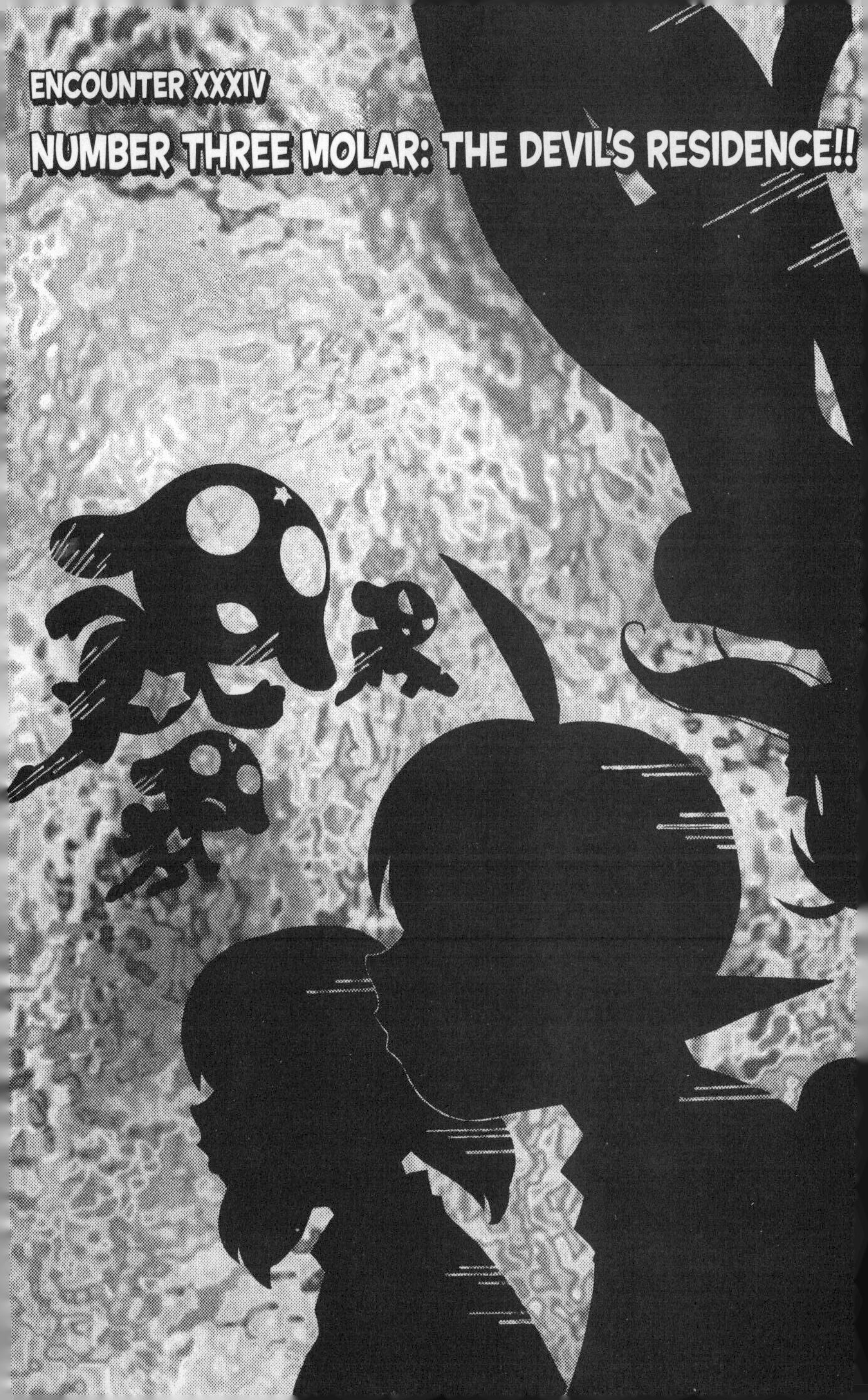
ENCOUNTER XXXIV
NUMBER THREE MOLAR: THE DEVIL'S RESIDENCE!!

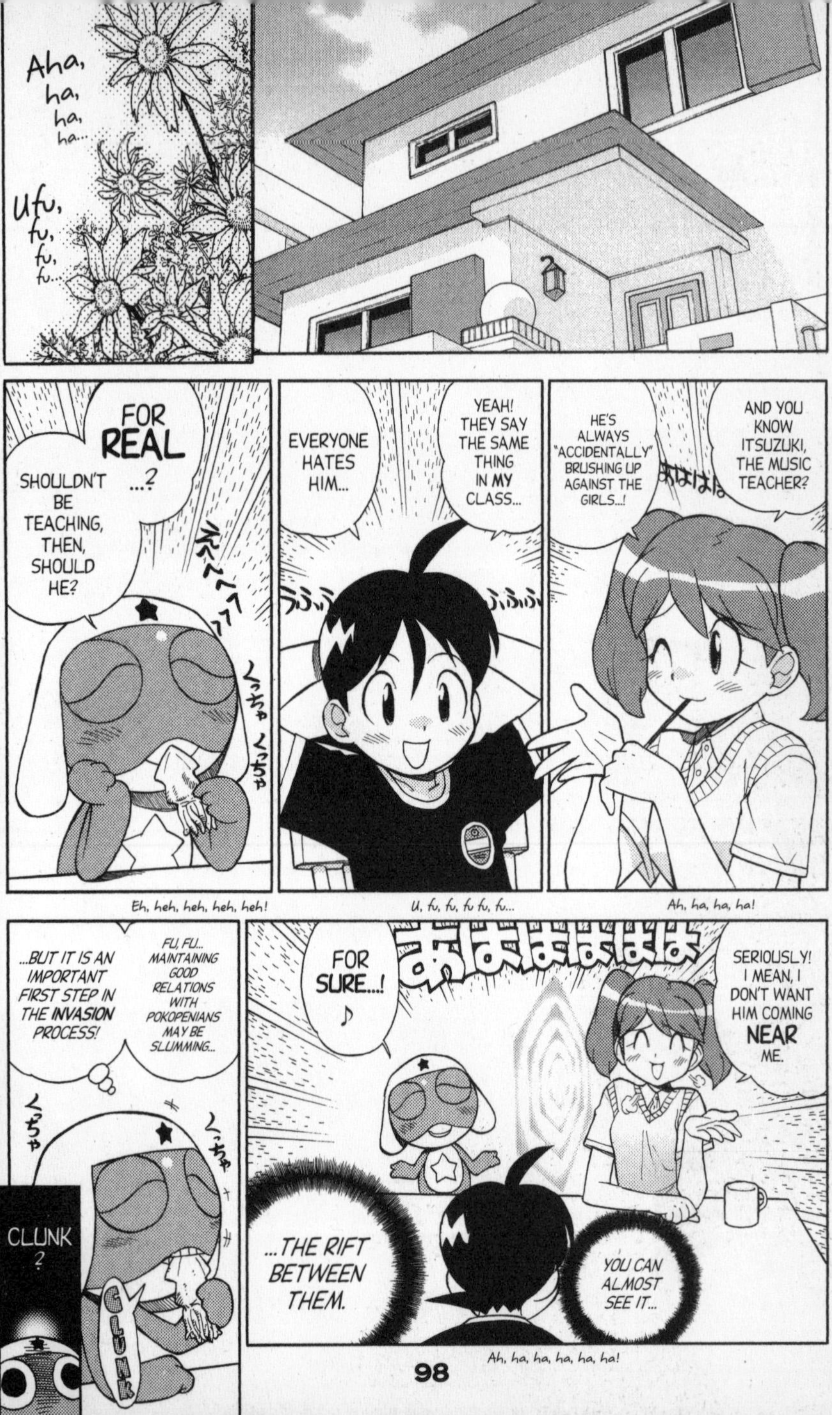
Aha, ha, ha, ha...
Ufu, fu, fu, fu...
AND YOU KNOW ITSUZUKI, THE MUSIC TEACHER?
HE'S ALWAYS "ACCIDENTALLY" BRUSHING UP AGAINST THE GIRLS...!
あははは
Ah, ha, ha, ha!
YEAH! THEY SAY THE SAME THING IN MY CLASS...
EVERYONE HATES HIM...
うふふ
ふふふ
U, fu, fu, fu fu, fu...
FOR REAL ...?
SHOULDN'T BE TEACHING, THEN, SHOULD HE?
えへへへへ
くっちゃ くっちゃ
Eh, heh, heh, heh, heh!
SERIOUSLY! I MEAN, I DON'T WANT HIM COMING NEAR ME.
あはははははは
FOR SURE...! ♪
YOU CAN ALMOST SEE IT...
...THE RIFT BETWEEN THEM.
Ah, ha, ha, ha, ha, ha!
FU, FU... MAINTAINING GOOD RELATIONS WITH POKOPENIANS MAY BE SLUMMING...
...BUT IT IS AN IMPORTANT FIRST STEP IN THE INVASION PROCESS!
くっちゃ
くっちゃ
CLUNK ?

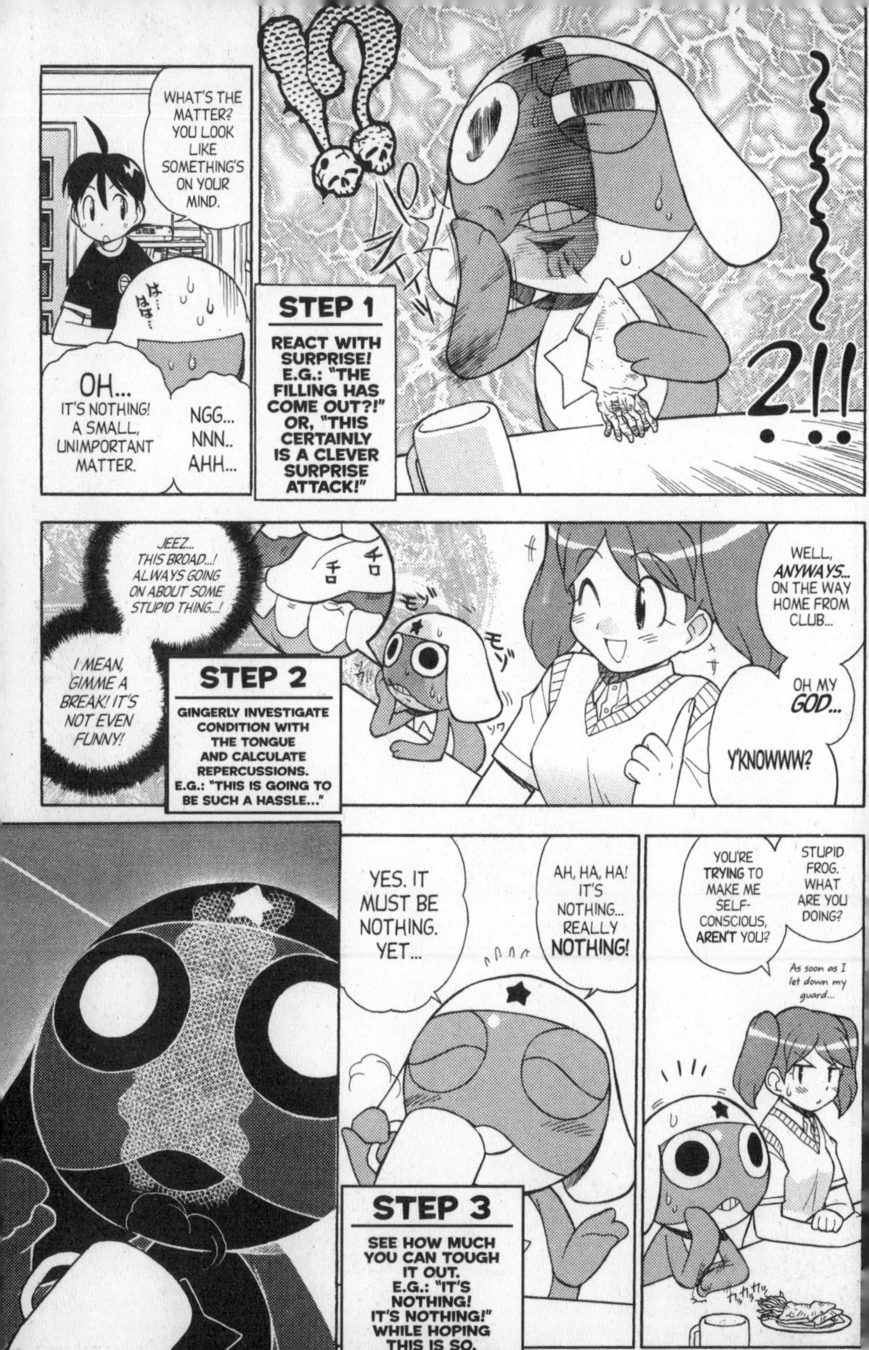
2!!...
STEP 1
REACT WITH SURPRISE! E.G.: "THE FILLING HAS COME OUT?!" OR, "THIS CERTAINLY IS A CLEVER SURPRISE ATTACK!"
WHAT'S THE MATTER? YOU LOOK LIKE SOMETHING'S ON YOUR MIND.
NGG... NNN.. AHH...
OH... IT'S NOTHING! A SMALL, UNIMPORTANT MATTER.
WELL, ANYWAYS... ON THE WAY HOME FROM CLUB...
OH MY GOD...
Y'KNOWWW?
STEP 2
GINGERLY INVESTIGATE CONDITION WITH THE TONGUE AND CALCULATE REPERCUSSIONS. E.G.: "THIS IS GOING TO BE SUCH A HASSLE..."
JEEZ... THIS BROAD...! ALWAYS GOING ON ABOUT SOME STUPID THING...!
I MEAN, GIMME A BREAK! IT'S NOT EVEN FUNNY!
STUPID FROG. WHAT ARE YOU DOING?
YOU'RE TRYING TO MAKE ME SELF-CONSCIOUS, AREN'T YOU?
As soon as I let down my guard...
AH, HA, HA! IT'S NOTHING... REALLY NOTHING!
YES. IT MUST BE NOTHING. YET...
STEP 3
SEE HOW MUCH YOU CAN TOUGH IT OUT. E.G.: "IT'S NOTHING! IT'S NOTHING!" WHILE HOPING THIS IS SO, FURTHER ASSESS THE SENSITIVITY!

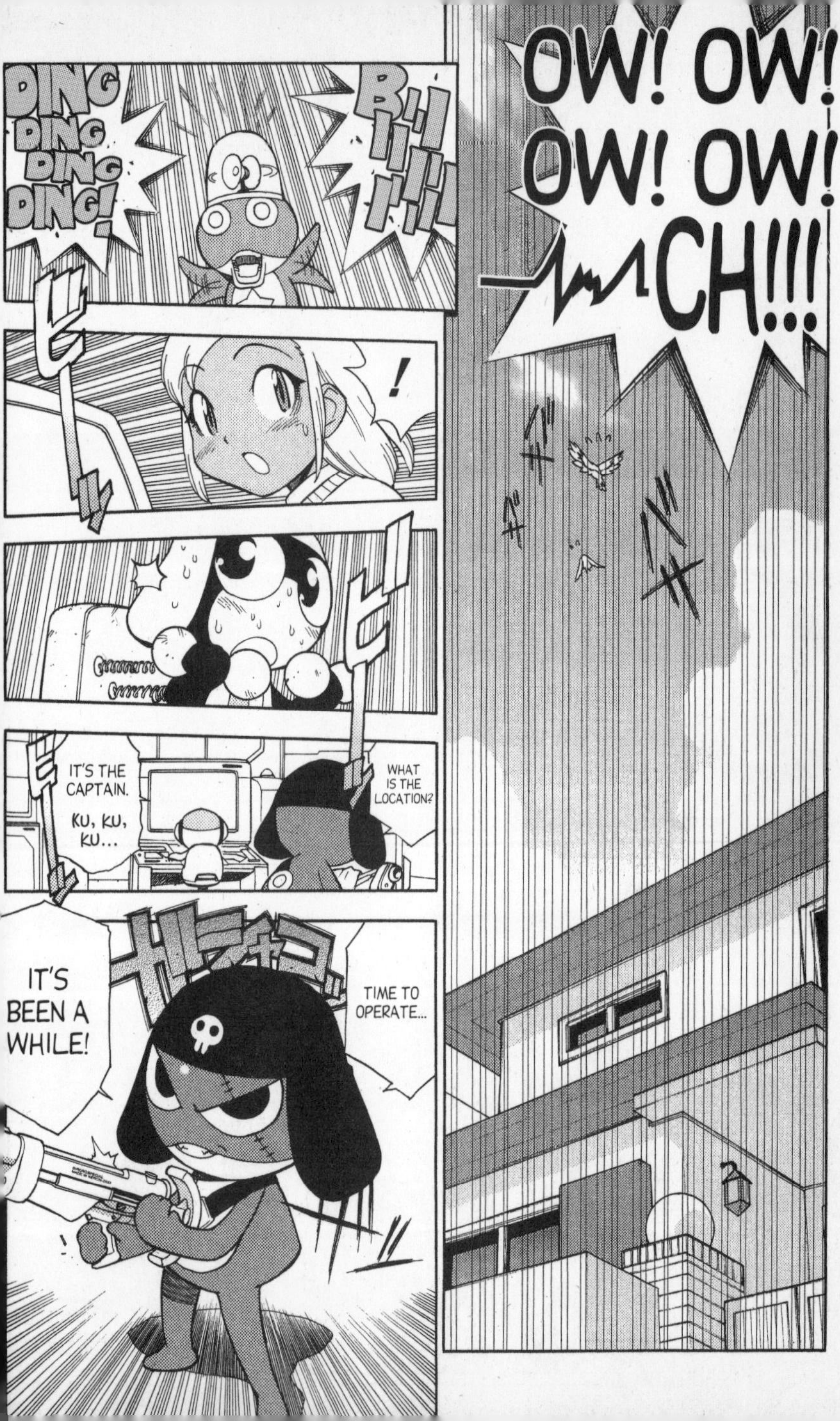
OW! OW! OW! OW!
CH!!!
DING DING DING DING!
!
WHAT IS THE LOCATION?
IT'S THE CAPTAIN.
KU, KU, KU...
TIME TO OPERATE...
IT'S BEEN A WHILE!

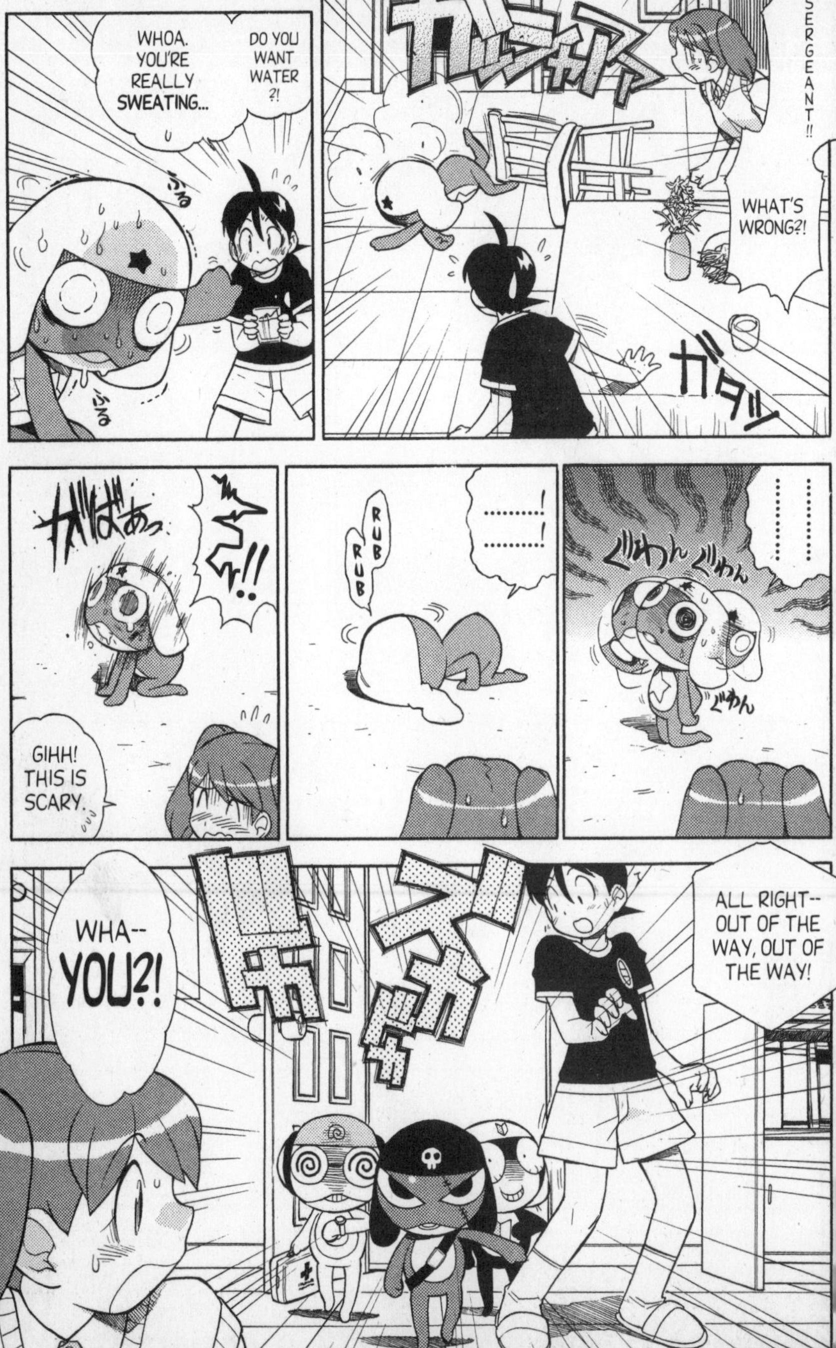
SERGEANT!!
WHAT'S WRONG?!
ガタッ
WHOA. YOU'RE REALLY SWEATING...
DO YOU WANT WATER?!
......
......!
......!
RUB RUB
GIHH! THIS IS SCARY.
ALL RIGHT-- OUT OF THE WAY, OUT OF THE WAY!
WHA-- YOU?!

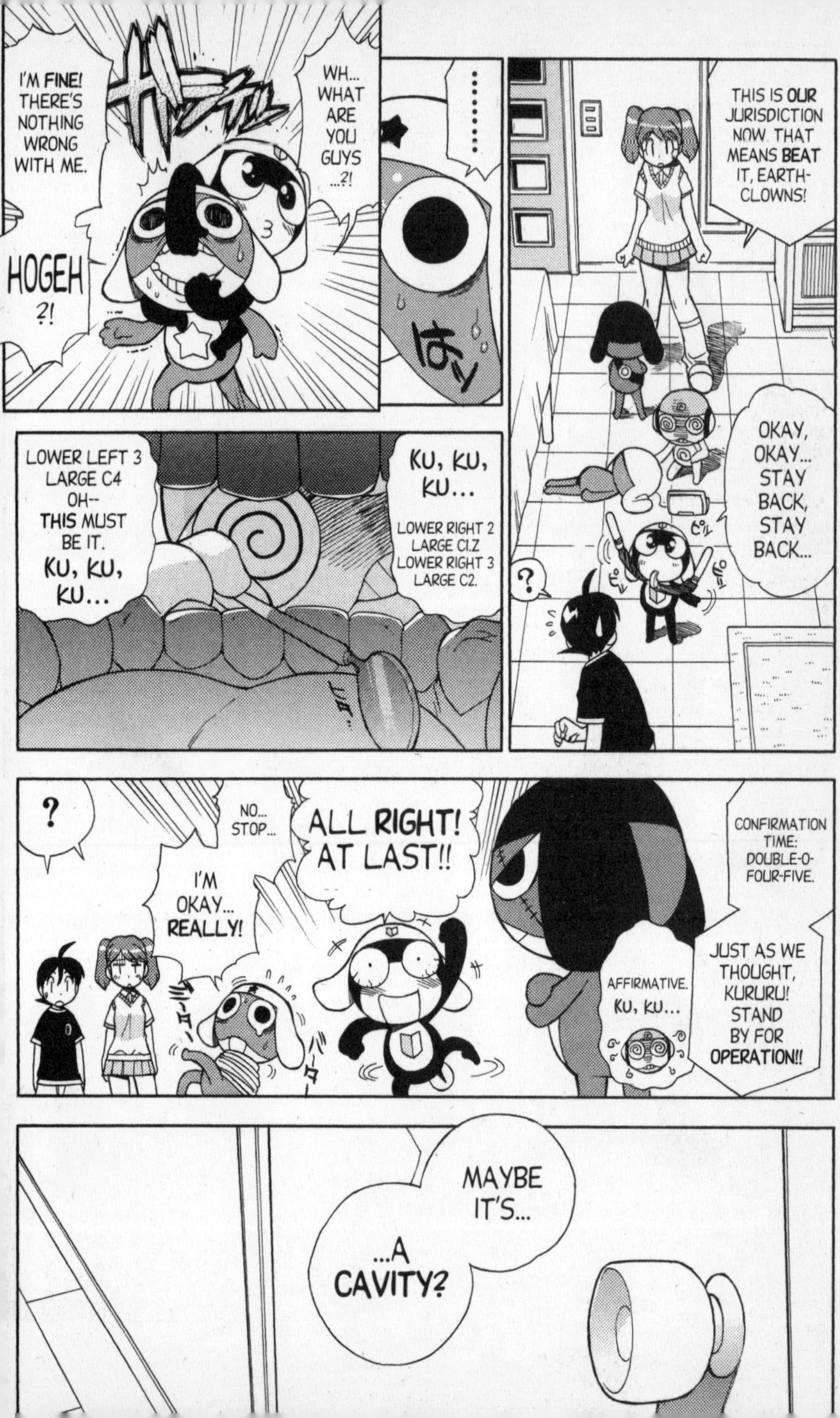
THIS IS OUR JURISDICTION NOW. THAT MEANS BEAT IT, EARTH-CLOWNS!
OKAY, OKAY... STAY BACK, STAY BACK...
?
......
はッ
WH... WHAT ARE YOU GUYS ...?!
I'M FINE! THERE'S NOTHING WRONG WITH ME.
HOGEH ?!
KU, KU, KU...
LOWER RIGHT 2 LARGE C1.Z LOWER RIGHT 3 LARGE C2.
LOWER LEFT 3 LARGE C4 OH-- THIS MUST BE IT.
KU, KU, KU...
CONFIRMATION TIME: DOUBLE-O-FOUR-FIVE.
JUST AS WE THOUGHT, KURURU! STAND BY FOR OPERATION!!
AFFIRMATIVE. KU, KU...
ALL RIGHT! AT LAST!!
NO... STOP...
I'M OKAY... REALLY!
?
MAYBE IT'S...
...A CAVITY?

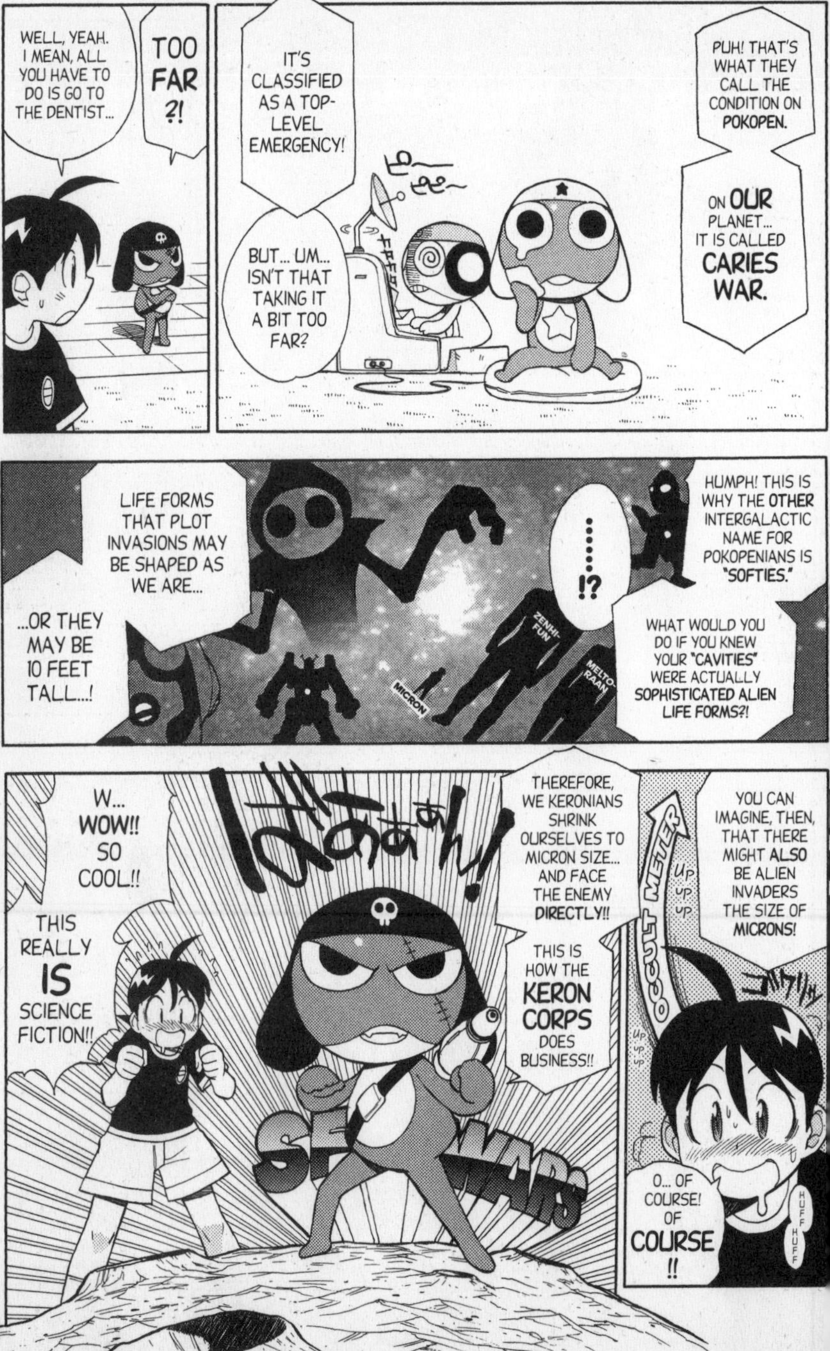
PUH! THAT'S WHAT THEY CALL THE CONDITION ON POKOPEN.
ON OUR PLANET... IT IS CALLED CARIES WAR.
IT'S CLASSIFIED AS A TOP-LEVEL EMERGENCY!
BUT... UM... ISN'T THAT TAKING IT A BIT TOO FAR?
TOO FAR?!
WELL, YEAH. I MEAN, ALL YOU HAVE TO DO IS GO TO THE DENTIST...
HUMPH! THIS IS WHY THE OTHER INTERGALACTIC NAME FOR POKOPENIANS IS "SOFTIES."
WHAT WOULD YOU DO IF YOU KNEW YOUR "CAVITIES" WERE ACTUALLY SOPHISTICATED ALIEN LIFE FORMS?!
......!?
ZENHI-FUN
MELTO-RAAN
MICRON
LIFE FORMS THAT PLOT INVASIONS MAY BE SHAPED AS WE ARE...
...OR THEY MAY BE 10 FEET TALL...!
YOU CAN IMAGINE, THEN, THAT THERE MIGHT ALSO BE ALIEN INVADERS THE SIZE OF MICRONS!
OCCULT METER
UP UP UP
UP UP UP
O... OF COURSE! OF COURSE!!
HUFF HUFF
THEREFORE, WE KERONIANS SHRINK OURSELVES TO MICRON SIZE... AND FACE THE ENEMY DIRECTLY!!
THIS IS HOW THE KERON CORPS DOES BUSINESS!!
W... WOW!! SO COOL!!
THIS REALLY IS SCIENCE FICTION!!

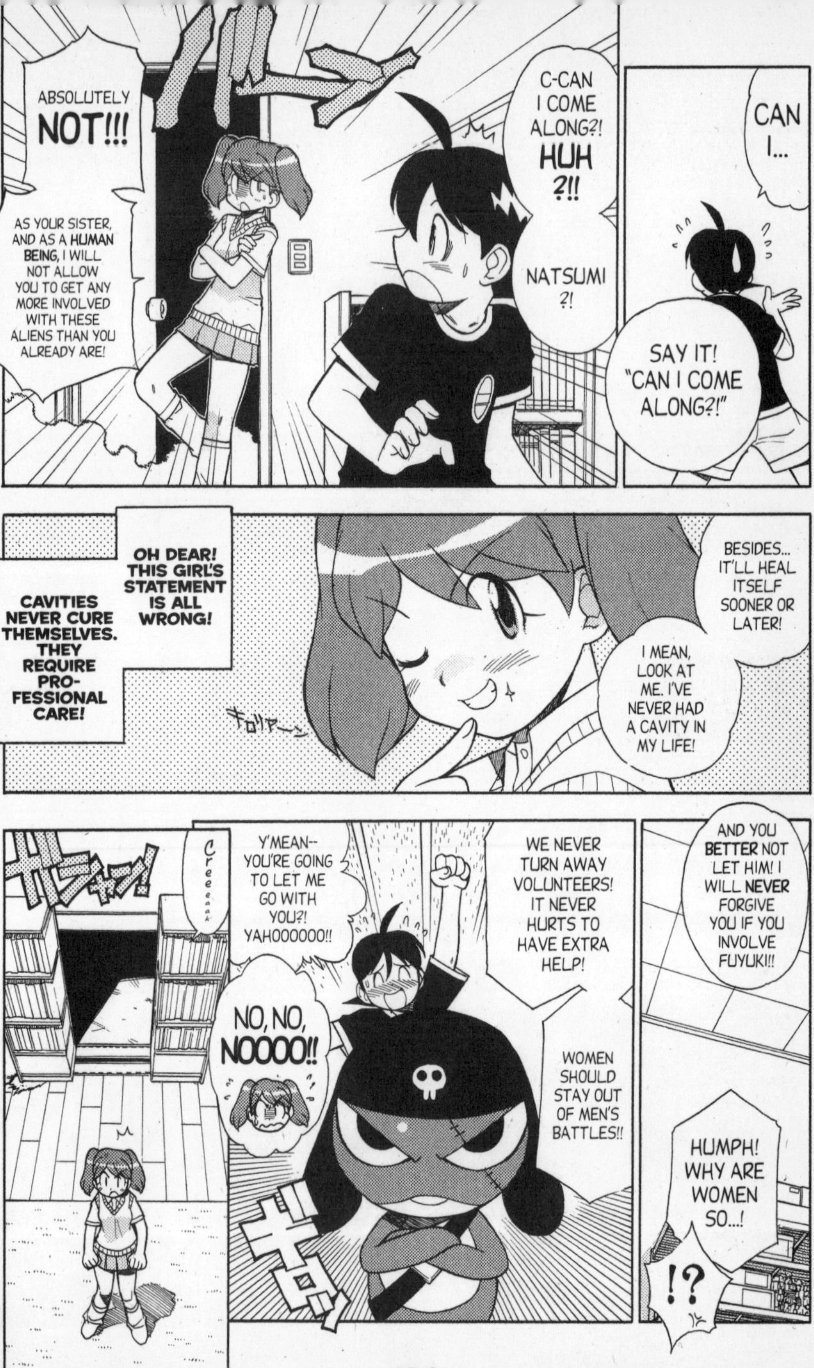
CAN I...
SAY IT! "CAN I COME ALONG?!"
C-CAN I COME ALONG?! HUH ?!!
NATSUMI ?!
ABSOLUTELY NOT!!!
AS YOUR SISTER, AND AS A HUMAN BEING, I WILL NOT ALLOW YOU TO GET ANY MORE INVOLVED WITH THESE ALIENS THAN YOU ALREADY ARE!
BESIDES... IT'LL HEAL ITSELF SOONER OR LATER!
I MEAN, LOOK AT ME. I'VE NEVER HAD A CAVITY IN MY LIFE!
OH DEAR! THIS GIRL'S STATEMENT IS ALL WRONG!
CAVITIES NEVER CURE THEMSELVES. THEY REQUIRE PRO-FESSIONAL CARE!
AND YOU BETTER NOT LET HIM! I WILL NEVER FORGIVE YOU IF YOU INVOLVE FUYUKI!!
HUMPH! WHY ARE WOMEN SO...!
!?
WE NEVER TURN AWAY VOLUNTEERS! IT NEVER HURTS TO HAVE EXTRA HELP!
WOMEN SHOULD STAY OUT OF MEN'S BATTLES!!
Y'MEAN-- YOU'RE GOING TO LET ME GO WITH YOU?! YAHOOOOOO!!
NO, NO, NOOOO!!
Creeeaak

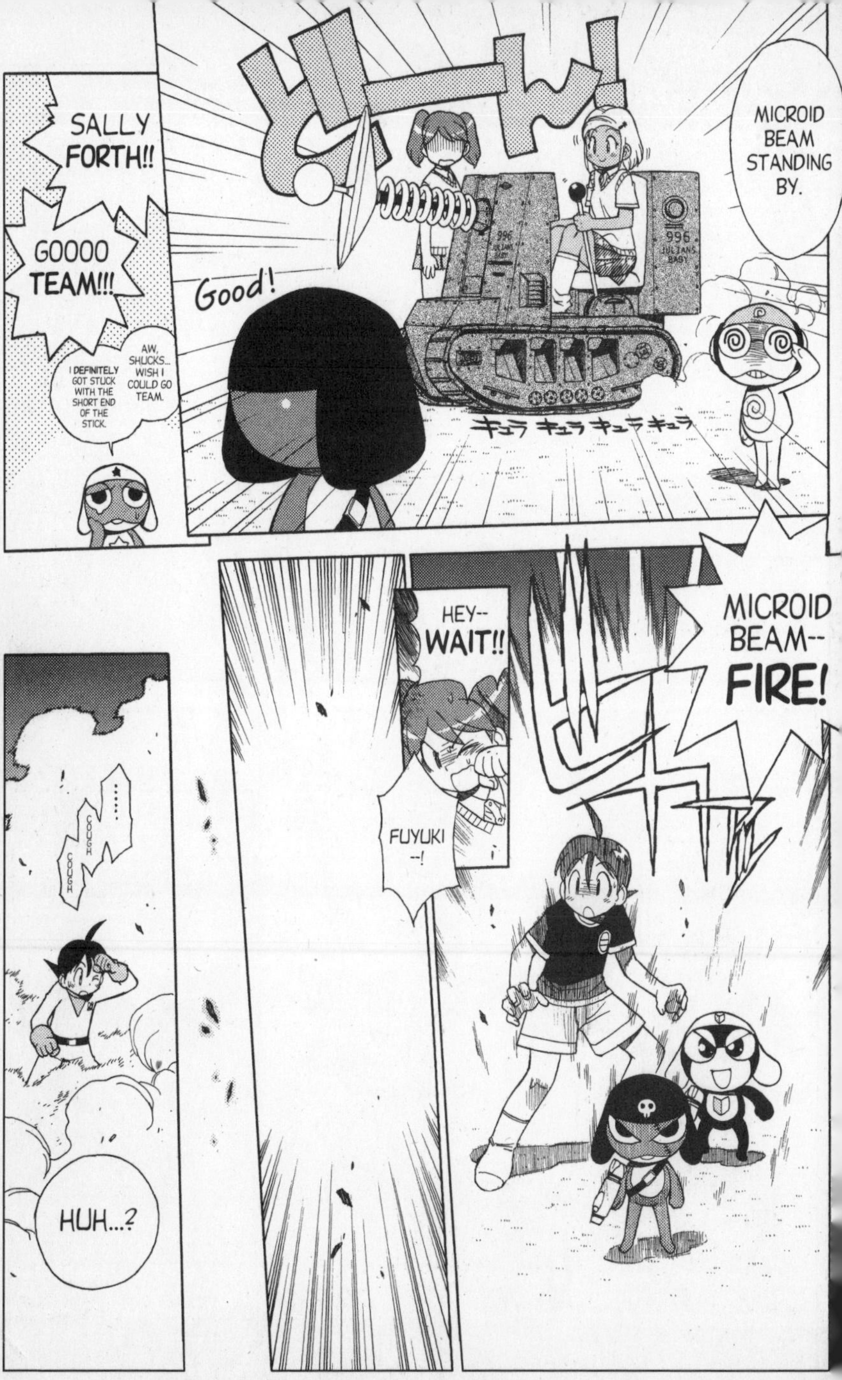
MICROID BEAM STANDING BY.
Good!
キュラ キュラ キュラ キュラ
SALLY FORTH!!
GOOOO TEAM!!!
AW, SHUCKS... WISH I COULD GO TEAM.
I DEFINITELY GOT STUCK WITH THE SHORT END OF THE STICK.
MICROID BEAM-- FIRE!
HEY-- WAIT!!
FUYUKI --!
......
COUGH COUGH
HUH...?

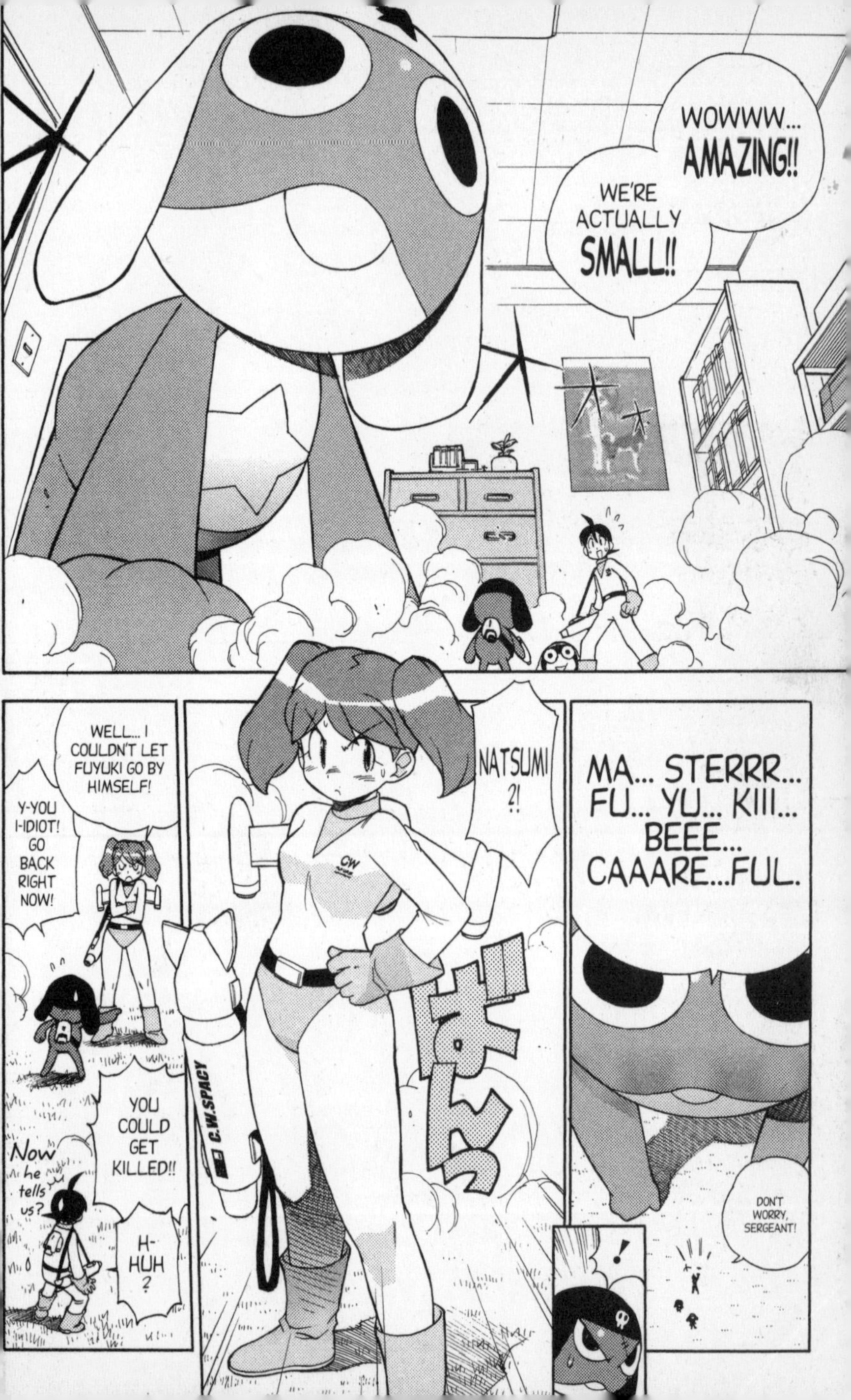

WOWWW... AMAZING!!
WE'RE ACTUALLY SMALL!!
MA... STERRR... FU... YU... KIII... BEEE... CAAARE...FUL.
DON'T WORRY, SERGEANT!
!
NATSUMI ?!
ぼん
WELL... I COULDN'T LET FUYUKI GO BY HIMSELF!
Y-YOU I-IDIOT! GO BACK RIGHT NOW!
YOU COULD GET KILLED!!
H-HUH ?
Now he tells us?
C.W.SPACY

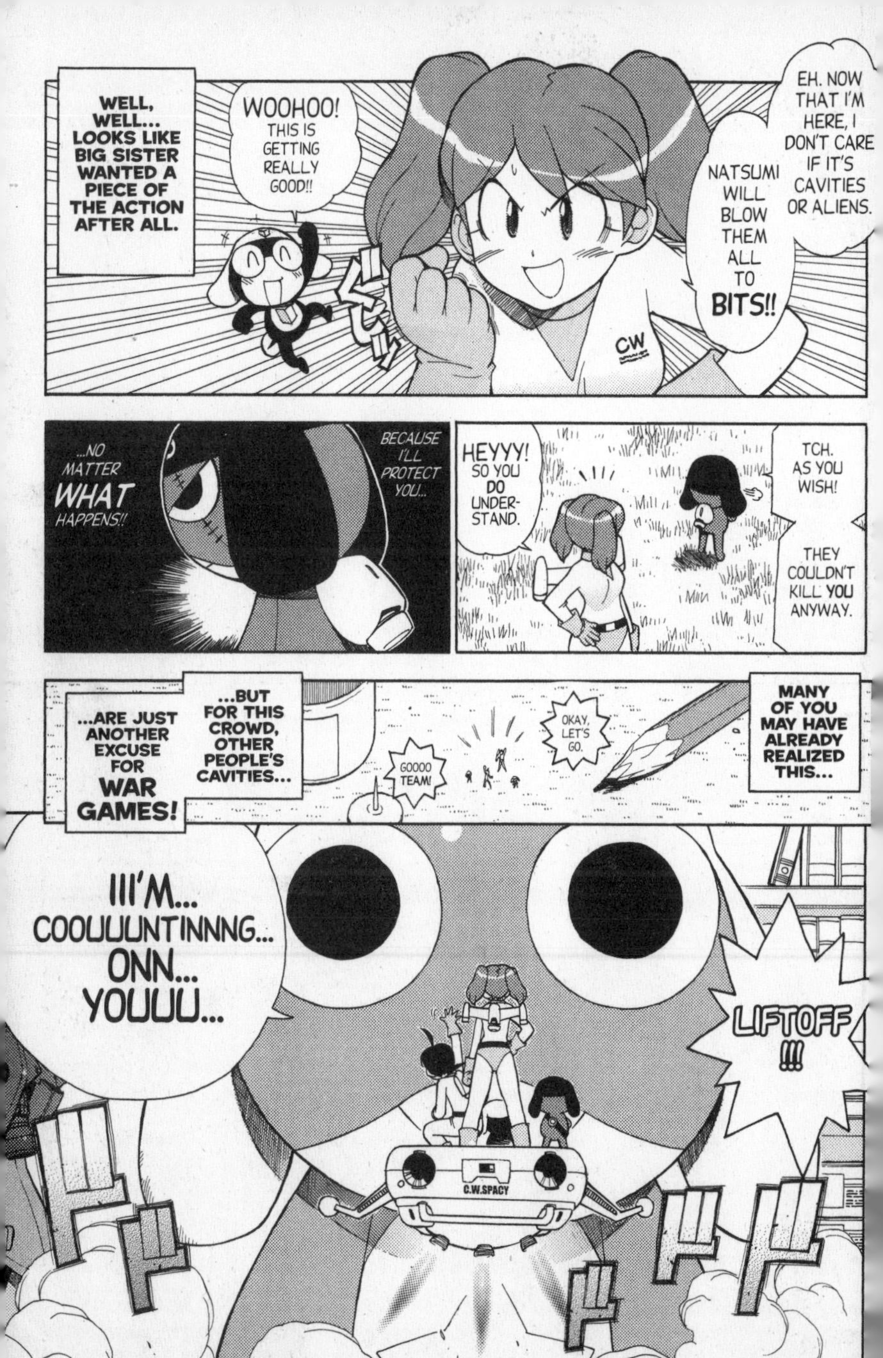
EH. NOW THAT I'M HERE, I DON'T CARE IF IT'S CAVITIES OR ALIENS.
NATSUMI WILL BLOW THEM ALL TO BITS!!
WOOHOO! THIS IS GETTING REALLY GOOD!!
WELL, WELL... LOOKS LIKE BIG SISTER WANTED A PIECE OF THE ACTION AFTER ALL.
CW
TCH. AS YOU WISH!
THEY COULDN'T KILL YOU ANYWAY.
HEYYY! SO YOU DO UNDER-STAND.
BECAUSE I'LL PROTECT YOU...
...NO MATTER WHAT HAPPENS!!
MANY OF YOU MAY HAVE ALREADY REALIZED THIS...
OKAY, LET'S GO.
GOOOO TEAM!
...BUT FOR THIS CROWD, OTHER PEOPLE'S CAVITIES...
...ARE JUST ANOTHER EXCUSE FOR WAR GAMES!
LIFTOFF!!!
III'M... COOUUUNTINNNG... ONN... YOUUU...
C.W.SPACY

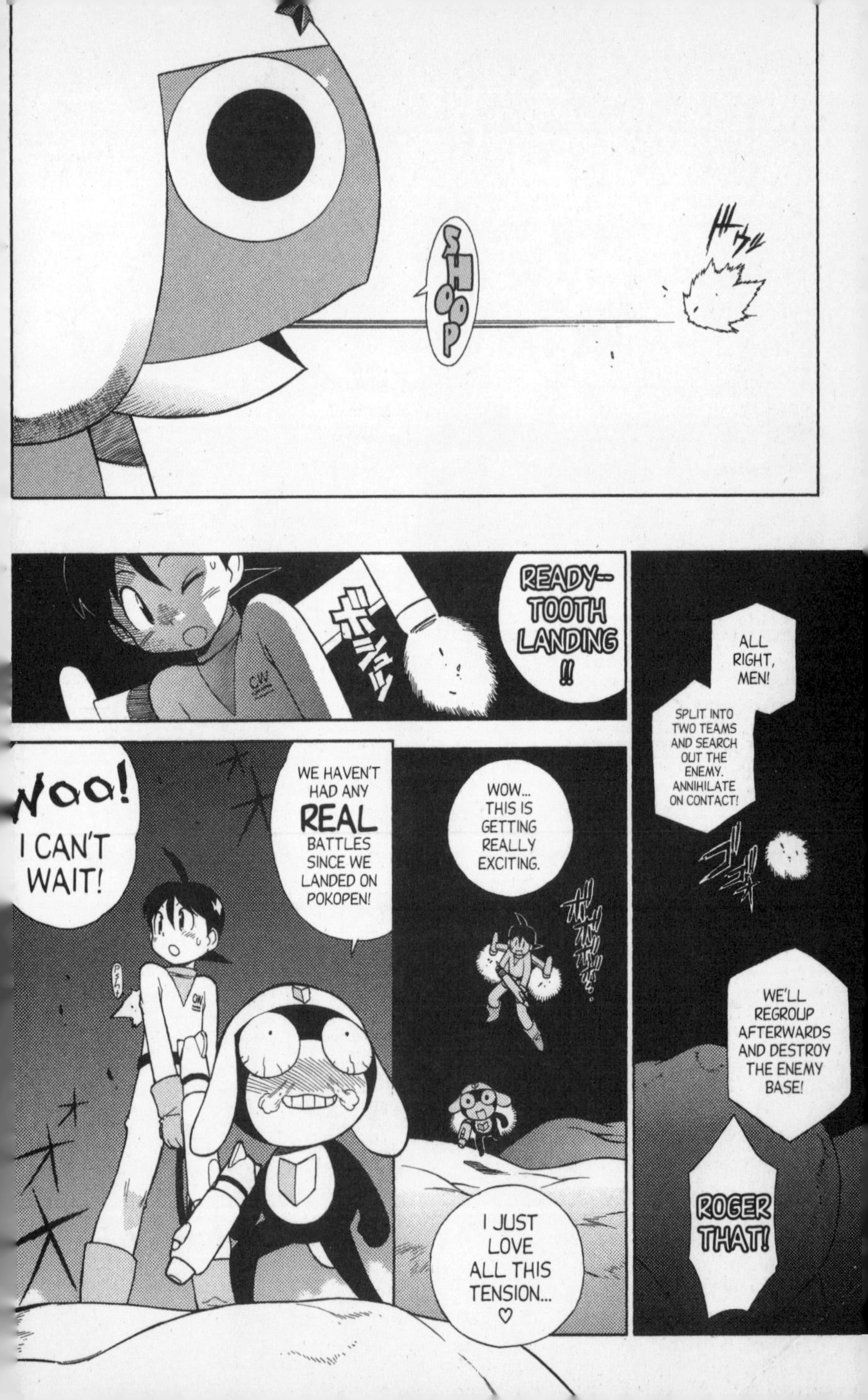
SHOOP
ALL RIGHT, MEN!
SPLIT INTO TWO TEAMS AND SEARCH OUT THE ENEMY. ANNIHILATE ON CONTACT!
WE'LL REGROUP AFTERWARDS AND DESTROY THE ENEMY BASE!
ROGER THAT!
READY-- TOOTH LANDING!!
WOW... THIS IS GETTING REALLY EXCITING.
I JUST LOVE ALL THIS TENSION... ♡
WE HAVEN'T HAD ANY REAL BATTLES SINCE WE LANDED ON POKOPEN!
Waa! I CAN'T WAIT!

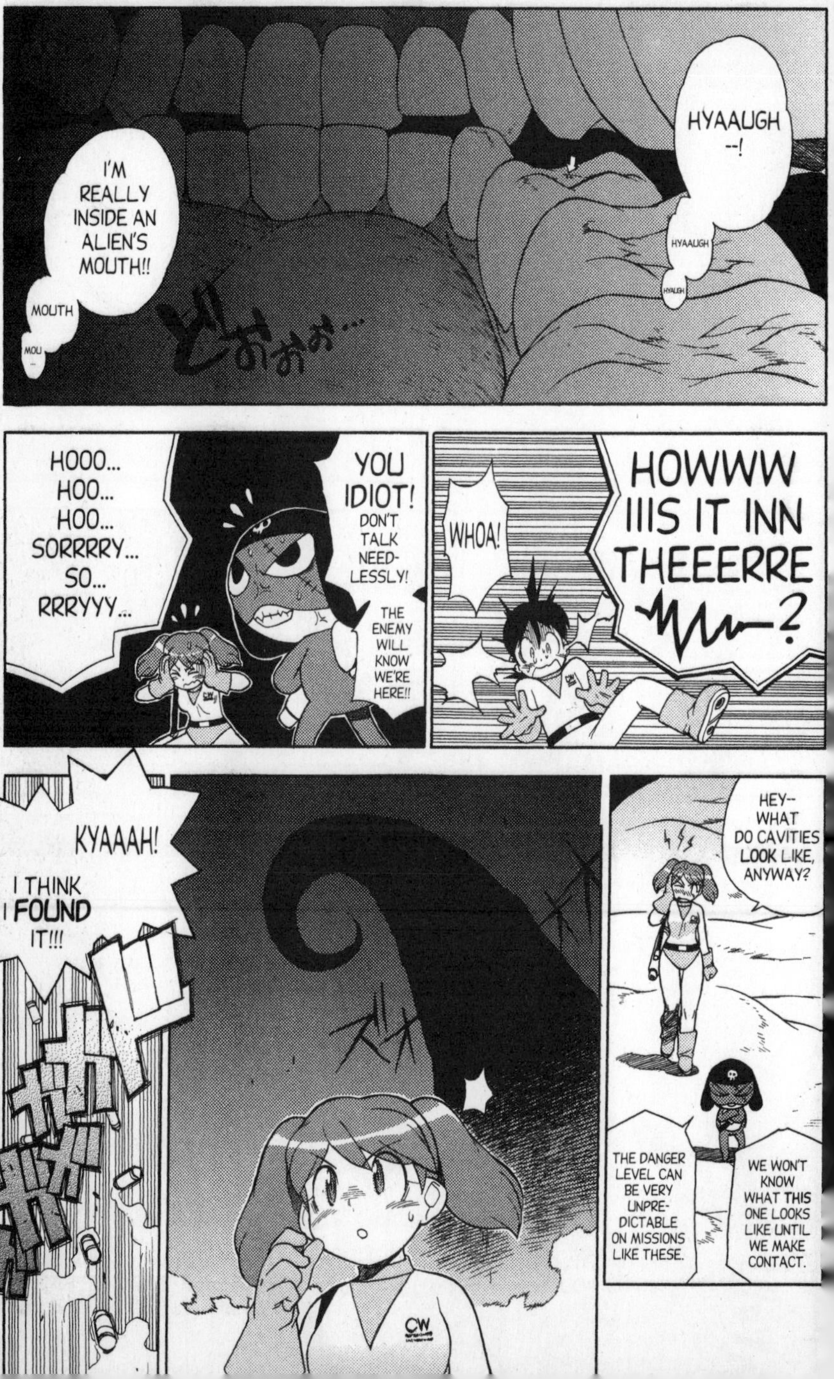
HYAAUGH --!
HYAAUGH
HYAUGH
I'M REALLY INSIDE AN ALIEN'S MOUTH!!
MOUTH
MOU...
HOWWW IIIS IT INN THEEERRE~?
WHOA!
YOU IDIOT! DON'T TALK NEEDLESSLY!
THE ENEMY WILL KNOW WE'RE HERE!!
HOOO... HOO... HOO... SORRRRY... SO... RRRYYY...
HEY-- WHAT DO CAVITIES **LOOK** LIKE, ANYWAY?
WE WON'T KNOW WHAT **THIS** ONE LOOKS LIKE UNTIL WE MAKE CONTACT.
THE DANGER LEVEL CAN BE VERY UNPREDICTABLE ON MISSIONS LIKE THESE.
KYAAAH!
I THINK I **FOUND** IT!!!

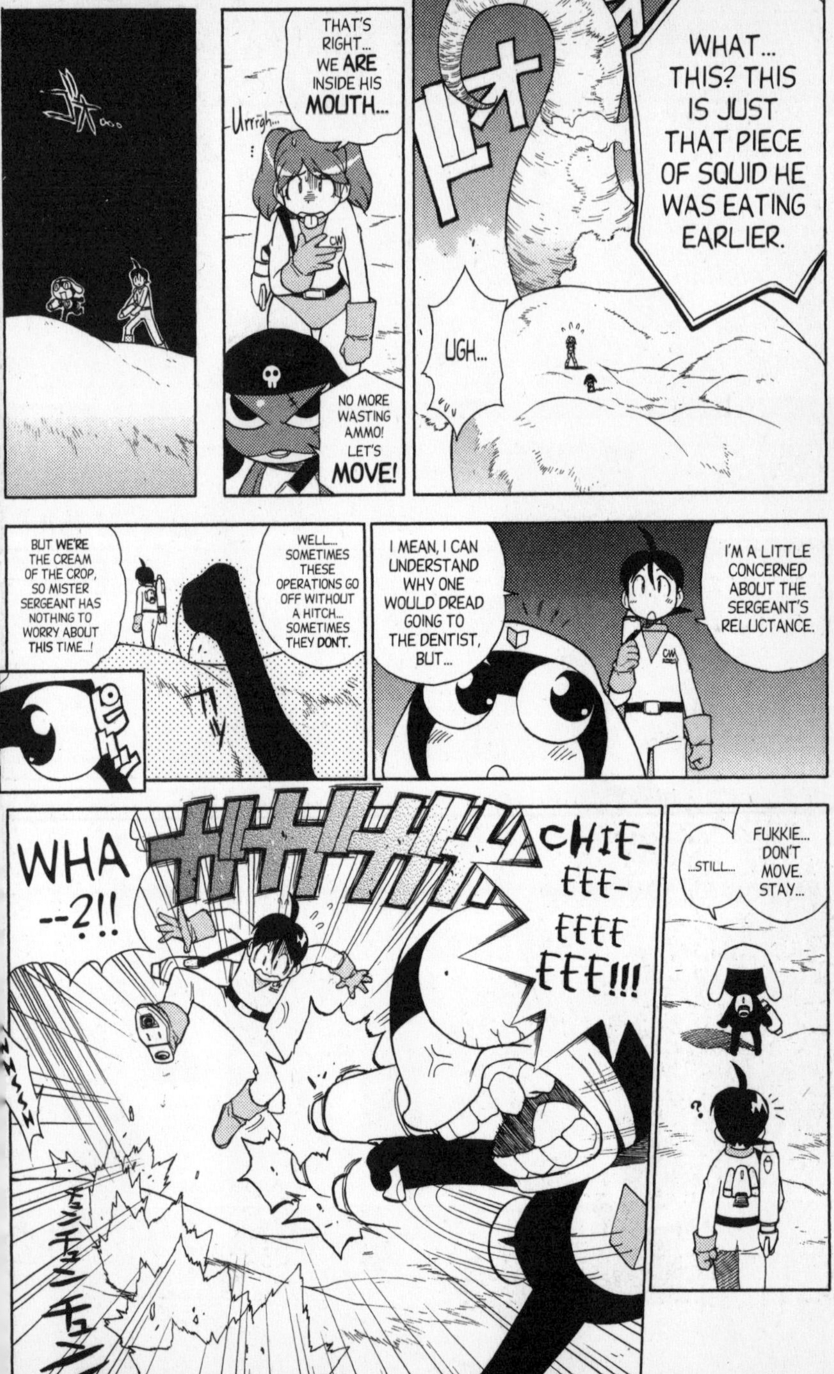
WHAT... THIS? THIS IS JUST THAT PIECE OF SQUID HE WAS EATING EARLIER.
UGH...
THAT'S RIGHT... WE ARE INSIDE HIS MOUTH...
Urrrgh...
NO MORE WASTING AMMO! LET'S MOVE!
I'M A LITTLE CONCERNED ABOUT THE SERGEANT'S RELUCTANCE.
I MEAN, I CAN UNDERSTAND WHY ONE WOULD DREAD GOING TO THE DENTIST, BUT...
WELL... SOMETIMES THESE OPERATIONS GO OFF WITHOUT A HITCH... SOMETIMES THEY DON'T.
BUT WE'RE THE CREAM OF THE CROP, SO MISTER SERGEANT HAS NOTHING TO WORRY ABOUT THIS TIME...!
FUKKIE... DON'T MOVE. STAY...
...STILL...
CHIE-EEE-EEEE EEE!!!
WHA --?!!

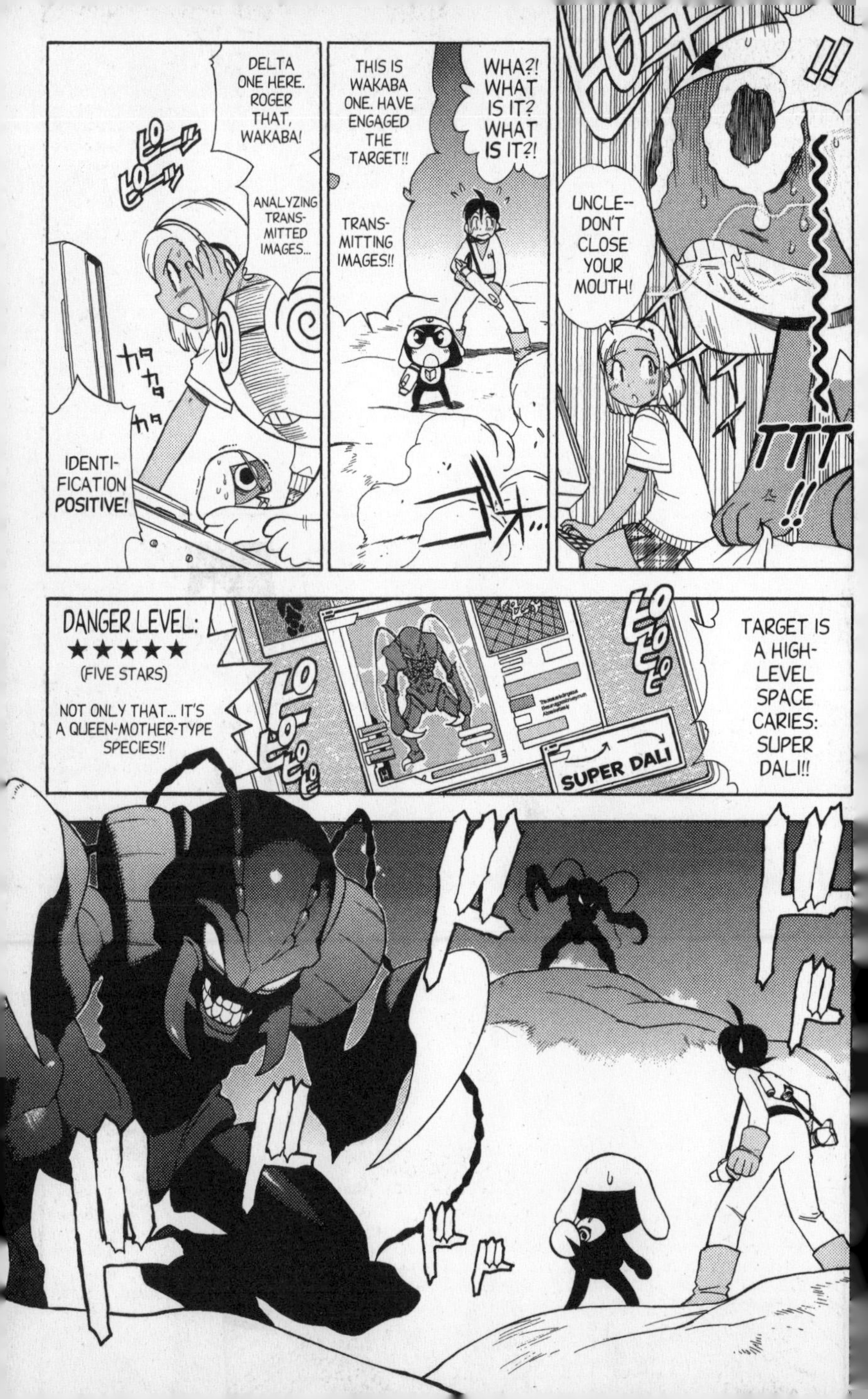
UNCLE-- DON'T CLOSE YOUR MOUTH!
TTT!!
WHA?! WHAT IS IT? WHAT IS IT?!
THIS IS WAKABA ONE. HAVE ENGAGED THE TARGET!!
TRANSMITTING IMAGES!!
DELTA ONE HERE. ROGER THAT, WAKABA!
ANALYZING TRANSMITTED IMAGES...
IDENTIFICATION POSITIVE!
TARGET IS A HIGH-LEVEL SPACE CARIES: SUPER DALI!!
SUPER DALI
DANGER LEVEL: ★★★★★ (FIVE STARS)
NOT ONLY THAT... IT'S A QUEEN-MOTHER-TYPE SPECIES!!

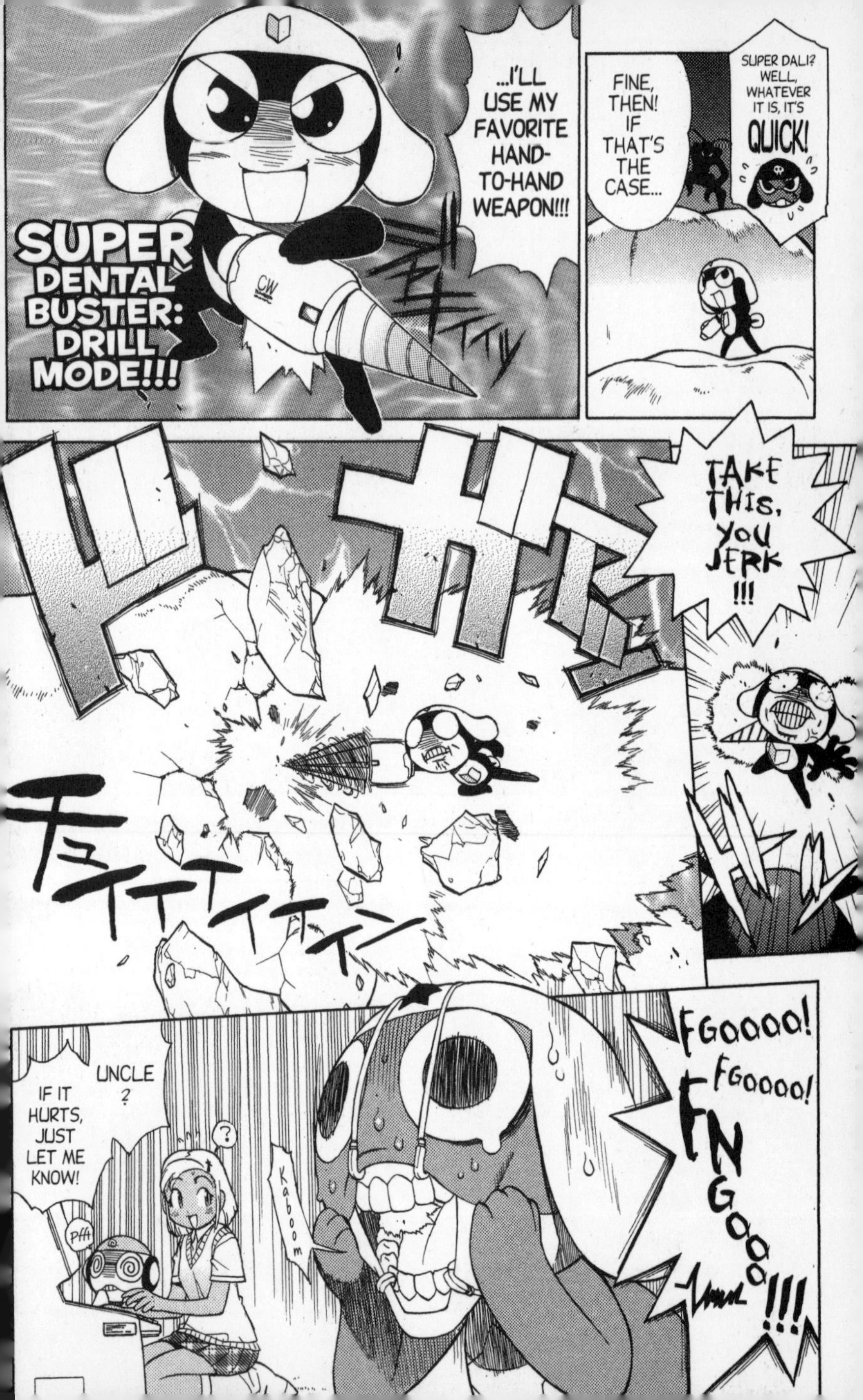
SUPER DALI? WELL, WHATEVER IT IS, IT'S QUICK!
FINE, THEN! IF THAT'S THE CASE...
...I'LL USE MY FAVORITE HAND-TO-HAND WEAPON!!!
SUPER DENTAL BUSTER: DRILL MODE!!!
TAKE THIS, YOU JERK!!!
FGaaaa! FGaaaa! FNGaaaa!!!
Kaboom
UNCLE ?
IF IT HURTS, JUST LET ME KNOW!
?
Pfft

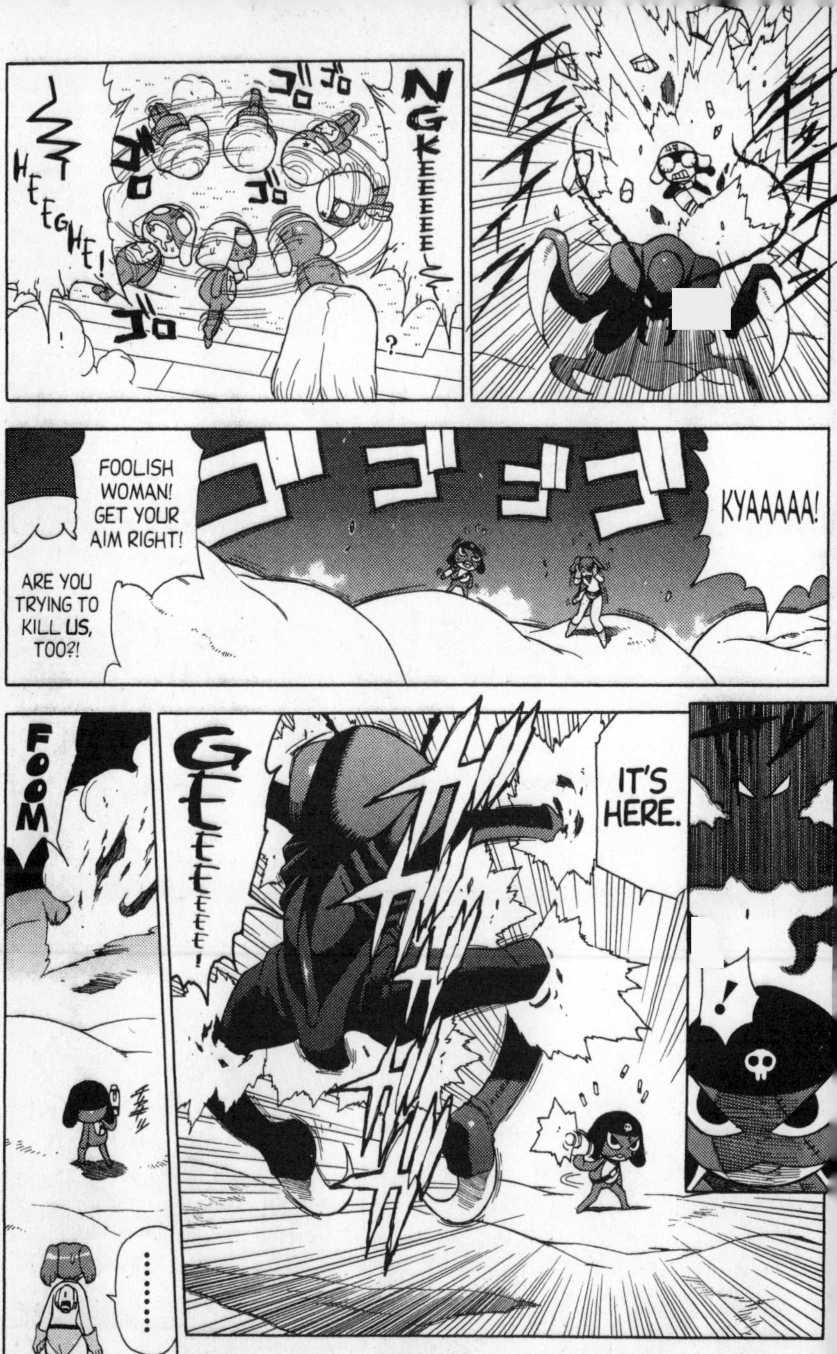
NGKEEEEEEE
HEEGHE!
?
KYAAAAA!
FOOLISH WOMAN! GET YOUR AIM RIGHT!
ARE YOU TRYING TO KILL US, TOO?!
!
IT'S HERE.
GEEEEEEEE!
FOOM
........

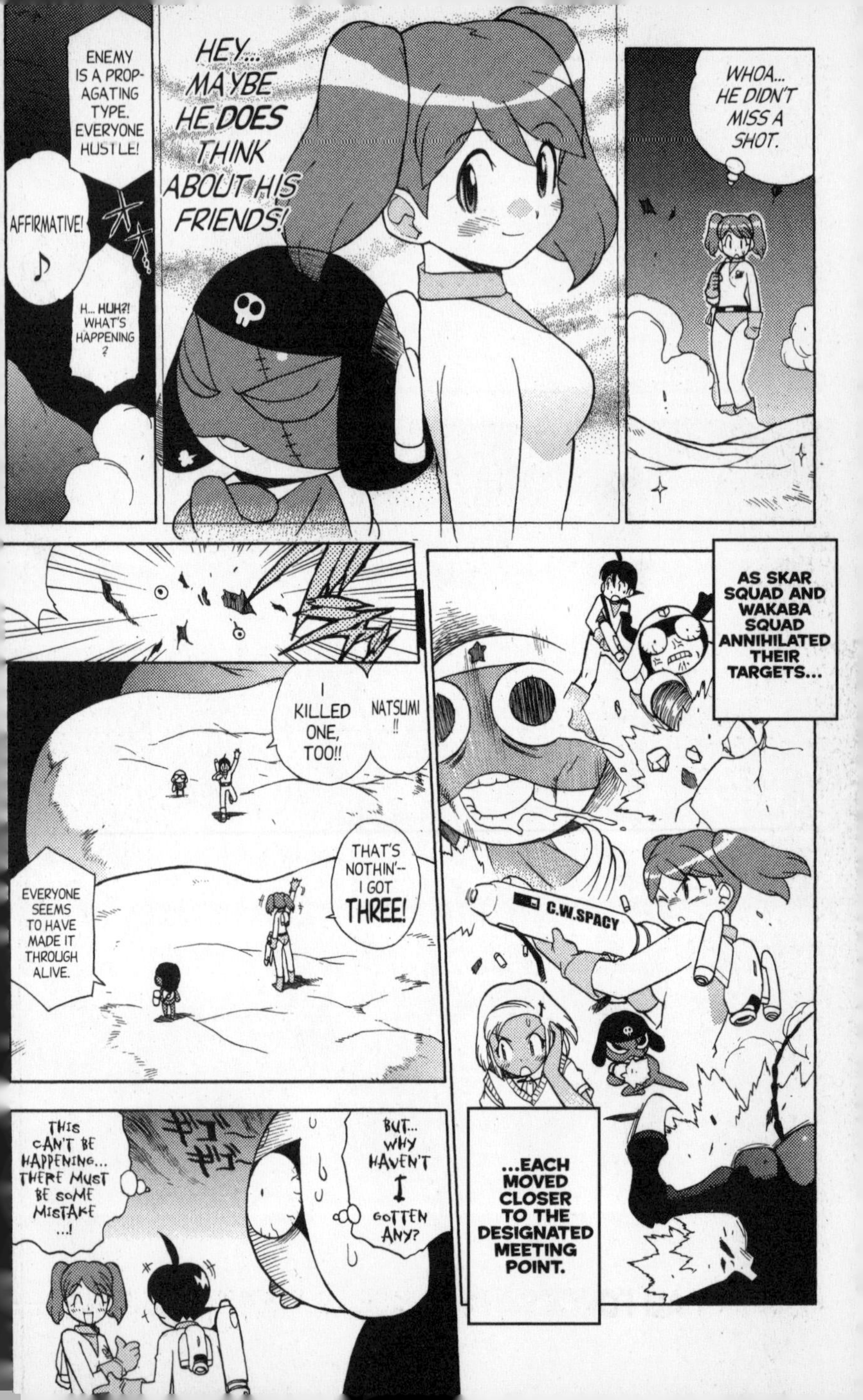
WHOA... HE DIDN'T MISS A SHOT.
HEY... MAYBE HE DOES THINK ABOUT HIS FRIENDS!
ENEMY IS A PROPAGATING TYPE. EVERYONE HUSTLE!
AFFIRMATIVE! ♪
H... HUH?! WHAT'S HAPPENING?
AS SKAR SQUAD AND WAKABA SQUAD ANNIHILATED THEIR TARGETS...
C.W.SPACY
NATSUMI!!
I KILLED ONE, TOO!!
THAT'S NOTHIN'-- I GOT THREE!
EVERYONE SEEMS TO HAVE MADE IT THROUGH ALIVE.
...EACH MOVED CLOSER TO THE DESIGNATED MEETING POINT.
BUT... WHY HAVEN'T I GOTTEN ANY?
THIS CAN'T BE HAPPENING... THERE MUST BE SOME MISTAKE...!

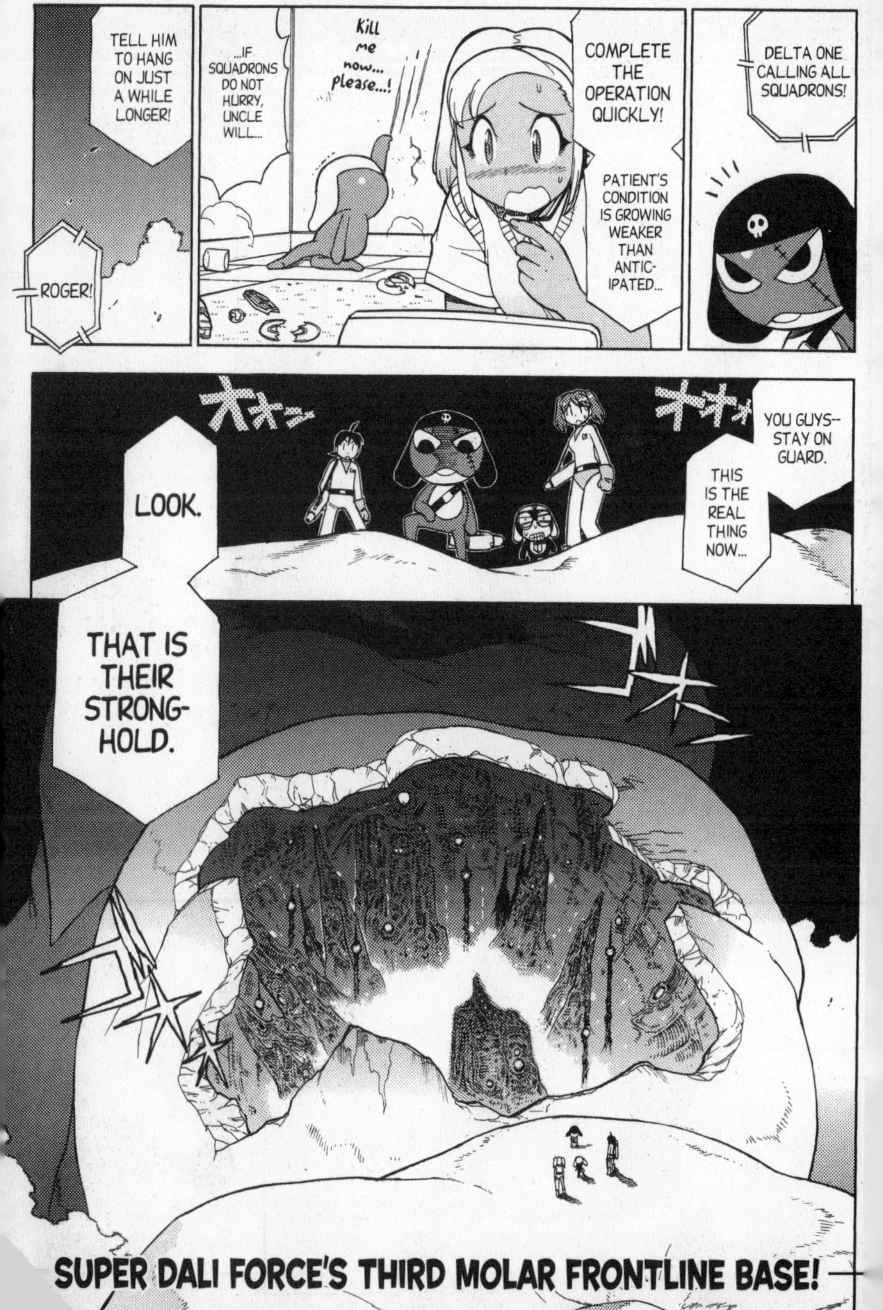
DELTA ONE CALLING ALL SQUADRONS!
COMPLETE THE OPERATION QUICKLY!
PATIENT'S CONDITION IS GROWING WEAKER THAN ANTIC-IPATED...
Kill me now... Please...!
...IF SQUADRONS DO NOT HURRY, UNCLE WILL...
TELL HIM TO HANG ON JUST A WHILE LONGER!
ROGER!
YOU GUYS-- STAY ON GUARD.
THIS IS THE REAL THING NOW...
LOOK.
THAT IS THEIR STRONG-HOLD.
SUPER DALI FORCE'S THIRD MOLAR FRONTLINE BASE!

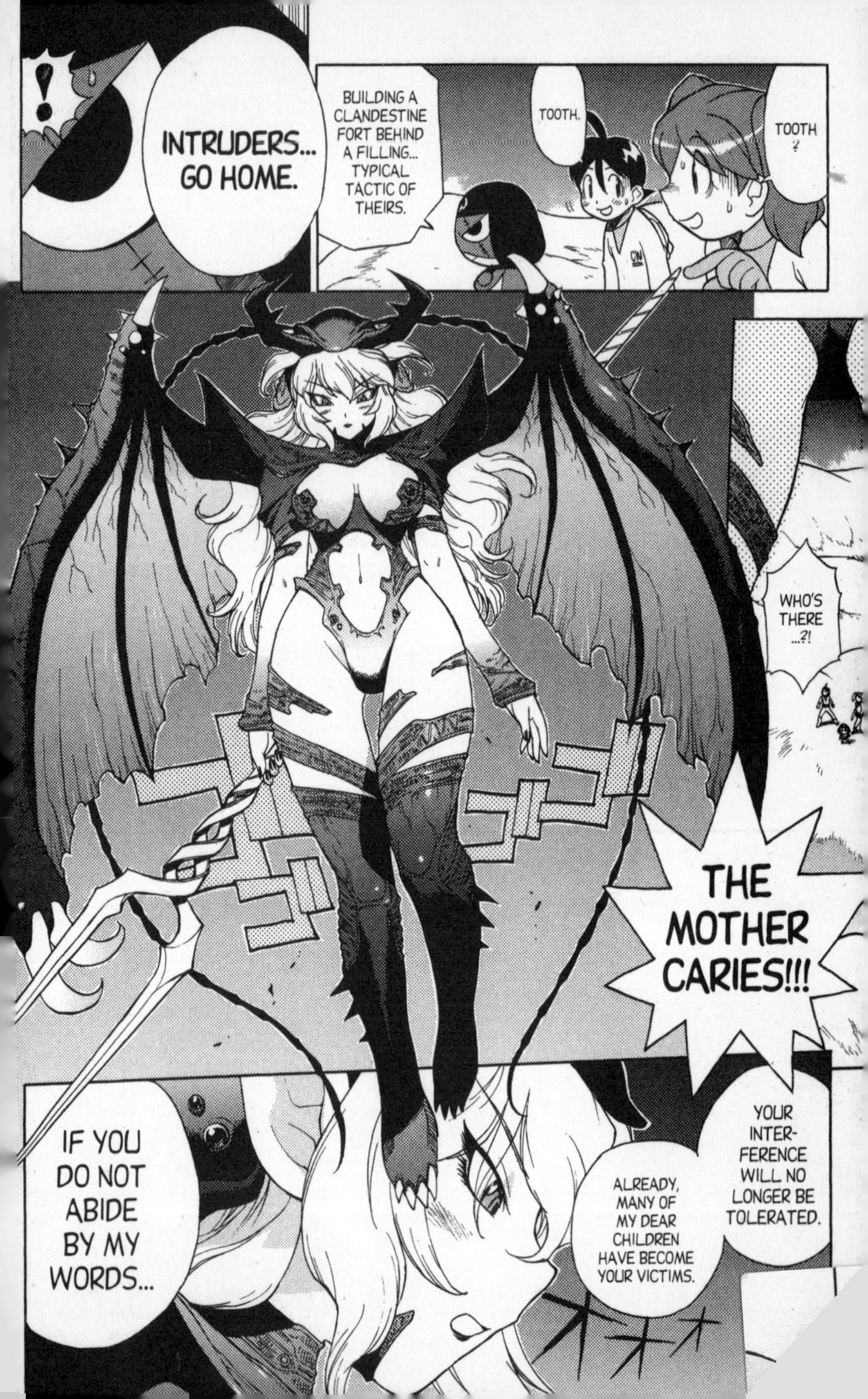
TOOTH ?
TOOTH.
BUILDING A CLANDESTINE FORT BEHIND A FILLING... TYPICAL TACTIC OF THEIRS.
INTRUDERS... GO HOME.
WHO'S THERE ...?!
THE MOTHER CARIES!!!
YOUR INTER-FERENCE WILL NO LONGER BE TOLERATED.
ALREADY, MANY OF MY DEAR CHILDREN HAVE BECOME YOUR VICTIMS.
IF YOU DO NOT ABIDE BY MY WORDS...

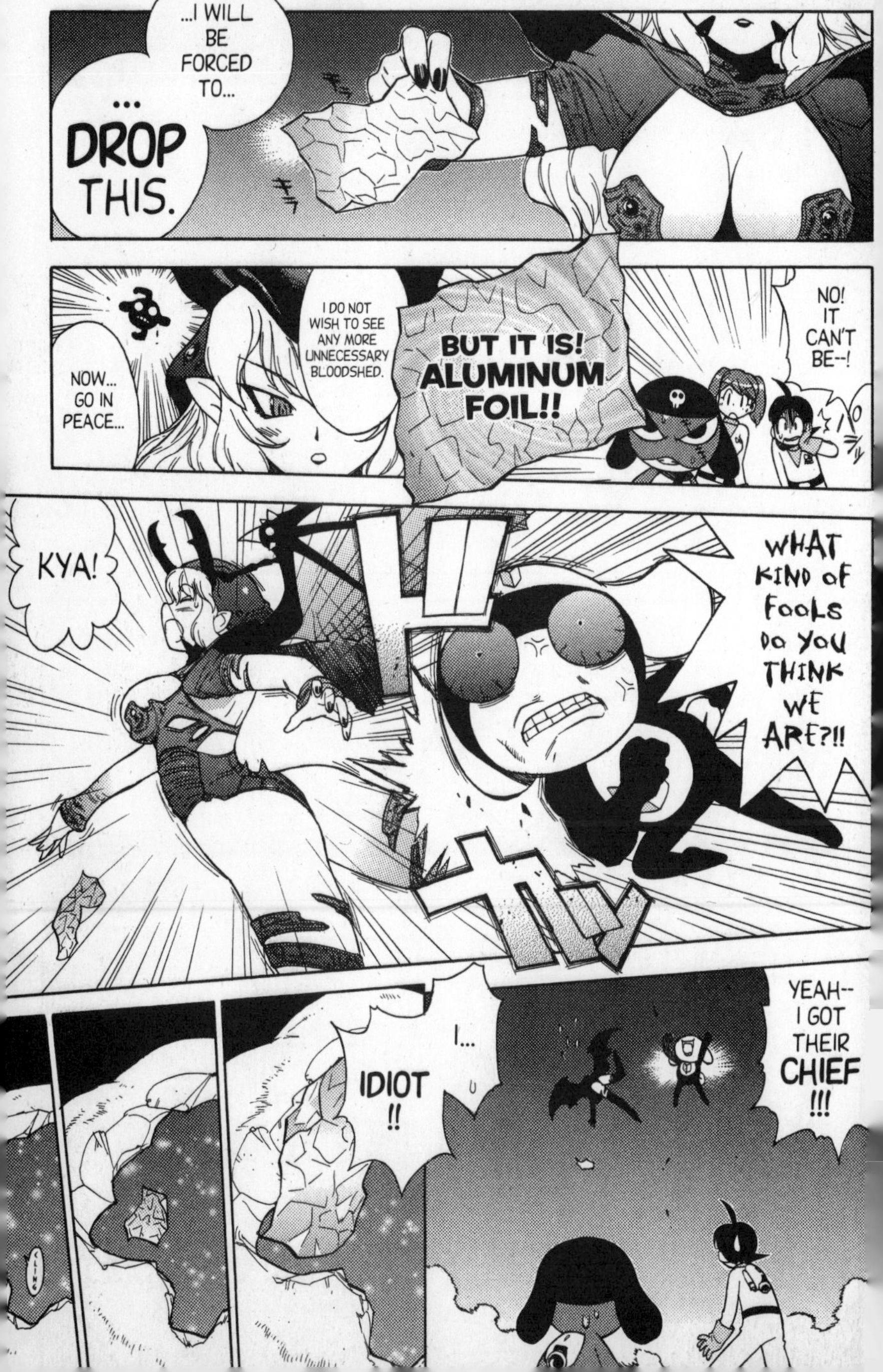
...I WILL BE FORCED TO...
...DROP THIS.
NO! IT CAN'T BE--!
BUT IT IS! ALUMINUM FOIL!!
I DO NOT WISH TO SEE ANY MORE UNNECESSARY BLOODSHED.
NOW... GO IN PEACE...
WHAT KIND OF FOOLS DO YOU THINK WE ARE?!!
KYA!
YEAH-- I GOT THEIR CHIEF!!!
I...
IDIOT!!
CLING

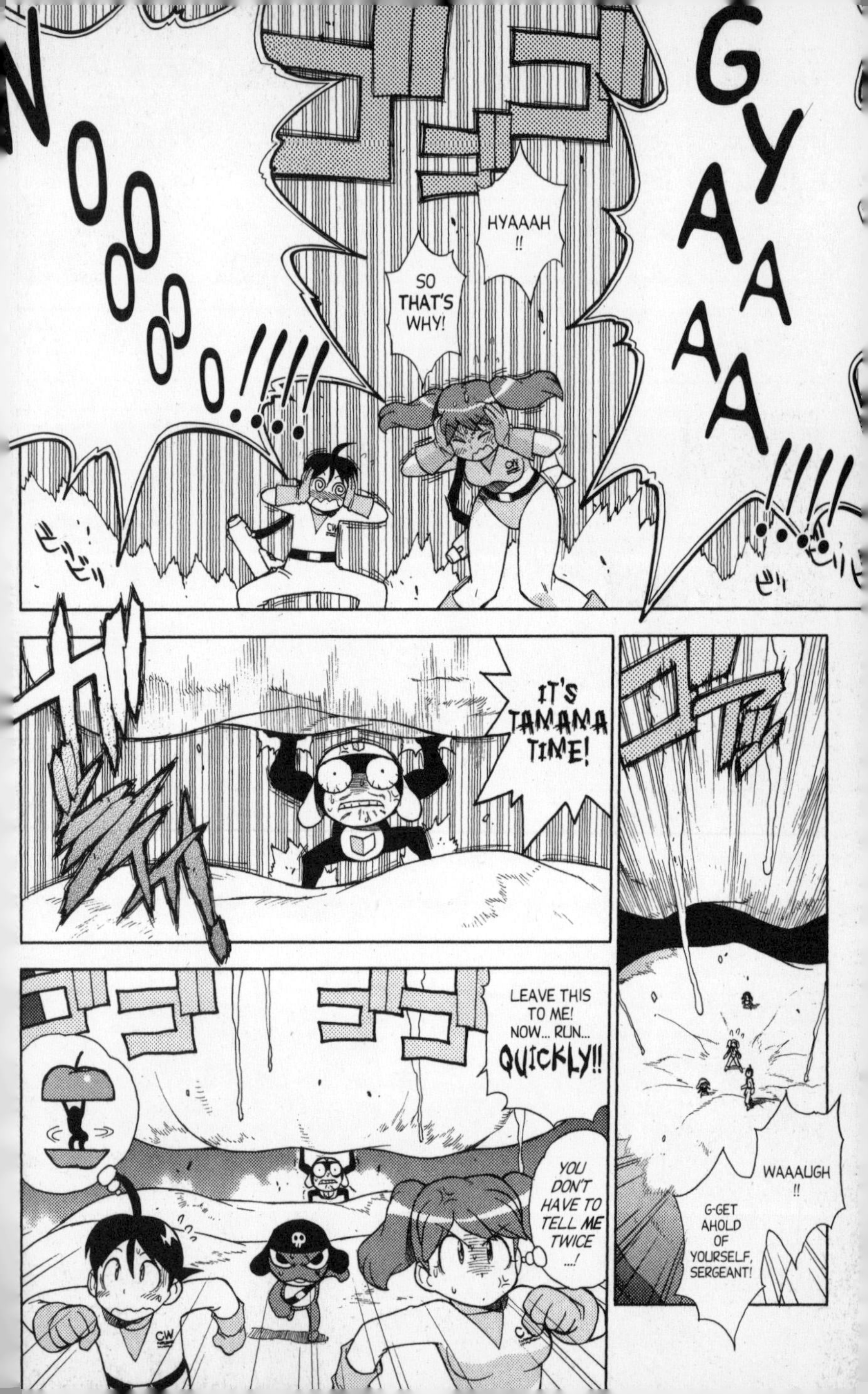
GYAAAAA!!!!...
HYAAAH!!
SO THAT'S WHY!
NOOOOOO!!!!...
WAAAUGH!!
G-GET AHOLD OF YOURSELF, SERGEANT!
IT'S TAMAMA TIME!
LEAVE THIS TO ME! NOW... RUN... QUICKLY!!
YOU DON'T HAVE TO TELL ME TWICE ...!

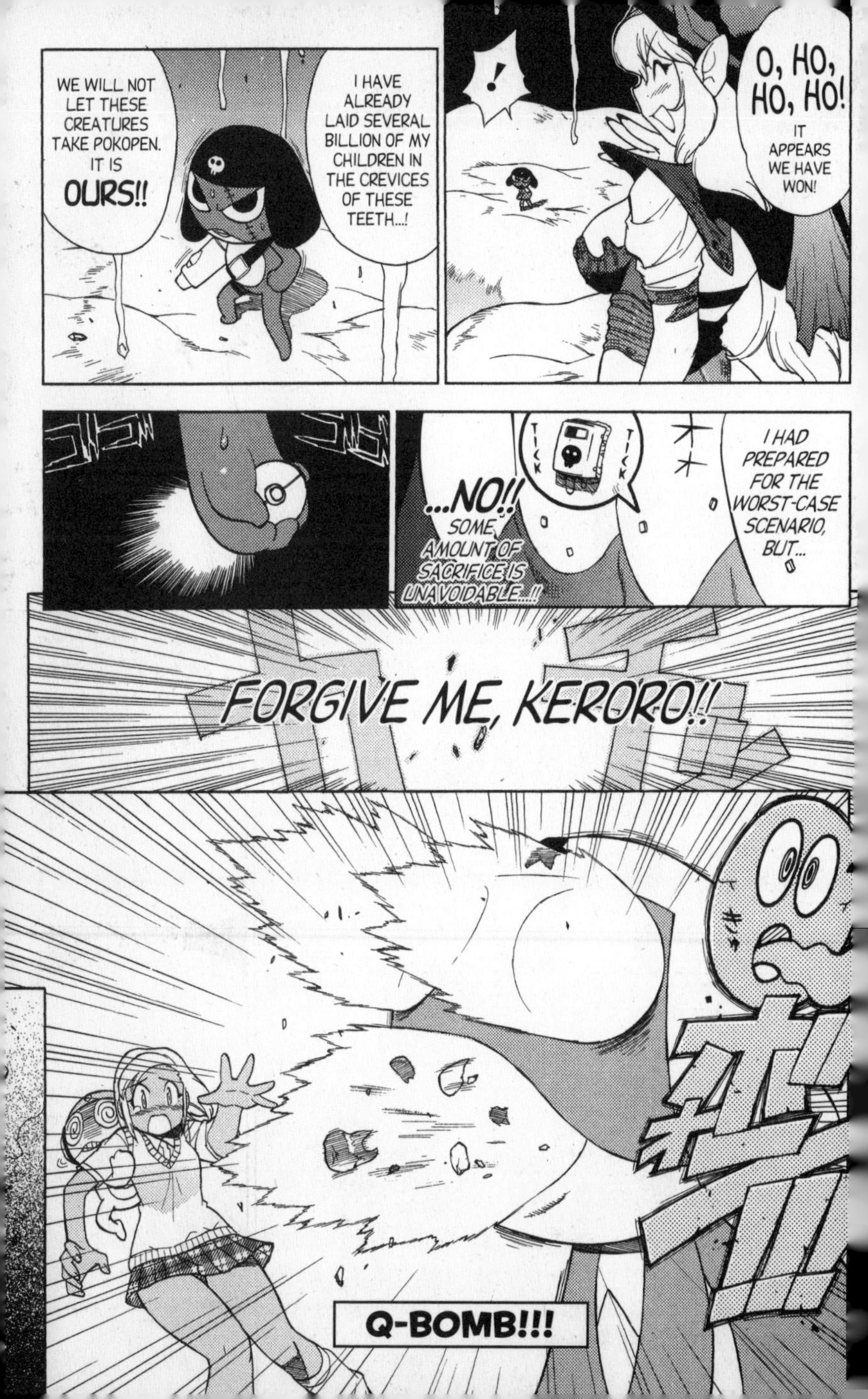
O, HO, HO, HO!
IT APPEARS WE HAVE WON!
!
I HAVE ALREADY LAID SEVERAL BILLION OF MY CHILDREN IN THE CREVICES OF THESE TEETH...!
WE WILL NOT LET THESE CREATURES TAKE POKOPEN. IT IS OURS!!
I HAD PREPARED FOR THE WORST-CASE SCENARIO, BUT...
TICK
TICK
...NO!! SOME AMOUNT OF SACRIFICE IS UNAVOIDABLE...!!
FORGIVE ME, KERORO!!
Q-BOMB!!!

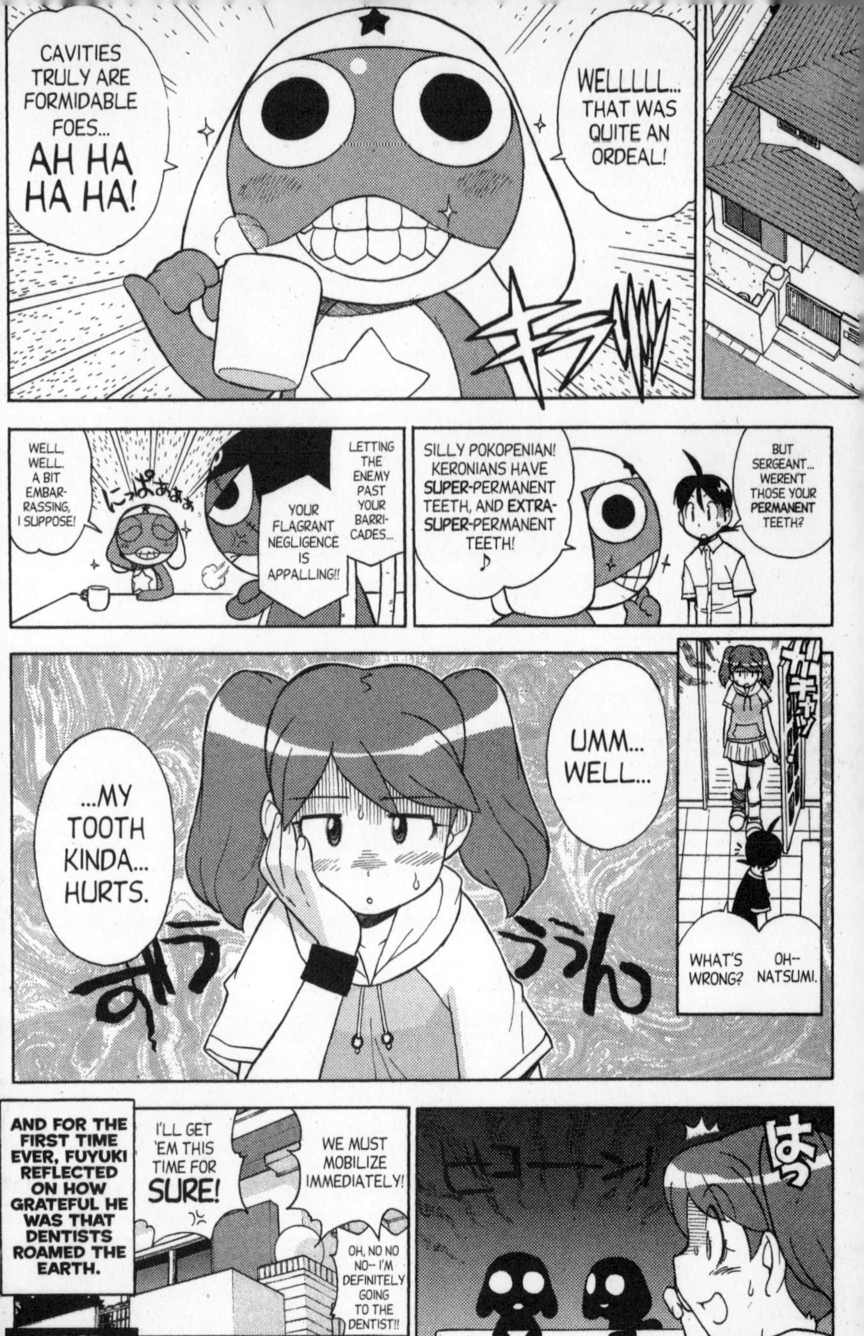
WELLLLL... THAT WAS QUITE AN ORDEAL!
CAVITIES TRULY ARE FORMIDABLE FOES... AH HA HA HA!
BUT SERGEANT... WEREN'T THOSE YOUR PERMANENT TEETH?
SILLY POKOPENIAN! KERONIANS HAVE SUPER-PERMANENT TEETH, AND EXTRA-SUPER-PERMANENT TEETH! ♪
LETTING THE ENEMY PAST YOUR BARRICADES...
YOUR FLAGRANT NEGLIGENCE IS APPALLING!!
WELL, WELL. A BIT EMBARRASSING, I SUPPOSE!
OH-- NATSUMI.
WHAT'S WRONG?
UMM... WELL...
...MY TOOTH KINDA... HURTS.
はっ
WE MUST MOBILIZE IMMEDIATELY!
I'LL GET 'EM THIS TIME FOR SURE!
OH, NO NO NO-- I'M DEFINITELY GOING TO THE DENTIST!!
AND FOR THE FIRST TIME EVER, FUYUKI REFLECTED ON HOW GRATEFUL HE WAS THAT DENTISTS ROAMED THE EARTH.
TO BE CONTINUED

## ENCOUNTER XXXV

# I AM YOU AND YOU ARE ME

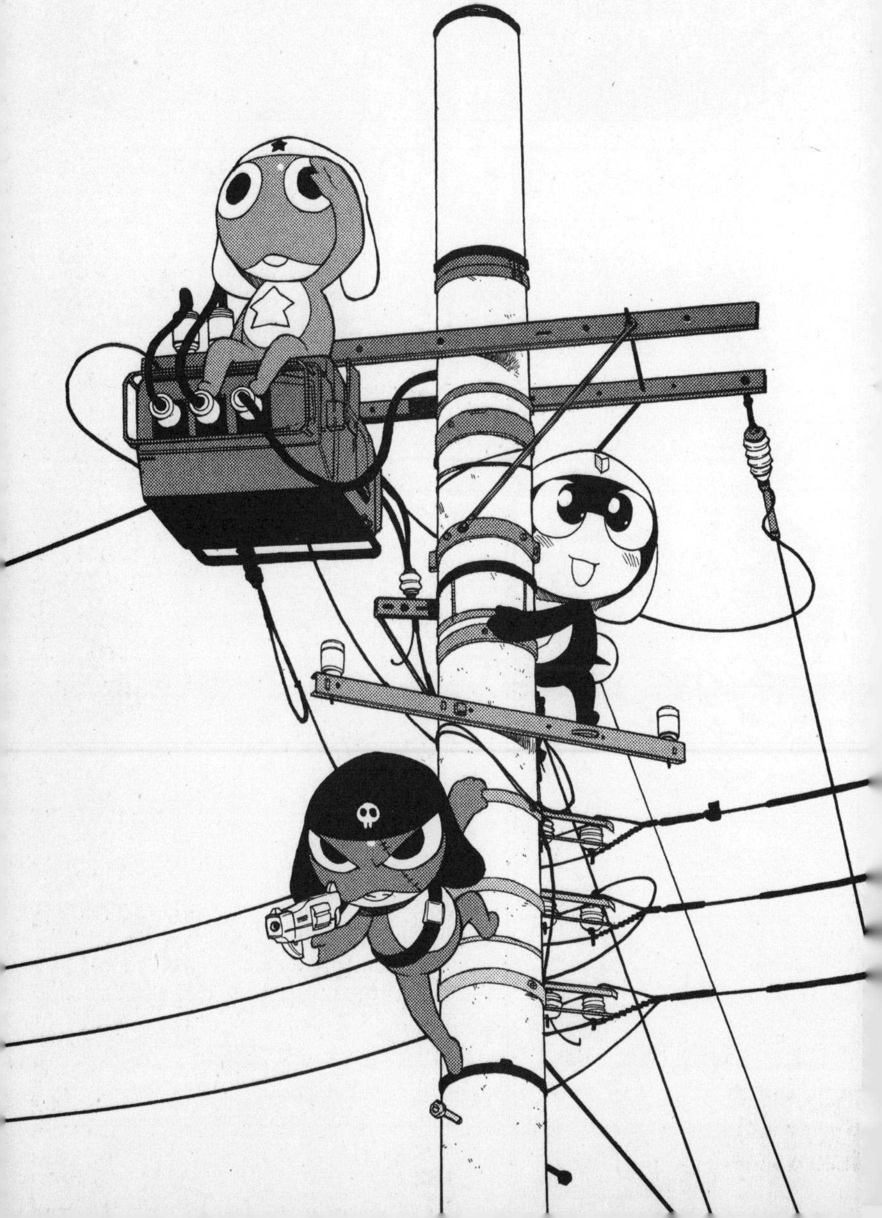

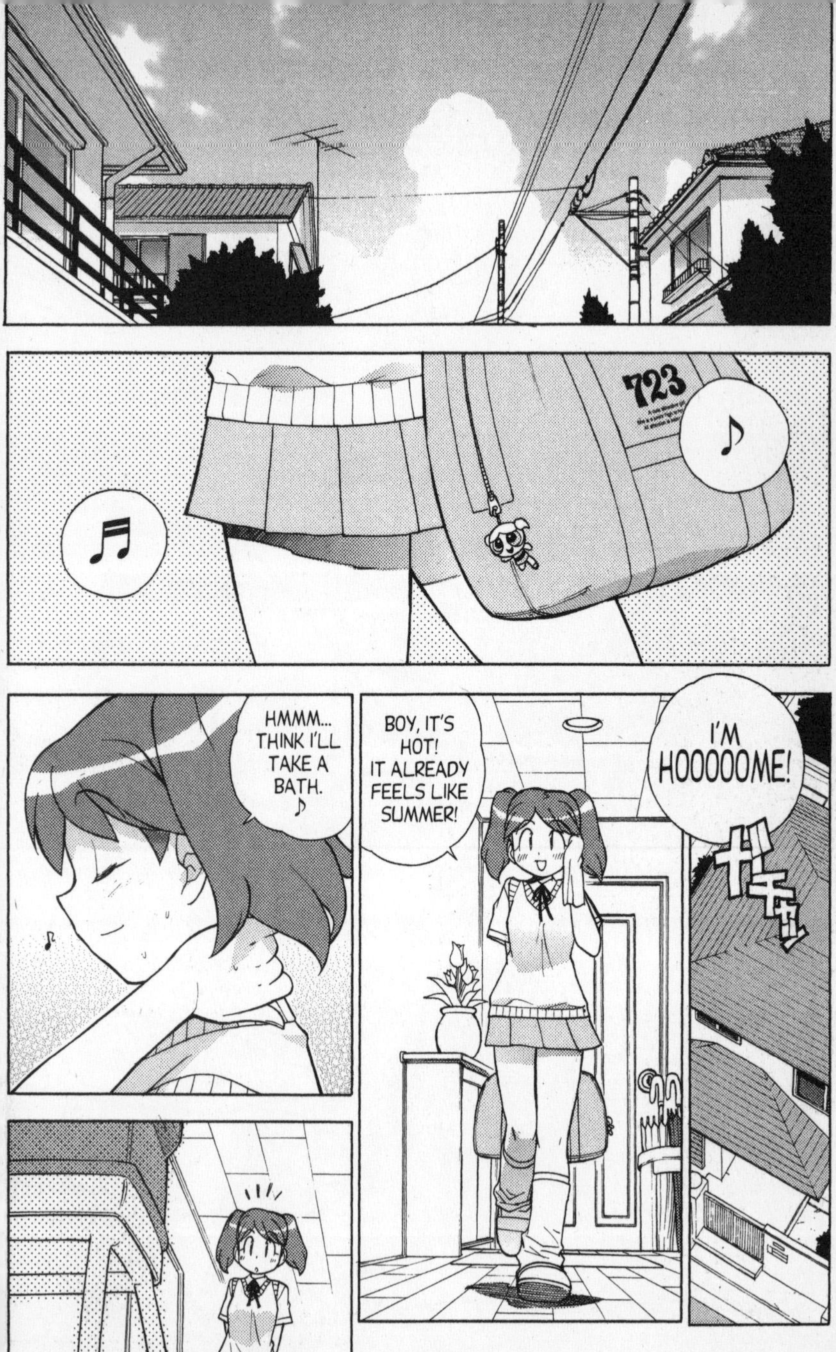

I'M HOOOOOME!
ガチャ
BOY, IT'S HOT! IT ALREADY FEELS LIKE SUMMER!
HMMM... THINK I'LL TAKE A BATH. ♪

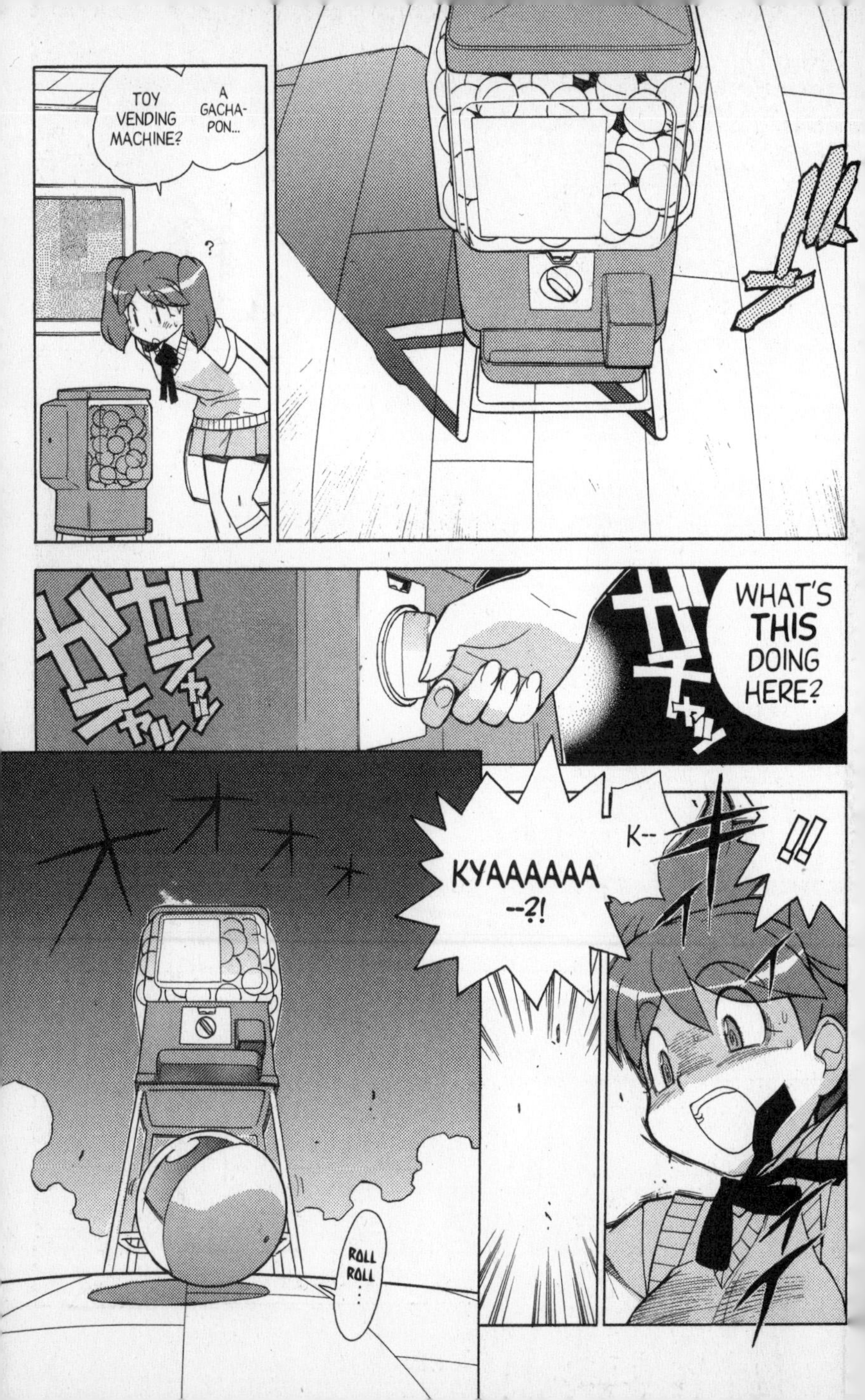
A GACHA-PON...
TOY VENDING MACHINE?
?
WHAT'S THIS DOING HERE?
!!
K--
KYAAAAAA --?!
ROLL ROLL ...

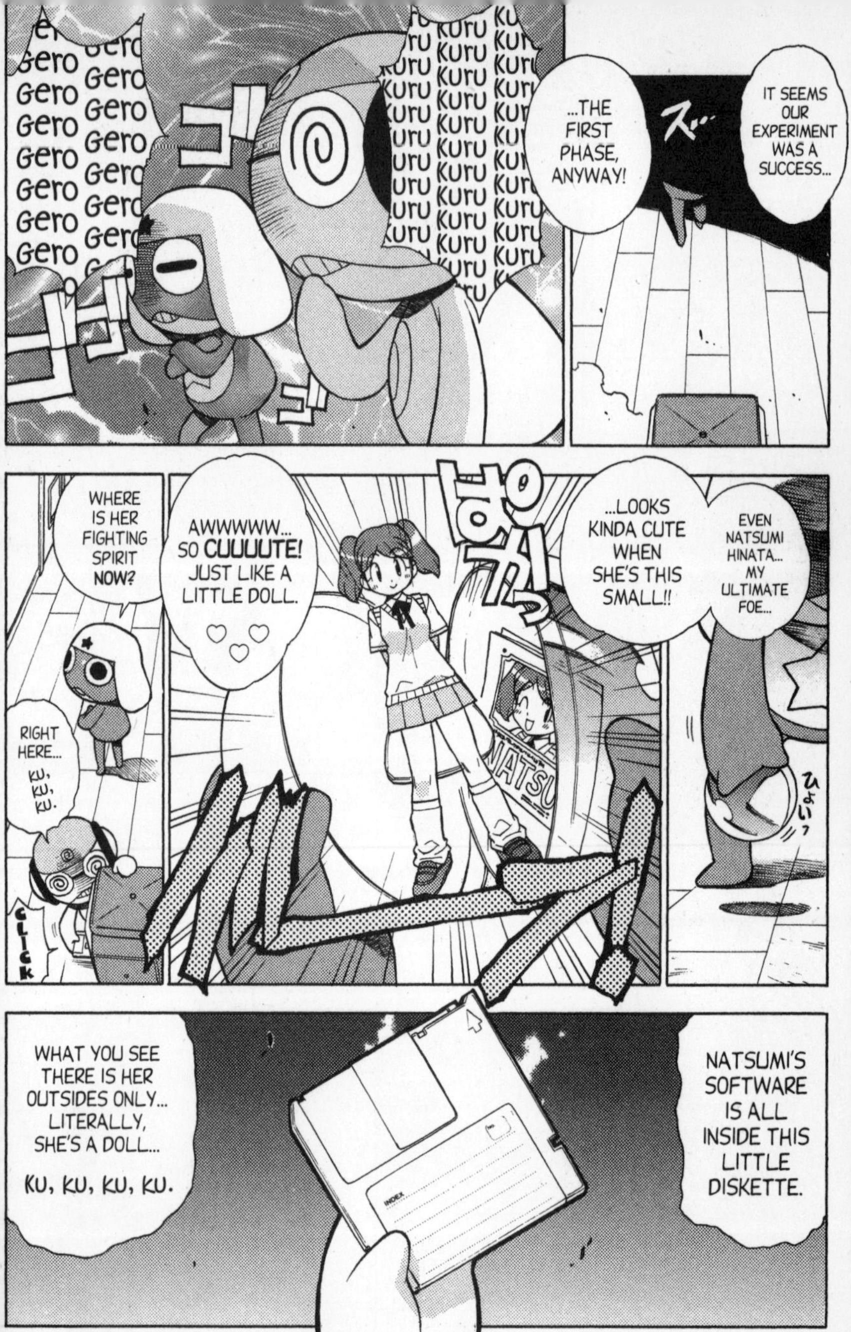
IT SEEMS OUR EXPERIMENT WAS A SUCCESS...
...THE FIRST PHASE, ANYWAY!
Kuru Kuru Kuru Kuru Kuru Kuru Kuru Kuru Kuru
Gero Gero Gero Gero Gero Gero Gero Gero
EVEN NATSUMI HINATA... MY ULTIMATE FOE...
...LOOKS KINDA CUTE WHEN SHE'S THIS SMALL!!
ぱかっ
ひょいっ
NATSU
AWWWWW... SO CUUUUTE! JUST LIKE A LITTLE DOLL.
WHERE IS HER FIGHTING SPIRIT NOW?
RIGHT HERE... KU, KU, KU.
CLICK
NATSUMI'S SOFTWARE IS ALL INSIDE THIS LITTLE DISKETTE.
INDEX
WHAT YOU SEE THERE IS HER OUTSIDES ONLY... LITERALLY, SHE'S A DOLL...
KU, KU, KU, KU.

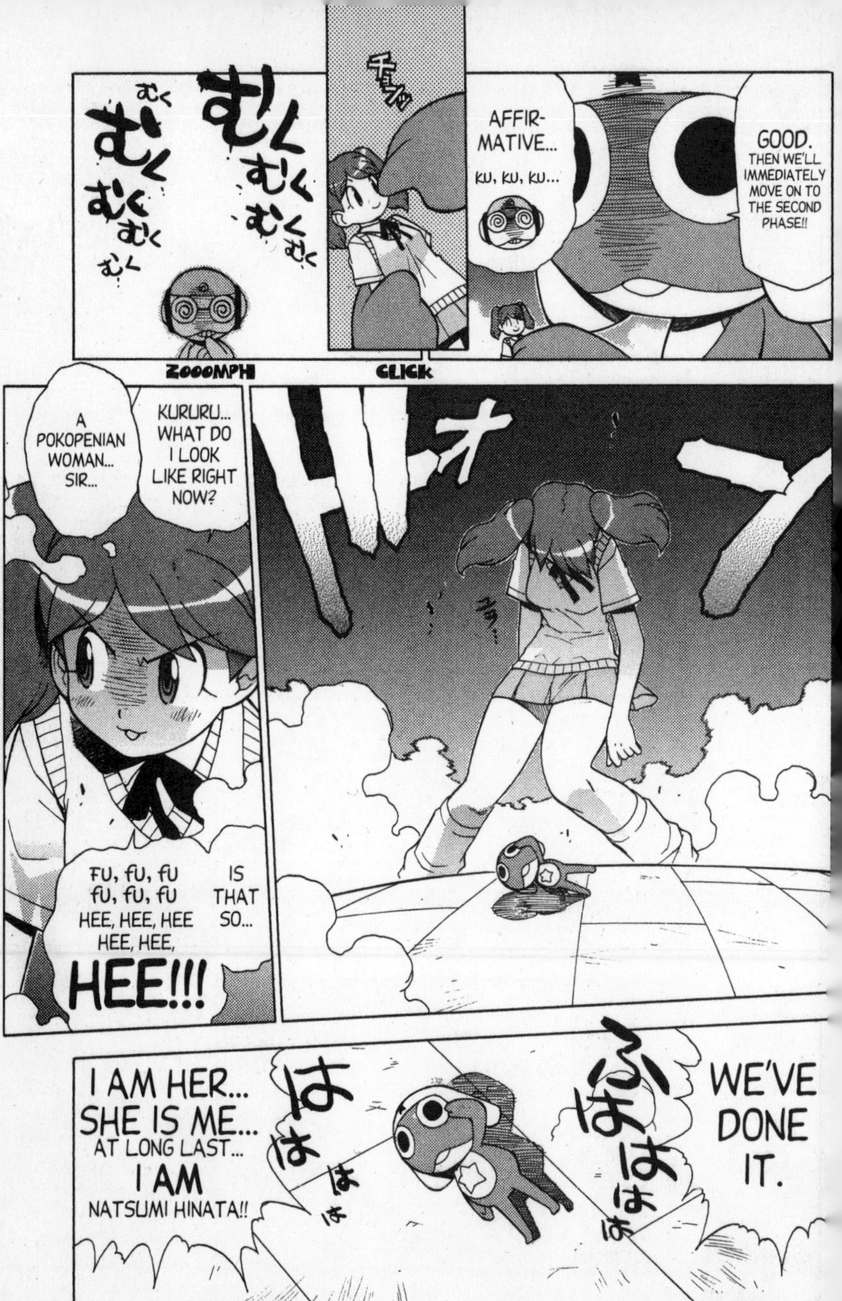
GOOD. THEN WE'LL IMMEDIATELY MOVE ON TO THE SECOND PHASE!!
AFFIRMATIVE...
KU, KU, KU...
CLICK
むく むく むく むく むく むく
むく むく むく むく
ZOOOMPH
KURURU... WHAT DO I LOOK LIKE RIGHT NOW?
A POKOPENIAN WOMAN... SIR...
IS THAT SO...
FU, FU, FU FU, FU, FU HEE, HEE, HEE HEE, HEE, HEE!!!
WE'VE DONE IT.
ふははは
FU, HA, HA, HA, HA!
I AM HER... SHE IS ME... AT LONG LAST... I AM NATSUMI HINATA!!
ははは
BWA, HA, HA, HA, HA!

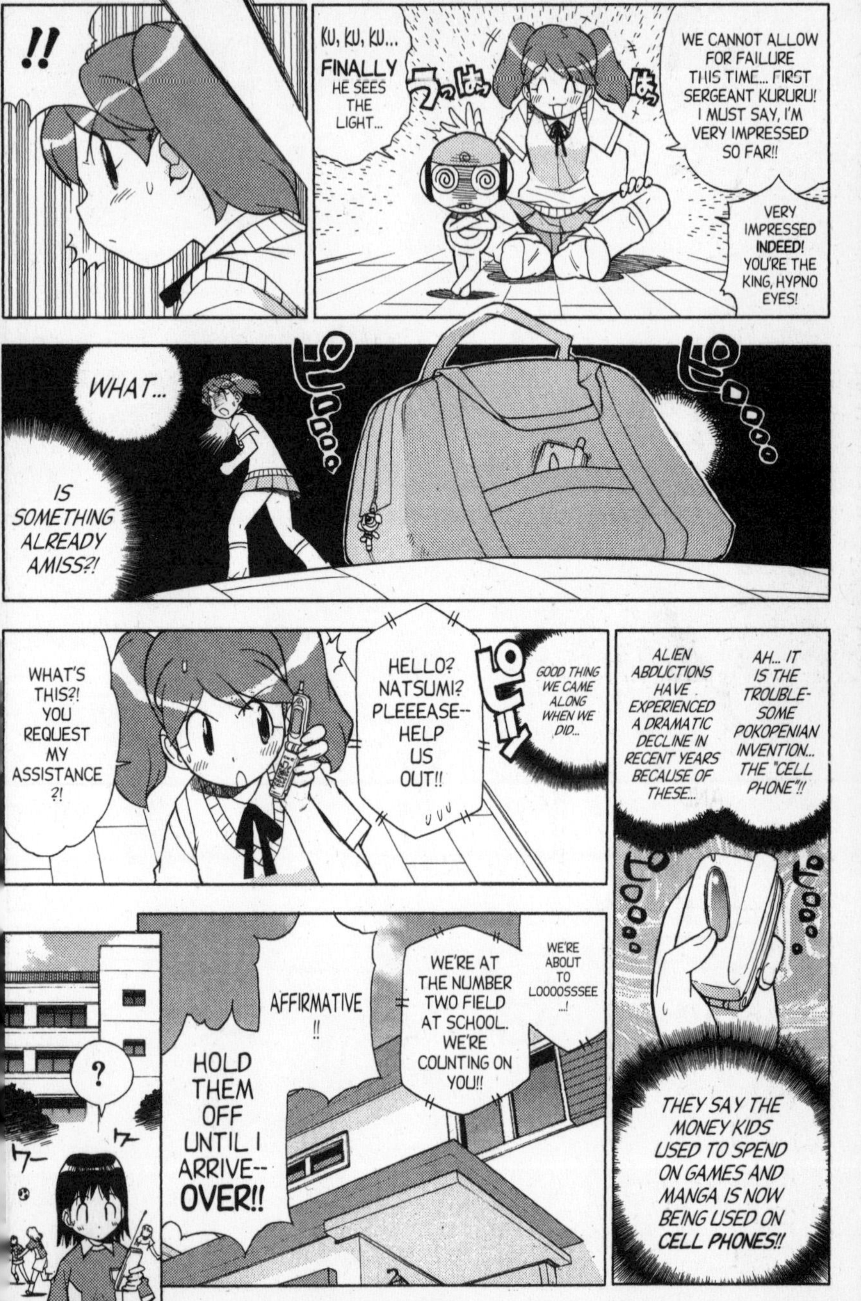
WE CANNOT ALLOW FOR FAILURE THIS TIME... FIRST SERGEANT KURURU! I MUST SAY, I'M VERY IMPRESSED SO FAR!!
VERY IMPRESSED INDEED! YOU'RE THE KING, HYPNO EYES!
KU, KU, KU... FINALLY HE SEES THE LIGHT...
うっはっ
はっ
!!
WHAT...
IS SOMETHING ALREADY AMISS?!
AH... IT IS THE TROUBLE-SOME POKOPENIAN INVENTION... THE "CELL PHONE"!!
ALIEN ABDUCTIONS HAVE EXPERIENCED A DRAMATIC DECLINE IN RECENT YEARS BECAUSE OF THESE...
THEY SAY THE MONEY KIDS USED TO SPEND ON GAMES AND MANGA IS NOW BEING USED ON CELL PHONES!!
HELLO? NATSUMI? PLEEEASE-- HELP US OUT!!
GOOD THING WE CAME ALONG WHEN WE DID...
WHAT'S THIS?! YOU REQUEST MY ASSISTANCE?!
WE'RE ABOUT TO LOOOOSSSEE...!
WE'RE AT THE NUMBER TWO FIELD AT SCHOOL. WE'RE COUNTING ON YOU!!
AFFIRMATIVE!!
HOLD THEM OFF UNTIL I ARRIVE-- OVER!!
?

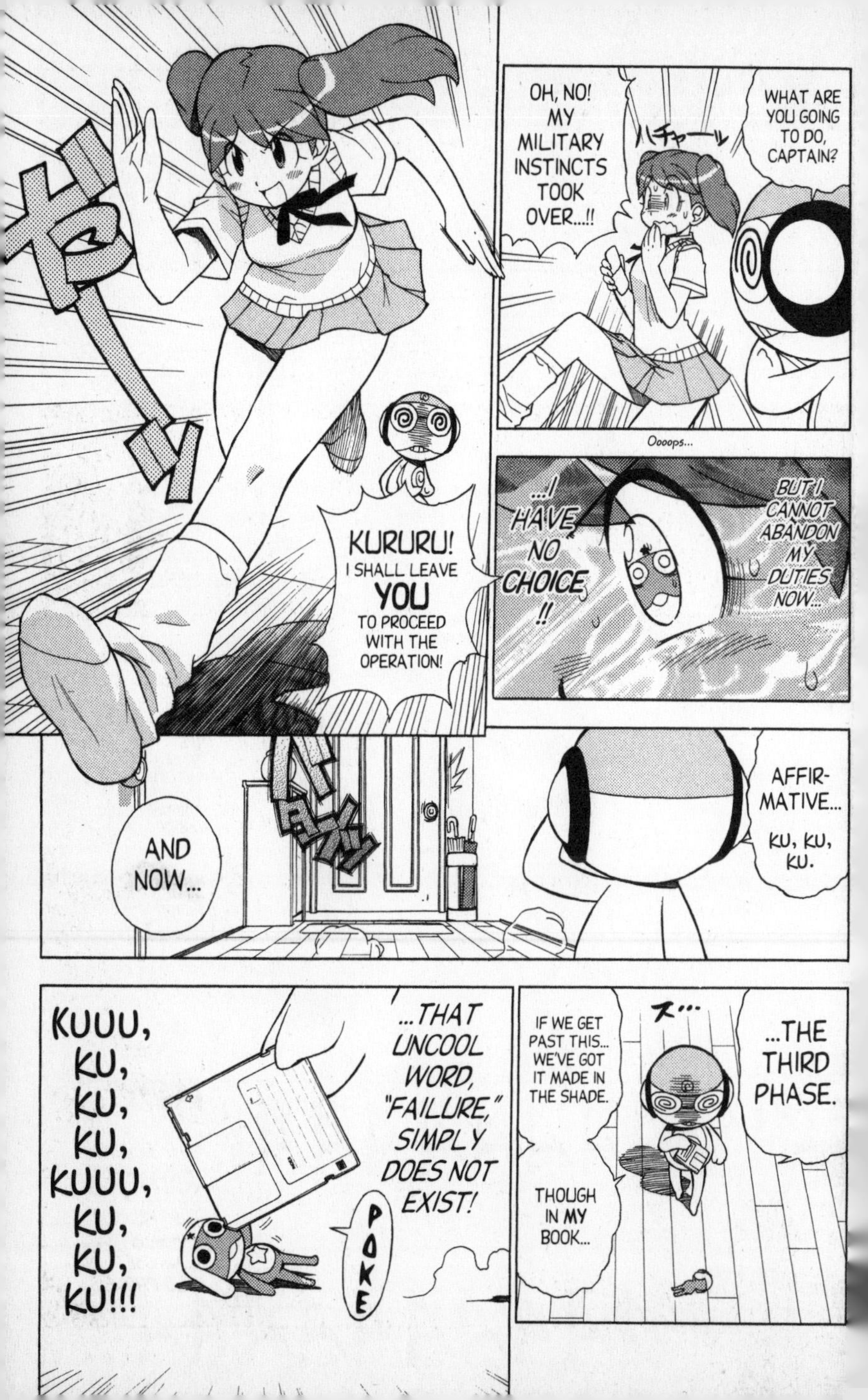
WHAT ARE YOU GOING TO DO, CAPTAIN?
ハチャーッ
OH, NO! MY MILITARY INSTINCTS TOOK OVER...!!
Oooops...
BUT I CANNOT ABANDON MY DUTIES NOW...
...I HAVE NO CHOICE!!
KURURU! I SHALL LEAVE YOU TO PROCEED WITH THE OPERATION!
AFFIRMATIVE...
KU, KU, KU.
AND NOW...
...THE THIRD PHASE.
ス…
IF WE GET PAST THIS... WE'VE GOT IT MADE IN THE SHADE.
THOUGH IN MY BOOK...
...THAT UNCOOL WORD, "FAILURE," SIMPLY DOES NOT EXIST!
POKE
KUUU, KU, KU, KU, KUUU, KU, KU, KU!!!

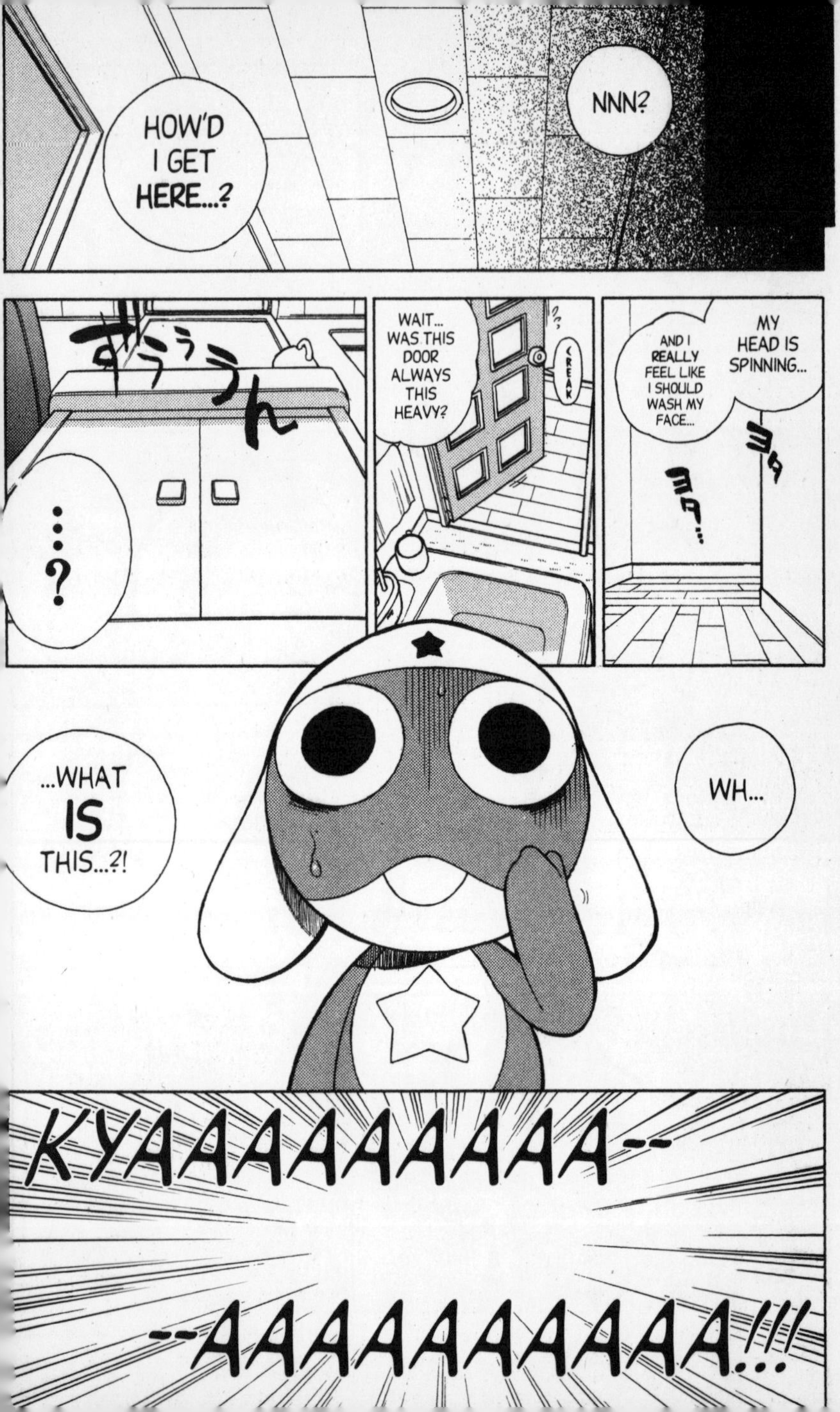
NNN?
HOW'D I GET HERE...?
MY HEAD IS SPINNING...
AND I REALLY FEEL LIKE I SHOULD WASH MY FACE...
ヨタ
ヨタ...
WAIT... WAS THIS DOOR ALWAYS THIS HEAVY?
CREAK
...?
WH...
...WHAT IS THIS...?!
KYAAAAAAAAAA--
--AAAAAAAAAAA!!!

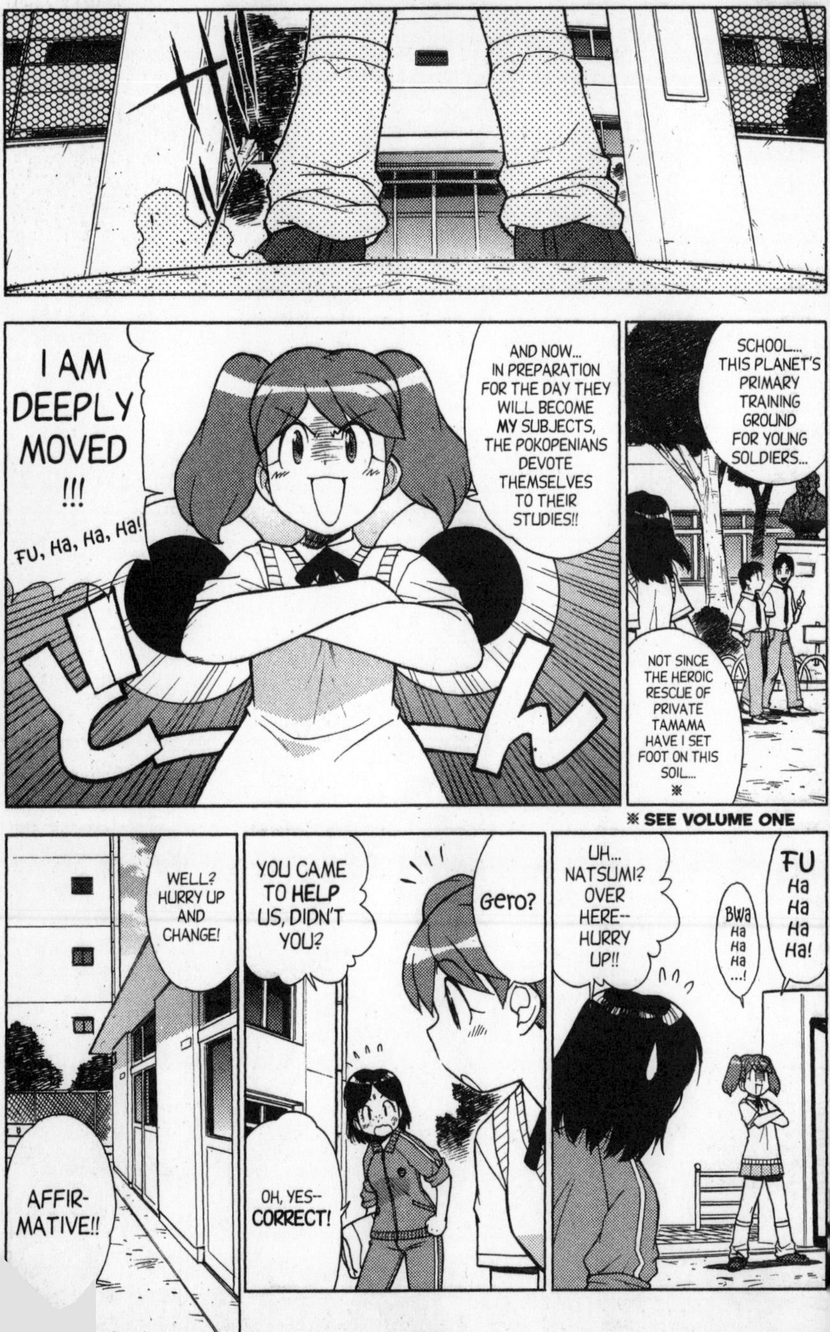

SCHOOL... THIS PLANET'S PRIMARY TRAINING GROUND FOR YOUNG SOLDIERS...
NOT SINCE THE HEROIC RESCUE OF PRIVATE TAMAMA HAVE I SET FOOT ON THIS SOIL... ※
AND NOW... IN PREPARATION FOR THE DAY THEY WILL BECOME MY SUBJECTS, THE POKOPENIANS DEVOTE THEMSELVES TO THEIR STUDIES!!
I AM DEEPLY MOVED !!!
FU, Ha, Ha, Ha!
※ SEE VOLUME ONE
FU Ha Ha Ha Ha!
Bwa Ha Ha Ha ...!
UH... NATSUMI? OVER HERE-- HURRY UP!!
Gero?
YOU CAME TO HELP US, DIDN'T YOU?
OH, YES-- CORRECT!
WELL? HURRY UP AND CHANGE!
AFFIR-MATIVE!!

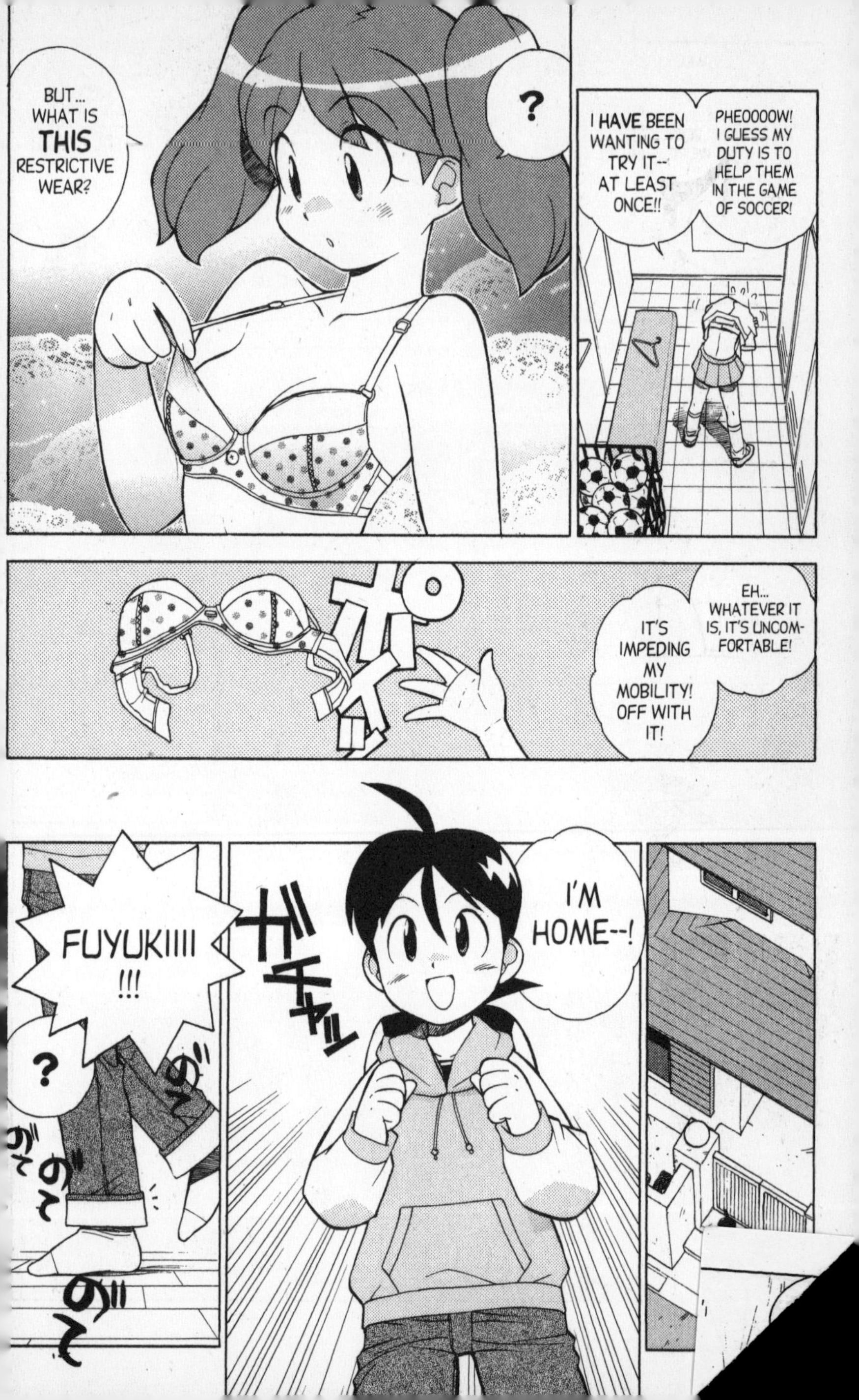
PHEOOOOW! I GUESS MY DUTY IS TO HELP THEM IN THE GAME OF SOCCER!
I **HAVE** BEEN WANTING TO TRY IT-- AT LEAST ONCE!!
?
BUT... WHAT IS **THIS** RESTRICTIVE WEAR?
EH... WHATEVER IT IS, IT'S UNCOMFORTABLE!
IT'S IMPEDING MY MOBILITY! OFF WITH IT!
I'M HOME--!
FUYUKIIII !!!
?

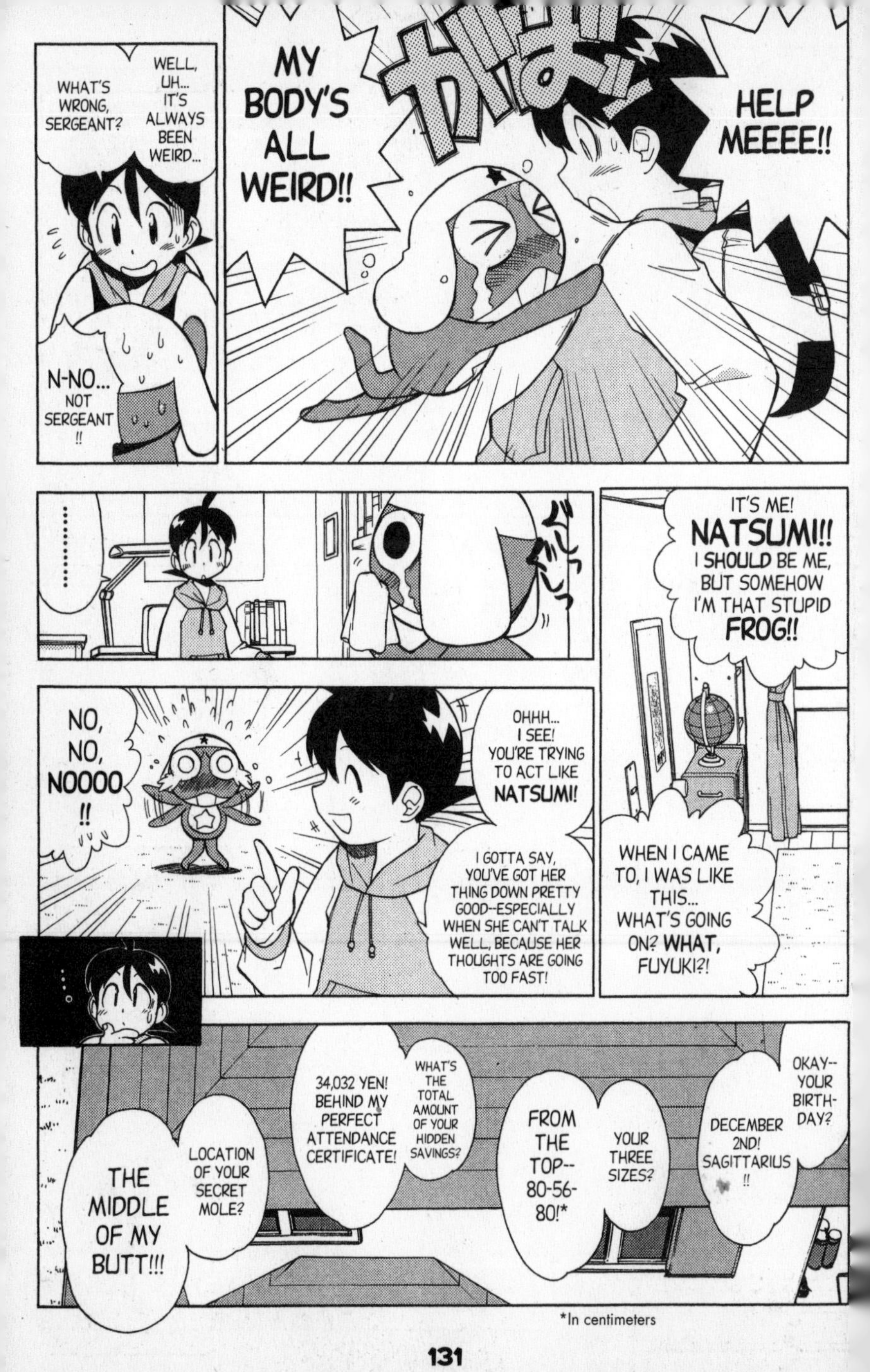

HELP MEEEE!!
MY BODY'S ALL WEIRD!!
WHAT'S WRONG, SERGEANT? WELL, UH... IT'S ALWAYS BEEN WEIRD...
N-NO... NOT SERGEANT!!
IT'S ME! NATSUMI!! I SHOULD BE ME, BUT SOMEHOW I'M THAT STUPID FROG!!
WHEN I CAME TO, I WAS LIKE THIS... WHAT'S GOING ON? WHAT, FUYUKI?!
..........
OHHH... I SEE! YOU'RE TRYING TO ACT LIKE NATSUMI!
I GOTTA SAY, YOU'VE GOT HER THING DOWN PRETTY GOOD--ESPECIALLY WHEN SHE CAN'T TALK WELL, BECAUSE HER THOUGHTS ARE GOING TOO FAST!
NO, NO, NOOOO!!
...
OKAY-- YOUR BIRTHDAY?
DECEMBER 2ND! SAGITTARIUS!!
YOUR THREE SIZES?
FROM THE TOP-- 80-56-80!*
WHAT'S THE TOTAL AMOUNT OF YOUR HIDDEN SAVINGS?
34,032 YEN! BEHIND MY PERFECT ATTENDANCE CERTIFICATE!
LOCATION OF YOUR SECRET MOLE?
THE MIDDLE OF MY BUTT!!!


*In centimeters

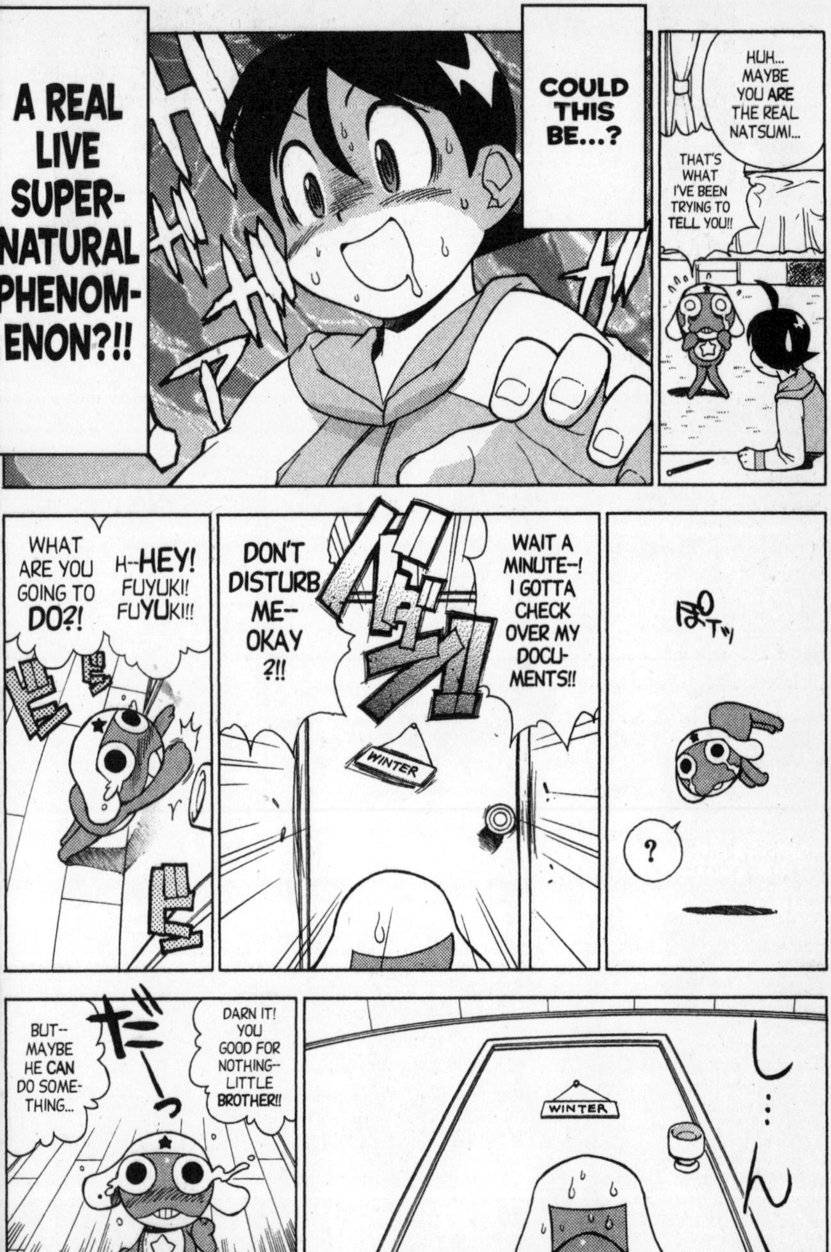
HUH... MAYBE YOU ARE THE REAL NATSUMI...
THAT'S WHAT I'VE BEEN TRYING TO TELL YOU!!
COULD THIS BE...?
A REAL LIVE SUPER-NATURAL PHENOM-ENON?!!
?
WAIT A MINUTE--! I GOTTA CHECK OVER MY DOCU-MENTS!!
DON'T DISTURB ME--OKAY?!!
WINTER
H--HEY! FUYUKI! FUYUKI!!
WHAT ARE YOU GOING TO DO?!
WINTER
し…ん
DARN IT! YOU GOOD FOR NOTHING--LITTLE BROTHER!!
だーっ
BUT--MAYBE HE CAN DO SOME-THING...

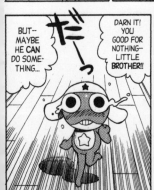

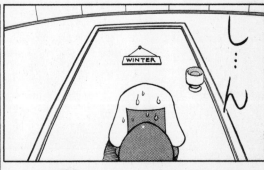

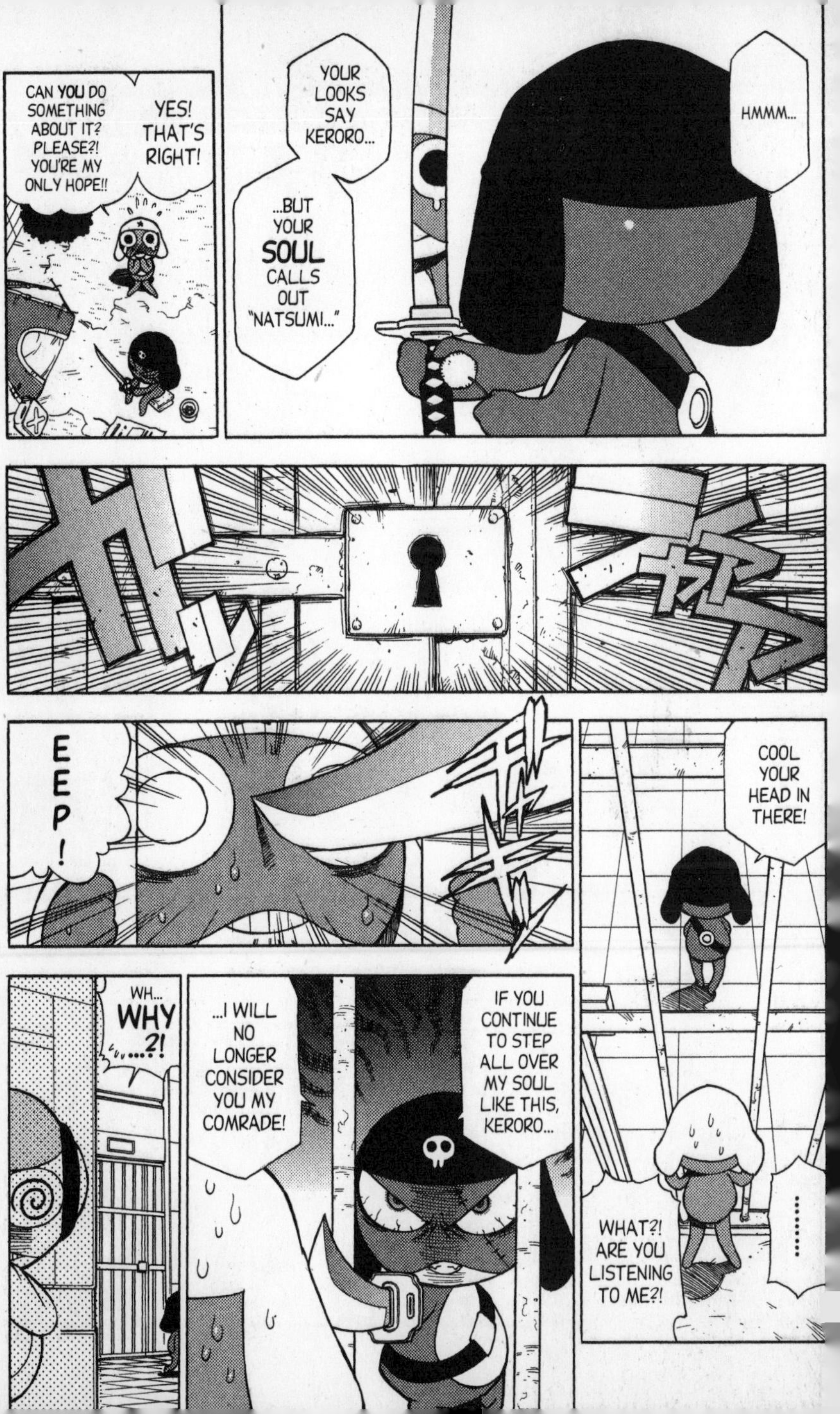
HMMM...
YOUR LOOKS SAY KERORO...
...BUT YOUR SOUL CALLS OUT "NATSUMI..."
YES! THAT'S RIGHT!
CAN YOU DO SOMETHING ABOUT IT? PLEASE?! YOU'RE MY ONLY HOPE!!
COOL YOUR HEAD IN THERE!
.......
WHAT?! ARE YOU LISTENING TO ME?!
EEP!
IF YOU CONTINUE TO STEP ALL OVER MY SOUL LIKE THIS, KERORO...
...I WILL NO LONGER CONSIDER YOU MY COMRADE!
WH... WHY ...?!

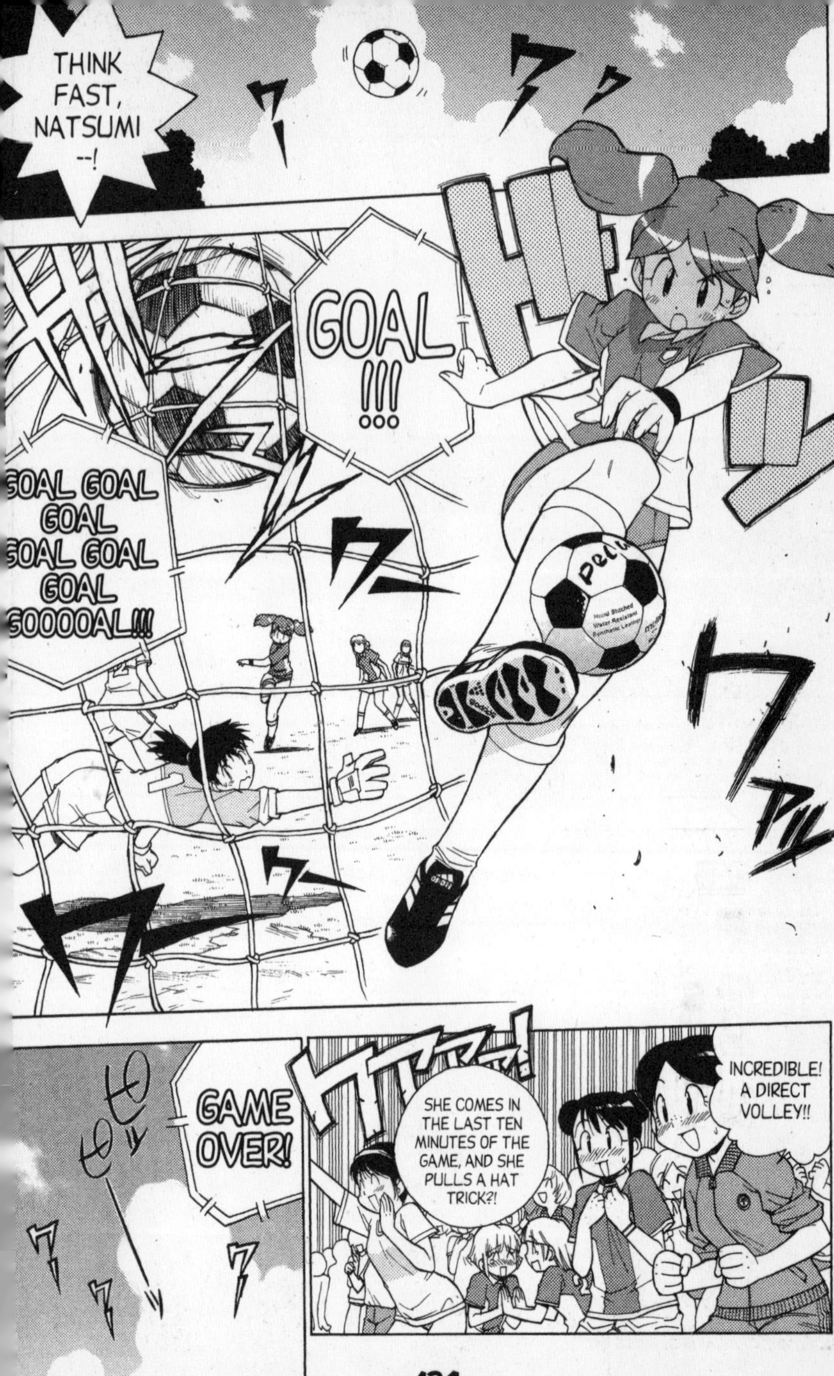
THINK FAST, NATSUMI --!
GOAL!!!
GOAL GOAL GOAL GOAL GOAL GOAL GOOOOAL!!!
INCREDIBLE! A DIRECT VOLLEY!!
SHE COMES IN THE LAST TEN MINUTES OF THE GAME, AND SHE PULLS A HAT TRICK?!
GAME OVER!

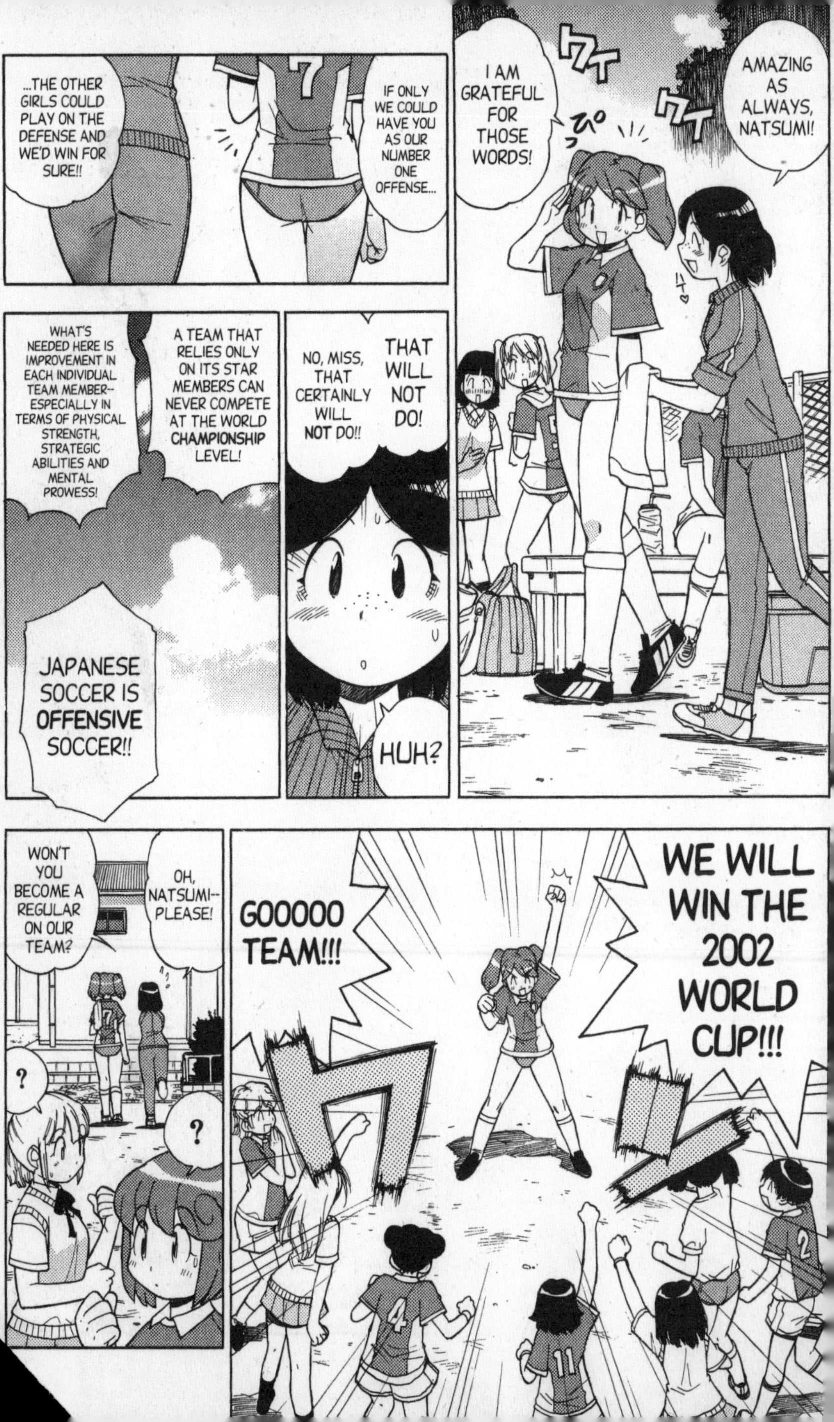
AMAZING AS ALWAYS, NATSUMI!
I AM GRATEFUL FOR THOSE WORDS!
IF ONLY WE COULD HAVE YOU AS OUR NUMBER ONE OFFENSE...
...THE OTHER GIRLS COULD PLAY ON THE DEFENSE AND WE'D WIN FOR SURE!!
THAT WILL NOT DO!
NO, MISS, THAT CERTAINLY WILL NOT DO!!
HUH?
A TEAM THAT RELIES ONLY ON ITS STAR MEMBERS CAN NEVER COMPETE AT THE WORLD CHAMPIONSHIP LEVEL!
WHAT'S NEEDED HERE IS IMPROVEMENT IN EACH INDIVIDUAL TEAM MEMBER--ESPECIALLY IN TERMS OF PHYSICAL STRENGTH, STRATEGIC ABILITIES AND MENTAL PROWESS!
JAPANESE SOCCER IS OFFENSIVE SOCCER!!
WE WILL WIN THE 2002 WORLD CUP!!!
GOOOOO TEAM!!!
OH, NATSUMI--PLEASE!
WON'T YOU BECOME A REGULAR ON OUR TEAM?
?
?

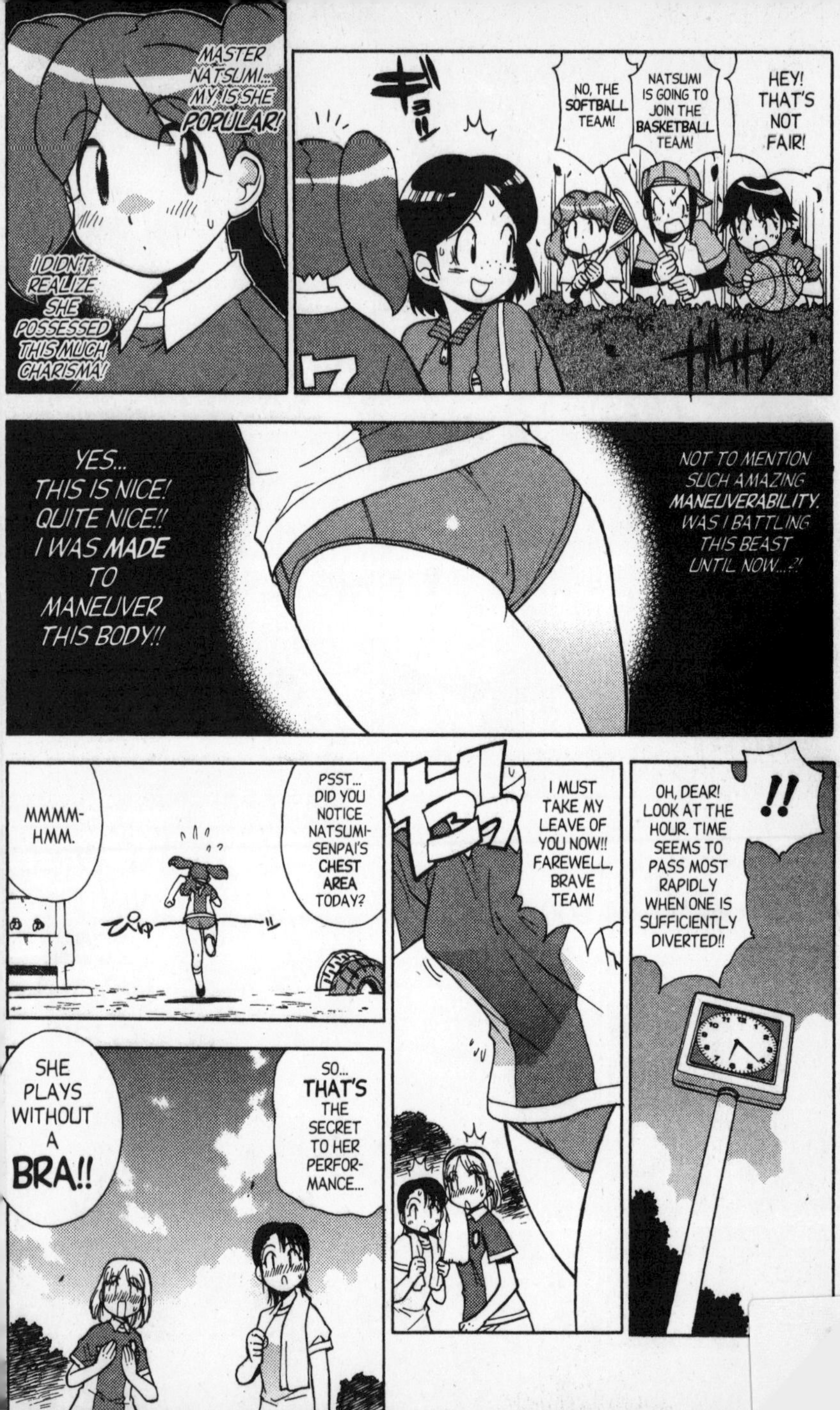
HEY! THAT'S NOT FAIR!
NATSUMI IS GOING TO JOIN THE BASKETBALL TEAM!
NO, THE SOFTBALL TEAM!
MASTER NATSUMI... MY, IS SHE POPULAR!
I DIDN'T REALIZE SHE POSSESSED THIS MUCH CHARISMA!
NOT TO MENTION SUCH AMAZING MANEUVERABILITY. WAS I BATTLING THIS BEAST UNTIL NOW...?!
YES... THIS IS NICE! QUITE NICE!! I WAS MADE TO MANEUVER THIS BODY!!
!!
OH, DEAR! LOOK AT THE HOUR. TIME SEEMS TO PASS MOST RAPIDLY WHEN ONE IS SUFFICIENTLY DIVERTED!!
I MUST TAKE MY LEAVE OF YOU NOW!! FAREWELL, BRAVE TEAM!
PSST... DID YOU NOTICE NATSUMI-SENPAI'S CHEST AREA TODAY?
MMMM-HMM.
SO... THAT'S THE SECRET TO HER PERFORMANCE...
SHE PLAYS WITHOUT A BRA!!

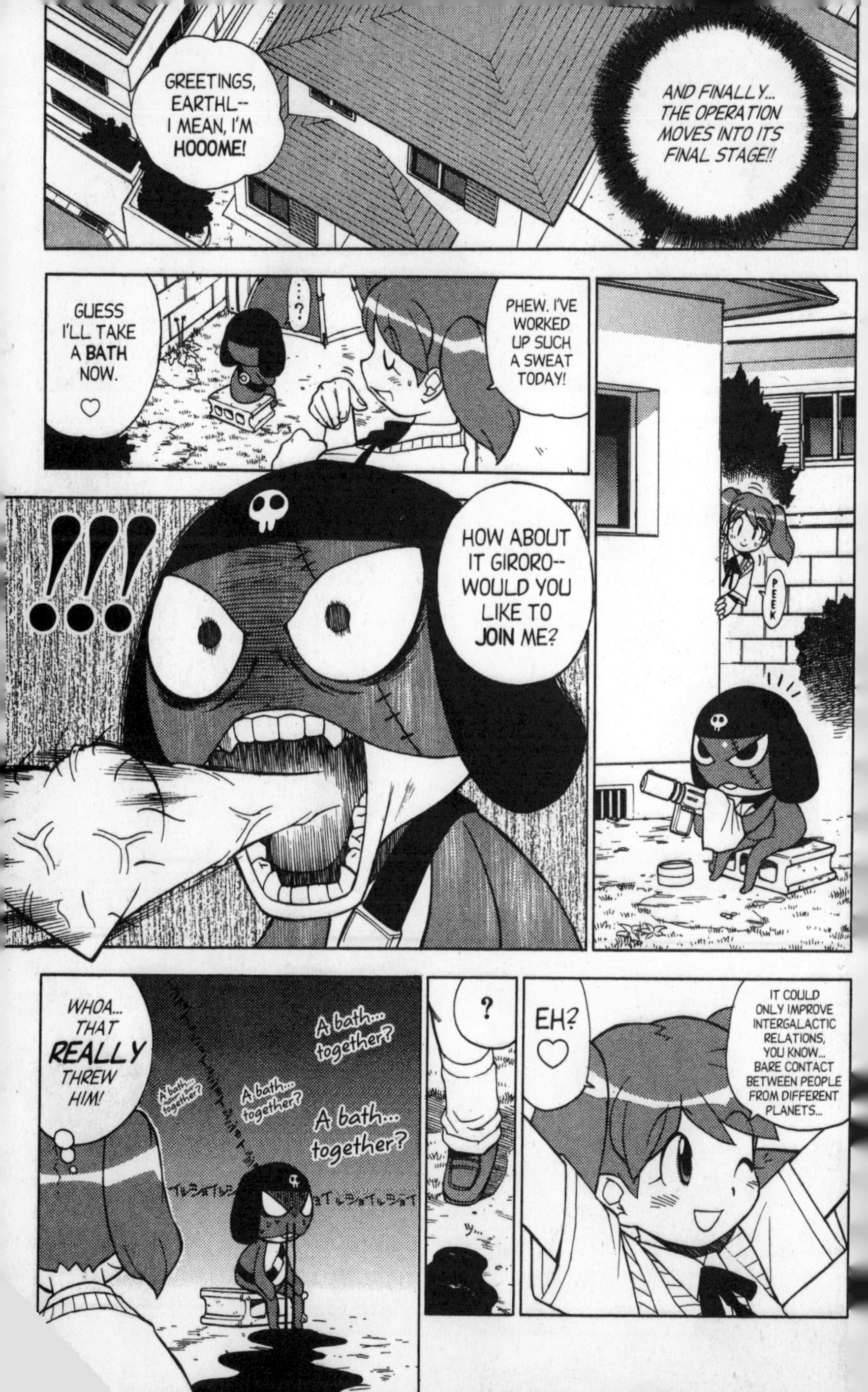
AND FINALLY... THE OPERATION MOVES INTO ITS FINAL STAGE!!
GREETINGS, EARTHL-- I MEAN, I'M HOOOME!
PEEK
PHEW. I'VE WORKED UP SUCH A SWEAT TODAY!
...?
GUESS I'LL TAKE A BATH NOW. ♡
HOW ABOUT IT GIRORO-- WOULD YOU LIKE TO JOIN ME?
!!!
IT COULD ONLY IMPROVE INTERGALACTIC RELATIONS, YOU KNOW... BARE CONTACT BETWEEN PEOPLE FROM DIFFERENT PLANETS...
EH? ♡
?
A bath... together?
A bath... together?
A bath... together?
A bath... together?
WHOA... THAT REALLY THREW HIM!

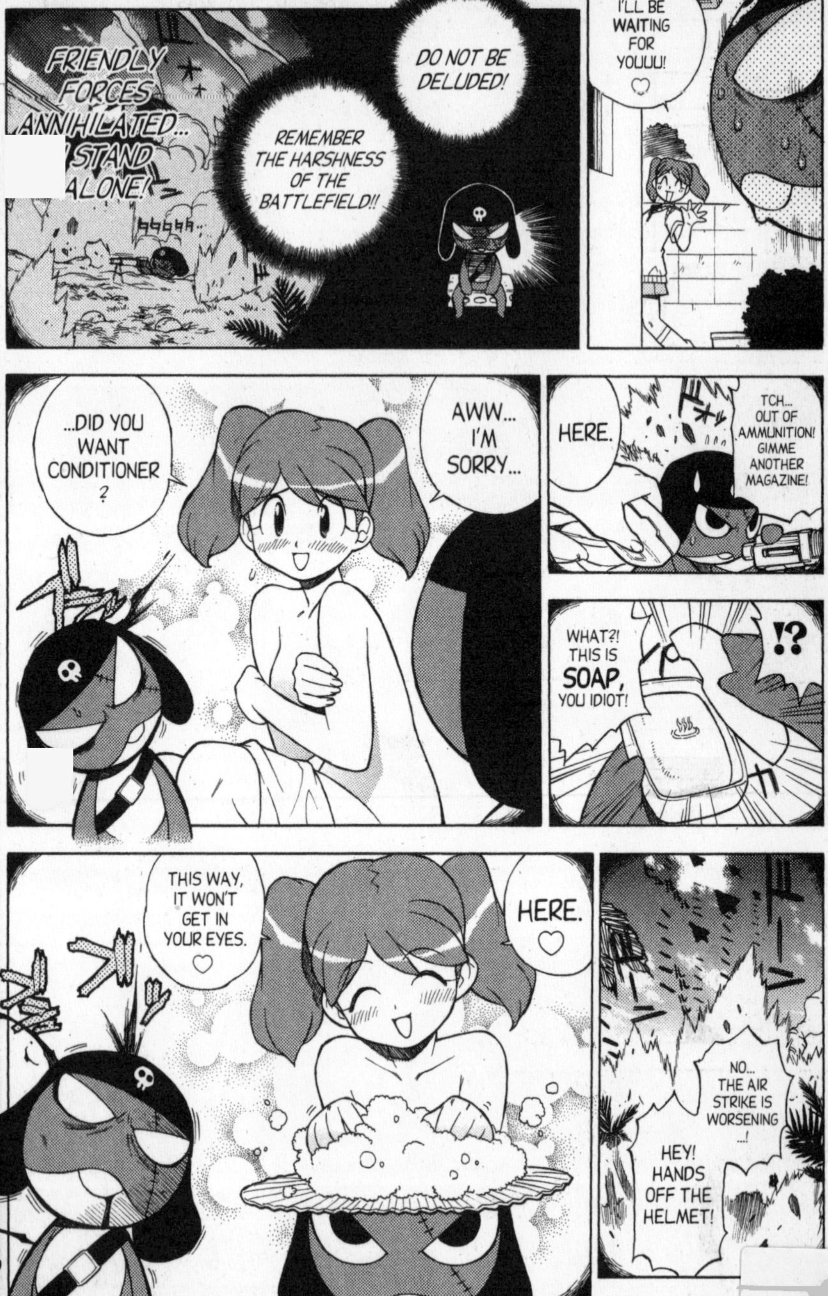
I'LL BE WAITING FOR YOUUU! ♡
DO NOT BE DELUDED!
REMEMBER THE HARSHNESS OF THE BATTLEFIELD!!
FRIENDLY FORCES ANNIHILATED... STAND ALONE!
TCH... OUT OF AMMUNITION! GIMME ANOTHER MAGAZINE!
HERE.
!?
WHAT?! THIS IS SOAP, YOU IDIOT!
AWW... I'M SORRY...
...DID YOU WANT CONDITIONER?
NO... THE AIR STRIKE IS WORSENING...!
HEY! HANDS OFF THE HELMET!
HERE. ♡
THIS WAY, IT WON'T GET IN YOUR EYES. ♡

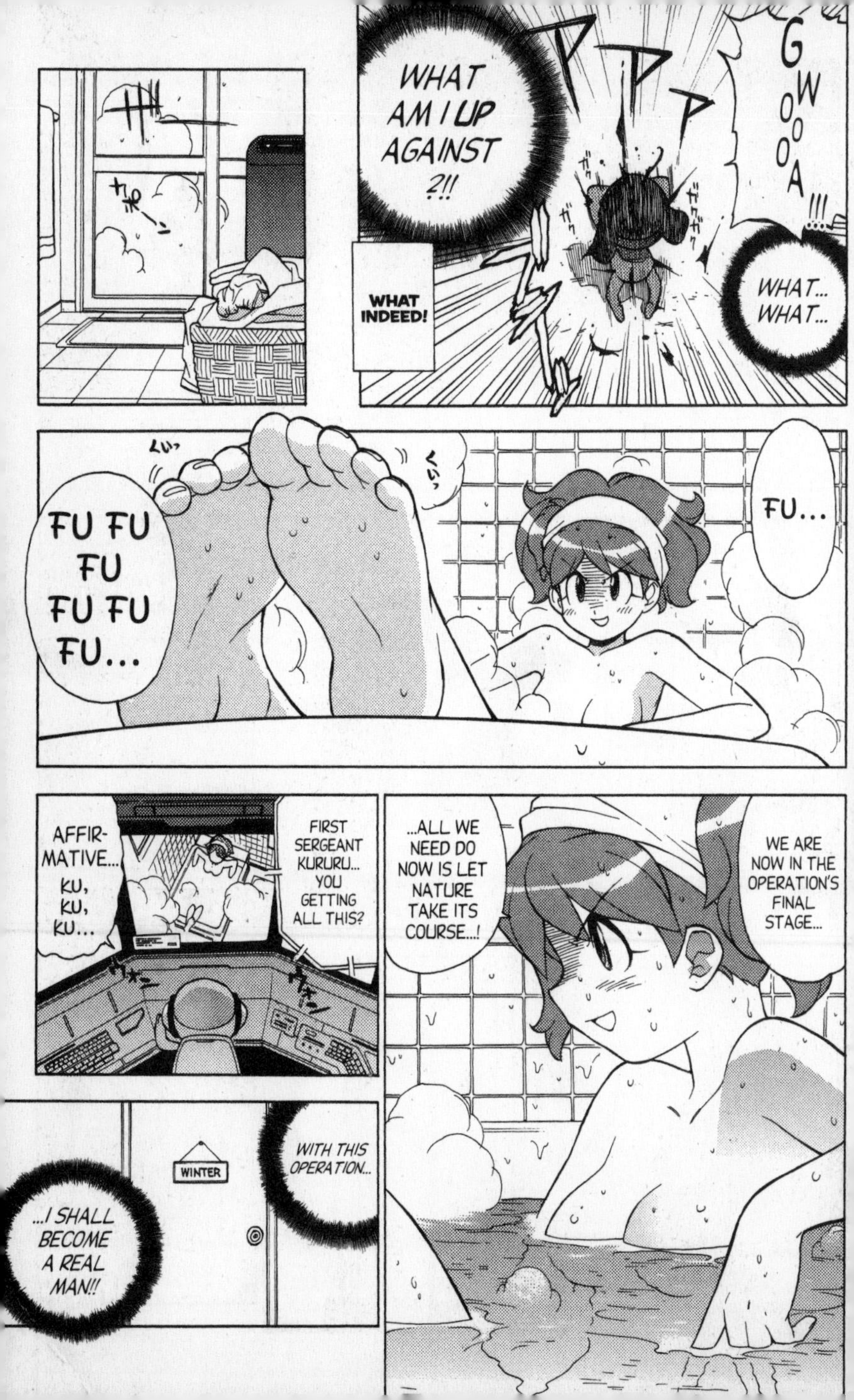
GWOOOA!!!
WHAT... WHAT...
WHAT AM I UP AGAINST ?!!
WHAT INDEED!
FU...
FU FU FU FU FU FU FU...
WE ARE NOW IN THE OPERATION'S FINAL STAGE...
...ALL WE NEED DO NOW IS LET NATURE TAKE ITS COURSE...!
FIRST SERGEANT KURURU... YOU GETTING ALL THIS?
AFFIRMATIVE... KU, KU, KU...
WINTER
WITH THIS OPERATION...
...I SHALL BECOME A REAL MAN!!

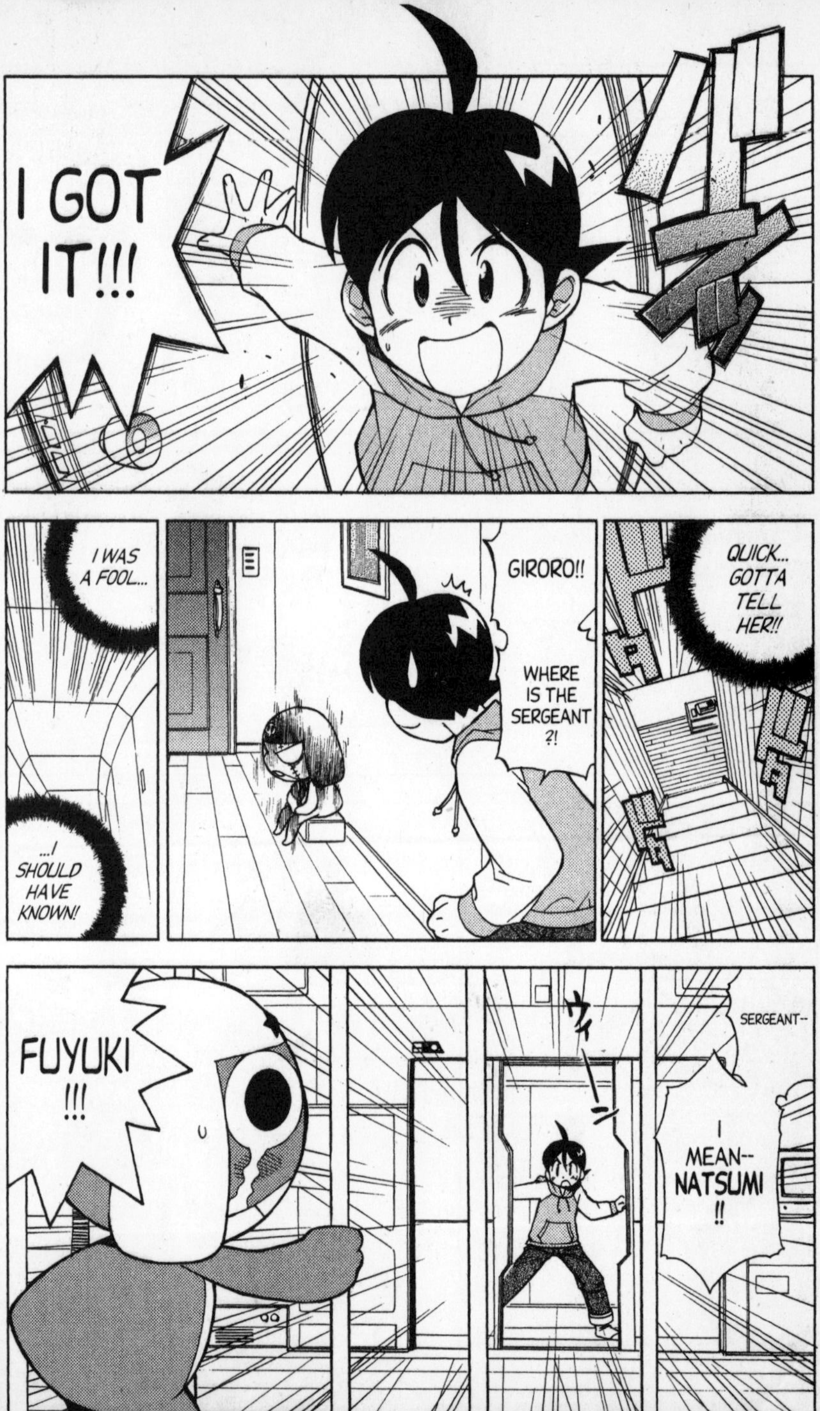
I GOT IT!!!
QUICK... GOTTA TELL HER!!
GIRORO!!
WHERE IS THE SERGEANT?!
I WAS A FOOL...
...I SHOULD HAVE KNOWN!
SERGEANT--
I MEAN--NATSUMI!!
FUYUKI!!!

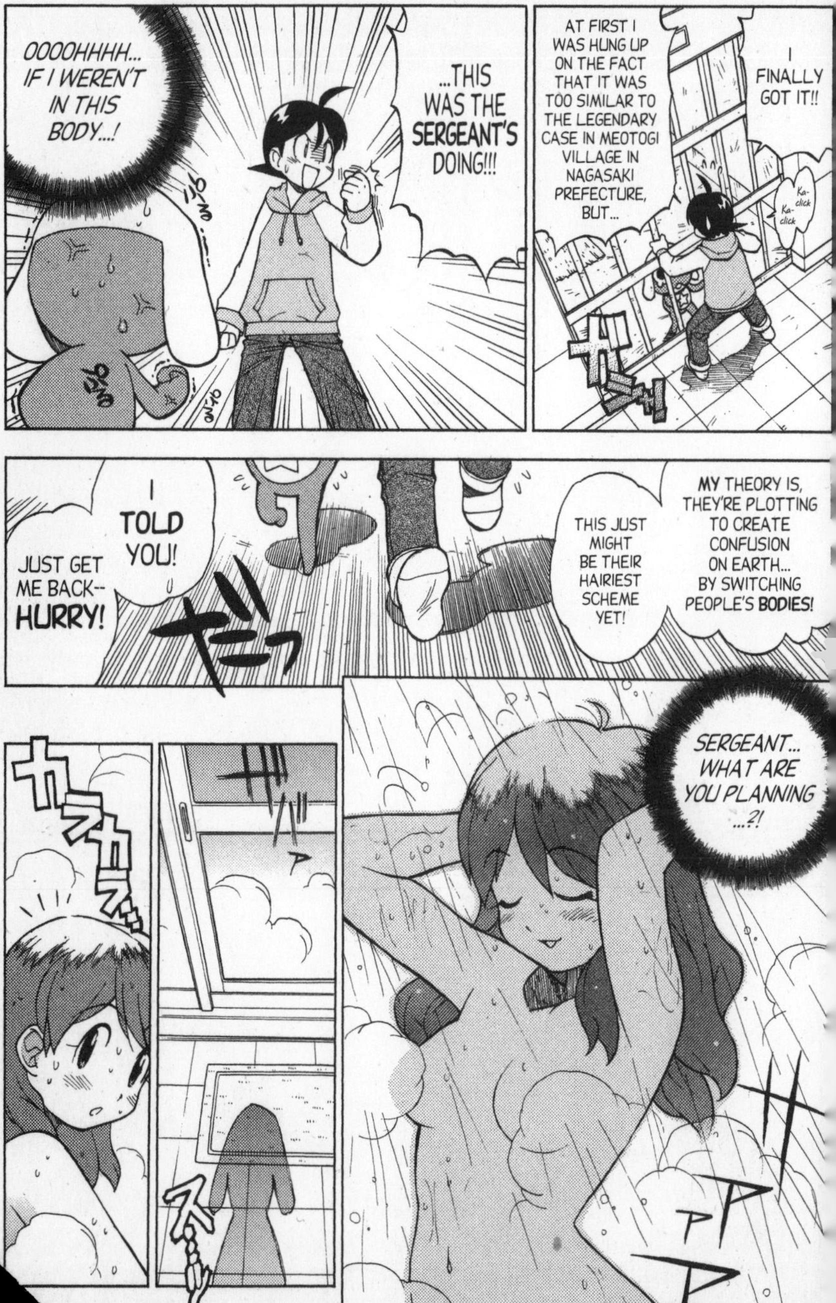
I FINALLY GOT IT!!
AT FIRST I WAS HUNG UP ON THE FACT THAT IT WAS TOO SIMILAR TO THE LEGENDARY CASE IN MEOTOGI VILLAGE IN NAGASAKI PREFECTURE, BUT...
Ka-click
Ka-click
...THIS WAS THE SERGEANT'S DOING!!!
OOOOHHHH... IF I WEREN'T IN THIS BODY...!
MY THEORY IS, THEY'RE PLOTTING TO CREATE CONFUSION ON EARTH... BY SWITCHING PEOPLE'S BODIES!
THIS JUST MIGHT BE THEIR HAIRIEST SCHEME YET!
I TOLD YOU!
JUST GET ME BACK-- HURRY!
SERGEANT... WHAT ARE YOU PLANNING ...?!

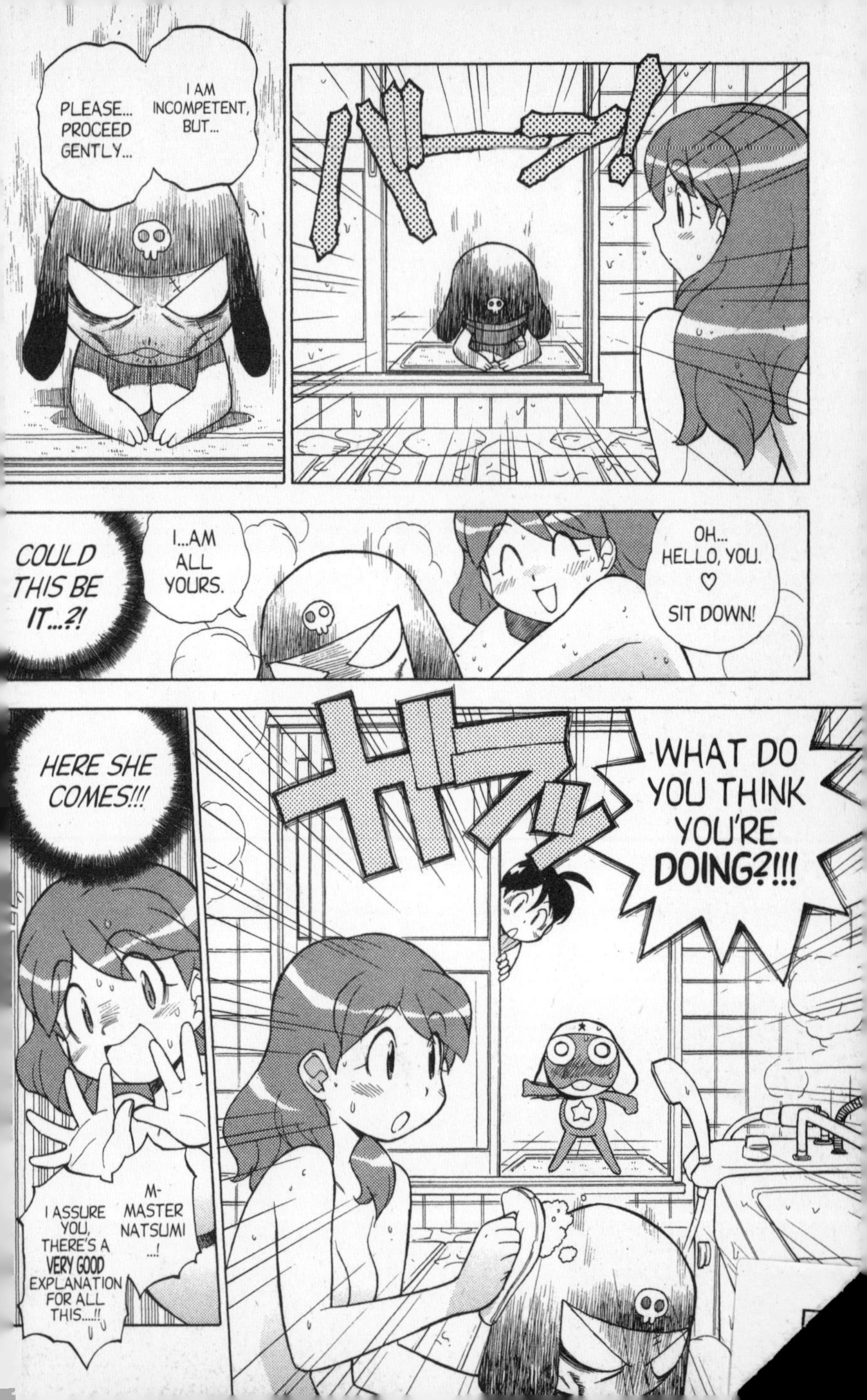

パーッ!
I AM INCOMPETENT, BUT...
PLEASE... PROCEED GENTLY...
OH... HELLO, YOU. ♡ SIT DOWN!
I...AM ALL YOURS.
COULD THIS BE IT...?!
ガラッ
WHAT DO YOU THINK YOU'RE DOING?!!!
HERE SHE COMES!!!
M-MASTER NATSUMI...!
I ASSURE YOU, THERE'S A VERY GOOD EXPLANATION FOR ALL THIS....!!

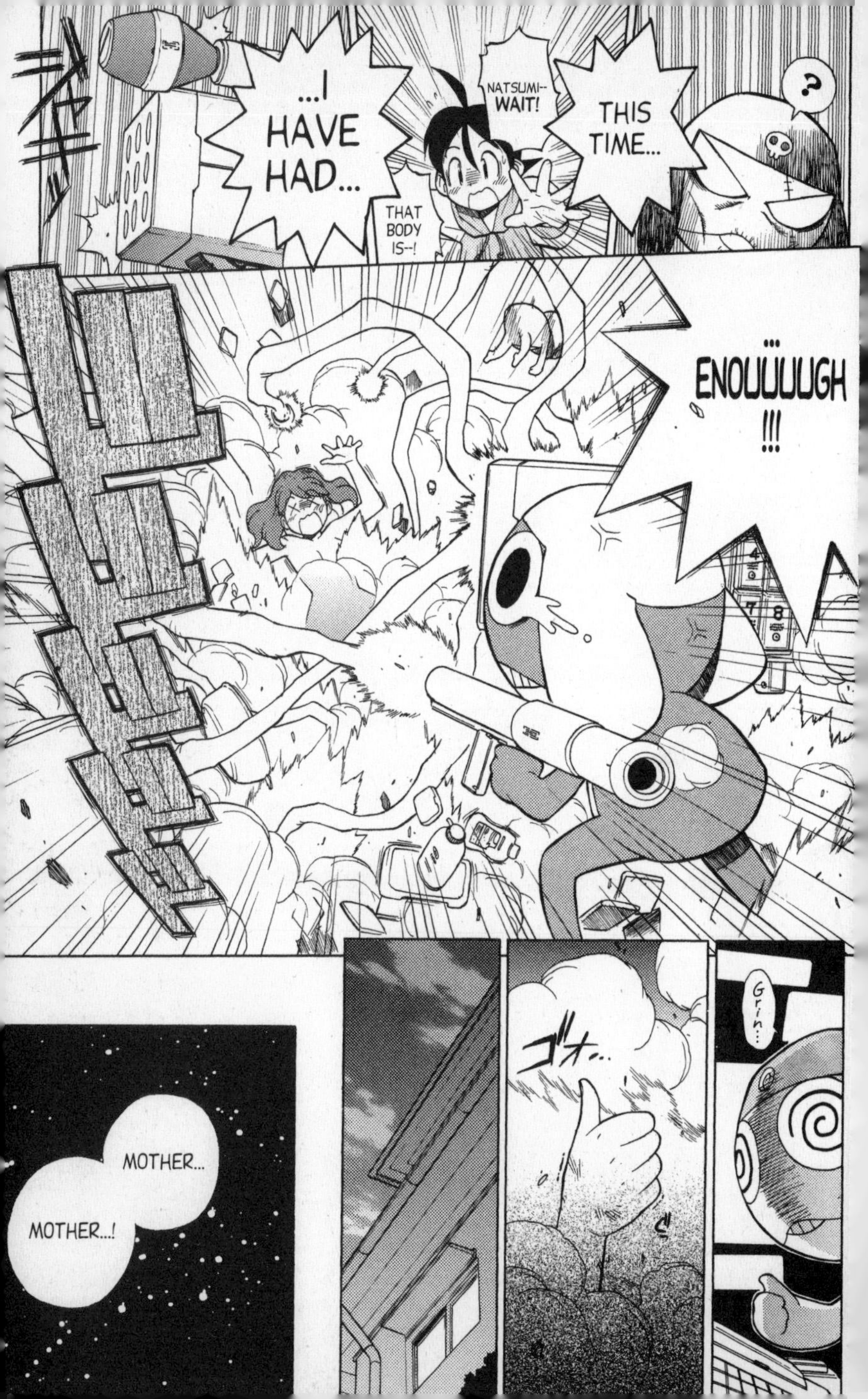

?
THIS TIME...
NATSUMI-- WAIT!
THAT BODY IS--!
...I HAVE HAD...
...ENOUUUUGH !!!
Grin...
MOTHER...
MOTHER...!

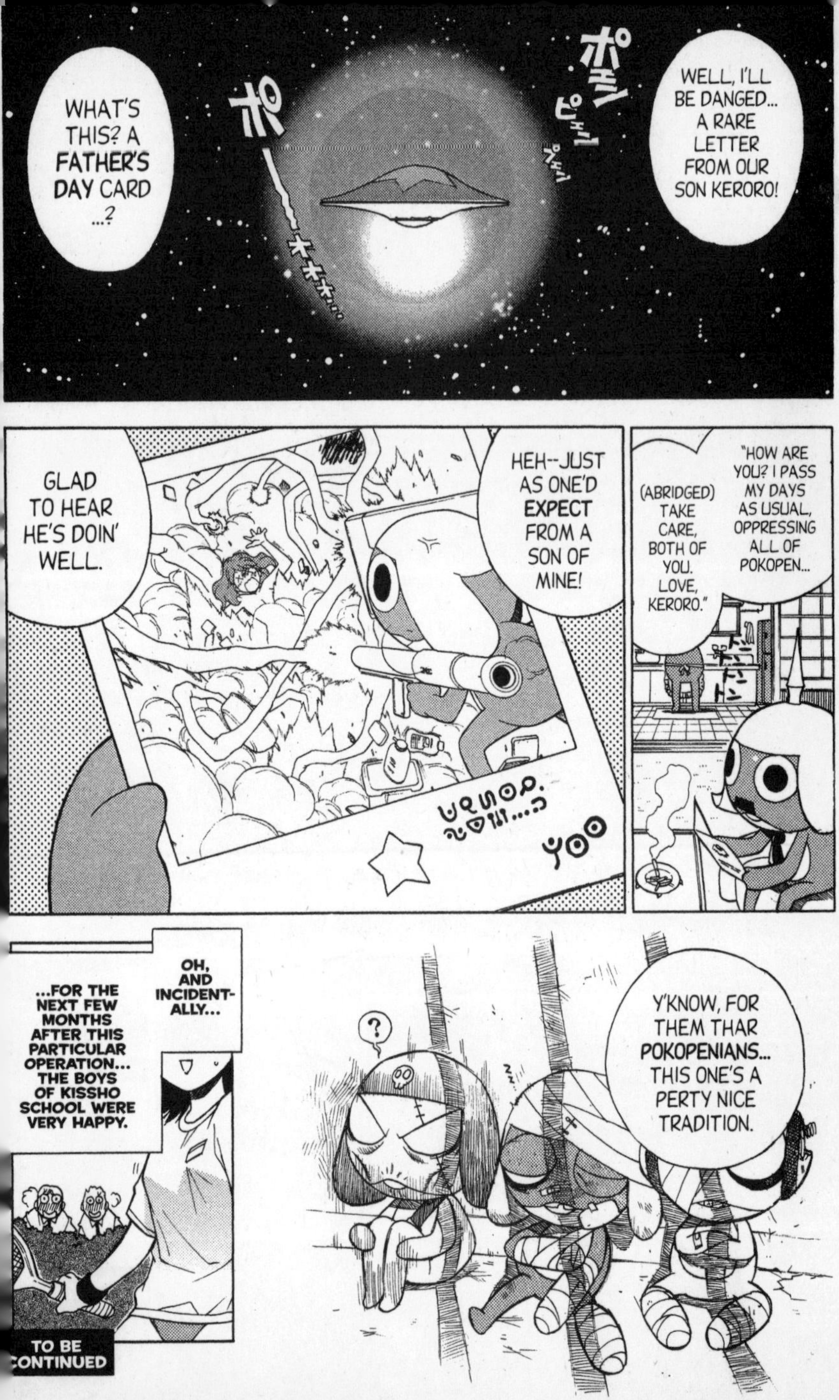

WELL, I'LL BE DANGED... A RARE LETTER FROM OUR SON KERORO!
WHAT'S THIS? A FATHER'S DAY CARD ...?
"HOW ARE YOU? I PASS MY DAYS AS USUAL, OPPRESSING ALL OF POKOPEN...
(ABRIDGED) TAKE CARE, BOTH OF YOU. LOVE, KERORO."
HEH--JUST AS ONE'D EXPECT FROM A SON OF MINE!
GLAD TO HEAR HE'S DOIN' WELL.
Y'KNOW, FOR THEM THAR POKOPENIANS... THIS ONE'S A PERTY NICE TRADITION.
?
OH, AND INCIDENT-ALLY...
...FOR THE NEXT FEW MONTHS AFTER THIS PARTICULAR OPERATION... THE BOYS OF KISSHO SCHOOL WERE VERY HAPPY.
TO BE CONTINUED

# ENCOUNTER XXXVI

# INCOMING!
# KERORO PLATOON'S NUMBER ONE FAN

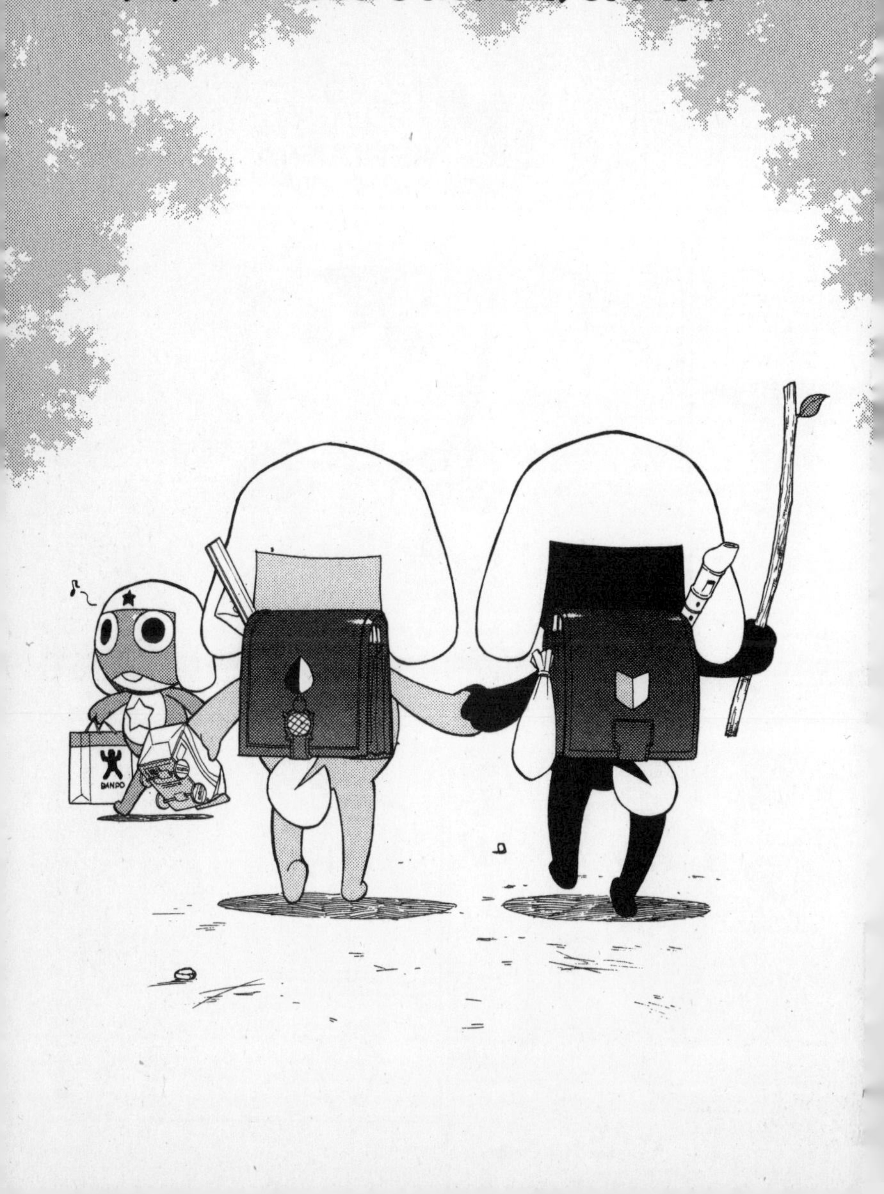

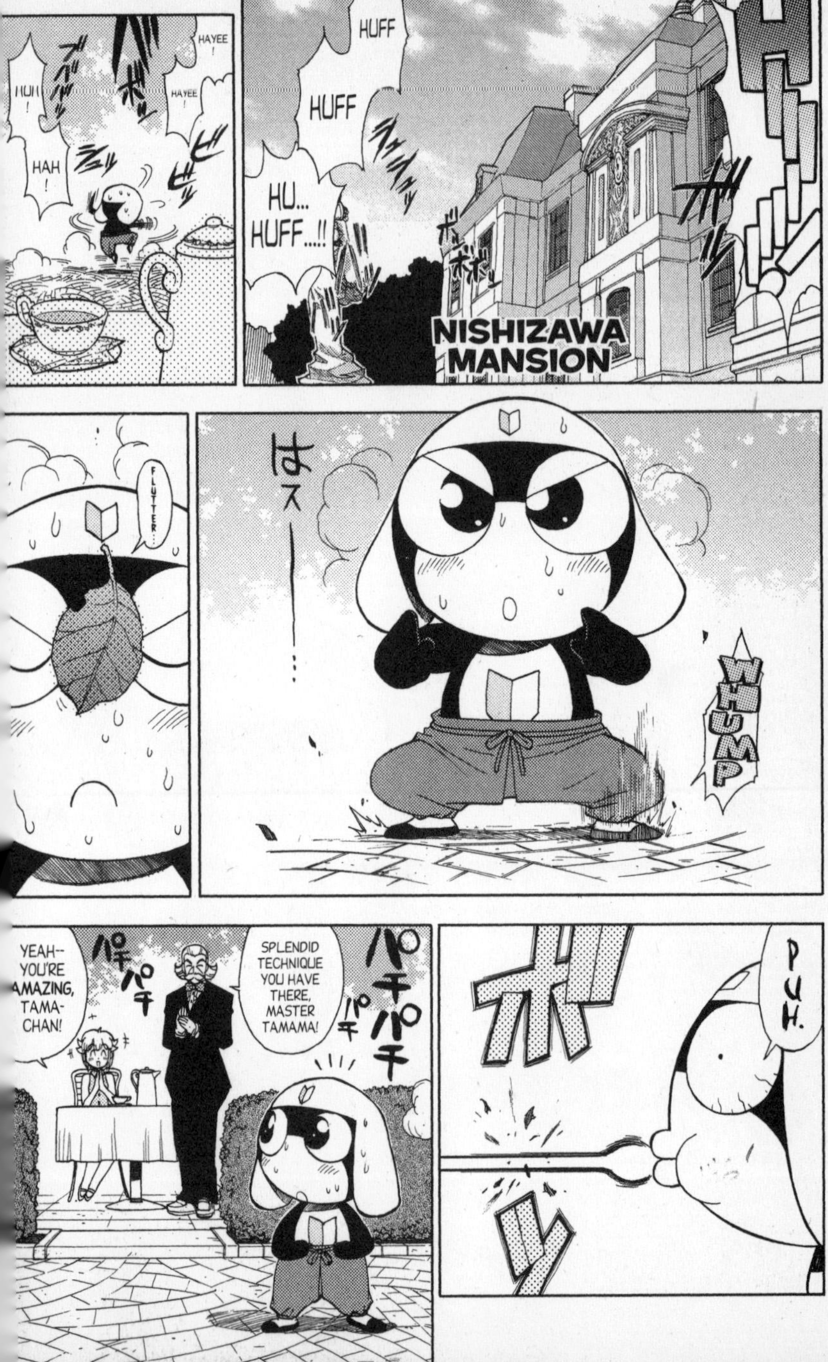
HUFF
HUFF
HU... HUFF...!!
NISHIZAWA MANSION
HAYEE!
HAYEE
HUH!
HAH!
はスー…
WHUMP
FLUTTER...
PUH.
パチパチ
SPLENDID TECHNIQUE YOU HAVE THERE, MASTER TAMAMA!
パチパチ
YEAH-- YOU'RE AMAZING, TAMA-CHAN!

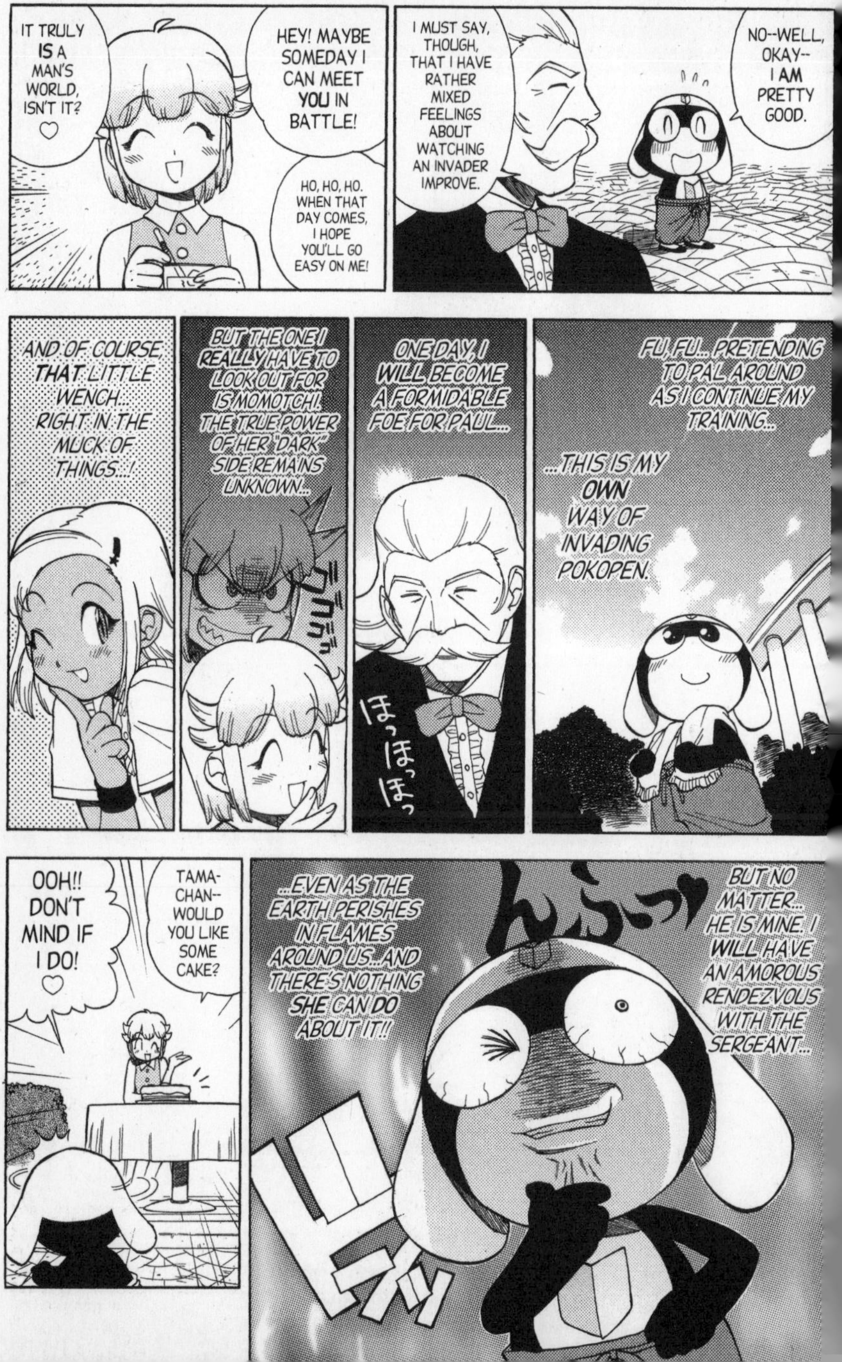
NO--WELL, OKAY-- I AM PRETTY GOOD.
I MUST SAY, THOUGH, THAT I HAVE RATHER MIXED FEELINGS ABOUT WATCHING AN INVADER IMPROVE.
HEY! MAYBE SOMEDAY I CAN MEET YOU IN BATTLE!
HO, HO, HO. WHEN THAT DAY COMES, I HOPE YOU'LL GO EASY ON ME!
IT TRULY IS A MAN'S WORLD, ISN'T IT? ♡
FU, FU... PRETENDING TO PAL AROUND AS I CONTINUE MY TRAINING...
...THIS IS MY OWN WAY OF INVADING POKOPEN.
ONE DAY, I WILL BECOME A FORMIDABLE FOE FOR PAUL...
ほっほっほっ
BUT THE ONE I REALLY HAVE TO LOOK OUT FOR IS MOMOTCHI. THE TRUE POWER OF HER "DARK" SIDE REMAINS UNKNOWN...
ゴゴゴ
AND OF COURSE, THAT LITTLE WENCH... RIGHT IN THE MUCK OF THINGS...!
BUT NO MATTER... HE IS MINE. I WILL HAVE AN AMOROUS RENDEZVOUS WITH THE SERGEANT...
んふっ♥
...EVEN AS THE EARTH PERISHES IN FLAMES AROUND US...AND THERE'S NOTHING SHE CAN DO ABOUT IT!!
TAMA-CHAN-- WOULD YOU LIKE SOME CAKE?
OOH!! DON'T MIND IF I DO! ♡

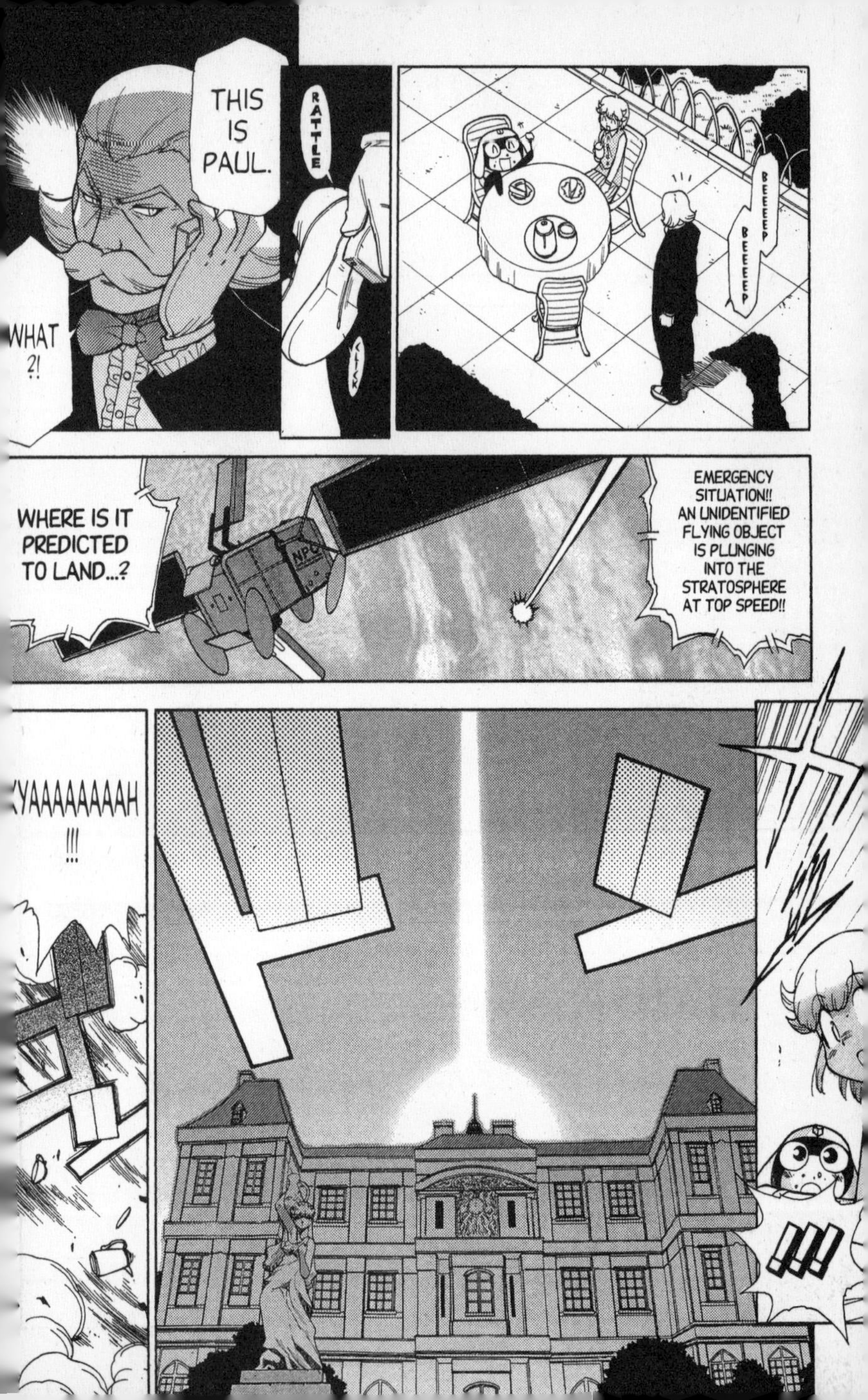
BEEEEP
BEEEEP
RATTLE
CLICK
THIS IS PAUL.
WHAT ?!
EMERGENCY SITUATION!! AN UNIDENTIFIED FLYING OBJECT IS PLUNGING INTO THE STRATOSPHERE AT TOP SPEED!!
WHERE IS IT PREDICTED TO LAND...?
!!!
YAAAAAAAAH !!!

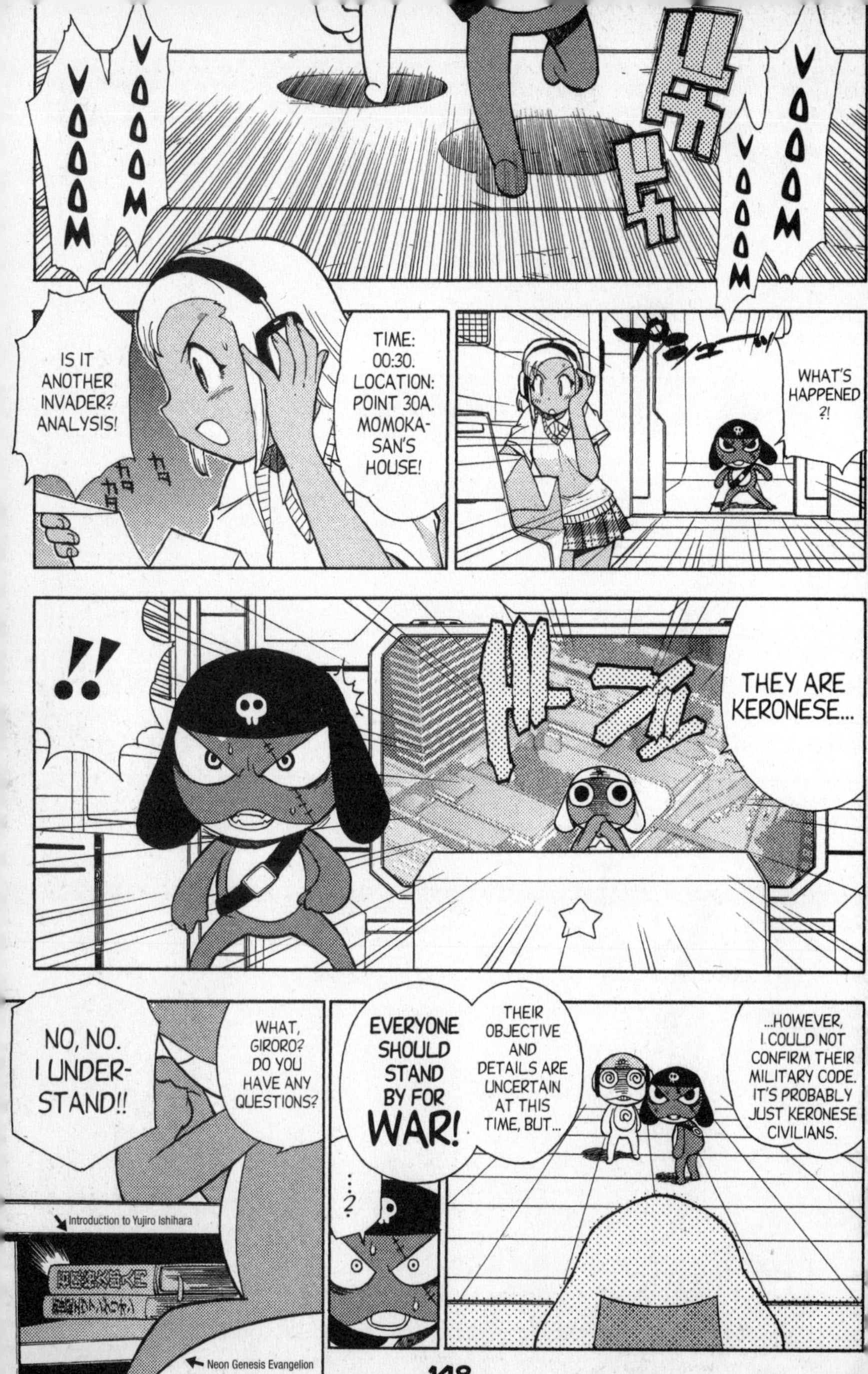
VOOOM
VOOOM
VOOOM
VOOOM
WHAT'S HAPPENED?!
TIME: 00:30. LOCATION: POINT 30A. MOMOKA-SAN'S HOUSE!
IS IT ANOTHER INVADER? ANALYSIS!
THEY ARE KERONESE...
!!
...HOWEVER, I COULD NOT CONFIRM THEIR MILITARY CODE. IT'S PROBABLY JUST KERONESE CIVILIANS.
THEIR OBJECTIVE AND DETAILS ARE UNCERTAIN AT THIS TIME, BUT...
EVERYONE SHOULD STAND BY FOR WAR!
...?
WHAT, GIRORO? DO YOU HAVE ANY QUESTIONS?
NO, NO. I UNDERSTAND!!
Introduction to Yujiro Ishihara
Neon Genesis Evangelion

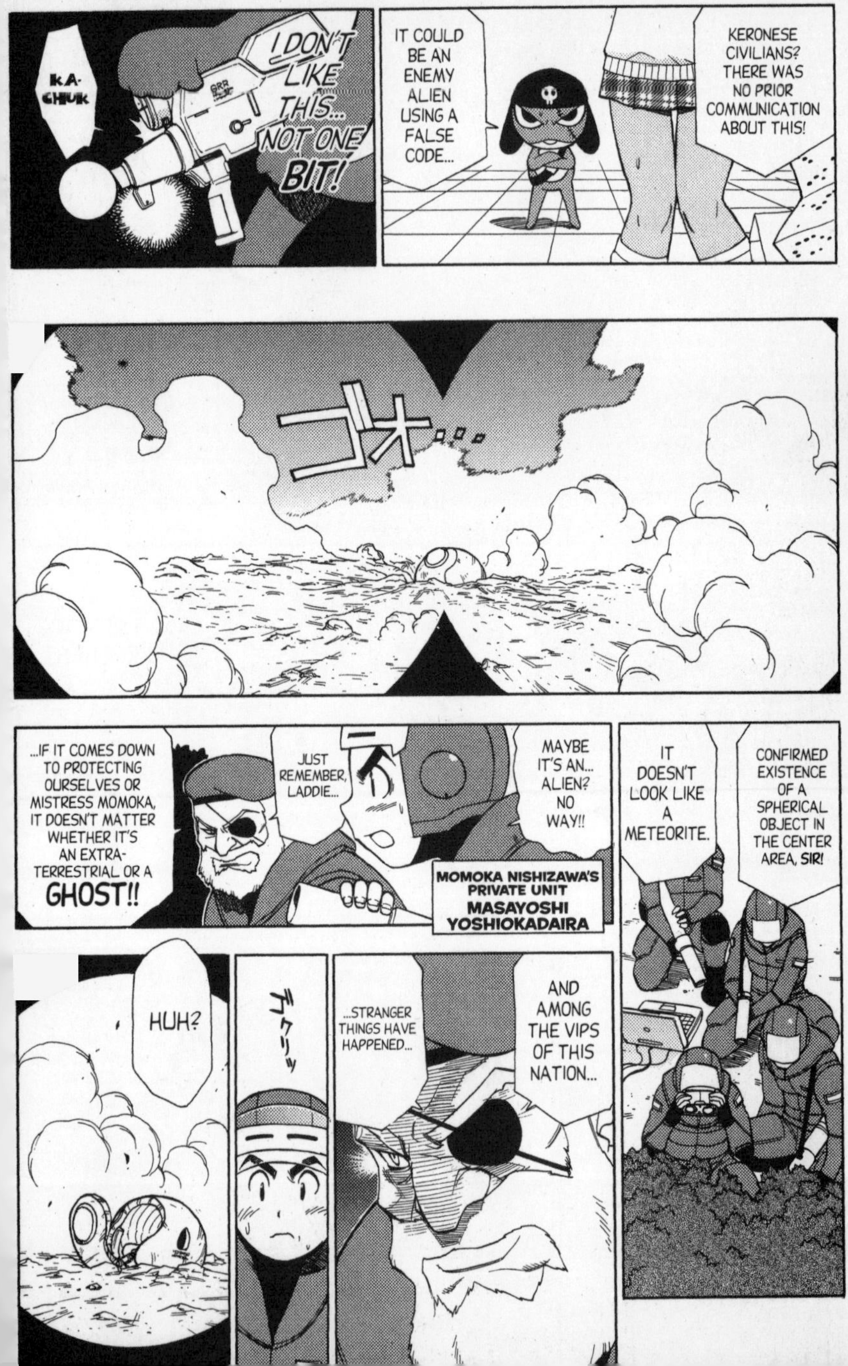
KERONESE CIVILIANS? THERE WAS NO PRIOR COMMUNICATION ABOUT THIS!
IT COULD BE AN ENEMY ALIEN USING A FALSE CODE...
I DON'T LIKE THIS... NOT ONE BIT!
KA-CHUK
ゴオ...
CONFIRMED EXISTENCE OF A SPHERICAL OBJECT IN THE CENTER AREA, SIR!
IT DOESN'T LOOK LIKE A METEORITE.
MAYBE IT'S AN... ALIEN? NO WAY!!
JUST REMEMBER, LADDIE...
...IF IT COMES DOWN TO PROTECTING OURSELVES OR MISTRESS MOMOKA, IT DOESN'T MATTER WHETHER IT'S AN EXTRA-TERRESTRIAL OR A GHOST!!
MOMOKA NISHIZAWA'S PRIVATE UNIT MASAYOSHI YOSHIOKADAIRA
AND AMONG THE VIPS OF THIS NATION...
...STRANGER THINGS HAVE HAPPENED...
ギクリッ
HUH?

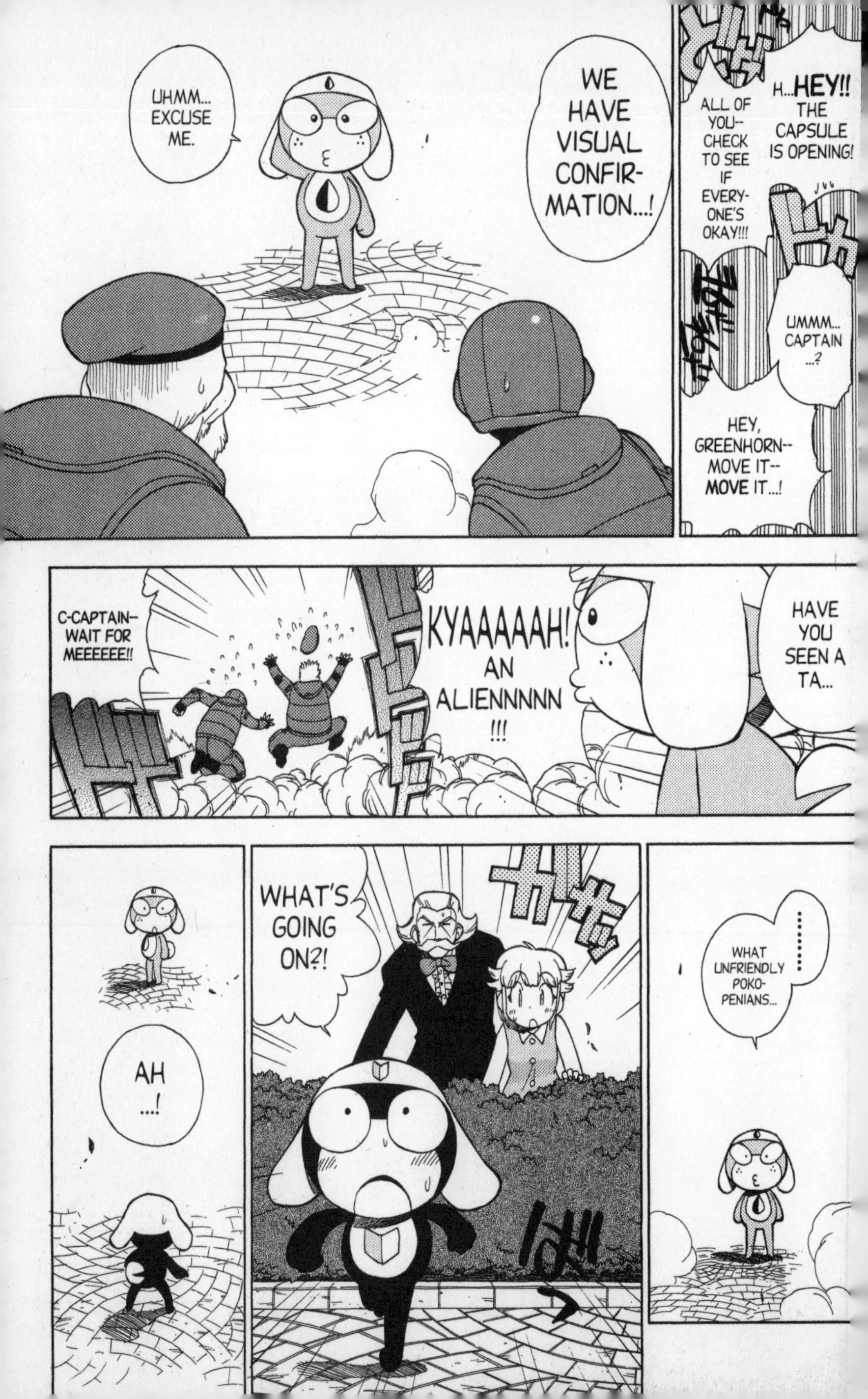
H...HEY!! THE CAPSULE IS OPENING!
ALL OF YOU-- CHECK TO SEE IF EVERY-ONE'S OKAY!!!
UMMM... CAPTAIN ...?
HEY, GREENHORN-- MOVE IT-- MOVE IT...!
WE HAVE VISUAL CONFIR-MATION...!
UHMM... EXCUSE ME.
HAVE YOU SEEN A TA...
KYAAAAAH! AN ALIENNNNN !!!
C-CAPTAIN-- WAIT FOR MEEEEEE!!
......
WHAT UNFRIENDLY POKO-PENIANS...
WHAT'S GOING ON?!
AH ...!

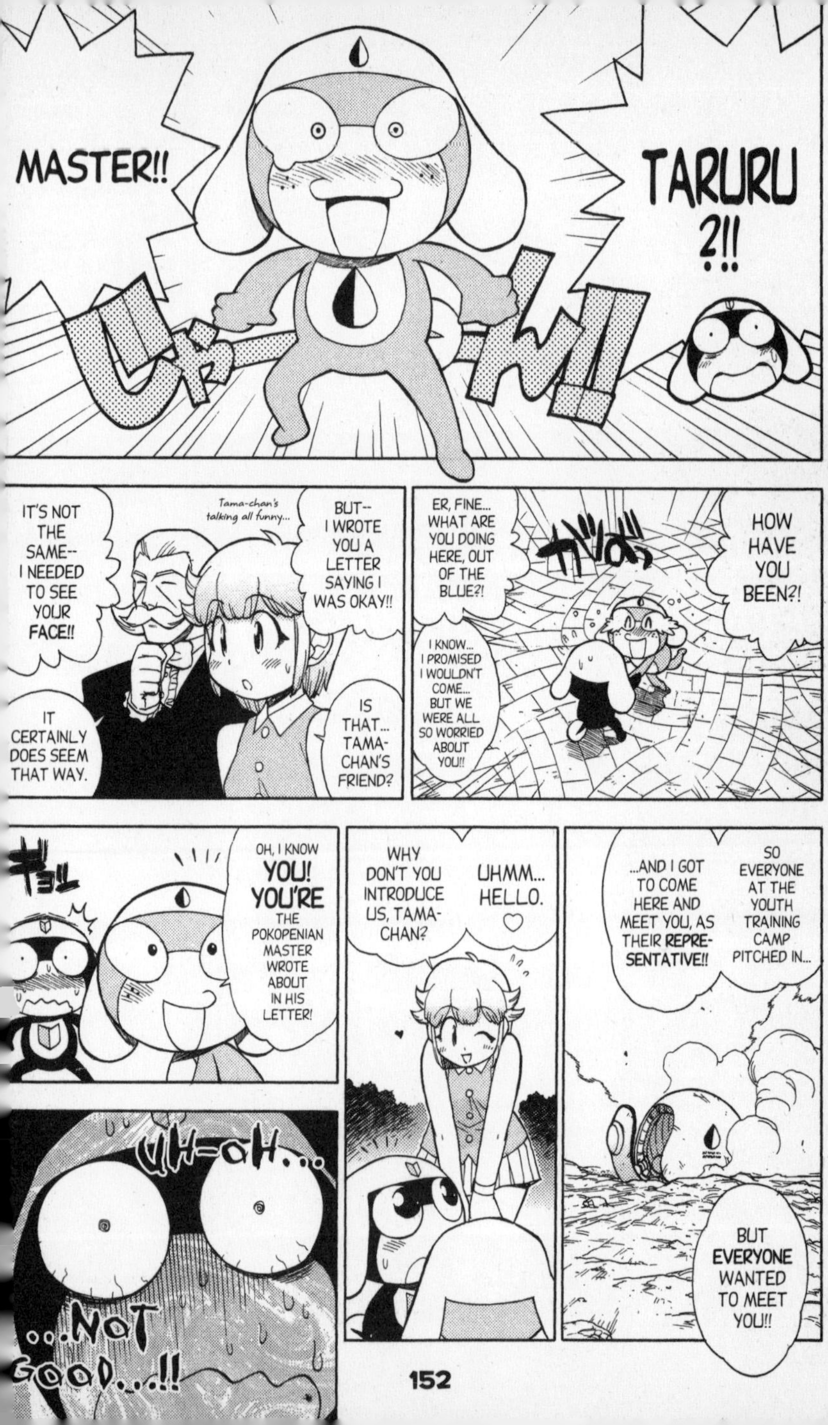
TARURU?!!
MASTER!!
HOW HAVE YOU BEEN?!
ER, FINE... WHAT ARE YOU DOING HERE, OUT OF THE BLUE?!
I KNOW... I PROMISED I WOULDN'T COME... BUT WE WERE ALL SO WORRIED ABOUT YOU!!
BUT-- I WROTE YOU A LETTER SAYING I WAS OKAY!!
Tama-chan's talking all funny...
IT'S NOT THE SAME-- I NEEDED TO SEE YOUR FACE!!
IS THAT... TAMA-CHAN'S FRIEND?
IT CERTAINLY DOES SEEM THAT WAY.
SO EVERYONE AT THE YOUTH TRAINING CAMP PITCHED IN...
...AND I GOT TO COME HERE AND MEET YOU, AS THEIR REPRESENTATIVE!!
BUT EVERYONE WANTED TO MEET YOU!!
UHMM... HELLO. ♡
WHY DON'T YOU INTRODUCE US, TAMA-CHAN?
OH, I KNOW YOU! YOU'RE THE POKOPENIAN MASTER WROTE ABOUT IN HIS LETTER!
UH-OH...
...NOT GOOD...!!

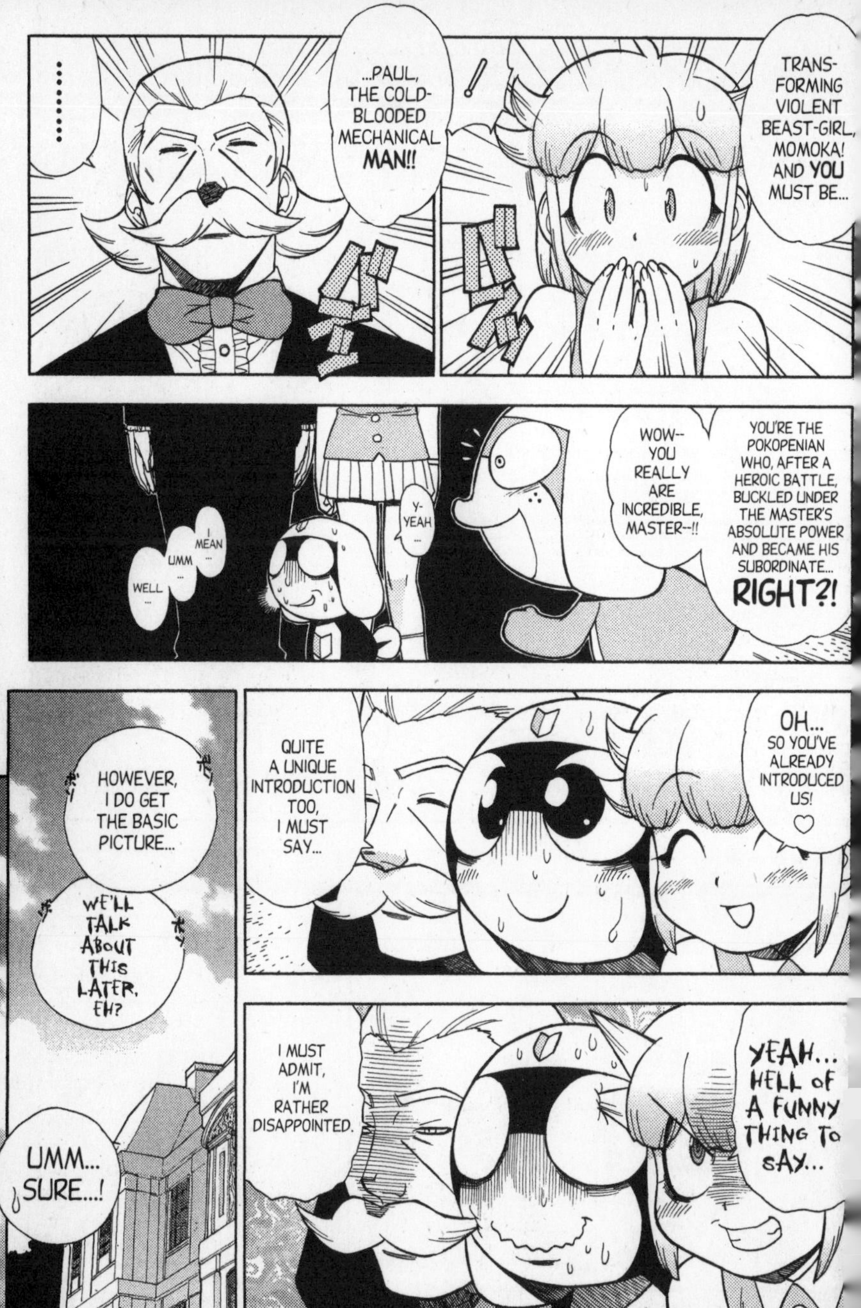
TRANS-FORMING VIOLENT BEAST-GIRL, MOMOKA! AND YOU MUST BE...
...PAUL, THE COLD-BLOODED MECHANICAL MAN!!
!
......
YOU'RE THE POKOPENIAN WHO, AFTER A HEROIC BATTLE, BUCKLED UNDER THE MASTER'S ABSOLUTE POWER AND BECAME HIS SUBORDINATE... RIGHT?!
WOW-- YOU REALLY ARE INCREDIBLE, MASTER--!!
Y-YEAH...
I MEAN...
UMM...
WELL...
OH... SO YOU'VE ALREADY INTRODUCED US! ♡
QUITE A UNIQUE INTRODUCTION TOO, I MUST SAY...
YEAH... HELL OF A FUNNY THING TO SAY...
I MUST ADMIT, I'M RATHER DISAPPOINTED.
HOWEVER, I DO GET THE BASIC PICTURE...
WE'LL TALK ABOUT THIS LATER, EH?
UMM... SURE...!

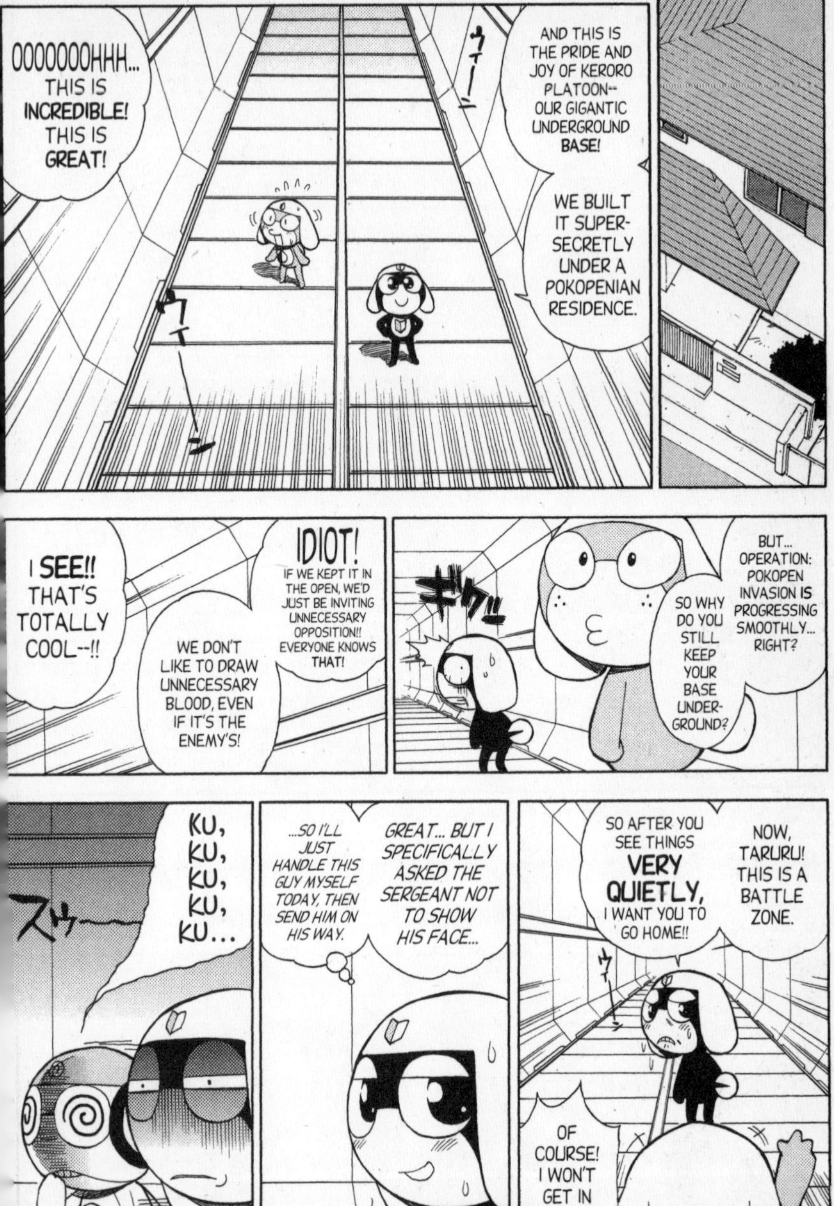
AND THIS IS THE PRIDE AND JOY OF KERORO PLATOON-- OUR GIGANTIC UNDERGROUND BASE!
WE BUILT IT SUPER-SECRETLY UNDER A POKOPENIAN RESIDENCE.
OOOOOOOHHH... THIS IS INCREDIBLE! THIS IS GREAT!
BUT... OPERATION: POKOPEN INVASION IS PROGRESSING SMOOTHLY... RIGHT?
SO WHY DO YOU STILL KEEP YOUR BASE UNDER-GROUND?
ギクッ!!
IDIOT! IF WE KEPT IT IN THE OPEN, WE'D JUST BE INVITING UNNECESSARY OPPOSITION!! EVERYONE KNOWS THAT!
WE DON'T LIKE TO DRAW UNNECESSARY BLOOD, EVEN IF IT'S THE ENEMY'S!
I SEE!! THAT'S TOTALLY COOL--!!
NOW, TARURU! THIS IS A BATTLE ZONE.
SO AFTER YOU SEE THINGS VERY QUIETLY, I WANT YOU TO GO HOME!!
OF COURSE! I WON'T GET IN MY MASTER'S WAY!
GREAT... BUT I SPECIFICALLY ASKED THE SERGEANT NOT TO SHOW HIS FACE...
...SO I'LL JUST HANDLE THIS GUY MYSELF TODAY, THEN SEND HIM ON HIS WAY.
KU, KU, KU, KU, KU...

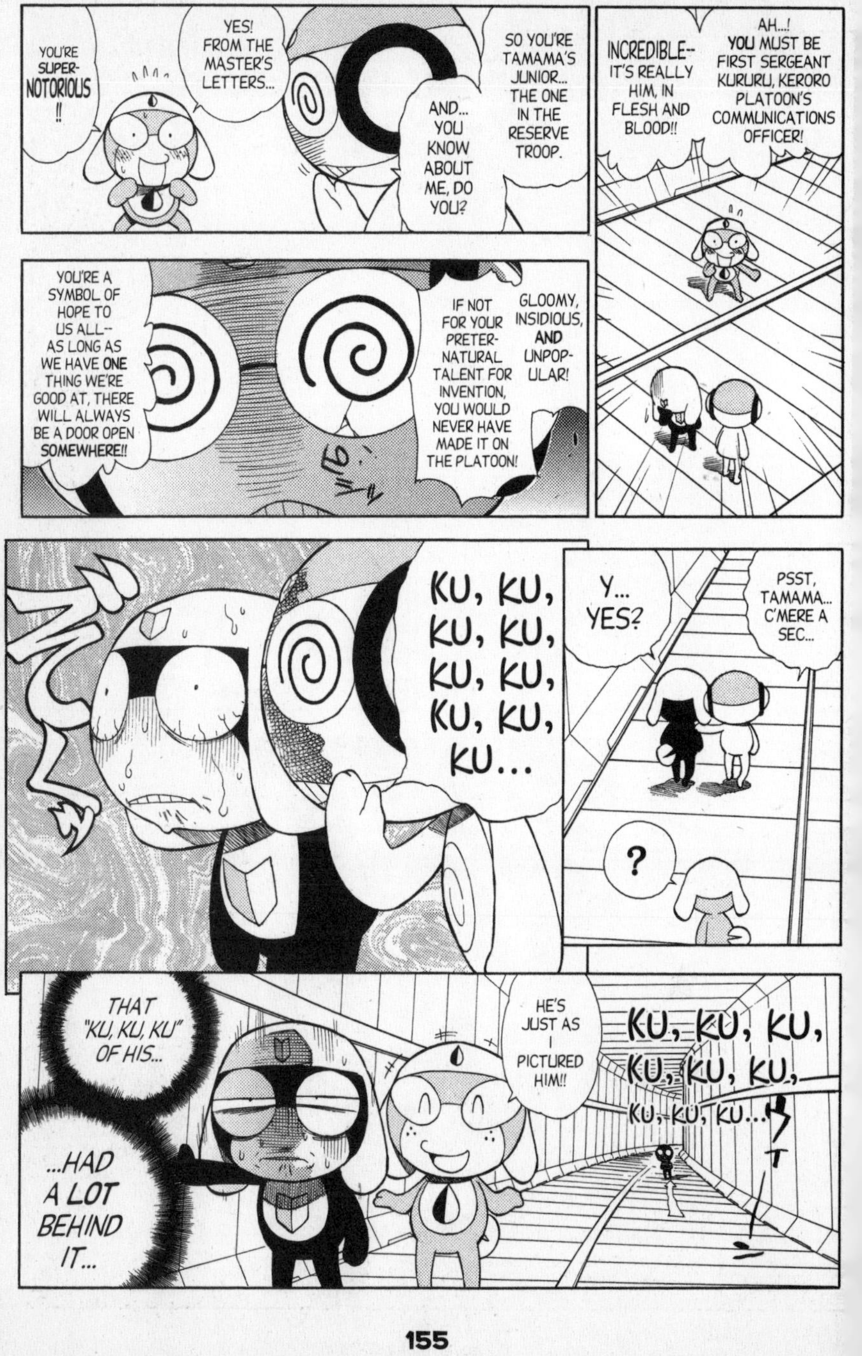

AH...! YOU MUST BE FIRST SERGEANT KURURU, KERORO PLATOON'S COMMUNICATIONS OFFICER!
INCREDIBLE-- IT'S REALLY HIM, IN FLESH AND BLOOD!!
SO YOU'RE TAMAMA'S JUNIOR... THE ONE IN THE RESERVE TROOP.
AND... YOU KNOW ABOUT ME, DO YOU?
YES! FROM THE MASTER'S LETTERS...
YOU'RE SUPER-NOTORIOUS!!
GLOOMY, INSIDIOUS, AND UNPOPULAR!
IF NOT FOR YOUR PRETER-NATURAL TALENT FOR INVENTION, YOU WOULD NEVER HAVE MADE IT ON THE PLATOON!
YOU'RE A SYMBOL OF HOPE TO US ALL-- AS LONG AS WE HAVE ONE THING WE'RE GOOD AT, THERE WILL ALWAYS BE A DOOR OPEN SOMEWHERE!!
PSST, TAMAMA... C'MERE A SEC...
Y... YES?
?
KU, KU, KU, KU, KU, KU, KU, KU, KU...
KU, KU, KU, KU, KU, KU, KU, KU, KU...
HE'S JUST AS I PICTURED HIM!!
THAT "KU, KU, KU" OF HIS...
...HAD A LOT BEHIND IT...

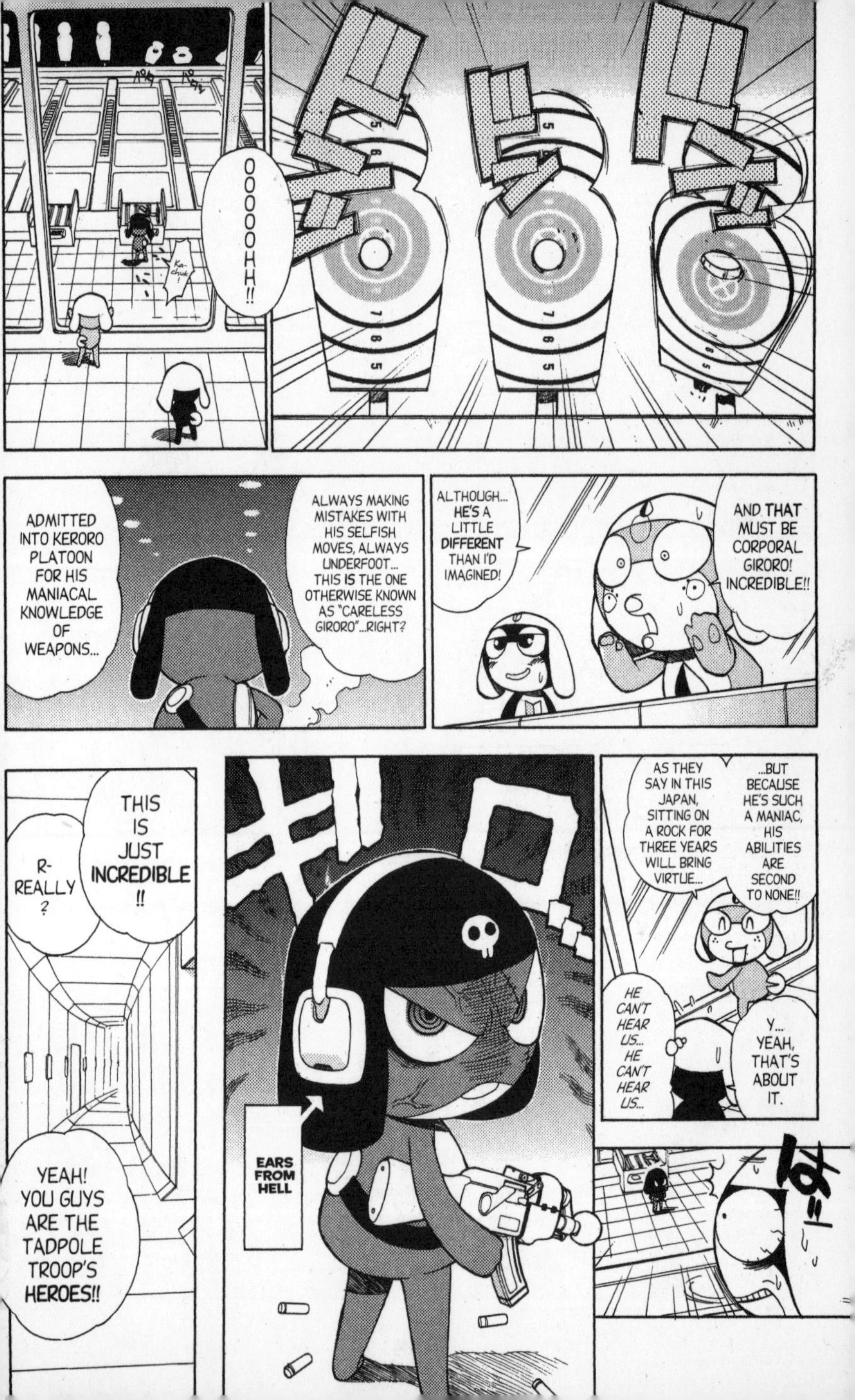
OOOOOOHH!!
Ka-chuk!
AND THAT MUST BE CORPORAL GIRORO! INCREDIBLE!!
ALTHOUGH... HE'S A LITTLE DIFFERENT THAN I'D IMAGINED!
ALWAYS MAKING MISTAKES WITH HIS SELFISH MOVES, ALWAYS UNDERFOOT... THIS IS THE ONE OTHERWISE KNOWN AS "CARELESS GIRORO"...RIGHT?
ADMITTED INTO KERORO PLATOON FOR HIS MANIACAL KNOWLEDGE OF WEAPONS...
AS THEY SAY IN THIS JAPAN, SITTING ON A ROCK FOR THREE YEARS WILL BRING VIRTUE...
...BUT BECAUSE HE'S SUCH A MANIAC, HIS ABILITIES ARE SECOND TO NONE!!
Y... YEAH, THAT'S ABOUT IT.
HE CAN'T HEAR US... HE CAN'T HEAR US...
は!!
EARS FROM HELL
THIS IS JUST INCREDIBLE!!
R-REALLY?
YEAH! YOU GUYS ARE THE TADPOLE TROOP'S HEROES!!

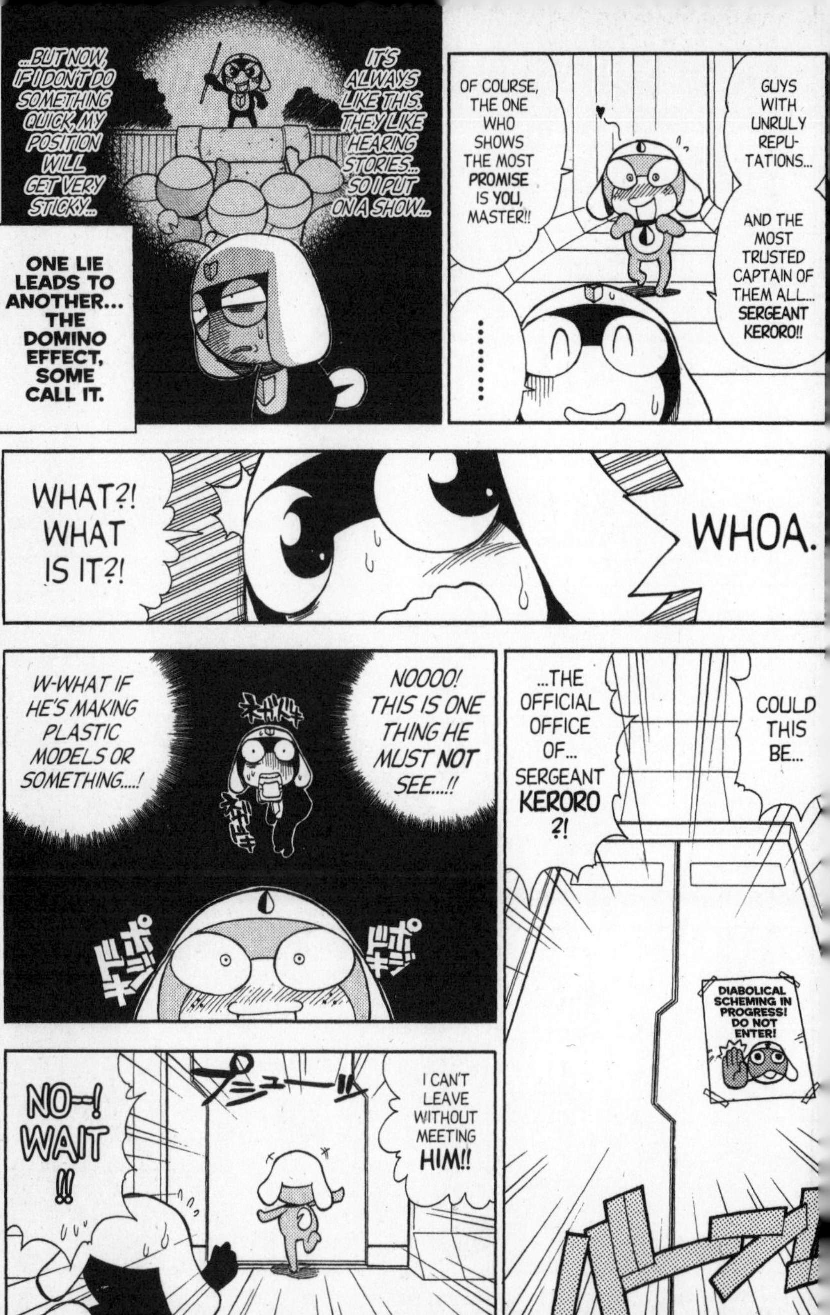
GUYS WITH UNRULY REPUTATIONS...
AND THE MOST TRUSTED CAPTAIN OF THEM ALL... SERGEANT KERORO!!
OF COURSE, THE ONE WHO SHOWS THE MOST PROMISE IS YOU, MASTER!!
.......
IT'S ALWAYS LIKE THIS. THEY LIKE HEARING STORIES... SO I PUT ON A SHOW...
...BUT NOW, IF I DON'T DO SOMETHING QUICK, MY POSITION WILL GET VERY STICKY...
ONE LIE LEADS TO ANOTHER... THE DOMINO EFFECT, SOME CALL IT.
WHOA.
WHAT?! WHAT IS IT?!
COULD THIS BE...
...THE OFFICIAL OFFICE OF... SERGEANT KERORO?!
DIABOLICAL SCHEMING IN PROGRESS! DO NOT ENTER!
NOOOO! THIS IS ONE THING HE MUST NOT SEE...!!
W-WHAT IF HE'S MAKING PLASTIC MODELS OR SOMETHING....!
I CAN'T LEAVE WITHOUT MEETING HIM!!
NO--! WAIT!!

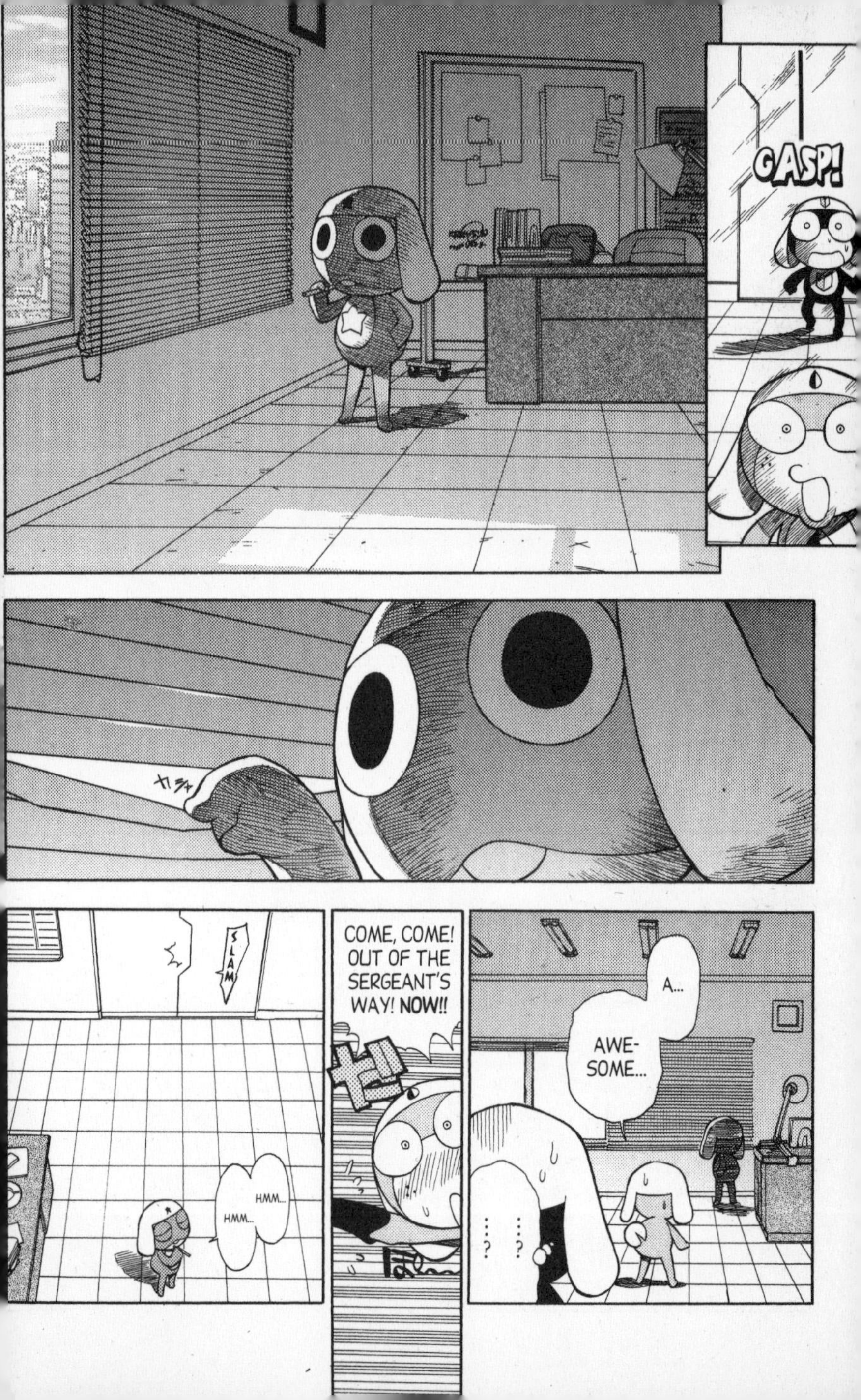
GASP!
A...
AWE-SOME...
...?
...?
COME, COME! OUT OF THE SERGEANT'S WAY! NOW!!
SLAM
HMM...
HMM...

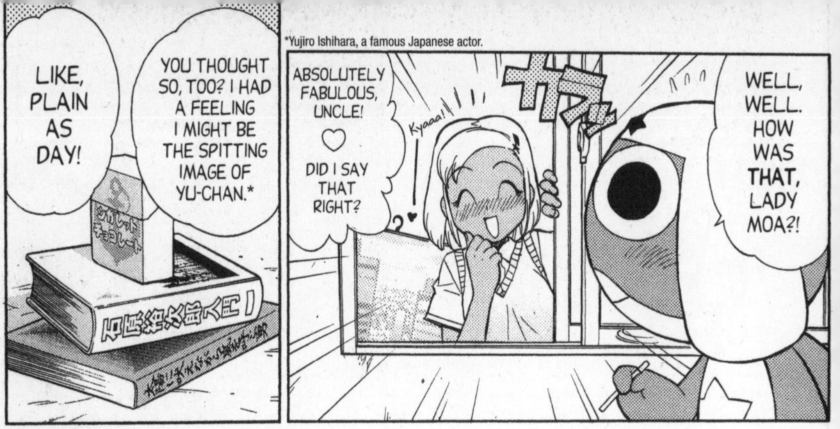
WELL, WELL. HOW WAS THAT, LADY MOA?!
ABSOLUTELY FABULOUS, UNCLE! ♥
DID I SAY THAT RIGHT?
Kyaaa!
YOU THOUGHT SO, TOO? I HAD A FEELING I MIGHT BE THE SPITTING IMAGE OF YU-CHAN.*
LIKE, PLAIN AS DAY!

*Yujiro Ishihara, a famous Japanese actor.

Chocolate Cigarettes
Introduction to Yujiro Ishihara
The Man who Barks at the Sun and Calls the Wind

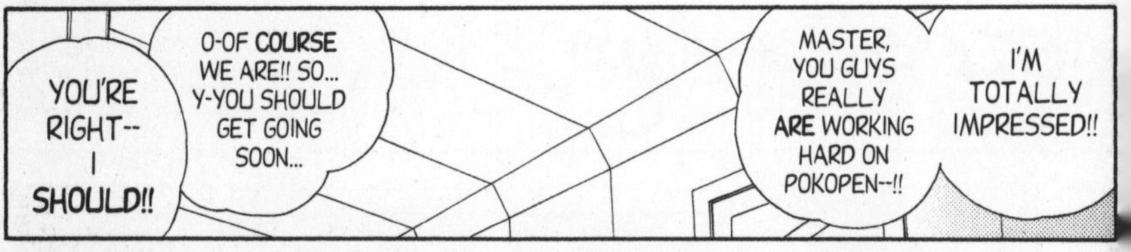
I'M TOTALLY IMPRESSED!!
MASTER, YOU GUYS REALLY ARE WORKING HARD ON POKOPEN--!!
O-OF COURSE WE ARE!! SO... Y-YOU SHOULD GET GOING SOON...
YOU'RE RIGHT-- I SHOULD!!

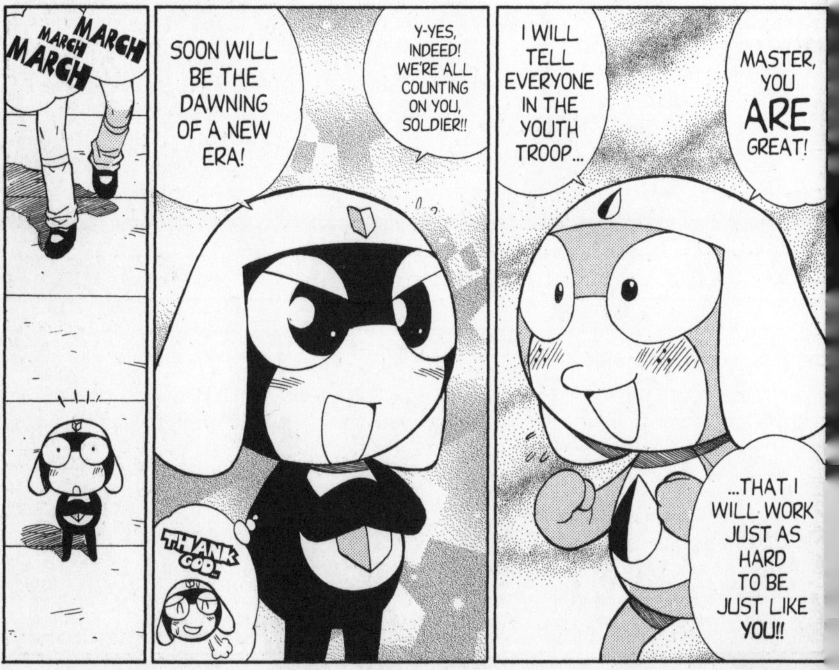
MASTER, YOU ARE GREAT!
I WILL TELL EVERYONE IN THE YOUTH TROOP...
...THAT I WILL WORK JUST AS HARD TO BE JUST LIKE YOU!!
Y-YES, INDEED! WE'RE ALL COUNTING ON YOU, SOLDIER!!
SOON WILL BE THE DAWNING OF A NEW ERA!
THANK GOD...
MARCH
MARCH
MARCH

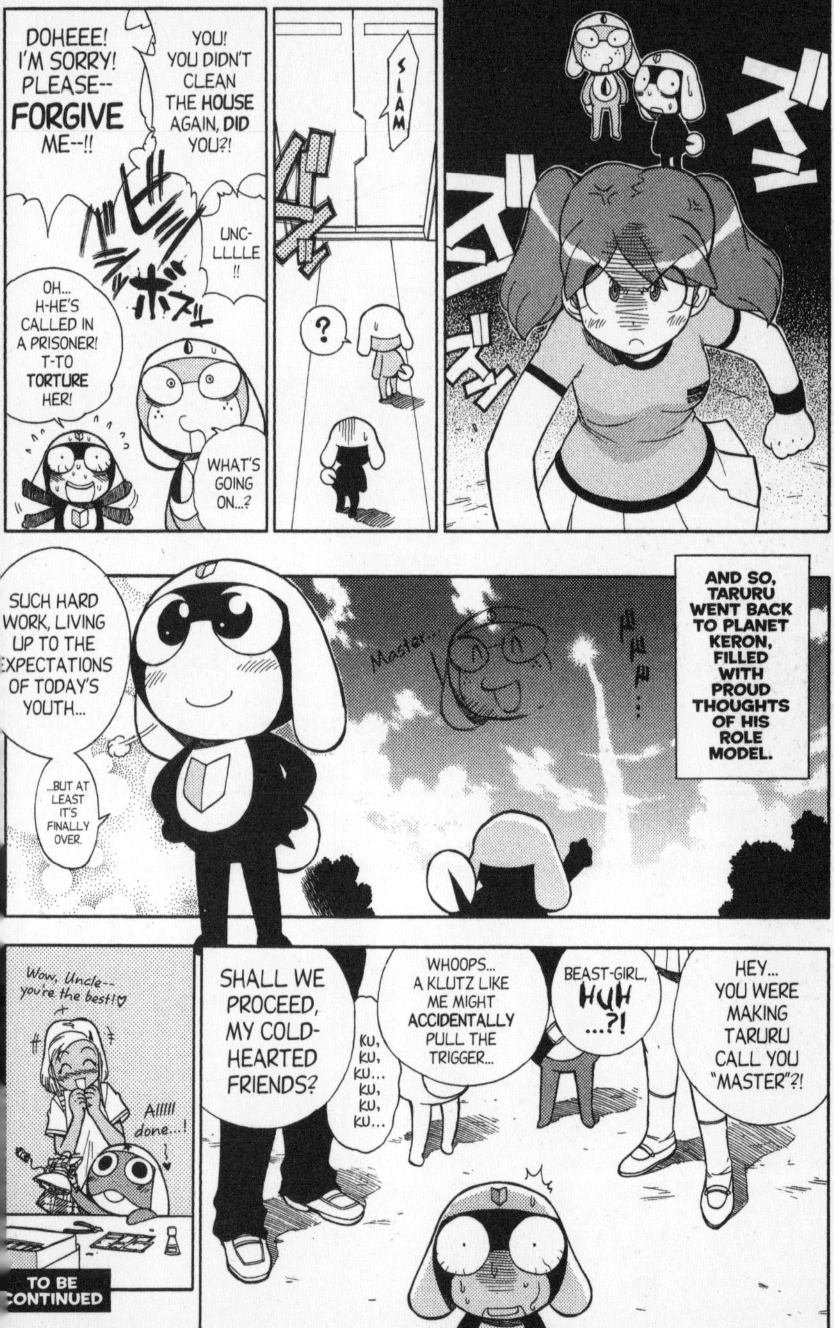
SLAM
?
YOU! YOU DIDN'T CLEAN THE HOUSE AGAIN, DID YOU?!
DOHEEE! I'M SORRY! PLEASE-- FORGIVE ME--!!
UNC- LLLLE !!
WHAT'S GOING ON...?
OH... H-HE'S CALLED IN A PRISONER! T-TO TORTURE HER!
AND SO, TARURU WENT BACK TO PLANET KERON, FILLED WITH PROUD THOUGHTS OF HIS ROLE MODEL.
Master...
SUCH HARD WORK, LIVING UP TO THE EXPECTATIONS OF TODAY'S YOUTH...
...BUT AT LEAST IT'S FINALLY OVER.
HEY... YOU WERE MAKING TARURU CALL YOU "MASTER"?!
BEAST-GIRL, HUH ...?!
WHOOPS... A KLUTZ LIKE ME MIGHT ACCIDENTALLY PULL THE TRIGGER...
KU, KU, KU... KU, KU, KU...
SHALL WE PROCEED, MY COLD-HEARTED FRIENDS?
Wow, Uncle-- you're the best!♡
Allll done...!
TO BE CONTINUED

## ENCOUNTER XXXVII

# A HINATA FAMILY REUNION

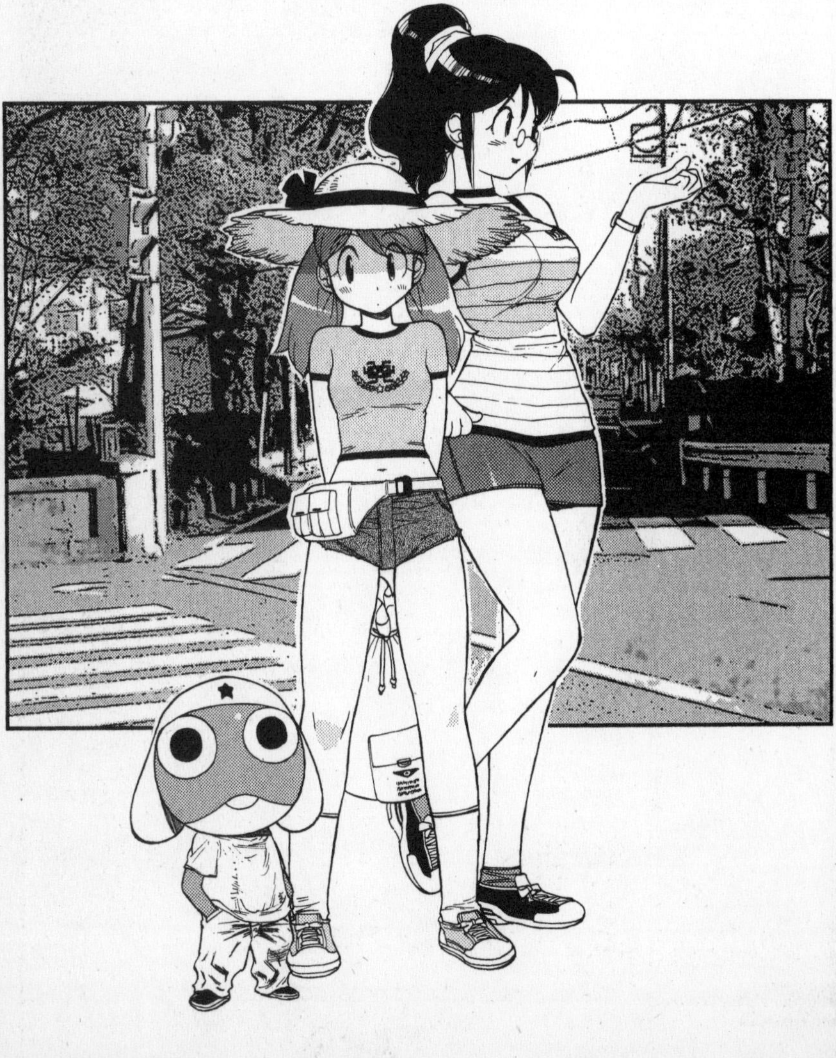

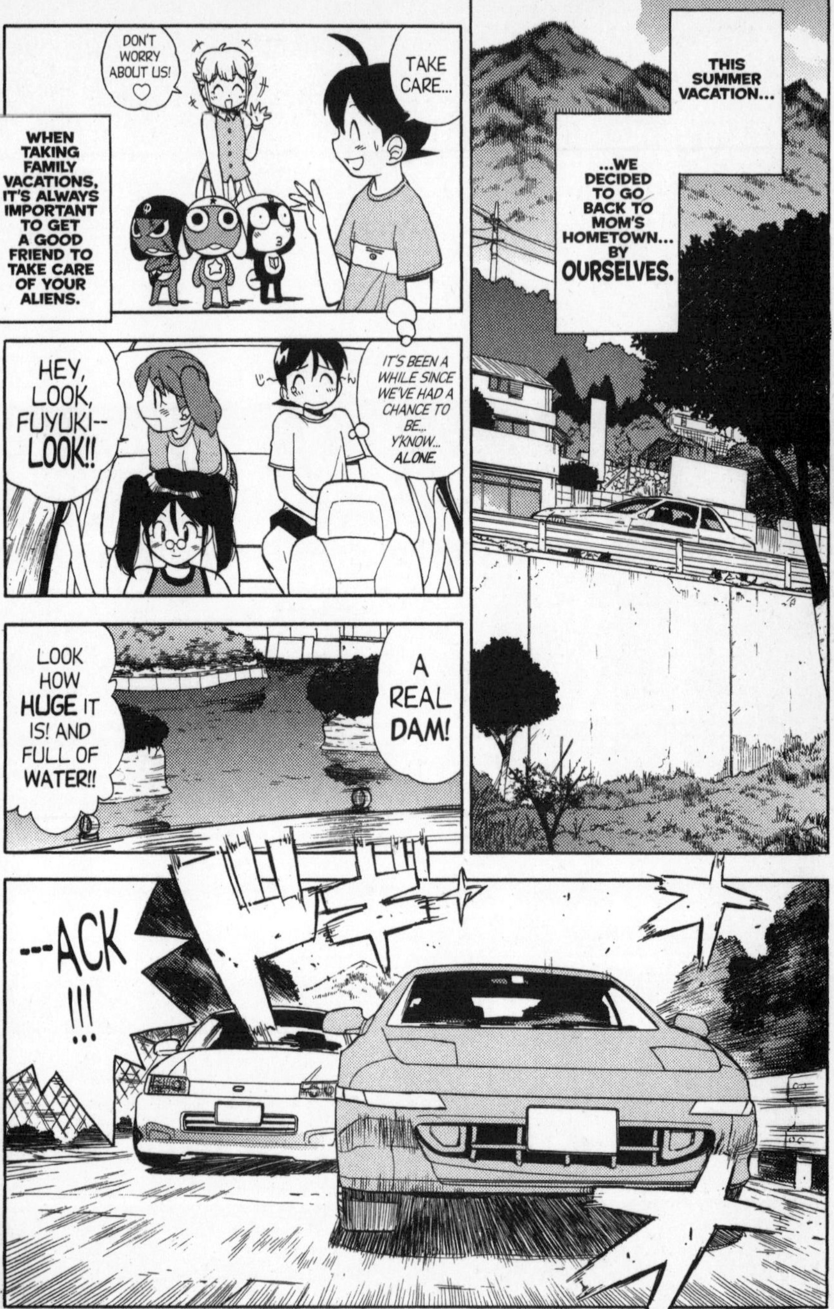
THIS SUMMER VACATION...
...WE DECIDED TO GO BACK TO MOM'S HOMETOWN... BY OURSELVES.
TAKE CARE...
DON'T WORRY ABOUT US! ♡
WHEN TAKING FAMILY VACATIONS, IT'S ALWAYS IMPORTANT TO GET A GOOD FRIEND TO TAKE CARE OF YOUR ALIENS.
IT'S BEEN A WHILE SINCE WE'VE HAD A CHANCE TO BE... Y'KNOW... ALONE.
HEY, LOOK, FUYUKI-- LOOK!!
A REAL DAM!
LOOK HOW HUGE IT IS! AND FULL OF WATER!!
---ACK !!!

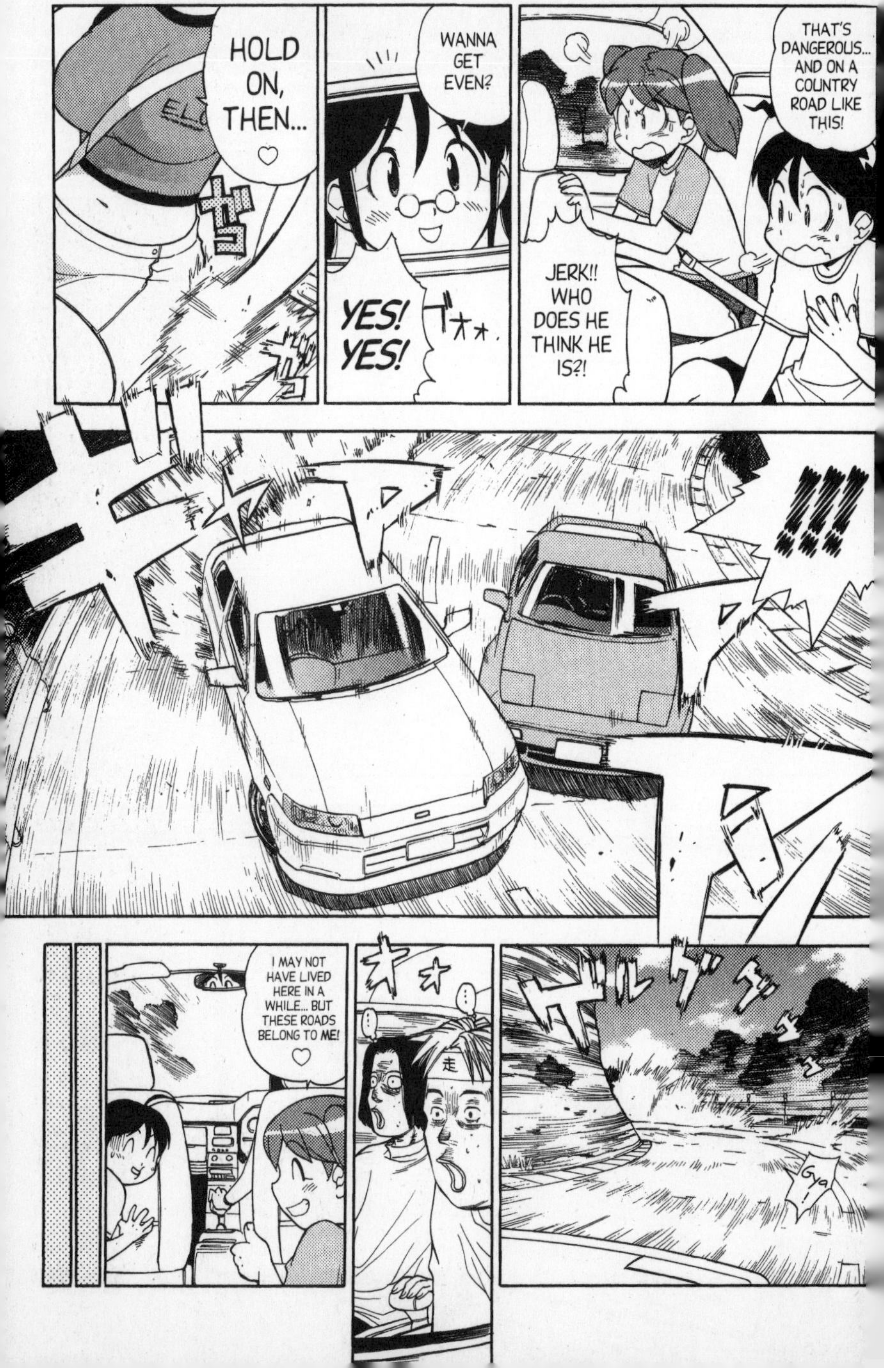
THAT'S DANGEROUS... AND ON A COUNTRY ROAD LIKE THIS!
JERK!! WHO DOES HE THINK HE IS?!
WANNA GET EVEN?
YES! YES!
HOLD ON, THEN... ♡
!!!
Gya!
...
...!
I MAY NOT HAVE LIVED HERE IN A WHILE... BUT THESE ROADS BELONG TO ME! ♡

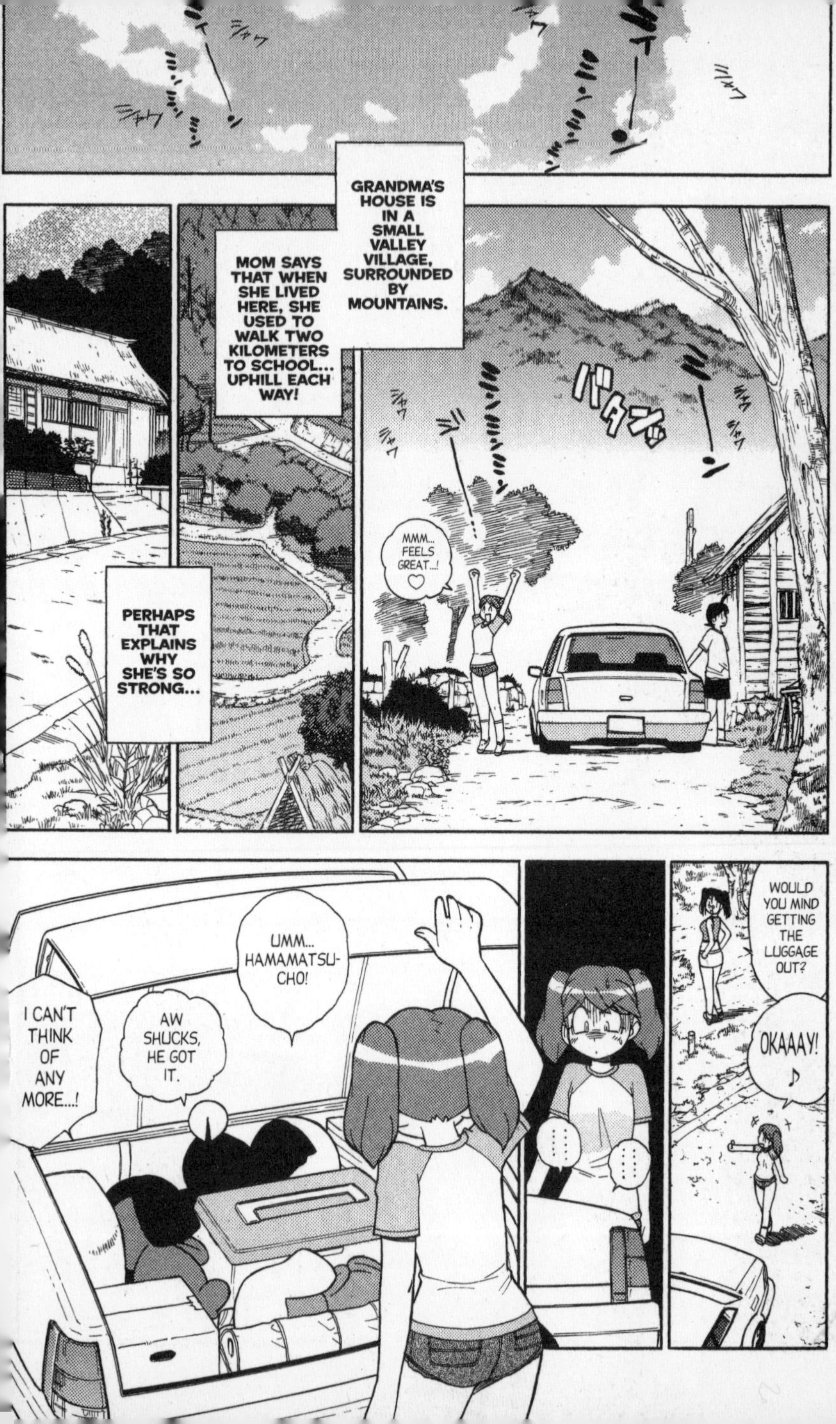
GRANDMA'S HOUSE IS IN A SMALL VALLEY VILLAGE, SURROUNDED BY MOUNTAINS.
MMM... FEELS GREAT...! ♡
MOM SAYS THAT WHEN SHE LIVED HERE, SHE USED TO WALK TWO KILOMETERS TO SCHOOL... UPHILL EACH WAY!
PERHAPS THAT EXPLAINS WHY SHE'S SO STRONG...
WOULD YOU MIND GETTING THE LUGGAGE OUT?
OKAAAY! ♪
......
......
UMM... HAMAMATSU-CHO!
AW SHUCKS, HE GOT IT.
I CAN'T THINK OF ANY MORE...!

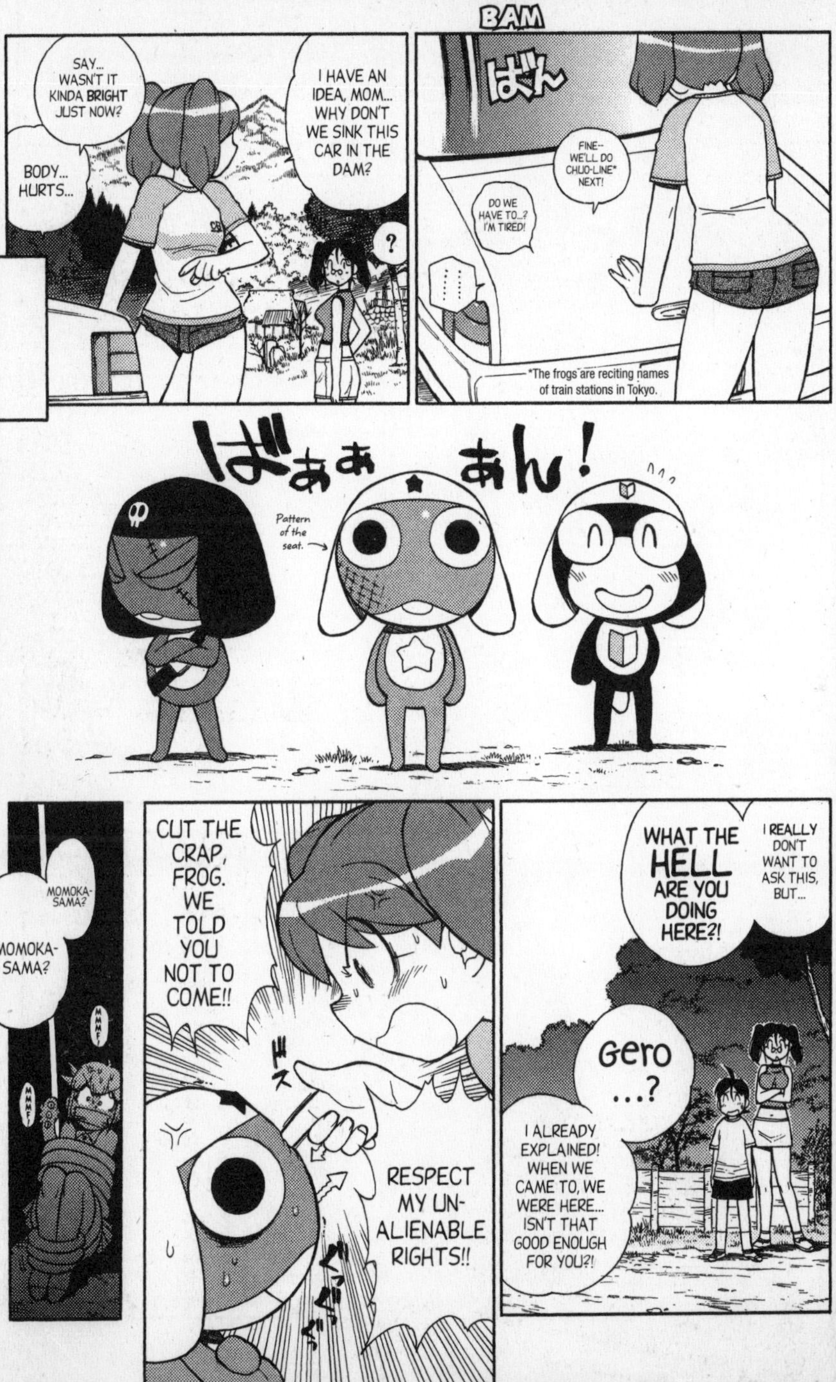
BAM
ばん
FINE-- WE'LL DO CHUO-LINE* NEXT!
DO WE HAVE TO...? I'M TIRED!
......
*The frogs are reciting names of train stations in Tokyo.
I HAVE AN IDEA, MOM... WHY DON'T WE SINK THIS CAR IN THE DAM?
?
SAY... WASN'T IT KINDA BRIGHT JUST NOW?
BODY... HURTS...
ばぁぁ　あん!
Pattern of the seat.
I REALLY DON'T WANT TO ASK THIS, BUT...
WHAT THE HELL ARE YOU DOING HERE?!
Gero ...?
I ALREADY EXPLAINED! WHEN WE CAME TO, WE WERE HERE... ISN'T THAT GOOD ENOUGH FOR YOU?!
CUT THE CRAP, FROG. WE TOLD YOU NOT TO COME!!
RESPECT MY UN-ALIENABLE RIGHTS!!
MOMOKA-SAMA?
MOMOKA-SAMA?
MMMF!
MMMF!

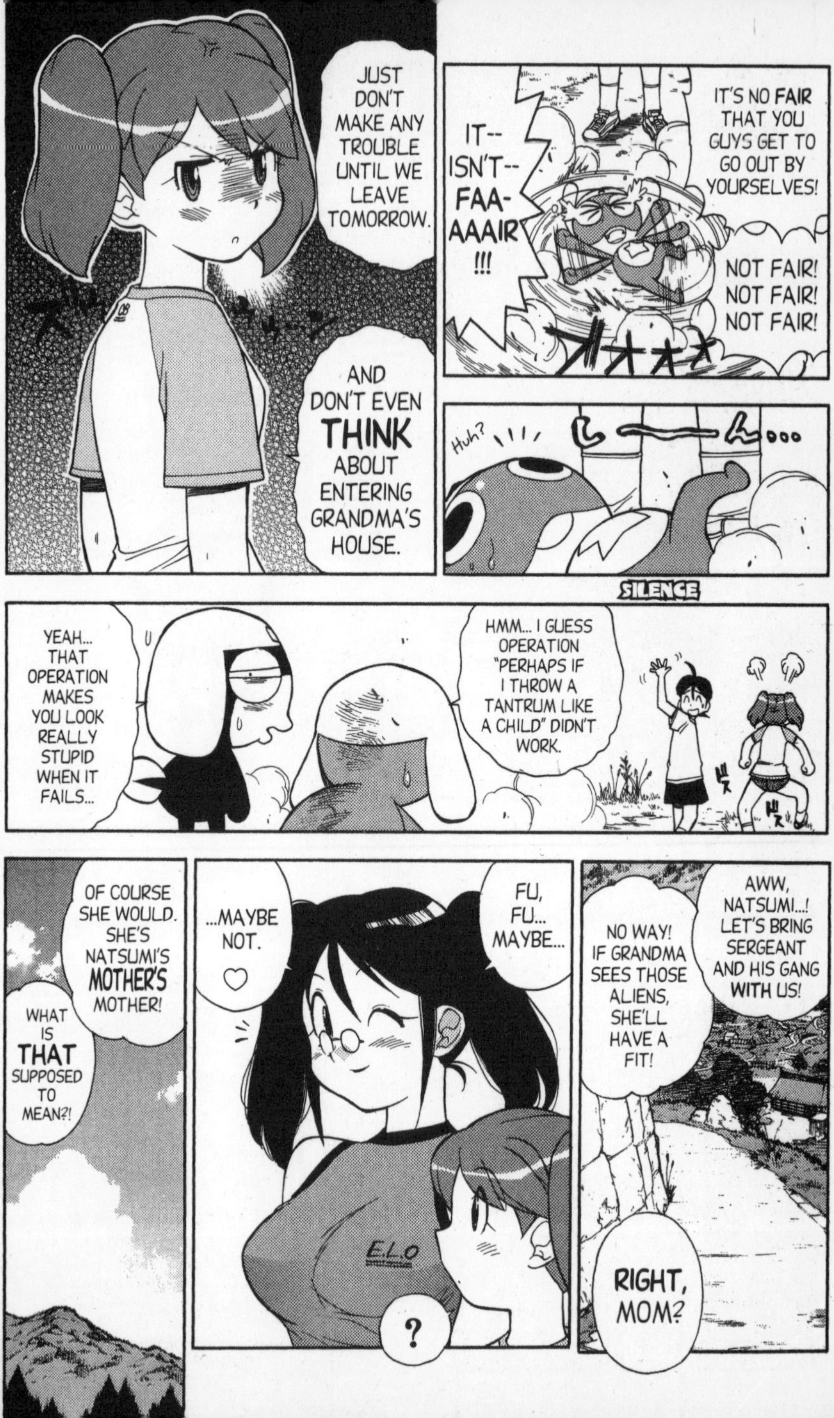
IT'S NO FAIR THAT YOU GUYS GET TO GO OUT BY YOURSELVES!
IT-- ISN'T-- FAA-AAAIR!!!
NOT FAIR! NOT FAIR! NOT FAIR!
Huh?
SILENCE
JUST DON'T MAKE ANY TROUBLE UNTIL WE LEAVE TOMORROW.
AND DON'T EVEN THINK ABOUT ENTERING GRANDMA'S HOUSE.
HMM... I GUESS OPERATION "PERHAPS IF I THROW A TANTRUM LIKE A CHILD" DIDN'T WORK.
YEAH... THAT OPERATION MAKES YOU LOOK REALLY STUPID WHEN IT FAILS...
AWW, NATSUMI...! LET'S BRING SERGEANT AND HIS GANG WITH US!
NO WAY! IF GRANDMA SEES THOSE ALIENS, SHE'LL HAVE A FIT!
RIGHT, MOM?
FU, FU... MAYBE...
...MAYBE NOT. ♡
?
OF COURSE SHE WOULD. SHE'S NATSUMI'S MOTHER'S MOTHER!
WHAT IS THAT SUPPOSED TO MEAN?!

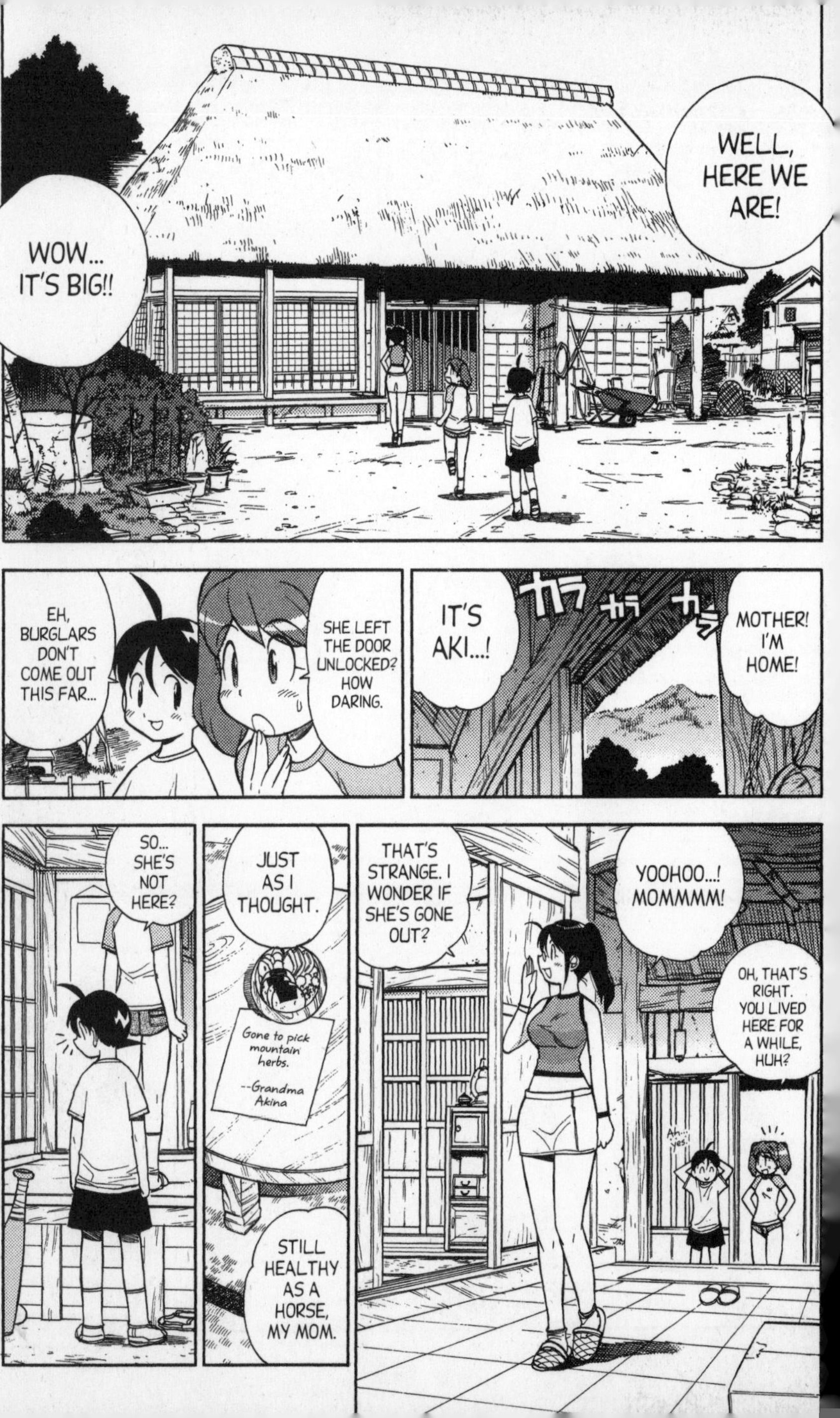
WELL, HERE WE ARE!
WOW... IT'S BIG!!
MOTHER! I'M HOME!
IT'S AKI...!
SHE LEFT THE DOOR UNLOCKED? HOW DARING.
EH, BURGLARS DON'T COME OUT THIS FAR...
YOOHOO...! MOMMMM!
THAT'S STRANGE. I WONDER IF SHE'S GONE OUT?
OH, THAT'S RIGHT. YOU LIVED HERE FOR A WHILE, HUH?
Ah... yes!
JUST AS I THOUGHT.
Gone to pick mountain herbs. --Grandma Akina
STILL HEALTHY AS A HORSE, MY MOM.
SO... SHE'S NOT HERE?

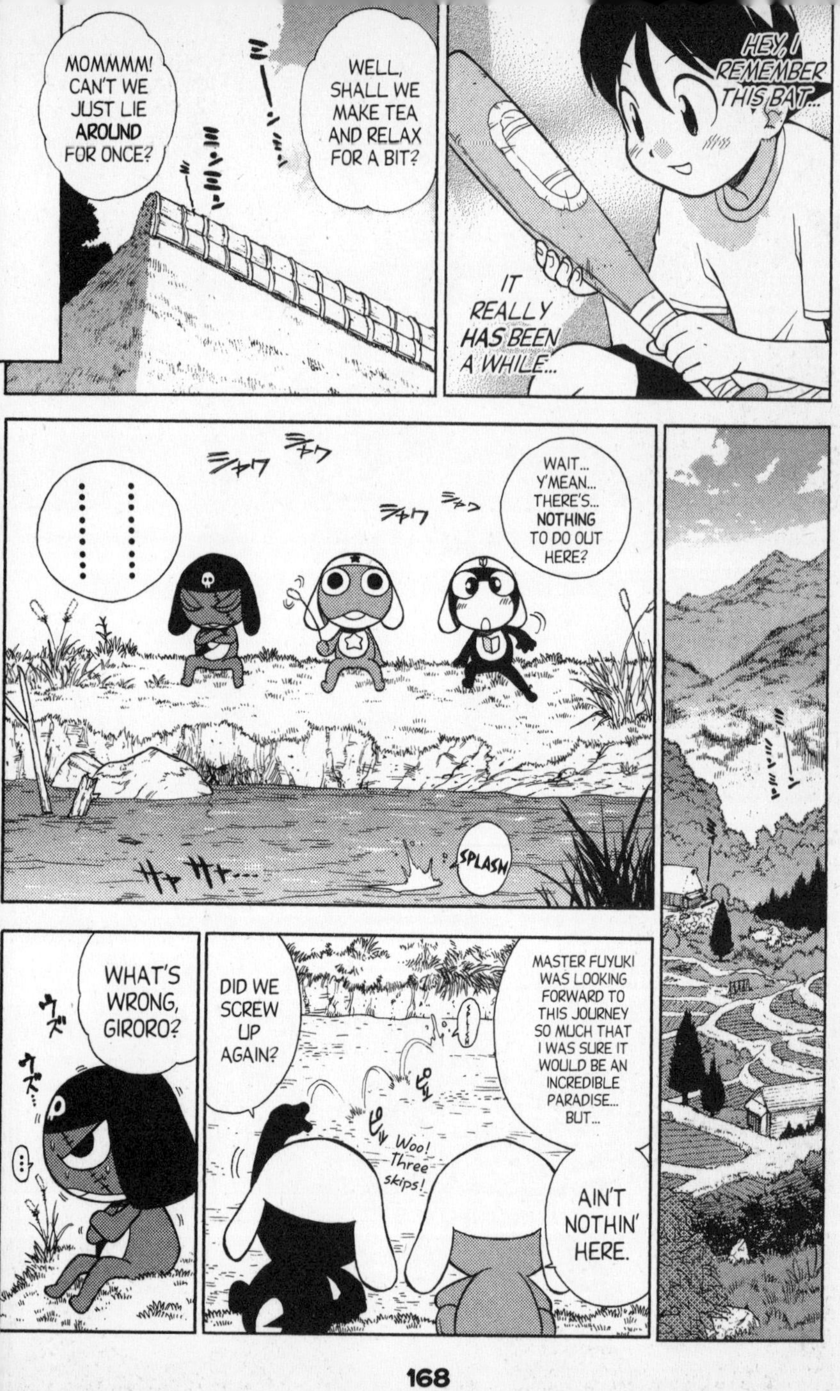
HEY, I REMEMBER THIS BAT...
IT REALLY HAS BEEN A WHILE...
WELL, SHALL WE MAKE TEA AND RELAX FOR A BIT?
MOMMMM! CAN'T WE JUST LIE AROUND FOR ONCE?
WAIT... Y'MEAN... THERE'S... NOTHING TO DO OUT HERE?
......
SPLASH
MASTER FUYUKI WAS LOOKING FORWARD TO THIS JOURNEY SO MUCH THAT I WAS SURE IT WOULD BE AN INCREDIBLE PARADISE... BUT...
AIN'T NOTHIN' HERE.
DID WE SCREW UP AGAIN?
Woo! Three skips!
WHAT'S WRONG, GIRORO?
...

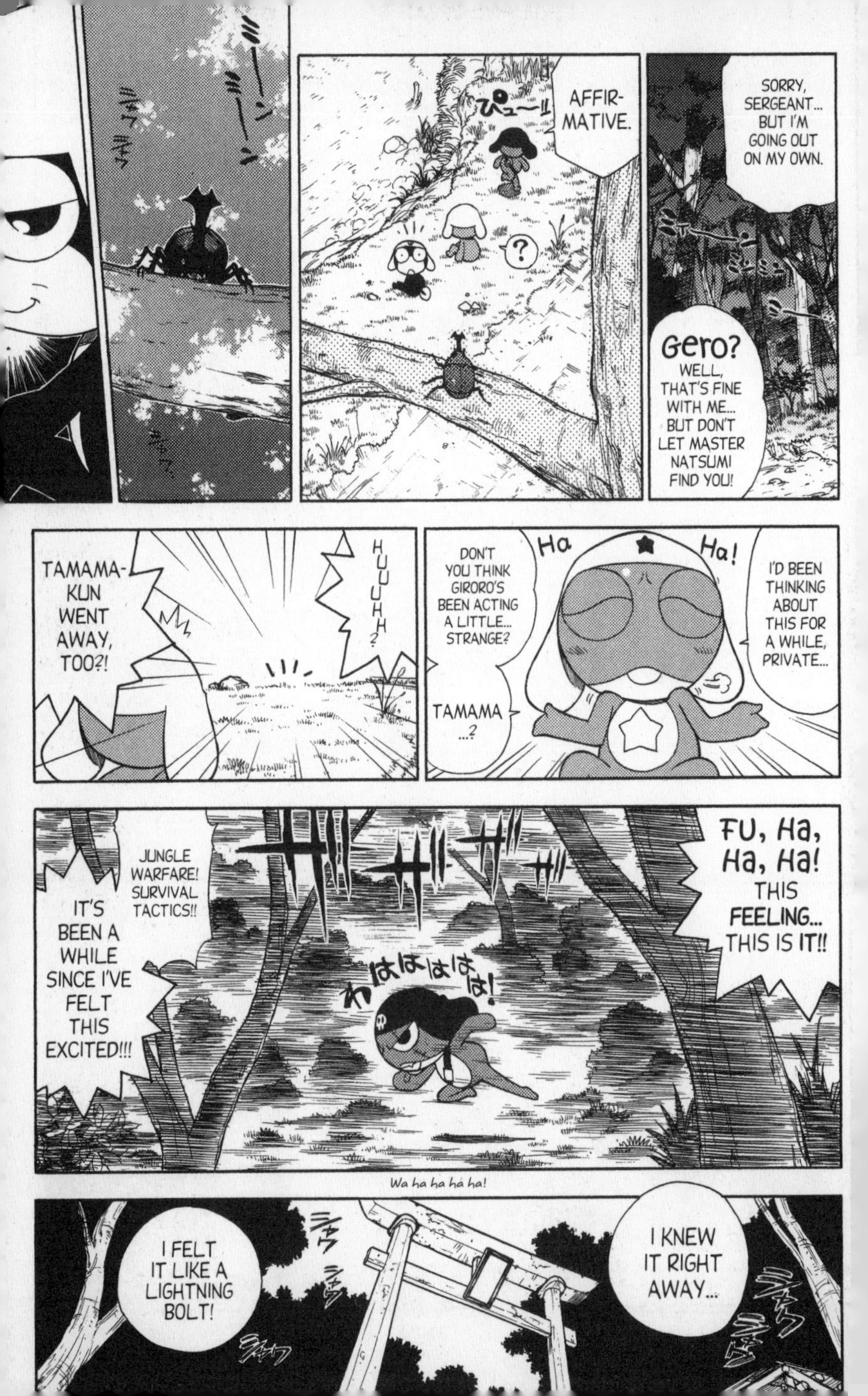
SORRY, SERGEANT... BUT I'M GOING OUT ON MY OWN.
Gero? WELL, THAT'S FINE WITH ME... BUT DON'T LET MASTER NATSUMI FIND YOU!
AFFIR-MATIVE.
ぴュ~!!
?
I'D BEEN THINKING ABOUT THIS FOR A WHILE, PRIVATE...
Ha Ha!
DON'T YOU THINK GIRORO'S BEEN ACTING A LITTLE... STRANGE?
TAMAMA ...?
HUUUUHH?
TAMAMA-KUN WENT AWAY, TOO?!
FU, Ha, Ha, Ha! THIS FEELING... THIS IS IT!!
JUNGLE WARFARE! SURVIVAL TACTICS!!
IT'S BEEN A WHILE SINCE I'VE FELT THIS EXCITED!!!
わはははは!
Wa ha ha ha ha!
I KNEW IT RIGHT AWAY...
I FELT IT LIKE A LIGHTNING BOLT!

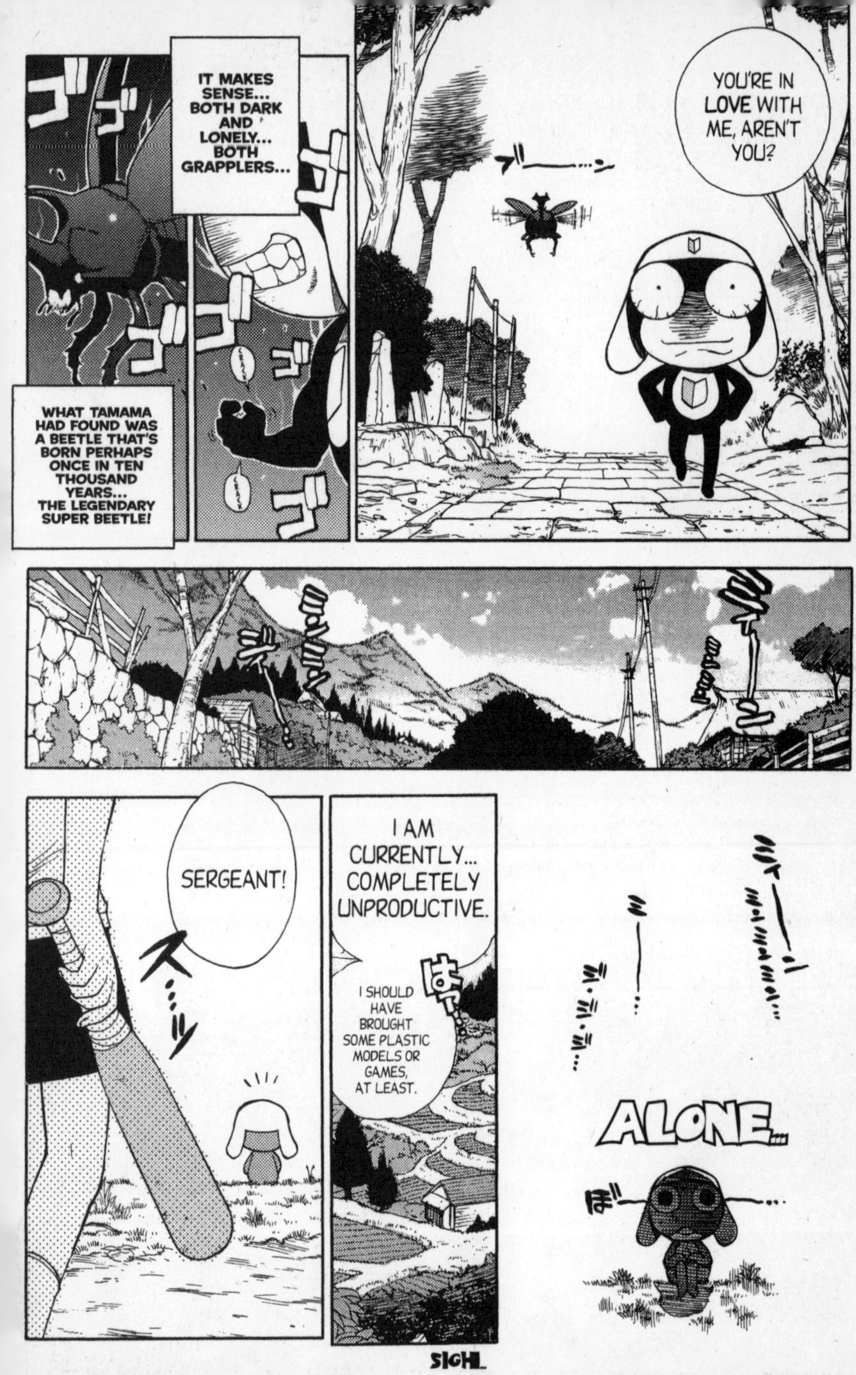
YOU'RE IN LOVE WITH ME, AREN'T YOU?
IT MAKES SENSE... BOTH DARK AND LONELY... BOTH GRAPPLERS...
WHAT TAMAMA HAD FOUND WAS A BEETLE THAT'S BORN PERHAPS ONCE IN TEN THOUSAND YEARS... THE LEGENDARY SUPER BEETLE!
ALONE...
I AM CURRENTLY... COMPLETELY UNPRODUCTIVE.
I SHOULD HAVE BROUGHT SOME PLASTIC MODELS OR GAMES, AT LEAST.
SIGH
SERGEANT!

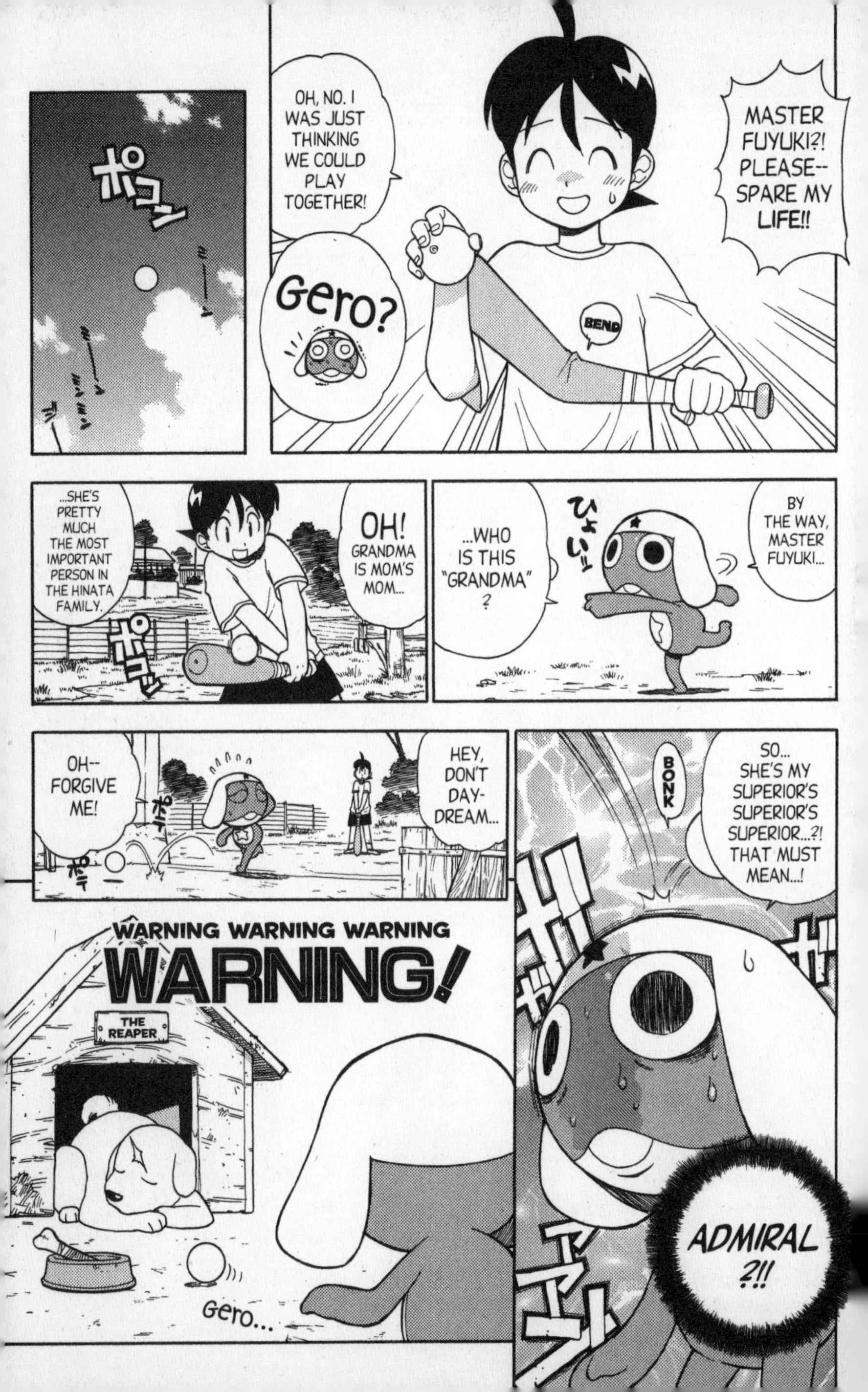
MASTER FUYUKI?! PLEASE-- SPARE MY LIFE!!
OH, NO. I WAS JUST THINKING WE COULD PLAY TOGETHER!
Gero?
BEND
ポコン
BY THE WAY, MASTER FUYUKI...
...WHO IS THIS "GRANDMA"?
ひょい
OH! GRANDMA IS MOM'S MOM...
...SHE'S PRETTY MUCH THE MOST IMPORTANT PERSON IN THE HINATA FAMILY.
SO... SHE'S MY SUPERIOR'S SUPERIOR'S SUPERIOR...?! THAT MUST MEAN...!
BONK
ADMIRAL ?!!
HEY, DON'T DAY-DREAM...
OH-- FORGIVE ME!
WARNING WARNING WARNING
WARNING!
THE REAPER
Gero...

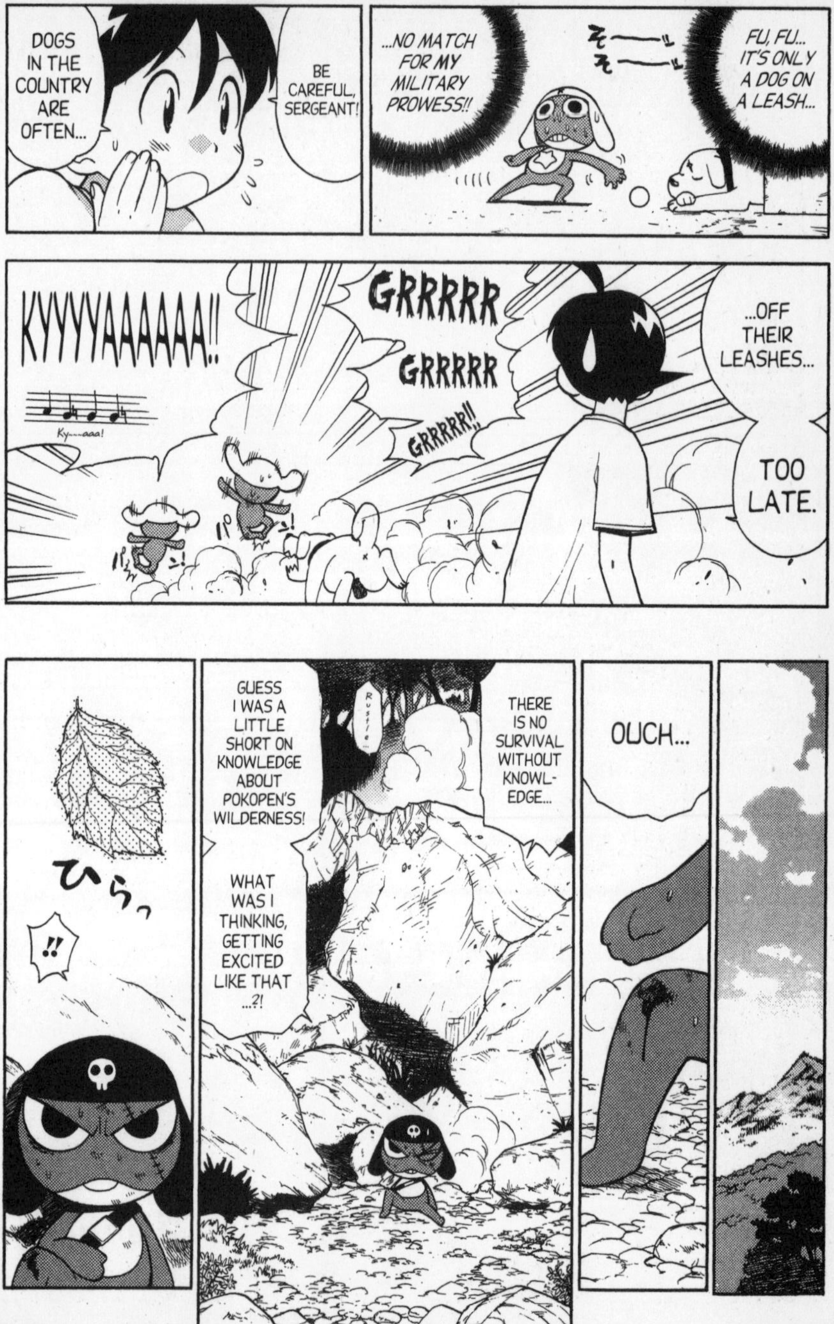
FU, FU... IT'S ONLY A DOG ON A LEASH...
...NO MATCH FOR MY MILITARY PROWESS!!
BE CAREFUL, SERGEANT!
DOGS IN THE COUNTRY ARE OFTEN...
...OFF THEIR LEASHES...
TOO LATE.
GRRRRR
GRRRRR
GRRRRR!!
KYYYYAAAAAA!!
Ky---aaa!
OUCH...
THERE IS NO SURVIVAL WITHOUT KNOWL-EDGE...
Rustle...
GUESS I WAS A LITTLE SHORT ON KNOWLEDGE ABOUT POKOPEN'S WILDERNESS!
WHAT WAS I THINKING, GETTING EXCITED LIKE THAT ...?!
ひらっ
!!

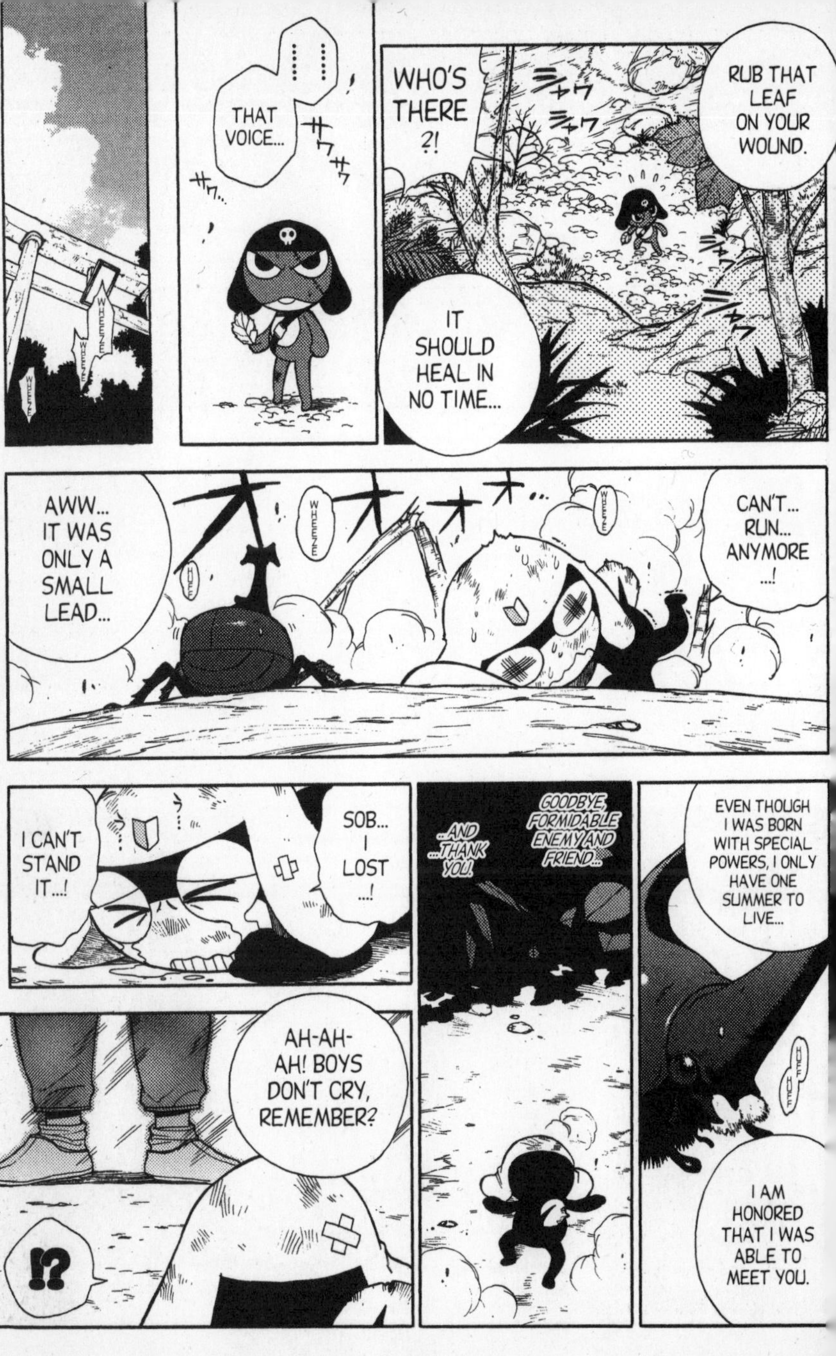
RUB THAT LEAF ON YOUR WOUND.
WHO'S THERE ?!
IT SHOULD HEAL IN NO TIME...
......
THAT VOICE...
WHEEZE
WHEEZE
WHEEZE
CAN'T... RUN... ANYMORE ...!
WHEEZE
WHEEZE
HUFF
AWW... IT WAS ONLY A SMALL LEAD...
EVEN THOUGH I WAS BORN WITH SPECIAL POWERS, I ONLY HAVE ONE SUMMER TO LIVE...
HUFF
HUFF
I AM HONORED THAT I WAS ABLE TO MEET YOU.
GOODBYE, FORMIDABLE ENEMY AND FRIEND...
...AND ...THANK YOU.
SOB... I LOST ...!
I CAN'T STAND IT...!
AH-AH-AH! BOYS DON'T CRY, REMEMBER?
!?

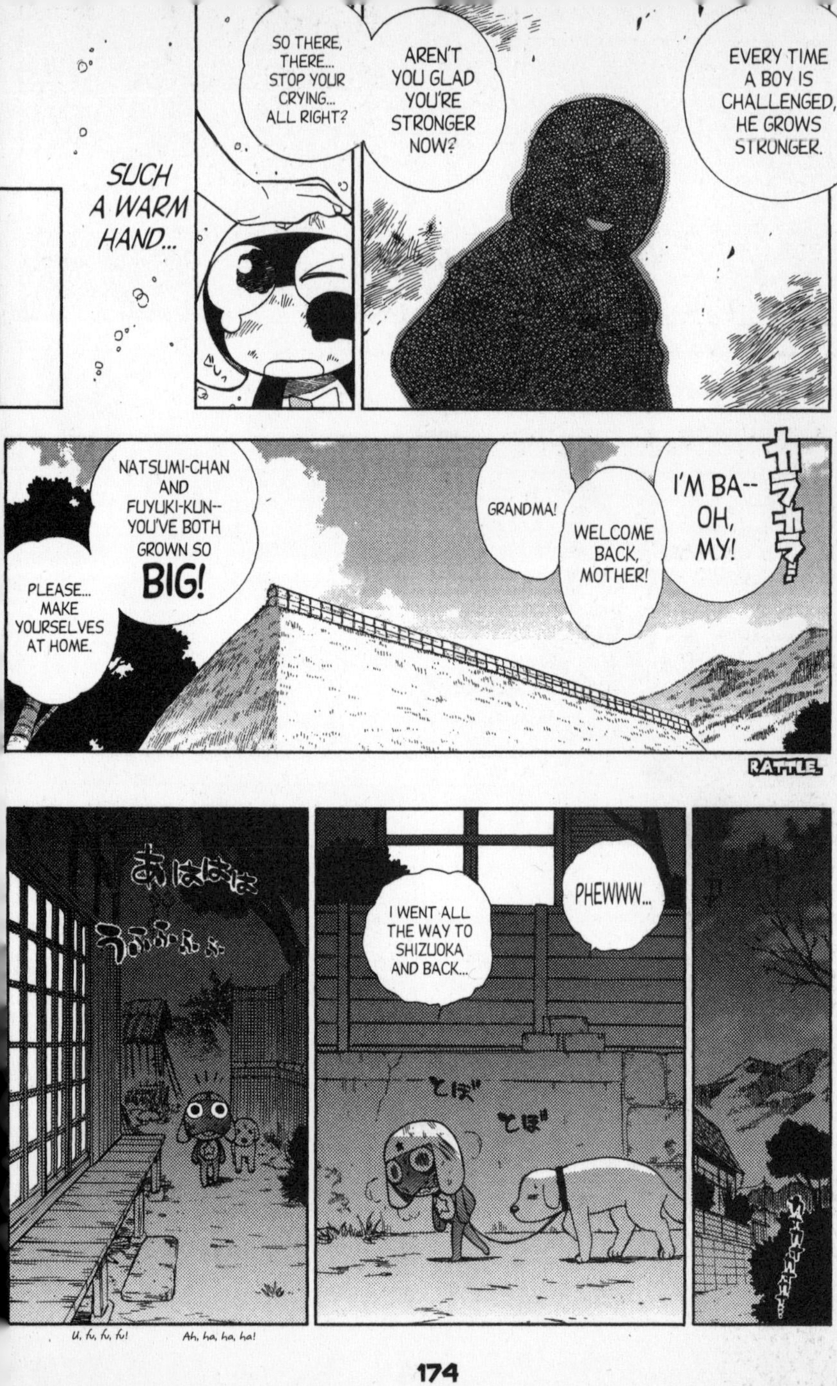
EVERY TIME A BOY IS CHALLENGED, HE GROWS STRONGER.
AREN'T YOU GLAD YOU'RE STRONGER NOW?
SO THERE, THERE... STOP YOUR CRYING... ALL RIGHT?
SUCH A WARM HAND...
カラカラ
RATTLE
I'M BA-- OH, MY!
WELCOME BACK, MOTHER!
GRANDMA!
NATSUMI-CHAN AND FUYUKI-KUN-- YOU'VE BOTH GROWN SO BIG!
PLEASE... MAKE YOURSELVES AT HOME.
PHEWWW...
I WENT ALL THE WAY TO SHIZUOKA AND BACK...
とぼ
とぼ
あははは
うふふふふ

U, fu, fu, fu!    Ah, ha, ha, ha!

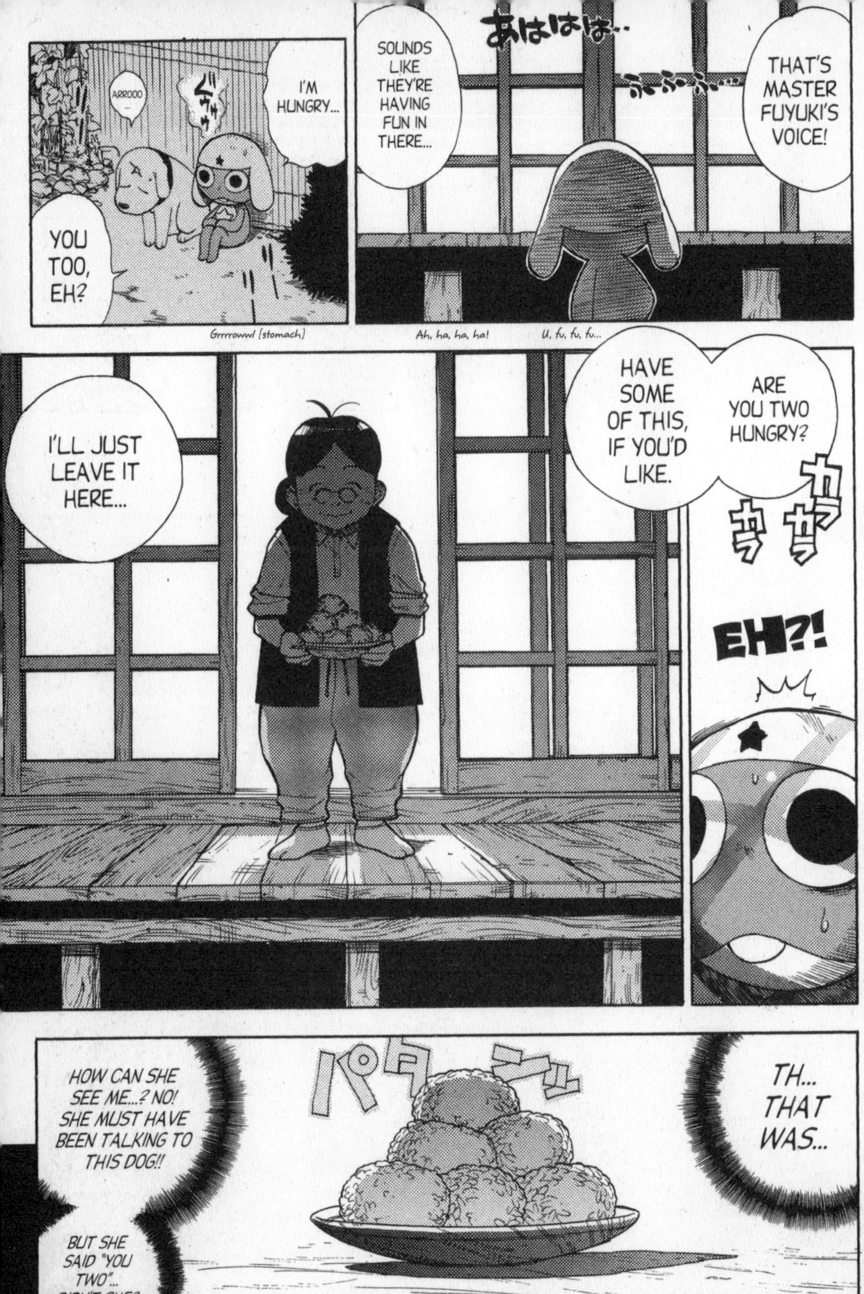
THAT'S MASTER FUYUKI'S VOICE!
あははは…
ふふふ…
SOUNDS LIKE THEY'RE HAVING FUN IN THERE...
Ah, ha, ha, ha!
U, fu, fu, fu...
I'M HUNGRY...
ぐぅぅ
ARROOO...
YOU TOO, EH?
Grrrrowwl [stomach]
EH?!
ARE YOU TWO HUNGRY?
HAVE SOME OF THIS, IF YOU'D LIKE.
カラカラ
I'LL JUST LEAVE IT HERE...
TH... THAT WAS...
パタン
HOW CAN SHE SEE ME...? NO! SHE MUST HAVE BEEN TALKING TO THIS DOG!!
BUT SHE SAID "YOU TWO"... DIDN'T SHE?

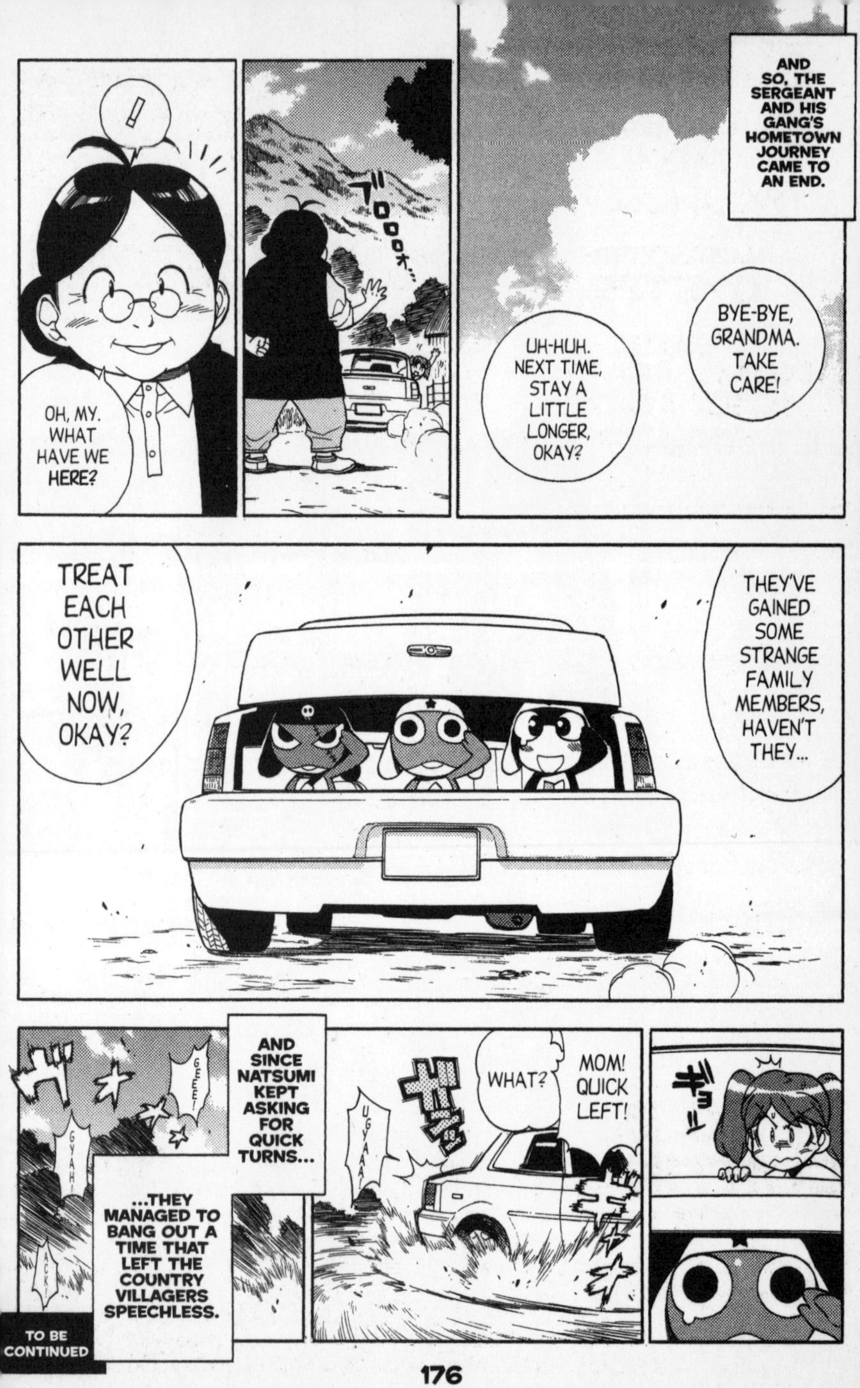
AND SO, THE SERGEANT AND HIS GANG'S HOMETOWN JOURNEY CAME TO AN END.
BYE-BYE, GRANDMA. TAKE CARE!
UH-HUH. NEXT TIME, STAY A LITTLE LONGER, OKAY?
!
OH, MY. WHAT HAVE WE HERE?
THEY'VE GAINED SOME STRANGE FAMILY MEMBERS, HAVEN'T THEY...
TREAT EACH OTHER WELL NOW, OKAY?
MOM! QUICK LEFT!
WHAT?
UGYAAA!
AND SINCE NATSUMI KEPT ASKING FOR QUICK TURNS...
...THEY MANAGED TO BANG OUT A TIME THAT LEFT THE COUNTRY VILLAGERS SPEECHLESS.
GEEE!
GYAH!
ACK!
TO BE CONTINUED

JAPAN STAFF

CREATOR
**MINE YOSHIZAKI**

BACKGROUNDS
**OYSTER**

FINISH
**GOMOKU AKATSUKI**
**ROBIN TOKYO**
**LISA LISA**

---

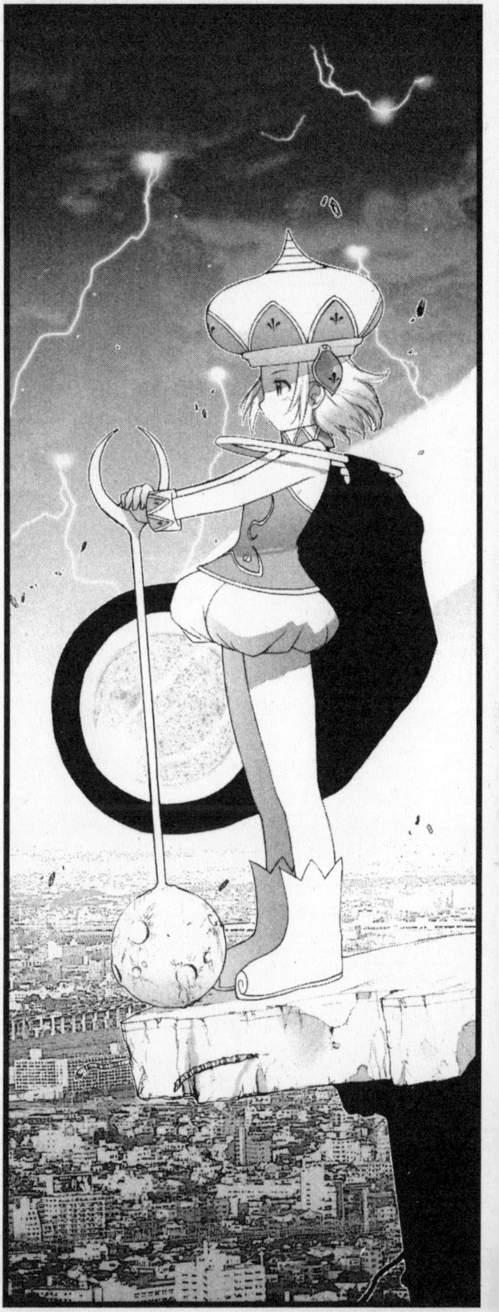

# TO BE CONTINUED IN VOLUME 5

ANGOL MOA

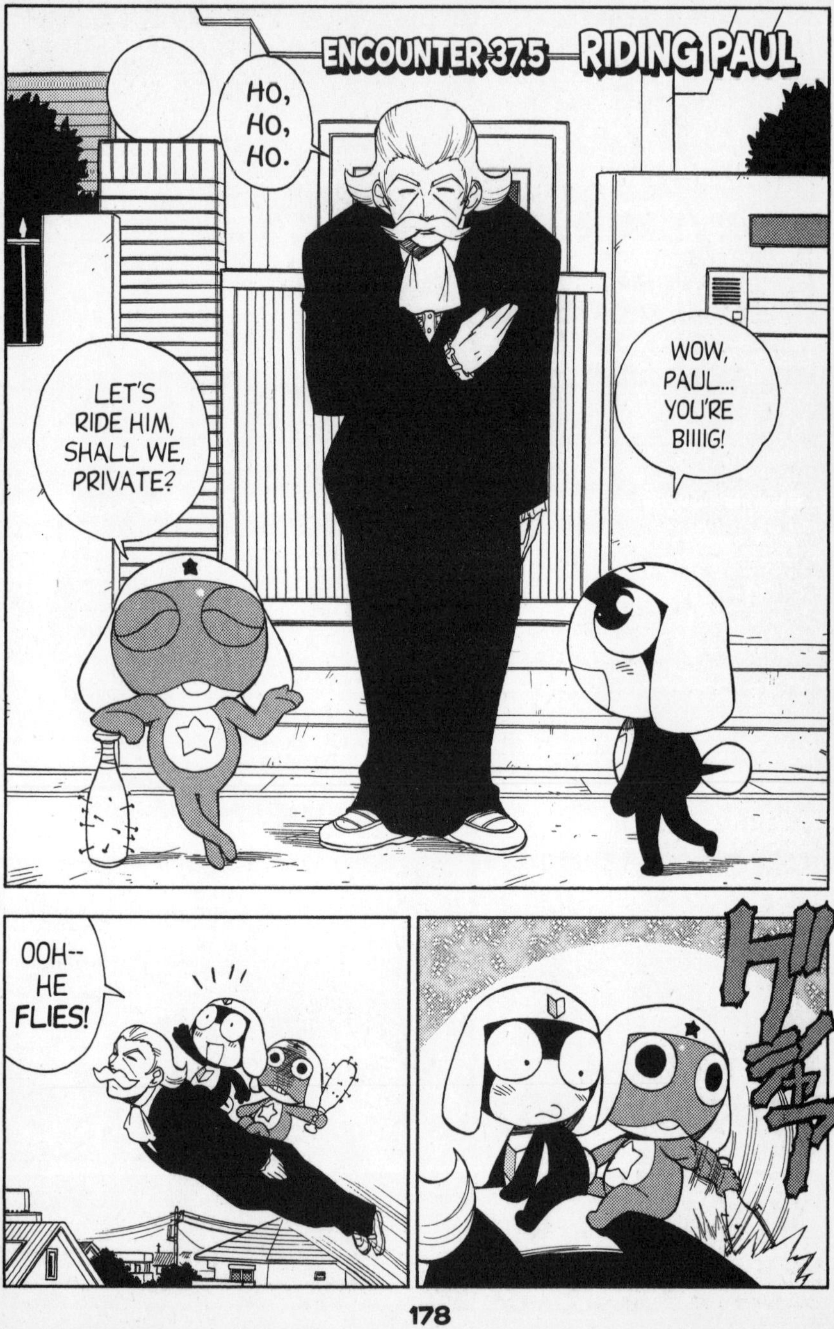
ENCOUNTER 37.5 RIDING PAUL
HO, HO, HO.
WOW, PAUL... YOU'RE BIIIG!
LET'S RIDE HIM, SHALL WE, PRIVATE?
OOH-- HE FLIES!

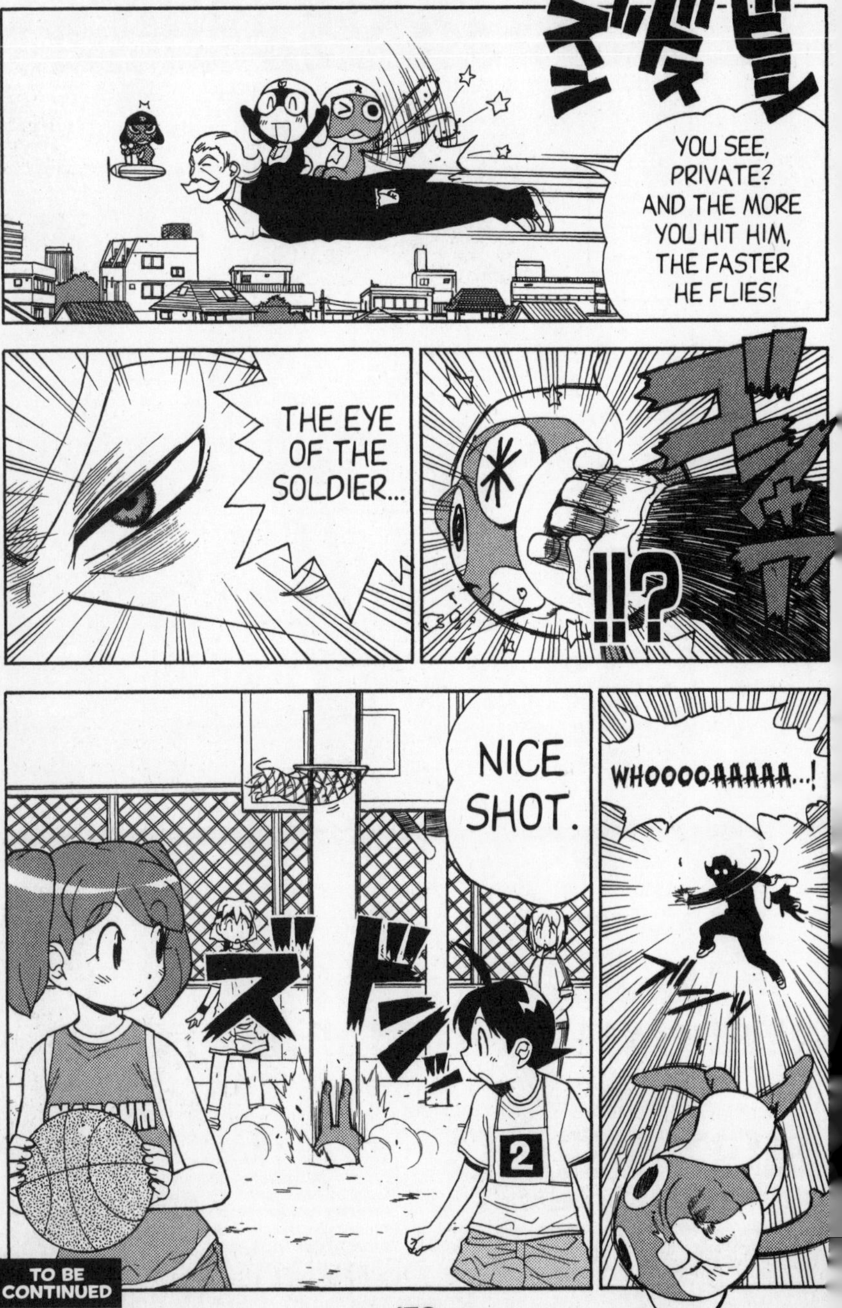
YOU SEE, PRIVATE? AND THE MORE YOU HIT HIM, THE FASTER HE FLIES!
!!?
THE EYE OF THE SOLDIER...
WHOOOOAAAAA...!
NICE SHOT.
TO BE CONTINUED

# SGT. Frog Vol. 4
## Created by Mine Yoshizaki

Translation - Yuko Fukami
English Adaptation - Carol Fox
Copy Editor - Hope Donovan
Retouch and Lettering - Jose Macasocol, Jr.
Production Artist - Vicente Rivera, Jr.
Cover Design - Raymond Makowski

Editor - Paul Morrissey
Digital Imaging Manager - Chris Buford
Pre-Press Manager - Antonio DePietro
Production Managers - Jennifer Miller and Mutsumi Miyazaki
Art Director - Matt Alford
Managing Editor - Jill Freshney
VP of Production - Ron Klamert
President and C.O.O. - John Parker
Publisher and C.E.O. - Stuart Levy

A **TOKYOPOP**® Manga

TOKYOPOP Inc.
5900 Wilshire Blvd. Suite 2000
Los Angeles, CA 90036

E-mail: info@TOKYOPOP.com
Come visit us online at www.TOKYOPOP.com

ISBN: 1-59182-706-X

First TOKYOPOP printing: September 2004
10  9  8  7  6  5  4  3  2  1
Printed in the USA

# ALSO AVAILABLE FROM TOKYOPOP

# ALSO AVAILABLE FROM

## MANGA

.HACK//LEGEND OF THE TWILIGHT
@LARGE
ABENOBASHI: MAGICAL SHOPPING ARCADE
A.I. LOVE YOU
AI YORI AOSHI
ANGELIC LAYER
ARM OF KANNON
BABY BIRTH
BATTLE ROYALE
BATTLE VIXENS
BOYS BE...
BRAIN POWERED
BRIGADOON
B'TX
CANDIDATE FOR GODDESS, THE
CARDCAPTOR SAKURA
CARDCAPTOR SAKURA - MASTER OF THE CLOW
CHOBITS
CHRONICLES OF THE CURSED SWORD
CLAMP SCHOOL DETECTIVES
CLOVER
COMIC PARTY
CONFIDENTIAL CONFESSIONS
CORRECTOR YUI
COWBOY BEBOP
COWBOY BEBOP: SHOOTING STAR
CRAZY LOVE STORY
CRESCENT MOON
CROSS
CULDCEPT
CYBORG 009
D•N•ANGEL
DEMON DIARY
DEMON ORORON, THE
DEUS VITAE
DIABOLO
DIGIMON
DIGIMON TAMERS
DIGIMON ZERO TWO
DOLL
DRAGON HUNTER
DRAGON KNIGHTS
DRAGON VOICE
DREAM SAGA
DUKLYON: CLAMP SCHOOL DEFENDERS
EERIE QUEERIE!
ERICA SAKURAZAWA: COLLECTED WORKS
ET CETERA
ETERNITY
EVIL'S RETURN
FAERIES' LANDING
FAKE
FLCL
FLOWER OF THE DEEP SLEEP
FORBIDDEN DANCE
FRUITS BASKET

G GUNDAM
GATEKEEPERS
GETBACKERS
GIRL GOT GAME
GIRLS EDUCATIONAL CHARTER
GRAVITATION
GTO
GUNDAM BLUE DESTINY
GUNDAM SEED ASTRAY
GUNDAM WING
GUNDAM WING: BATTLEFIELD OF PACIFISTS
GUNDAM WING: ENDLESS WALTZ
GUNDAM WING: THE LAST OUTPOST (G-UNIT)
HANDS OFF!
HAPPY MANIA
HARLEM BEAT
HYPER RUNE
I.N.V.U.
IMMORTAL RAIN
INITIAL D
INSTANT TEEN: JUST ADD NUTS
ISLAND
JING: KING OF BANDITS
JING: KING OF BANDITS - TWILIGHT TALES
JULINE
KARE KANO
KILL ME, KISS ME
KINDAICHI CASE FILES, THE
KING OF HELL
KODOCHA: SANA'S STAGE
LAMENT OF THE LAMB
LEGAL DRUG
LEGEND OF CHUN HYANG, THE
LES BIJOUX
LOVE HINA
LUPIN III
LUPIN III: WORLD'S MOST WANTED
MAGIC KNIGHT RAYEARTH I
MAGIC KNIGHT RAYEARTH II
MAHOROMATIC: AUTOMATIC MAIDEN
MAN OF MANY FACES
MARMALADE BOY
MARS
MARS: HORSE WITH NO NAME
MINK
MIRACLE GIRLS
MIYUKI-CHAN IN WONDERLAND
MODEL
MOURYOU KIDEN
MY LOVE
NECK AND NECK
ONE
ONE I LOVE, THE
PARADISE KISS
PARASYTE
PASSION FRUIT
PEACH GIRL
PEACH GIRL: CHANGE OF HEART

06.21.04T

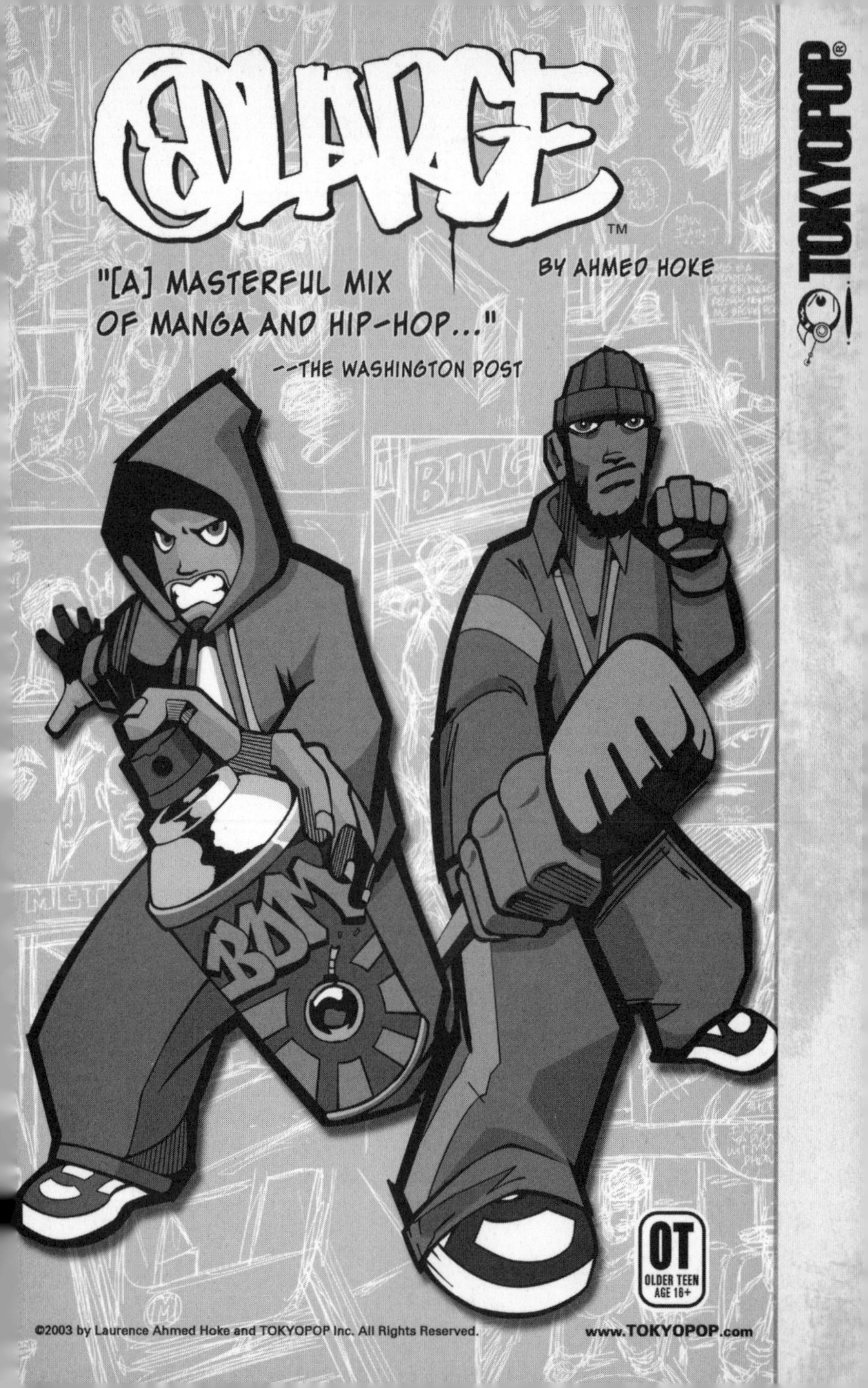

@LARGE™
BY AHMED HOKE
"[A] MASTERFUL MIX OF MANGA AND HIP-HOP..."
--THE WASHINGTON POST
TOKYOPOP®
OT OLDER TEEN AGE 16+
©2003 by Laurence Ahmed Hoke and TOKYOPOP Inc. All Rights Reserved.
www.TOKYOPOP.com

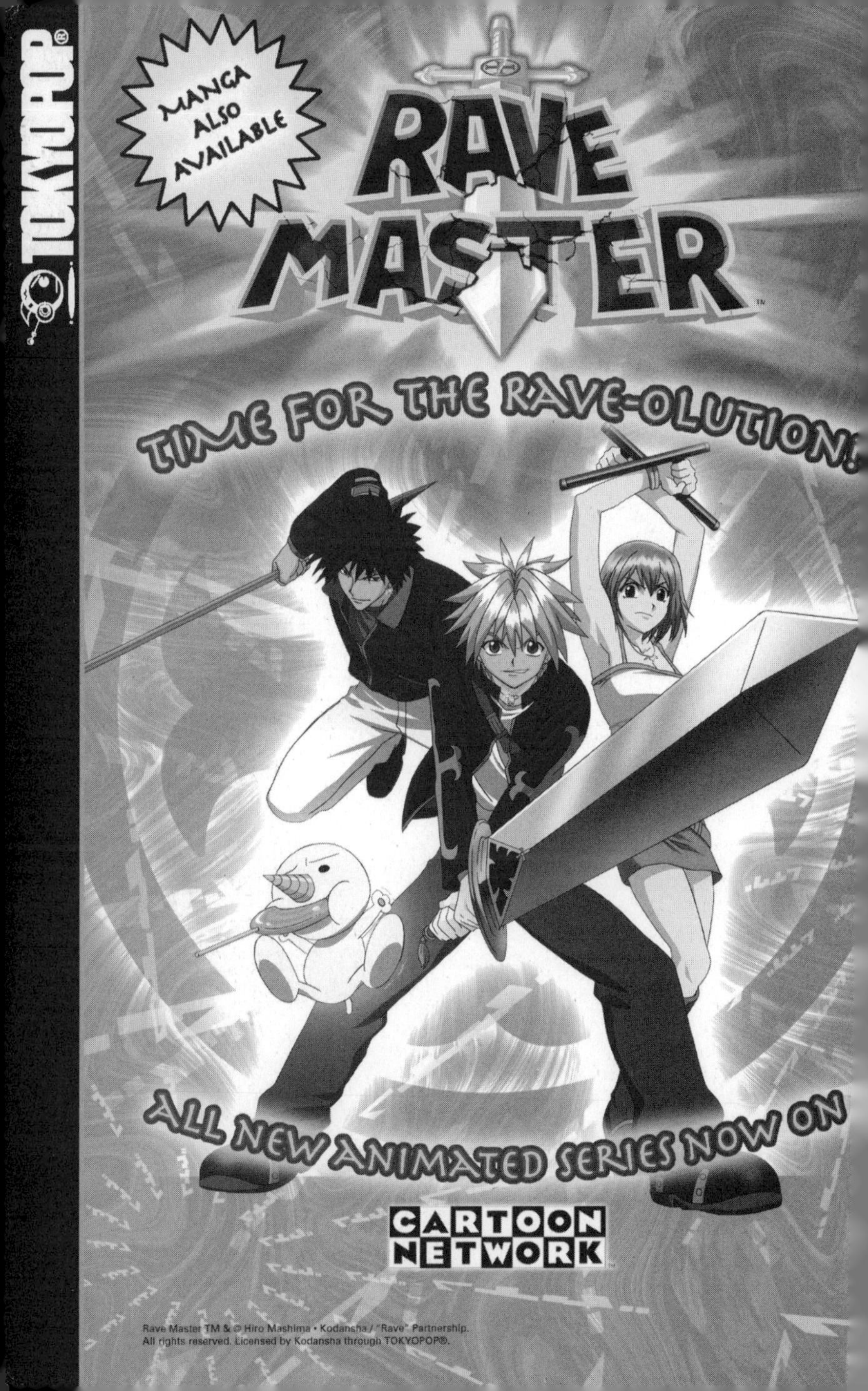
TOKYOPOP®
MANGA ALSO AVAILABLE
RAVE MASTER™
TIME FOR THE RAVE-OLUTION!
ALL NEW ANIMATED SERIES NOW ON
CARTOON NETWORK
Rave Master TM & © Hiro Mashima • Kodansha / "Rave" Partnership.
All rights reserved. Licensed by Kodansha through TOKYOPOP®.

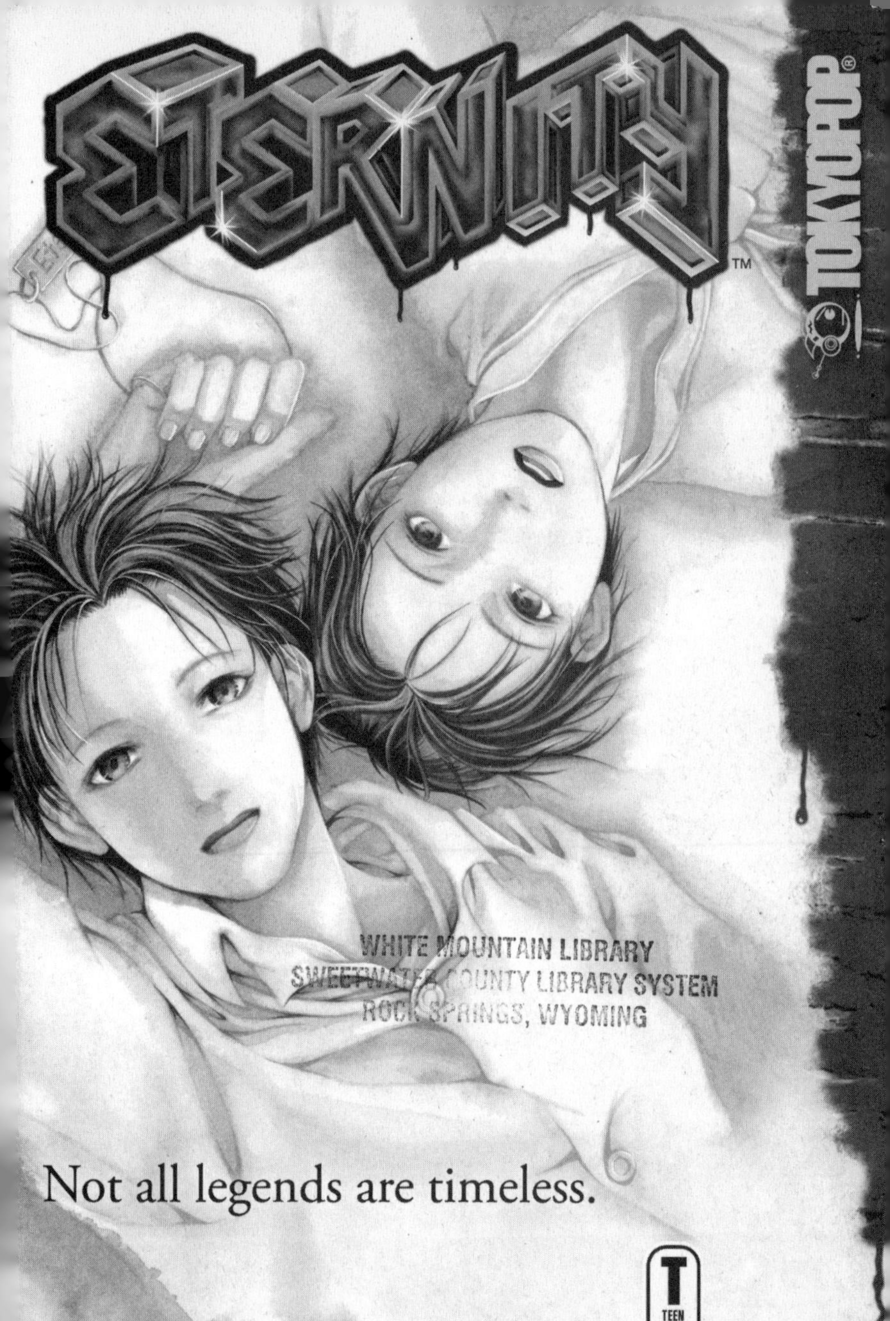
ETERNITY™
TOKYOPOP®
Not all legends are timeless.
T
TEEN
AGE 13+
www.TOKYOPOP.com

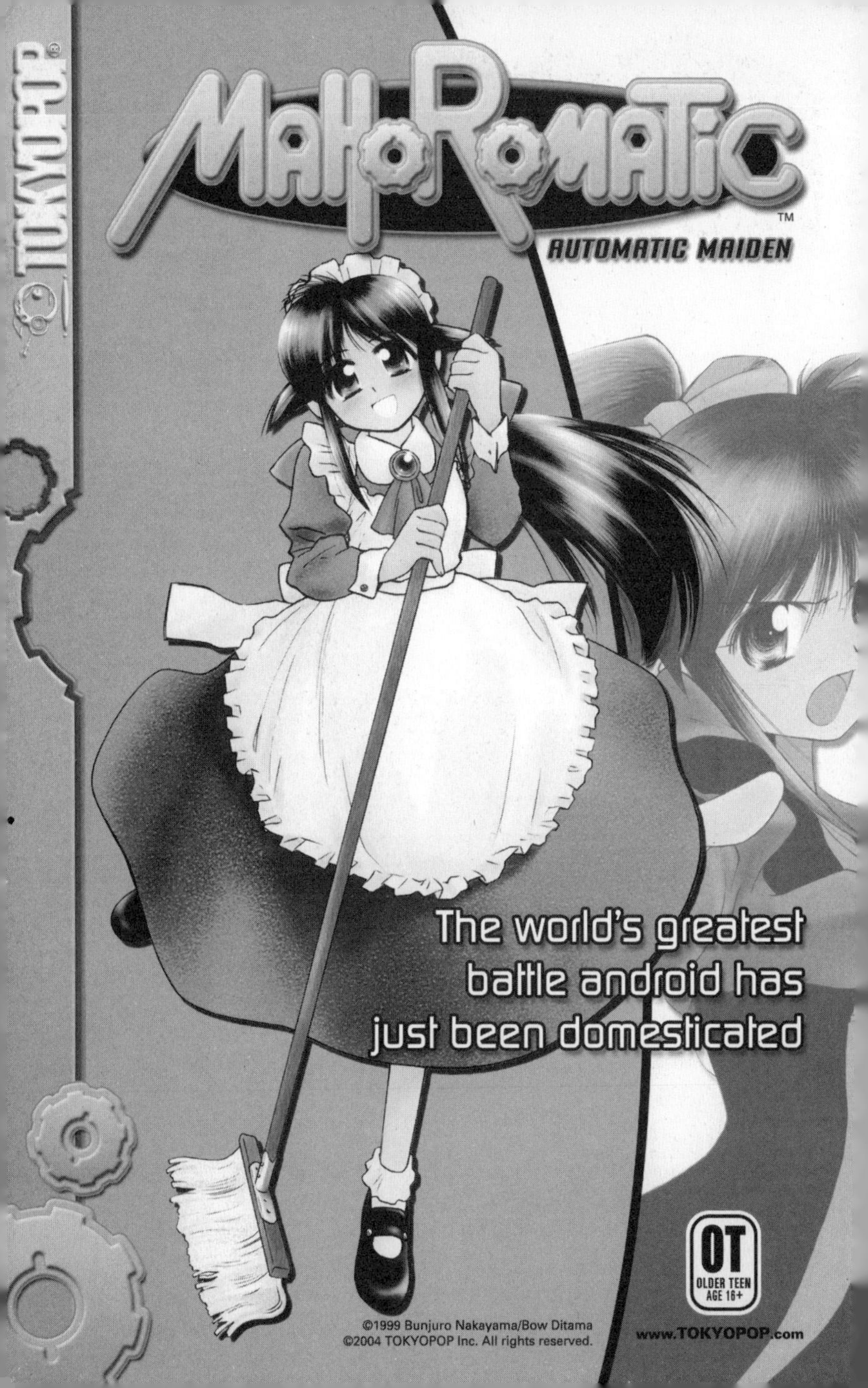
TOKYOPOP®
MAHOROMATIC™
AUTOMATIC MAIDEN
The world's greatest battle android has just been domesticated
OT
OLDER TEEN
AGE 16+
©1999 Bunjuro Nakayama/Bow Ditama
©2004 TOKYOPOP Inc. All rights reserved.
www.TOKYOPOP.com

# STOP!

## This is the back of the book.
## You wouldn't want to spoil a great ending!

This book is printed "manga-style," in the authentic Japanese right-to-left format. Since none of the artwork has been flipped or altered, readers get to experience the story just as the creator intended. You've been asking for it, so TOKYOPOP® delivered: authentic, hot-off-the-press, and far more fun!

# DIRECTIONS

If this is your first time reading manga-style, here's a quick guide to help you understand how it works.

It's easy... just start in the top right panel and follow the numbers. Have fun, and look for more 100% authentic manga from TOKYOPOP®!